D1603306

BEFORE AND AFTER MUḤAMMAD

BEFORE AND AFTER MUḤAMMAD

THE FIRST MILLENNIUM REFOCUSED

Garth Fowden

PRINCETON UNIVERSITY PRESS
PRINCETON AND OXFORD

Published by Princeton University Press, 41 William Street,
Princeton, New Jersey 08540
In the United Kingdom: Princeton University Press, 6 Oxford Street,
Woodstock, Oxfordshire OX20 1TW

press.princeton.edu

ISBN 978-0-691-15853-2

Library of Congress Control Number 2013942727

British Library Cataloging-in-Publication Data is available

This book has been composed in Garamond Premier Pro

Printed on acid-free paper. ∞

Printed in the United States of America

1 3 5 7 9 10 8 6 4 2

aug. mmix

Contents

Prefatory Note and Acknowledgments

Before and after Muḥammad develops my attempt in *Empire to commonwealth* (1993) to view Arsacid and Sasanid Iran, Rome, and the Caliphate within a single frame. Since then I have approached the early Caliphate by way of its material culture in *Quṣayr ʿAmra* (2004), and through philosophy (especially the Arabic Plotinus) in an uncompleted book titled *Rational Islam and the reinvention of Aristotle*. Except in its definition of the geographical framework, *Before and after Muḥammad* barely overlaps with *Empire to commonwealth*; but it has been much fertilized by *Rational Islam*. It lays out, and in its last two chapters somewhat schematically exemplifies, a new historical periodization, whose practical demonstration will be provided, in due course, by a large-scale narrative to be titled *The First Millennium: From Augustus to Avicenna*.

Unless specified otherwise, all dates are CE, and translations listed in the notes are into English. There is no bibliography. All references are given in full at their first occurrence and in abbreviated form thereafter, with their first occurrence indicated in square brackets by chapter and footnote number separated by a colon (e.g., [2:32]). The chapter 2 epigraph excerpt is reprinted by permission of the publisher from *Interpreting late Antiquity: Essays on the postclassical world*, edited by G. W. Bowersock, Peter Brown, and Oleg Grabar, p. ix: Cambridge, Mass.: The Belknap Press of Harvard University Press, Copyright © 1999, 2001 by the President and Fellows of Harvard College. The chapter 5 first epigraph excerpt is from Sebastian Brock's article "From antagonism to assimilation: Syriac attitudes to Greek learning", © 1982, Dumbarton Oaks Research Library and Collection, Trustees for Harvard University. Originally published in *East of Byzantium: Syria and Armenia in the formative period,* edited by Nina G. Garsoïan, Thomas F. Mathews, and Robert W. Thomson.

I would like to thank Johann Arnason for his early interest in and encouragement of my First Millennium project, and Glenn Most for inviting me to give three lectures, titled "Beyond late Antiquity," at the Scuola Normale Superiore, Pisa, in April 2009. Rob Tempio, of Princeton University Press, suggested I turn these into a short book. I wrote a first draft during three intense weeks of August 2009 at Katounia, Limni, in the pine woods by the Euboean Gulf, where forty years earlier Dimitri Obolensky composed *The Byzantine Commonwealth* (1971), and Philip Sherrard worked until his untimely death in 1995. I am grateful to Denise Sherrard for her ever-generous hospitality.

Otherwise, *Before and after Muḥammad* was conceived and written in the uniquely favorable environment provided by the Department of Greek and Roman Antiquity at the Institute of Historical Research, National Research Foundation, Athens, and in particular by Anna Mihailidou (Acting Director) and Harikleia Papageorgiadou (Head of Department), who sacrificed time and energy to protecting their colleagues from the worst effects of the Greek economic collapse. The book was completed in the winter of 2012–13, when I was fortunate to be a fellow of the Wissenschaftskolleg zu Berlin, and finally caught up with many publications not available in Greece.

Among those who have read part or all of this book, or otherwise assisted at its birth, the following deserve special thanks: Nadia Ali, Aziz al-Azmeh, Kamal Boullata, Hariclia Brecoulaki, Peter Brown, Elizabeth Key Fowden, Luca Giuliani, Anthony Kaldellis, Myrto Malouta, and Walter Pohl. I also thank all those who organized (Johann Arnason, Bo Stråth) and took part in the meeting on "The European foundation myth: A critical assessment and a relativisation of the European origo," which was convened at the University of Helsinki in May 2011 in order to discuss the Before and After Muḥammad/First Millennium project.

Finally, I thank Elizabeth and Gabriel for the good humor and solidarity that have kept us going through the last three and a half difficult years of crisis in Greece and temporary departure.

Wissenschaftskolleg zu Berlin
30th January 2013

Abbreviations

ASAP	*Arabic sciences and philosophy* (Cambridge)
CAH	*The Cambridge ancient history* vol. 12², ed. A. K. Bowman and others (Cambridge 2005); vol. 14, ed. Av. Cameron and others (Cambridge 2000)
DPA	R. Goulet (ed.), *Dictionnaire des philosophes antiques* (Paris 1989–)
EIr	E. Yarshater (ed.), *Encyclopaedia Iranica* (London; Costa Mesa, Calif.; New York1985–); and www.iranicaonline.org, including supplements to printed volumes and content for forthcoming volumes
EIs²	H. A. R. Gibb, J. H. Kramers, E. Lévi-Provençal, and J. Schacht (eds.), *The encyclopaedia of Islam* (Leiden 1960–2009²)
EIs³	M. Gaborieau and others (eds.), *The encyclopaedia of Islam three* (Leiden 2007–)
EQ	J. D. McAuliffe (ed.), *Encyclopaedia of the Qurʾān* (Leiden 2001–6)
Gibbon	E. Gibbon (ed. D. Womersley), *The history of the decline and fall of the Roman Empire* (London 1994); citations consist of the chapter number followed by the volume and page in Womersley's edition (e.g., 7: 1.195, 15: 1.480 n. 96, 40: 2.565 n. 24)
IBALA	J. Lössl and J. W. Watt (eds.), *Interpreting the Bible and Aristotle in late Antiquity: The Alexandrian commentary tradition between Rome and Baghdad* (Farnham 2011)
JLA	*Journal of late Antiquity* (Baltimore)
PIW	U. Rudolph (ed.), *Philosophie in der islamischen Welt* 1: *8.-10. Jahrhundert* (Basel 2012)
Pocock	J. G. A. Pocock, *Barbarism and religion* (Cambridge 1999–)
SEP	E. N. Zalta (ed.), *The Stanford encyclopedia of philosophy*, http://plato.stanford.edu
SFIM	C. D'Ancona (ed.), *Storia della filosofia nell' Islam medievale* (Turin 2005)
SODebate	P. Brown and others, "*SO Debate*: The world of late Antiquity revisited," *Symbolae Osloenses* 72 (1997) 5–90
ZRG	*Zeitschrift der Savigny-Stiftung für Rechtsgeschichte, Romanistische Abteilung* (Vienna)

BEFORE AND AFTER MUḤAMMAD

1

INCLUDING ISLAM

Although the divide between Islam and Europe will always be deeper than that between the different European peoples, there are two reasons why we simply cannot do without Islam in the construction of European cultural history: namely the unique opportunity to compare its assimilation of the same [antique] heritage, and on account of the abundance of [the two sides'] historical interactions.

—C. H. Becker, *Islamstudien* (1924–32) 1.39 (lecture delivered in 1921)

THE WEST AND THE REST

In this brief programmatic book, I contribute a new angle to the debate about "the West and the Rest." One party is eager to explain how Europe and eventually North America—the North Atlantic world—left the rest in the dust from about 1500. The other side argues that Asia—China, Japan, and the Islamic trio of Mughals, Safavids, and Ottomans—remained largely free of European encroachment until the mid-1700s, but then either collapsed for internal reasons, or else were gradually undermined by colonial powers' superior technological, economic, and military clout. Europe is relativized and its supposedly exceptional destiny undermined; but it still wins in the end, along with its North American offshoot.[1]

This is all just the latest phase in other long-standing debates about America's destiny and Europe's identity, the latter a focus of particular concern now given the impetus toward European integration—or disintegration—provided by the economic crisis that broke out in 2007. North Atlantic hegemony is no longer a given—it is more and more shadowed by two great Asian powers, China and India. It appears that the dominance of the West is on the

1 See for example M. G. S. Hodgson, *The venture of Islam* (Chicago 1974) 3, esp. 3–15; J. Darwin, *After Tamerlane* (London 2007); S. F. Dale, *The Muslim empires of the Ottomans, Safavids, and Mughals* (Cambridge 2010). I use the term "North Atlantic" to denote the shared heritage and attitudes of Europe and North America, and "Eurocentric" to refer to a particular European emphasis apparent in many histories of Europe and/or Asia dealing with periods before—and even after—the two sides of the Atlantic came into regular contact, irrespective of whether they are written by Europeans or North Americans.

way to becoming one more historical period, and that future historians will be as much concerned to explain its loss as its rise.

If Asian economic competition is one cloud on the North Atlantic world's horizon, another is Islam—both the religion that goes under that name even though it has many branches sometimes bitterly hostile to each other, and the cultural region created by it, the "Islamic world," which has in most phases of its history included large non-Muslim populations. Asiatic economic competition can be faced with some equanimity or at least resignation by societies that have benefited (as well as suffered) for decades now from a deluge of cheap consumer goods. The Islamic world, by contrast, represents not an economic challenge but something more insidious, a moral and spiritual competitor offering different norms of conduct and a variant vision of man and God unnervingly close—yet at the same time a challenge, as the Qur'ān makes explicit—to the values espoused by "Judeo-Christian" civilization. (The ideal reader will forgive essentializing references to "Judaism," "Christianity," and "Islam" for ease of general exposition, be aware that all three emerged gradually not ready-made as distinct identities,[2] and take due account of allusions, especially in my later chapters, to "orthodox" and "heretics," Latin, Greek, Syriac, and Armenian strands in Christianity, and Sunnis, Shiites, and different traditions of law in Islam.)

My purpose here is not to join this debate directly, but to overhaul its foundations, especially as regards the role of Islam and the Islamic world. In doing this, I hope to contribute to a sounder and more generous understanding of Islam's historical and intellectual contribution. I do not believe this can be attained by compiling a balance sheet of what the North Atlantic and Islamic worlds have achieved, or done to each other, since 1500. The sum total of what these civilizations are—and may come to be—cannot be grasped only in terms of the last half millennium. Instead we have to go back to the First Millennium, during which Christianity was born and matured, roughly in the middle of which the Prophet[3] Muḥammad received or conceived the Qur'ān, and by the end of which Islam had matured sufficiently to be compared with patristic Christianity.[4]

2 On Islam see recently F. M. Donner, *Muhammad and the believers* (Cambridge, Mass. 2010). With A. W. Hughes, *Abrahamic religions* (New York 2012), I eschew the hold-all "Abrahamic" terminology. Is using it for writing history (e. g. J. Goody, *Renaissances* [Cambridge 2010]) the price we pay for a global perspective?

3 While the Qur'ān calls Muḥammad both "messenger" (rasūl) and "prophet" (nabī), the consecrated English usage is adopted here.

4 The period and region here addressed are determined by the basic question about Islam. M. Mann, *The sources of social power* (Cambridge 1986–2013; 1²: 2012) 1.301–3, poses a more general sociological question, about the emergence and articulation of "transcendent power," and locates four relevant religions born "in about one thousand years from the birth of Buddha to the death of Muḥammad" (Christianity and Hinduism being the other two). Naturally, the relevant geographical region extends

In the first place we need to reformulate the history of the First Millennium in order to fit Islam into it, for the Arabian doctrine is excluded from the conventional narrative by historians eager to draw a direct line from late Antiquity, through the European Middle Ages, to the Renaissance and Modernity. Next we need to ask this: what was the nature of this new Islamic religion whose features, however debatably fast or slow to emerge, were quite discernible by 1000 CE? How did it relate to other contemporary civilizations, and those of Antiquity? Viewed from our present-day vantage point, does it make sense that Islam's "classical" moment is excluded from North Atlantic educational curricula, while the European Middle Ages, even though less taught than they were a generation or so ago, still constitute the indispensable conceptual and historical link between us and the foundations of a European culture conceived of as Greek, Roman, Jewish, and Christian—but nothing much to do with Islam? After all, the European Union now has a Muslim population that some put at twenty million, around twice the size of a middling member country such as Portugal or Greece.

As with China and India, an already visible future in which Islam will be increasingly prominent has to be brought into play if historians are to formulate questions that elucidate our ongoing quandaries rather than reinforcing Eurocentric stereotypes about the past and present. History is engagement with the past not just as it was then but as it confronts and molds us now. And beyond the historian's contribution to the public debate with its mainly social and political parameters, there are intellectual and spiritual benefits to be had from a contextualized approach to early Islam. It may, for example, uncover fertile dimensions of the tradition forgotten or misapprehended even by Muslims themselves, for they too write history selectively. Arabic philosophy, to take just one example, turns out to have been far from exclusively Muslim: there were also Christians and Jews and Mazdeans/Zoroastrians who philosophized in Arabic. Philosophy both contextualizes and provides fresh approaches to a tradition that, if entered through the austerities of Qur'anic scholarship and theology, may seem alien and impenetrable to the non-Muslim. Muslims too may benefit from reading their orthodoxies against the grain, which the philosophical tradition tends to encourage. The more rational and therefore philosophical strains of Muslim theology, "Mu'tazilism" or "Neo-Mu'tazilism," are under attack from fundamentalists in the contemporary Islamic world, as part of general pressure for social and political purification.[5] But understanding of these controversies is hard to achieve without the historian's perspective and context.

---

farther into Asia than does mine: see below, n. 11. But Mann is not very interested in geography; nor would it make sense to study Islam only up to the death of its founder.

5 R. C. Martin and M. R. Woodward, *Defenders of reason in Islam: Mu'tazilism from medieval school to modern symbol* (Oxford 1997). T. Bauer, *Die Kultur der Ambiguität* (Berlin 2011) 385–87, points out that Mu'tazilism has not been exempt from dogmatism.

It may be objected that philosophy was and remains a minority pursuit. But more general study of early Islam can improve our appreciation of its interaction with the imaginative worlds of Biblical and rabbinic Judaism and Eastern, especially Syriac, Christianity. Note particularly the Corpus Coranicum project at the Berlin-Brandenburg Academy of Sciences, which aims, by "realigning the Qur'ān into Late Antiquity" and tracking Jewish and Christian parallels to the Qur'anic text, to present it as part of the European heritage and illuminate the range of possible relationships between these monotheistic belief systems, not just then but now too.[6] Through the Qur'anic Jesus, for instance, we grow to appreciate the shared prophetic heritage of all three religions, obscured by Christian insistence on the uniqueness of God's son. By studying the debates between Muslims and Christians in the Abbasid Caliphate, Christians may be helped to see their teachings in ways that bring out their essential compatibility with Islam's strict monotheism. If one starts from what both religions—and Judaism—affirm, namely the unity of God, then what Muslims see as Christianity's two stumbling blocks, namely the Trinity and Incarnation, may be understood as means of communicating that unity to humans. Although the modern study of comparative religion originated in Christian European scholars' investigations of Judaism and the Greco-Roman tradition, Islam offers a still better vantage point, as was already apparent in the work of, for example, the Eastern Iranian polymath and historian of—among much else—religion, Bīrūnī (d. 1048).[7]

Going back to the First Millennium makes sense, then, in terms of defining and securing the foundations of the contemporary debate with and about Islam. Non-Muslim scholarship on Islam has rightly been criticized for obsession with origins, and neglect of the living tradition with its distinctive view of the foundational phase.[8] But it is also true that failure to look behind later orthodoxies and rigidified dogmatic formulations (especially fundamentalist ones, which tend to simplify a diverse, un-self-consciously polyvalent, "ambiguous" tradition in response to criticism contained in universalizing, hegemonial Western discourse[9]) can suggest Islam is by its very nature inflexible and closed to the world around it. No student of Islamic origins, at least in the manner of the Corpus Coranicum project, will easily fall into this trap. Nor

6 See contributions by A. Neuwirth and M. J. Marx to D. Hartwig and others (eds), *"Im vollen Licht der Geschichte": Die Wissenschaft des Judentums und die Anfänge der kritischen Koranforschung* (Würzburg 2008) 11–53; A. Neuwirth, *Der Koran als Text der Spätantike: Ein europäischer Zugang* (Berlin 2010); http://koran.bbaw.de; www.corpuscoranicum.de.

7 G. G. Stroumsa, *A new science* (Cambridge, Mass. 2010) 10–11, 22, 41; F. de Blois, "Bīrūnī, Abū Rayḥān vii," *EIr* 4.283–85.

8 Cf. A. Hourani, *Islam in European thought* (Cambridge 1991) 41, 42, 50, 59–60. Beginning in the 1970s, Anglo-Saxon skepticism about the formative phase led to neglect of that too: N. Sinai, *Fortschreibung und Auslegung: Studien zur frühen Koraninterpretation* (Wiesbaden 2009) IX.

9 This is the argument of Bauer, *Ambiguität* [1:5], e.g., 186–87, 268–69.

will any sociologist of religion aware of the fluidity of ordinary Christian and Muslim identities, and the hybridity of both religions outside the compartmentalized minds of intellectuals.[10] Going back to the First Millennium also provides a logical and helpful frame for studying the last phases of Antiquity in conjunction with the "Byzantine" Greek, Latin, and Arabic civilizations as they emerged from it. Although the Islamic world plays a prominent role in the argument of this book, it is by no means my only focus of attention. Islam's coming served still further to diversify—as well as harmonize—the already existing pre-Islamic polyphony of Judaism, Christianity, Greek philosophy (to which I attach special importance), Mazdaism, Manicheism, and so on.

Greco-Roman Antiquity, symbolized by the Parthenon and Colosseum, and the Middle Ages and Renaissance—Chartres and Florence—still dominate our view of premodern history. But in recent decades another, more than merely intermediate or transitional vista has opened up, that of the "long" late Antiquity from 200 to 800 CE, which I here further expand into the First Millennium from Augustus to Bīrūnī's contemporary and correspondent, Ibn Sīnā (Avicenna). Our world, even if we define it in the narrowest North Atlantic terms, is now and will increasingly be indebted to *all* the various and entangled cultural strands that place the Eurasian[11] First Millennium at the crossroads of history, and the career of the Prophet Muḥammad at the heart of the First Millennium. I propose the First Millennium not as an alternative to the traditional tripartite periodization of history into ancient, medieval, and modern, but as a new focus within the existing framework. If taken seriously, this will have consequences for how we look at the two traditional periods it overlaps, namely Antiquity and the Middle Ages (a question I address in the closing pages of my last chapter). But the concern of the present book is to argue the intrinsic merits of the First Millennium.

EDWARD GIBBON

In writing *Before and after Muḥammad* I have come to a better appreciation of Edward Gibbon. He is renowned for his account of Rome's decline from her Antonine Golden Age to her sack in 410 by Alaric's Goths, thirty-one out of seventy-one chapters. Indeed, some whose researches get no further

10 J. B. V. Tannous, *Syria between Byzantium and Islam* (diss. Princeton 2010) 430–80.

11 Eurasia: By this fashionable, ill-defined term I mean neither the whole landmass, nor "west of India," but Europe plus Asia to the extent they share cultural traditions, notably Christianity and Islam. Therefore India and China are included, but only for the sake of religions that originated on the far western rim of Asia (though Chinese Christianity is expanding spectacularly at the moment). Similarly, I define the North Atlantic world primarily in terms of shared culture, the result of European conquest and/or mission in America. In chapter 4 I identify a more focused sector of Eurasia, the region from Afghanistan to the East Mediterranean basin with which this book is mainly concerned, as the "Eurasian Hinge."

than the title-page believe that *The history of the decline and fall of the Roman Empire* concerns only the Roman Mediterranean and excludes both Asiatic Christianity and Islam.[12] Gibbon's undeniable conviction that the European civilization of his day was the pinnacle of human achievement[13] makes him a clear-cut Eurocentrist too. Yet reading the whole work, one sees him setting an agenda that today seems more valid than ever. Gibbon was obliged to retain the attention of a classically educated audience, while conveying his own response (evolving as he wrote) to the story of an already more than millennial Rome renewed on the Bosphorus, and compelled to face victorious Arab armies in the seventh century and the encroachments of the Turks from the eleventh. Present-day historians, at least in Europe and North America, have to deal with a comparable tension between a public informed only about the history of the North Atlantic world, and their own appreciation of the consequences globalization must have for the formulation of meaningful historical questions.

An exit from both dead ends—fixation with Rome Old and New, Latin and Greek,[14] or with the North Atlantic world—is offered by the study of Islamic history. To justify neglecting Rome on the Tiber for alien, Greek Rome on the Bosphorus, Gibbon argued in chapter 48 (1788) that "the fate of the Byzantine monarchy is *passively* connected with the most splendid and important revolutions which have changed the state of the world." By this he meant especially the rise of Islam and the empires of the Arabs and then the Turks—of whom he observed that "like Romulus, the founder of that martial people was suckled by a she-wolf."[15] Gibbon reassured his readers that, while "the excursive line may embrace the wilds of Arabia and Tartary," still "the circle [of the *Decline and fall*] will be ultimately reduced to the decreasing limit of the Roman monarchy."[16] Hence, the great work's coda offers a prospect of the ruins of Old Rome at the dawn of the Renaissance, and it can even be argued that Rome's "firm edifice" has been present throughout the excursus, an "absent centre" implicitly contrasted to "the transient dynasties

12 E.g., S. F. Johnson, "Preface: On the uniqueness of late Antiquity," in id. (ed.), *The Oxford handbook of late Antiquity* (New York 2012) xii–xiii, xv, xx ("the intra-Roman narrative of Gibbon has largely been abandoned in every quarter of the field"; but in the pre-Islamic period alone Gibbon discusses, sometimes for an entire chapter, Persians, Germans, Huns, Goths, Germanic successor states, Slavs, Turks, Avars, Ethiopians, etc.). And, in the same volume, R. Hoyland, "Early Islam as a late antique religion," 1054–55.

13 Gibbon, "General observations on the fall of the Roman Empire in the West": 2.511.

14 I set aside the extreme position according to which Europe is a *Latin* Roman assimilation and synthesis of Hebraism, Hellenism, and Christianity, sidelining East Rome ("Byzantium") as well as Islam: R. Brague, *Europe, la voie romaine* (Paris 1999, revised ed. with "Postface") 28–36, 46, 159–63; cf. F. G. Maier, *Die Verwandlung der Mittelmeerwelt* (Frankfurt am Main 1968) 359. Pocock 4.208 observes that the exclusion of Spain from the traditional European master narrative removed a chance to insert Islam.

15 Gibbon 48: 3.25 (first quotation), and cf. 42: 2.694 (she-wolf), 50: 3.151, 64: 3.791, 69: 3. 978.

16 Gibbon 48: 3.25; cf. 48: 3.26, 51: 3.237.

of Asia."[17] Nevertheless, the space and extended narrative Gibbon devotes to the Islamic world, in a book whose declared subject is Rome and Europe, can only impress. This was a historian who could praise, repeatedly, the rationality of the Muslim Prophet and his Qur'ān,[18] and devote long chapters to the Arab, Turkish, and Mongol Empires, on his way to Mehmed II's capture of Constantinople, which offered the formal excuse for these accounts.

After the last volume was published in 1788, Gibbon went back to the first page of volume 1, where he had defined his purpose as "to deduce the most important circumstances of its [Rome's] decline and fall; a revolution which will ever be remembered, and is still felt by the nations of the earth." He took out his pen and, in the margin of his copy, rephrased his objective as "to prosecute the decline and fall of the Empire of Rome: of whose language, Religion and laws the impression will be long preserved in our own, and the neighbouring countries of Europe." And having in this way shifted his emphasis away from "wars, and the administration of public affairs, . . . the principal subjects of history," toward the durability of culture, and from the whole world to Europe alone as the field of Rome's influence, he added an "NB" to himself: "Have Asia and Africa, from Japan to Morocco, any feeling or memory of the Roman Empire?"[19] Without underestimating the extent to which *Decline and fall* already enlarges European into Eurasian history,[20] one appreciates that in this note Gibbon is moving on, not denying Rome but certainly relativizing it.

Succumbing to that perspective would have made a quite different book;[21] but even reading the account Gibbon did give us, of the inexorable rise and titanic conquests of the Arabs, Turks, and Mongols, one is struck by what a Pandora's box his attempt to explain the East Roman Emperor Heraclius's defeats in the 630s turned out to be.[22] Still more remarkable is the realization that in writing it, Gibbon was harking very far back indeed, to his "blind and

17 P. Ghosh, "The conception of Gibbon's *History*," in R. McKitterick and R. Quinault (eds), *Edward Gibbon and Empire* (Cambridge 1997) 309, 311–12 (the first and last phrases are Gibbon's).

18 See below, 22–23.

19 Gibbon 9: 1.252; 3.1094.

20 Cf. Pocock 1.3–4, 113. Note also Gibbon's undated draft "Outlines of the history of the world," ed. P. B. Craddock, *The English essays of Edward Gibbon* (Oxford 1972) 163–98; cf. J. G. A. Pocock, "The "Outlines of the history of the world,"" in A. T. Grafton and J. H. M. Salmon (eds), *Historians and ideologues* (Rochester, NY 2001) 211–30.

21 The same would be true of the present book if, instead of focusing on the First Millennium, it addressed the full implications of non-Eurocentricity for the history of the second and third millennia. Cf. K. Blankinship, "Islam and world history: Toward a new periodization," *American journal of Islamic social sciences* 8 (1991) 433–35. (My thanks to Peter O'Brien for knowledge of this article.) The interaction of Christian and Muslim worldviews is nonetheless a global phenomenon, as, for example, in Indonesia or Nigeria.

22 An intimately related problem, Iran's defeat by Heraclius in the 620s, has given rise to another *Decline and fall*: P. Pourshariati, *Decline and fall of the Sasanian Empire* (London 2008), esp. 2.

boyish taste for the pursuit of exotic history" in such as Simon Ockley and the *Universal history* (1736–68), among whose contributors was George Sale the translator of the Qur'ān—Gibbon held both these early English Orientalists in lasting esteem.[23] In the decades during which *The history of the decline and fall of the Roman Empire* gestated, both Arabic and Persian studies were expanding in several parts of Europe; but then as now the dominant historical narrative ran from Rome, through medieval Christendom and especially the relations of Papacy and empire, to the reemergence of civil society and the modern European system of nation-states variously enlightened. Gibbon was leading his public into ill-charted territory, and for reasons that he does not fully explain or perhaps even understand. European economic, political, and military encroachment on Asia was entering its crucial phase, though, as Gibbon wrote. He knew the broader issues through both his readings and his grandfather's disastrous involvement in the 1720 South Sea Bubble.[24] Arguably, the implication of his book was that these vast new horizons, especially the Islamic empires of the Mughals, Safavids, and Ottomans, could be reframed as a part, however excursively, of Europe's foundational Roman history. But did he actually intend this, or his readers grasp it? Gibbon and Islam remains a blind spot in scholarship.[25]

23 J. Murray (ed.), *The autobiographies of Edward Gibbon* (London 1897^2) 56–58, 79, 121, 224, characteristically emphasizing the inadequacy of his formal education in order to explain how his masterpiece transgressed so many conventional scholarly boundaries. Cf. on Ockley and Sale the Bibliographical Index to Womersley's edition of the *Decline and fall*, also therein Gibbon's less favorable view of the *Universal history*, despite its attention to the East.

24 Pocock 4.229–45 on the Abbé Raynal's *Histoire des deux Indes*; Murray (ed.), *Autobiographies of Edward Gibbon* [1:23] 11–17.

25 For a few suggestive pages, see A. Momigliano, "Eighteenth-century prelude to Mr. Gibbon," in id., *Sesto contributo alla storia degli studi classici e del mondo antico* (Rome 1980) 257–63, but also Ghosh, in McKitterick and Quinault (eds), *Edward Gibbon and Empire* [1:17: a volume largely neglectful of Islam] 294 n. 127. Ghosh well discusses, 300–316, the structural problems of books 4–6 (1788) and their "abjuration of a master narrative" (305); also their dismissal of the "transient dynasties of Asia" compared to Rome's "firm edifice" (311–12). For Pocock, *Barbarism and religion*, Gibbon's eastward turn is "the strangest of his decisions": 1.3, 3.1; also 1.2, on Gibbon's trajectory from the Germanic successor states "in whose barbarism may be found the seeds of European liberty" to "*the less rewarding question* of with what (if anything) Slav and Turkish barbarians have replaced the empire in the east" (my italics). See also, in a similar vein, 1.304; 2.4, 121, 303, 371, 373–74, 379–80, 390, 393–94, 402; 4.230; 5.374. Pocock bases his work on the three volumes Gibbon published from 1776 to 1781, accepts the conventional judgment that *Decline and fall* climaxes with the collapse of the Roman Empire in the West, and still at the end of his latest installment observes of the 1788 volumes, "These were radically different histories; it is far from certain that Gibbon resolved on ways of dealing with them, or that European historiography . . . offered him the means of doing so": 5.385–86. Ghosh's explaining where Gibbon went wrong is more interesting than Pocock's lamenting or patronizing it; but neither gets to grips with the eastward turn. D. Womersley's analysis of the whole work, *The transformation of The decline and fall of the Roman Empire* (Cambridge 1988), expatiates on Eastern Rome but not the Islamic empires, though note 209–11 on Gibbon's echoing of his account of Rome's fall in his description of the Caliphate's collapse (and his implicitly more ironical stance toward theories of historical causality—see below, 14–15). One might imagine that ne-

By singling out certain durable, "longue durée" currents in human experience—notably Greco-Roman rationalism and the Jewish-Christian-Muslim monotheistic traditions—which I consider to be crucially important both in their historical origins and development, and in their influence over us now, I too end up offering the reader what is sometimes derisively referred to as a "grand narrative"—what is more, one based on concepts, and in particular religious concepts. I make no apology. The past has enormous intrinsic interest, including at the purely antiquarian level; and for some that interest is sufficient motive for study.[26] But there are others who come to history with questions about its role in making us what we are now. To help make sense of the unfolding present in relation to the past, historians must cast a wide net, while searching the past for alternative ways of thinking to those now prevalent. An eminent Marxist historian recently deplored the two grand narratives to which, he believes, early medieval Europe falls victim, "the narrative of nationalism and the narrative of modernity."[27] His omission of "the formation of Christendom" serves to double-underline what separates his approach from the one I offer here, which is shy neither of large-scale narrative nor of ideas, notably religious and philosophical ideas.[28]

ISLAM AND LATE ANTIQUITY

My fundamental question about history and thought "before and after Muḥammad" can be put in various ways: Was Islam, as has usually been assumed, a perversion—or the nemesis—of the (late) ancient and early Christian world from which North Atlantic civilization derives its identity? Or was it perhaps its further evolution, or at least a viable alternative line of development? Does the Muslims' hijra era beginning in 622 denote a decisive turn in

---

glect of these chapters is best overcome by a separate publication: E. Gibbon (tr. J. Sporschil), *Der Sieg des Islam* (Frankfurt am Main 2003, with an essay on "Gibbons Muhammad" by R. Schulze) ; id. (tr. F. Guizot), *Mahomet et la naissance de l'islam* (Paris 2011). Within months of their appearance in London, excerpts were translated by A. H. W. von Walterstern, "Die Eroberung von Mekka", *Neue Literatur und Völkerkunde* 2–2 (1788) 400–410, and C. G Körner, "Mahomet: Ein Fragment," *Der Teutsche Merkur* (April 1789) 70–93, 217–42. My thanks to Reinhart Meyer-Kalkus and Gustav Seibt for this information.

26 J.-M. Carrié, "'Bas-Empire' ou 'Antiquité tardive'?," in J.-M. Carrié and A. Rousselle, *L'empire romain en mutation* (Paris 1999) 21 (quoting Paul Veyne); C. Wickham, *The inheritance of Rome* (London 2009) 553 (by way of repudiating "metahistorical narrative").

27 Wickham, *Inheritance* [1:26] 3.

28 Cf. D. Armitage, "What's the big idea? Intellectual history and the *longue durée*," *History of European ideas* 38 (2012) 1–15, drawing attention to revived interest among historians in both ideas and their diachronic, transmissional aspect (while exemplifying, in excluding fitna from his discussion of the concept of civil war, the continuing blind spot toward Islam, and in particular the direct bearing of the early fitnas on faith values).

history, perhaps even a completely fresh start? Or is it just one identity marker in a world full already of identities to which early Muslims were as much indebted as averse? And linked to these questions about the meaning of the new Muslim era are others about the dates and events commonly seen as marking the end of Antiquity.

What about, for example, the murder of the Emperor Maurice at Constantinople in 602? This is now widely taken to mark the end of the shorter—and more generally accepted—"late Antiquity," deemed to run from roughly 300 to 600.[29] And yet the "Last Great War of Antiquity" between Rome and Iran, which Maurice's death provoked, mirrored numerous other such conflicts between Iran and the lands to the west of it, which had molded history and mentalities ever since the Battle of Marathon in 490 BCE. Xerxes torching the Athens acropolis in 480, Alexander incinerating Persepolis in 331, Heraclius destroying fire temples and Khosrow II's palaces at Ctesiphon a millennium later in the 620s,[30] all were links in an ever more self-conscious tradition of East-West hostility. Indeed the story of Alexander was remodeled in Syriac to make him a Christian king subduing Iran in the image of Heraclius. Parts of this Syriac version echo in sura 18 of the Qur'ān, while sura 30 begins with a direct evocation of the Great War.[31] And the late antique empires of Qayṣar (Caesar) and Kisrā (Khosrow) continued long after this to be a vivid presence to Muslims, whether through constant contact with the lands and peoples still ruled from Constantinople, or through a more artistic and literary memory of the Sasanid court at Ctesiphon. One thinks of some of the best-known material evidence from the Umayyad period (661–750): the Caliph 'Abd al-Malik's (685–705) "Arab-Byzantine" and "Arab-Sasanian" coins; his Dome of the Rock in Jerusalem, so indebted to Christian architecture; and the Sasanian-style relief carvings on the Mushattā facade now in Berlin.[32]

In the course of the seventh century the East Roman Empire did indeed go through a damaging socioeconomic as well as political crisis, while the Sasanian state crumbled into dust. But no power vacuum was allowed to develop; urban life in the Caliphate continued, often along quite familiar lines; and once the crisis had passed, even battered Constantinople re-

29 Already in the Renaissance, the sixth century was regarded as still a part of Antiquity: P. R. Ghosh, "Gibbon's Dark Ages," *Journal of Roman studies* 73 (1983) 17 n. 109, to which add that only Le Nain de Tillemont's death prevented him from carrying his *Mémoires pour servir à l'histoire ecclésiastique des six premiers siècles* (Brussels 1693–1712), much exploited by Gibbon, down to the end of the sixth century.

30 Sebeos (attributed), *Armenian history* [tr. R. W. Thomson (Liverpool 1999)] 124, 127.

31 K. van Bladel, "The *Alexander legend* in the Qur'ān 18:83–102," in G. S. Reynolds (ed.), *The Qur'ān in its historical context* (London 2008) 175–203.

32 Cf. G. Fowden, *Quṣayr 'Amra* (Berkeley 2004), Index s.vv. "East Roman Empire," "Sasanian Irān."

mained not just an imperial capital, but the capital of the "Romans";[33] while the Sasanians arguably returned in the guise of the Abbasids. At least in part, 602 is a popular termination for Antiquity because most ancient historians are culturally as well as educationally unprepared for either Arabic or Islam. The 602 terminus tells us more about our (post-)Jewish/Christian selves than about the seventh century.

If 602 hardly convinces as either end or beginning, what of 529, with Justinian's closing of the Athens philosophy schools? Visitors to the new Acropolis Museum opened in 2009 are firmly informed that this and the triumph of Christianity mark the end of Antiquity. Yet we know philosophy continued to be studied after that date at Alexandria, which was a far more influential center.[34] The year 529 has proven a durable red herring because Plato, on whom late Athenian philosophers concentrated, seems a more plainly pagan figure, and therefore more representative of Antiquity, than Aristotle, on whom the Alexandrians focused. This highlighting of the Platonists has chimed all too well with historians' urge to find as richly symbolic as possible an end point for late Antiquity. What better than the Christian absolutist Justinian's assault on the very heart of Antiquity, the Athens philosophy schools, already adulterated and weakened by a mixture of magic (or "theurgy") and Orphic or Chaldaean revelation? But the evolving strength of Aristotelianism, not just after 529 but after Muḥammad as well, undermines this convenient periodization.

Latterly, Aristotelianism's role in the indispensable intellectual underpinnings of the period we are concerned with has been underlined by the Ancient commentators on Aristotle project guided by Richard Sorabji, which has liberated this whole thought world from the dignified obscurity imposed by the Berlin edition's twenty-three stout, austere volumes (themselves originally intended, and used, mainly as a mine for fragments of the Presocratics, Peripatetics, and Stoics[35]). In tandem with Sorabji's project, research has intensified on the Syriac and Arabic Aristotle translations and commentaries.[36] What is emerging is a picture of a coherent and profoundly

33 Hence the use in this book of "East Rome" not "Byzantium," which implies the foundation of a new empire. Gibbon writes of "Romans" or "Greeks," where modern scholars have "Byzantines," an epithet Gibbon reserves for the instruments of empire and Church, notably the "Byzantine court/palace/throne."

34 P. Hoffmann, "Damascius," *DPA* 2.556–59; C. Wildberg, "Philosophy in the reign of Justinian," in M. Maas (ed.), *The Cambridge companion to the age of Justinian* (Cambridge 2005) 316–40; M. di Branco, *La città dei filosofi: Storia di Atene da Marco Aurelio a Giustiniano* (Florence 2006) 192–97; E. J. Watts, *City and school in late antique Athens and Alexandria* (Berkeley 2006) 111–42, 232–56.

35 S. Fazzo, "Aristotelianism as a commentary tradition," in P. Adamson and others (eds), *Philosophy, science and exegesis in Greek, Arabic and Latin commentaries* (London 2004) 1.1–2.

36 On the importance of the ACA project for Arabic philosophy, see R. Wisnovsky, "The nature and scope of Arabic philosophical commentary in post-classical (ca. 1100–1900 AD) Islamic intellectual history," in Adamson and others (eds), *Philosophy, science and exegesis* [1:35] 2.149–52.

influential Aristotelian tradition that did not become prominent until after the beginning of the First Millennium, matured among the commentators of fifth- to sixth-century Alexandria, and broke through the commentary stage to a new synthesis, less tied to the Aristotelian texts, around the turn of the millennium thanks to the learned but also innovative mind of Ibn Sīnā. Of all this there will be more to say in chapter 5. Meanwhile, if one is looking for something truly epoch making that happened in 529, it is ready to hand in the first publication of the *Justinianic code*, a compilation of Roman law from the reign of Hadrian up to Justinian himself. The second, revised edition, issued in 534, of this summation of Rome's social and political wisdom accumulated during the first half of the First Millennium was also to mold whoever used Roman law subsequently, down to the present day.[37] The year 529 was a major point of transmission, and stage of transformation, in Roman civilization, not the catastrophic end of Antiquity; and this would have been more widely grasped, had ancient historians been in the habit of incorporating law in their curriculum (Gibbon is again the outstanding exception).

Admittedly it is easier to discern the end of Antiquity in the West, as Germanic kingdoms establish themselves during the fifth century on territories once ruled direct from Rome, as Latin becomes the language of the conquered not the victors, and as the Church annexes the legacy of Romanitas. But our fundamental question is about the relationship between the Islamic world and Antiquity, so our primary concern must be with the East. And there, the end of Antiquity is far from easy to nail down. In any case our interest in Islam, and its relationship with Judaism and Christianity, means that neither Greece and Rome, nor even the formation of Christendom, can any more be the *sole* determinant of our periodization. The traditional division among Antiquity, the Middle Ages, and Modern Times no longer responds to our most pressing question—unless you think Islam enjoyed a "medieval" phase, or is even by definition "medieval."[38] We become aware of the need to redefine, at least partially, the framework of our history, and to refocus its contents. This reframing and refocusing will affect space as well as time, the geographical as well as chronological parameters, as we shall see in the next three chapters.

With the effect induced on our view of Antiquity, and indeed the whole of history both before and after Muḥammad, by taking due account of Islam,

37 C. Humfress, "Law and legal practice in the age of Justinian," in Maas (ed.), *Age of Justinian* [1:34] 161–84. On Roman law's retreat in the later twentieth century, see A. Schiavone (tr. J. Carden and A. Shugaar), *The invention of law in the West* (Cambridge, Mass. 2012) 16–18.

38 Cf. D. Varisco, "Making 'medieval' Islam meaningful," *Medieval encounters* 13 (2007) 385–412; D. Ali, "The historiography of the medieval in South Asia," *Journal of the Royal Asiatic Society* 22 (2012) 7–8. The phrase "medieval Islam" may sometimes be innocent of ill will but never of unintentional irony, given the civilizational gap between Baghdad and Aachen.

compare the consequences for European thought of discovering the Americas.[39] In the New World, Europeans acquired not just a vast access of fresh knowledge, but an awareness of their ability to turn that knowledge to their own account, transforming it into power and wealth. They found people living at what seemed a more primitive stage of history, who inspired them to project themselves back, imaginatively, into their own remotest past, hitherto dominated by the account in Genesis.[40] An Englishman might find rudiments of heraldry in the war paints of Virginian Indians, and deduce "that Heraldry was ingrafted *naturally* into the sense of humane race."[41] Another Englishman might dream of finding a whole Iroquois literature, which would offer a unique encounter with the human mind, placed in circumstances we have never experienced and governed by manners and religious opinions utterly contrary to our own.[42]

Not that the reasons for Europeans' ignorance of Islam and America were the same. Islam was "terra incognita" because Europeans had chosen to ignore it, not because they had not found it. Today, taking it on board entails an acknowledgment of omission, or even error. One pays a certain psychological price. In particular, the relativizing of a whole set of absolute (Christian) truth claims in the light of another, long deliberately neglected set of absolute (Muslim) truth claims is no small thing. Enthusiasts for religious verity may be led thereby to embrace Islam, or reject it and reaffirm their Christian identity. The historian, by contrast, will be led to a better-founded skepticism of dogmatic religion in general, but also to a warmer appreciation of the rational, often more or less explicitly Aristotelian, undergirding which is part of the Jewish-Christian-Muslim monotheisms—not from their original formulation, but acquired since, often to meet the demands of controversy and polemic. This is an area of religious doctrine less dependent on arbitrary assertion and more relevant to the wider, ongoing philosophical and scientific debate about reality and how we may approach it.

The question is, ultimately, not just how Islam can be fitted in to a refocused, more generous, and open view of history, but also how much of the monotheist and ancient philosophical traditions generally can or ought to be

39 The comparison was suggested by Momigliano, *Sesto contributo* [1:25] 262–63. Others have compared Europe's reaction to Amerindian religions with its medieval incomprehension of Islam: G. Stroumsa, *New science* [1:7] 19–20 (and chap. 1 generally, on the shocking impact of the discovery of America on the study of religion). See also A. Grafton, *Joseph Scaliger* (Oxford 1983–93) 2.361–62, on the effect on Scaliger's scholarship of widening Chinese as well as American horizons.

40 Cf. Darwin, *After Tamerlane* [1:1] 209; and N. Giakovaki, *Ευρώπη μέσω Ελλάδας* (Athens 2006) 275–77, for the discovery of Greece and especially Athens in the 1670s, contextualized by contemporaries in contrast with New World primitiveness.

41 John Gibbon, quoted by his great-grandnephew Edward Gibbon: Murray (ed.), *Autobiographies of Edward Gibbon* [1:23] 8, 213, 368 (but cf. J. Gawthorp, "A history of Edward Gibbon's six autobiographical manuscripts", *British Library journal* 25 (1999) 188).

42 E. Gibbon, *Essai sur l'étude de la littérature* (London 1761) 61–62, §47, tr. Pocock 1.230.

part of our contemporary intellectual armory. Numerous exponents of modernity have been hostile to any form of religion, especially to Islam, which has so far responded to Enlightenment concerns much less than either Christianity or Judaism. Monotheism may legitimately be accused of encouraging a dangerous anthropocentricity and indifference to nature,[43] and being obsessed both with closed and petrified "canonical" collections of sacred texts, and with the resultant "orthodoxy"/"heresy" binary. The associated tyranny of Aristotle and rationalism, especially logic, has often been resented. So too the grip of religion-based law, especially on certain varieties of Judaism and Islam. The airtight "identities" that such authoritarian traditions foster have been a bane as well as a blessing, while the technological shrinking of our world throws these identities onto the defensive and makes them still more aggressive. But there is also a more constructive side to the debate. Looking afresh at the First Millennium in particular may, as already suggested, help us recover neglected but fertile aspects of the Muslim intellectual heritage, while taking seriously the shared patristic heritage helps bridge gaps in understanding between the churches. Reinvigorating the monotheist traditions opens up, in turn, the possibility of a richer, less constrictedly materialist approach to well-worn controversies such as the value of human life or the natural environment. In other words, religious and secular thought can be made to work creatively together.

By posing if not necessarily solving problems such as these, we engage more closely with some of the profounder issues of intellectual orientation that preoccupy our age. We also demonstrate a type of "philosophic history" (as opposed to antiquarian erudition) not driven by ideological agendas as Ernst Stein feared,[44] but instead, as was Gibbon's ideal, concerned to establish a sound and critical, not merely serialistic or annalistic narrative in order to explain the causes of things on as wide a canvas as possible, to illuminate the differing characters of nations, and to trace the emergence and improvement of modern (European) secular and commercial societies.[45] On the maximalist view, philosophic history studies the past in order to reflect on the existential issues which preoccupy the historian as a participant in his or her own times. But it must not be polemical or politically engaged; it may indeed subvert the patterns imposed by theory, system, and causality. It must resist the tendency toward zeal and rigidity inherent in philosophy itself, as Gibbon was painfully aware from the example of the Emperor Julian; and it

43 Cf., e.g., Neuwirth, *Koran als Text* [1:6] 431, 440.

44 E. Stein, *Geschichte des spätrömischen Reiches* 1 (Vienna 1928) VII = p. XV of the French translation.

45 Gibbon, "General observations": 2.511–16; 48: 3.26, 49: 3.95 (on freedom and knowledge expanding the faculties of man), 53: 3.409, 61: 3.728 with n. 69, 64: 3.791, 810 n. 41; cf. A. Momigliano, *Studies in historiography* (London 1966) 40–55; D. Womersley, "Introduction" to Gibbon 1.xx–xxiv; Pocock 1.111–12.

must not stifle the irreducible individuality of historical actors. It is not the least of the rewards to be had from reading Gibbon's account of East Rome and Islam, that we see him gradually adjusting himself to this more complex understanding of the historian's art.[46] The student of the past, having received there "an education in irony,"[47] may permit himself or herself, at most, "a philosophic smile."[48] In the end it is the painstaking and accurate historian who must prevail.

SUMMARY

At the end of this introductory chapter, some brief indication of how the argument will proceed may be found helpful.

Chapter 2, "Time: Beyond late Antiquity," investigates the role late antique scholarship has occasionally assigned to Islam. Among the protagonists: Alois Riegl, Josef Strzygowski, Henri Pirenne, and Peter Brown. Art history has played a conspicuous part. Brown's influential synthesis tracing continuities across a broad periodization up to c. 800 has of late bred a reaction by scholars eager to reassert the dimensions of catastrophe and decline he—and his pupils—are felt to have neglected. The materialist orientation of this new work fails, though, to take due account of the conceptual dimension of human experience. And for the concepts with which we are here concerned, especially their Arabic articulation, even the long late Antiquity to c. 800 is not an adequate canvas.

Chapter 3, "A new periodization: The First Millennium," presents my case for the First Millennium as an alternative or parallel periodization. Besides the three major monotheisms, the First Millennium also sees Greek philosophy, Roman law, Mazdaism, and Manicheism attaining intellectual and institutional maturation. By this I mean the completion of three successive stages of development: prophetic, scriptural, and exegetical, the last involving distillation of systematic doctrine from a textual/scriptural canon derived from prophecy, revelation, philosophical teaching, or law giving. I then focus on certain Greek and Arabic/Syriac historians who, taken together, may be seen as adumbrating the First Millennium periodization along with its conceptual, specifically monotheist, emphasis.

Chapter 4, "Space: An eastward shift," turns from time to space, revising the geographical framework—no longer the Mediterranean world of the Greeks and Romans, but what I call the "Eurasian Hinge," a triptych of re-

46 Cf. Womersley's "Introduction," esp. xxiv–xxxix, xlv–xlviii, liv–lv, lxvi, xciv–civ; id., *Transformation* [1:25] 203, 209–13, 237, 242–74, 287, 296–97; and above, n. 25.

47 Pocock 1.230; cf. 238–39.

48 Gibbon 69: 3.1012 and n. 90.

gions with the Iranian plateau and the Eastern Mediterranean as its wings, and as its centerpiece that cradle of monotheisms, the "Mountain Arena" stretching from the Zagros to the Mediterranean and from South Arabia to the Taurus. These vast horizons nourished two world empires no other could challenge: the Achaemenids with their continuator Alexander, and a millennium later the Islamic Caliphate of the Umayyads and Abbasids, of central importance to the argument presented here. Both, along with Christian Rome, spawned political and cultural "commonwealths" too, within the same frame.

Chapters 5 and 6, both devoted to "Exegetical cultures," aim to impart a clearer contour to the First Millennium's crucial conceptual aspects. Chapter 5 focuses on "Aristotelianism" both as an autonomous philosophy and as a denominator common to several of the traditions I am concerned with. Harmonized, especially in the Alexandrian schools, with Plato, Aristotle came to be seen as the distillation of Greek thought, while his logic, in particular, proved indispensable to the formulation of "orthodoxy" and the demolition of "heresy" within Christianity and Islam alike. Alexandrian Aristotelianism was then conveyed to Baghdad thanks largely to Syriac Christian translators. At the turn of the millennium Ibn Sīnā took a decisive step beyond the Alexandrian commentary tradition into a new, personal synthesis of Islamic theology and Aristotle.

Chapter 6, on "Law and religion," examines several other major learned or religious traditions which flourished during the First Millennium, in order to demonstrate their maturation through exegesis of and commentary on authoritative texts. Roman law, rabbinic Judaism, Christianity, and Islam are successively considered from this angle, in order to consolidate our portrait of the First Millennium as the source not only of the three great texts that have most deeply molded Eurasian civilization (the Christian Bible, the *Justinianic code*, and the Qur'ān), but also of the exegetical traditions through which these often recalcitrant books were transformed into usable public doctrine.

The final chapter, "Viewpoints around 1000: Ṭūs, Baṣra, Baghdad, Pisa," treats the years around 1000 as a viewing point from which to look mainly back but also a little bit forward, and consolidate our sense of the First Millennium's distinctiveness. It picks out and elaborates certain themes broached earlier in the book, associating each one with a particular city. Ṭūs stands for Iran, notably the composition of its national epic, the *Shahname*, at the close of the millennium. Baṣra stands for the encyclopedic erudition of the Brethren of Purity at the end of the tenth century, drawing on the whole heritage of the First Millennium to offer a way of salvation to the Muslim soul. Baghdad stands for the Abbasid capital's learned circles and their openness to reasoned argument and Aristotelian logic to facilitate debate between members of the many different faiths espoused by its inhabitants. In conclusion,

I consider what effect adoption of the First Millennium as an alternative periodization might have on study of ancient and medieval history. Pisa stands for the eleventh-century reemergence of Latin Europe, still in the shadow of Islam but bursting already with aggressive energy and a new cultural self-confidence.

2

TIME

BEYOND LATE ANTIQUITY

The time has come for scholars, students, and the educated public in general to treat the period between around 250 and 800 as a distinctive and quite decisive period of history that stands on its own.

—G. W. Bowersock, P. Brown, and O. Grabar (eds.), *Interpreting late Antiquity* (2001) ix

Will the periodization of history itself be cast aside, and will we see the rise of an entirely new paradigm that reframes these centuries in a radically different way? Whatever occurs, it is a sobering reflection that, as the twenty-first century draws to a close, the Late Antiquity with which the new generation engages (if, that is, "Late Antiquity" as a concept still exists) may well look significantly different from the Late Antiquity with which we engage now in the first decade of the same century.

—W. Mayer, "Approaching late Antiquity," in P. Rousseau (ed.), *A companion to late Antiquity* (2009) 13

THE ROOTS OF LATE ANTIQUE STUDIES

Just as what Europeans thought of as their discovery of "America" turned out to have had forerunners, so too the realization that Islam is to be read in the light of Antiquity long antedates the heightened American and European awareness of the Muslim world that has prevailed since 2001, and the concurrent reassessment of the historical narrative. This chapter shows questions about Islam were present at the very birth of modern late antique studies.

Discussion of periodization can seem arid because periods are so obviously our creation imposed retrospectively. Yet they are indispensable: historians must divide time into periods if they are to make any sense to each other let alone their pupils. Furthermore, historians' handling of the periods they construct, and their preferences among them, tell us much about their own times, particularly about issues of social, cultural, and political identity. This is certainly true of the problems I touched on in chapter 1: the difficulty of fitting the Islamic world into the conventional North Atlantic narrative of history ancient, medieval, and modern, and the more specific issues of how Islam relates to late Antiquity, and when late Antiquity ends. Recent intensive discussion of all this reflects the widespread uncertainty about whether to include Islam in our contemporary worldview, or go on excluding it.

Now is not the first time historians of later Antiquity have been faced with a more or less political choice between inclusive and exclusive understandings of what they study and teach. In the past, it was usually Christianity that provided the stumbling block, whether to Gibbon in Enlightenment England or educationalists in nineteenth-century Greece uncertain about what role to allot Christian Rome or "Byzantium" alongside the ancient Greeks.[1] In the Italy of the 1930s the young Arnaldo Momigliano felt called upon to assert that

> no fully self-aware historian of the ancient world, that is, no person conscious of the fact of living in a civilization of Christian origin, can get away with the refusal to recognize that ancient history makes sense only when it is seen to evolve in such a way as to end naturally in the rise of Christianity.[2]

And indeed we can find Fergus Millar even today asking ancient historians,

> Why do we exclude from the standard conception of what a classical education is about Jewish and Christian texts in Greek, and Christian texts in Latin?

Millar also makes the daring suggestion that

> we might even read in Greek classes those vivid views of provincial society in the Roman Empire provided by the Gospels and Acts.[3]

Millar accompanies this opening to Jewish and Christian Antiquity with a firm exclusion of Islam.[4] My concern here is to argue that it is now Islam's turn to be seen as Antiquity's "natural end," albeit thanks to the drift of the

1 Cf. C. Mango, *Byzantium and its image* (London 1984) III.53–55; C. Koulouri, *Dimensions idéologiques de l'historicité en Grèce (1834–1914)* (Frankfurt 1991) 319–28, 335–42, 491–96; A. Politis, "From Christian Roman emperors to the glorious Greek ancestors," in D. Ricks and P. Magdalino (eds), *Byzantium and the modern Greek identity* (Aldershot 1998) 1–14 (my thanks to Christina Angelidi for this last reference).

2 A. Momigliano, *Contributo alla storia degli studi classici* (Rome 1979) 186–87, quoted by P. Brown, "Arnaldo Dante Momigliano," *Proceedings of the British Academy* 74 (1988) 408.

3 F. Millar (ed. H. M. Cotton and G. M. Rogers), *Rome, the Greek world, and the East* (Chapel Hill 2002–6) 1.34; cf. 3.505–8.

4 Millar, *Rome, the Greek world, and the East* [2:3] 3.489, 506.

historical evidence itself rather than because our society is or ever can be Muslim in the sense Momigliano's was Christian. And although, in quoting the Italian historian, I have adopted Peter Brown's translation of "sfocia" as "to end naturally," it might also be rendered "to lead to," "to debouch" (as a river into a lake), which would better convey my view that Islam did not, as has been imagined, kill Antiquity, but grew out of it and even developed some of its major preoccupations. I would like to suggest that such a reconception of Islam's relation to late Antiquity—which actually takes us "beyond late Antiquity" in the sense in which the term is most commonly understood—is implicit not only in the Qur'ān's intense dialogue with rabbinic Judaism and Christianity, but also in the origins of late Antiquity as an independent academic discipline, as we see if we go back to Vienna—in particular—at the very beginning of the twentieth century. The example set then was not, though, consistently or effectively followed up.

But before considering the crucial books that came out in 1900 to 1901, we need to take firmly on board that, long before late Antiquity became an independent discipline, major aspects of the period were already at the focus of Renaissance and Reformation thought. In particular, Constantine's religious revolution resonated so deeply that we can claim late Antiquity as a fundamental contributor to European thought, long previous to its formal "invention" as a separate period.

It goes without saying that, throughout the Middle Ages both Greek and Latin, the theological and ecclesiological legacy of late Antiquity was what was uppermost in the mind of all educated people. Still, late Antiquity meant "paganism" as well as Christianity. Within a restricted circle in the Greek world, much of the secular literature of Antiquity remained familiar right down to the Ottoman capture of Constantinople in 1453, and indeed beyond. As for the Latin world, to begin with it made do with only a thin trickle of secular texts: Virgil, Livy, Cicero, and a few others, to judge for example from Carolingian library catalogues.[5] Although the situation much improved from the twelfth and especially the thirteenth century onward, it was only during the Italian Renaissance of the fifteenth century that non-Christian ancient thought began to be widely studied in its own right—not merely for how it could spice theology—and sometimes in Greek as well as Latin. Particularly the contribution of Marsilio Ficino (d. 1499), in unveiling Plato and the Hermetica through Latin translations, can hardly be overestimated.

No less important than these new ways of thinking was the inclination toward *critical* reading of texts, including Christian ones. When Lorenzo Valla (d. 1457) exposed as a forgery the *Donation of Constantine*, on which papal claims to temporal dominion were built, that brought about (eventu-

5 R. McKitterick, *The Carolingians and the written word* (Cambridge 1989) 153–54, 169–96.

ally, with the Protestant Reformation) a revolution in European thought[6]—more so than Thomas Aquinas's proving in 1272 that the *Book of causes* was by the late Platonist Proclus not Aristotle,[7] or Isaac Casaubon's demonstration in 1614 that "Hermes Trismegistus" was no Egyptian coeval of Moses, but a cover for Greek writers of the first Christian centuries.[8]

Exiled scholars from Constantinople played a part in this dazzling Renaissance reevaluation of Antiquity; but it was far more a Latin than a Greek achievement, while its protagonists are the direct ancestors of our own scholarly world. If one were to pick a single individual as exemplifying this catholic and critical approach to both the Greco-Roman and Christian traditions, it might be Erasmus of Rotterdam (d. 1536), of whom it has recently been said that

> Erasmus' return *ad fontes* is largely free of nostalgia for lost worlds.... [He] has the best claim of any Renaissance or "early modern" man to have anticipated our latter-day science of "Late Antiquity."[9]

This heady mixture of Platonism and patristics[10] did not suffice the scholars of the Renaissance and Reformation, unless accompanied by a hearty helping of ecclesiastical history. Catholics such as Cesare Baronius (d. 1607) or Le Nain de Tillemont (d. 1698) asserted Rome's traditions and privileges, Protestants such as Baronius's critic Casaubon (d. 1614) burrowed behind the imperial Papacy of the fifth and subsequent centuries to excavate a more pristine, authentic state of affairs. Before the eighteenth century, only a very few were interested in writing secular histories of any period of Antiquity.[11] For that to happen, and in particular for something nonconfessional and recognizable to us as late antique studies to emerge, a greater distance from Christianity was needed. Still in Gibbon the strife of Catholics and Protestants rumbles constantly through the footnotes, while the critical and rational historian flatters himself that he may "poise the balance with philosophic

6 M. Cortesi, "Valla, Laurentius," in H. R. Balz and others (eds), *Theologische Realenzyklopädie* (Berlin 1977–2007) 34.500–504; L. Valla (tr. G. W. Bowersock), *On the Donation of Constantine* (Cambridge, Mass. 2007).

7 H. D. Saffrey (ed.), *Thomas d'Aquin, Super Librum de causis expositio* (Paris 2002²).

8 A. Grafton, "Protestant versus Prophet: Isaac Casaubon on Hermes Trismegistus," *Journal of the Warburg and Courtauld Institutes* 46 (1983) 78–93 (noting, 86–87, that Casaubon was not the first to express skepticism about Trismegistus).

9 M. Vessey, "Cities of the mind: Renaissance views of early Christian culture and the end of Antiquity," in P. Rousseau (ed.), *A companion to late Antiquity* (Chichester 2009) 57; cf. id., "Jerome and the *Jeromanesque*," in A. Cain and J. Lössl (eds), *Jerome of Stridon* (Farnham 2009) 229–31. Gibbon made Erasmus "the father of rational theology" as well: 54: 3.438 n. 38.

10 Now renamed, especially in North America, "early Christian studies," registering a decline in philological as much as a rise in socio-anthropological competence.

11 Momigliano, *Sesto contributo* [1:25] 254–55. For some early accounts of late Antiquity, see A. Demandt, *Die Spätantike* (Munich 2007²) XV–XVII.

indifference" between the two camps.[12] In his *Vindication*, Gibbon expands on the historiographical juncture at which he finds himself:

> About two hundred years ago, the Court of Rome discovered that the system which had been erected by ignorance must be defended and countenanced by the aid, or at least by the abuse, of science. The grosser legends of the middle ages were abandoned to contempt, but the supremacy and infallibility of two hundred Popes, the virtues of many thousand Saints, and the miracles which they either performed or related, have been laboriously consecrated in the Ecclesiastical Annals of Cardinal Baronius. A Theological Barometer might be formed, of which the Cardinal and our countryman Dr. [Conyers] Middleton [d. 1750] should constitute the opposite and remote extremities, as the former sunk to the lowest degree of credulity, which was compatible with learning, and the latter rose to the highest pitch of scepticism, in any wise consistent with Religion. . . . It would be amusing enough to calculate the weight of prejudice in the air of Rome, of Oxford, of Paris, and of Holland; and sometimes to observe the irregular tendency of Papists towards freedom, sometimes to remark the unnatural gravitation of Protestants towards slavery.[13]

Even Gibbon necessarily remained, to a great extent, an ecclesiastical historian. But while acknowledging this, the most eminent present-day student of his thought can also recognize in him an Enlightened historian of late Antiquity.[14] In fact Gibbon's originality goes still further, for part of his attempt to get beyond the impasse described in the passage just quoted is the generous narrative attention he pays—already noted in chapter 1—to the Islamic empires, in "total ignorance of the Oriental tongues."[15] As for his opinion of Muḥammad and his religion, it is inflected by Enlightenment irony and a wish to tar Christianity by comparison—or at least orthodox Anglicanism as distinct from Unitarianism. (When Dr Johnson imagined Gibbon once a "Mahometan," he no doubt meant by that a Unitarian.)[16] Yet

12 E.g., Gibbon 49: 3.90 n. 11, 93 n. 18 (whence the quotation), 58: 565 n. 22; and the important passage, 54: 436–39.

13 E. Gibbon, *A Vindication* [ed. D. Womersley, in Gibbon 37: 3.1108–84] 1151; cf. Gibbon 37: 2.442 n. 115.

14 Pocock 1.4–5, 30, 42; 2.378–79, 402; 5.89–212.

15 Gibbon 50: 3.151 n. 1, 52: 3.353.

16 D. Womersley, *Gibbon and the "Watchmen of the Holy City"* (Oxford 2002) 147–72, placing Gibbon's composition of his account of Islam in the 1780s against the background of the Trinitarian controversies raging at that time. Gibbon describes Muslims as "Unitarians" at 3.178, 191, 550, etc. On radical Protestant anti-Trinitarian/Socinian/Unitarian sympathy for Islam, from the later sixteenth to the early eighteenth centuries, see M. Mulsow, "Socinianism, Islam and the radical uses of Arabic scholarship," *Al-Qantara* 31 (2010) 549–86.

Gibbon can almost be said to show true sympathy for the Prophet's rationality.[17] "The Mahometans have uniformly withstood the temptation of reducing the object of their faith and devotion to a level with the senses and imagination of man."[18] No project designed to assert Islam's relevance to study of the closing phase of Antiquity can afford to ignore Gibbon.

After 1800, the traditional preeminence of theology ceded place to philology and history. The critical, contextualizing approach already applied to the admired literature of Greek and Roman Antiquity began to be deployed on the Bible too. The consequences were not necessarily reductive, and the preoccupation with scripture continued to be immensely fertilizing. This was especially the case in Germany, whose academic culture was less agnostic than that of the French, less utilitarian and present-oriented than that of the British and Dutch. Especially in the Protestant theology faculties, exegesis of the Old Testament remained a major concern, and this entailed knowledge at the very least of Hebrew, and also of the other peoples on whom Israelite history touched: Egyptians, Assyrians, Babylonians, and Iranians. The main issue was the uniqueness—or not—of the Jews and their scriptures. It was inevitable that the New Testament too would eventually be historicized and contextualized; and when this happened, toward the end of the nineteenth century, there was an efflorescence of interest in rabbinic Judaism, Gnosticism, and the other religious currents of the Greek and Roman worlds. This was the so-called religious-historical school, which exhumed a vast range of Hellenistic and Roman spiritual and intellectual experience from neglect imposed by generations of "classical" purists, and cleared the way for broader study of comparative religion at the end of Antiquity.[19]

BURCKHARDT TO STRZYGOWSKI

In short, the impetus theological and philosophical concerns gave to interest in late Antiquity up to and including the nineteenth century can hardly be exaggerated. One might in principle imagine that this emphasis on ideas—the world of the mind—would favor a relatively generous chronological definition of late Antiquity. Do not Judaism and Christianity lead naturally on toward Islam? In practice, though, Christian scholarship followed its patristic sources and took inordinate interest in the destruction of paganism, seen as well under way by 400 and complete by the time of Justinian (529!). It also

17 Gibbon 50: 3.177–78, 184, 187, 190, 192, 212, 230, 51: 3.316. His esteem for Muḥammad's rationality was not without recent precedent: B. Lewis, *Islam and the West* (New York 1993) 89–90.

18 Gibbon 50: 3.230.

19 M. Mazza, *Tra Roma e Costantinopoli* (Catania 2009) 16–35; S. L. Marchand, *German Orientalism in the age of empire* (Cambridge 2009), esp. 259–70, 282–91.

had a rather restrictive view of its own intellectual formation, which most held to have been completed by the Council of Chalcedon in 451. So there was, in reality, little motivation coming from this quarter to paint late Antiquity on a broader canvas.

The emergence, in the mid-nineteenth century, of more secular approaches did not necessarily open up broader chronological horizons. If one lacked the believing scholar's conviction that the formation of Christianity was a development with living significance down to one's own day, one might find oneself composing a lament for another ideal—lost or corrupted Classicism. In fact, the first emergence of the precise expression "*late* Antiquity" is linked with the work of an historian who, far more than Gibbon, took literally late pagan and early Christian writers' harping on the old age and decline—explicitly conceived in biological terms—of the Roman world, especially in the fourth century.[20] When Jakob Burckhardt's *Die Zeit Constantins des Grossen* (translated into English as *The age of Constantine the Great*) appeared in 1853, his readers encountered a much more calculating, political figure than the Christian hero many were accustomed to; and this unvarnished portrait was accompanied by a consistently deflationary view of the period generally, explicitly presented in the famous central chapters (5–7) as Antiquity's senescence ("Alterung"). Not only does Burckhardt appear to have been the first to make explicit use of the concept "late Antiquity,"[21] but his generally pessimistic evaluation was to exercise notable influence, as we shall see at the end of this chapter.

Burckhardt showed considerable interest in such material evidence as was available at the time in the form of architecture, sculpture, and painting, seen as symptomatic of decline. Another generation was to pass before archaeologists began to uncover large quantities of new material and change the way late Antiquity was understood. Whole new areas of late antique experience—besides its aesthetics—were revealed for the first time: the fate of cities, the countryside, and the economy through—to single out one major discovery—the papyri from Oxyrhynchus; or the widespread and popular cult of the Iranian god Mithras, barely mentioned in literary sources. Chance played a part too. Until the American excavation of the Athens agora started

20 Cf. A. Demandt, "Das Ende des Altertums in metaphorischer Deutung," *Gymnasium* 87 (1980) 178–204.

21 Mazza, *Tra Roma e Costantinopoli* [2:19] 8–16. G. W. Bowersock, *From Gibbon to Auden* (New York 2009) 109–22, presents Burckhardt as a forerunner of the cultural-historical approach to late Antiquity popular from the 1970s onward, except of course in his emphasis on its decline (though that too is now coming back). On interest in late Antiquity during the decades before Burckhardt's book, see R. Herzog, *"Wir leben in der Spätantike": Eine Zeiterfahrung und ihre Impulse für die Forschung* (Bamberg 1987) 8–16 (the Oxford Movement, Chateaubriand, the decadent aesthetic); id., "Epochenerlebnis 'Revolution' und Epochenbewusstsein 'Spätantike': Zur Genese einer historischen Epoche bei Chateaubriand', in id. and R. Koselleck (eds), *Epochenschwelle und Epochenbewusstsein* (Munich 1987) 195–219.

in the 1930s, excavation levels from after c. 200 CE were usually discarded. But occasional mistakes were made, as for example Kaiser Wilhelm II's acquisition in 1903 of the whole facade of the supposedly Sasanid or Ghassanid, in any event pre-Islamic, palace of Mushattā near Amman, which once it arrived in Berlin turned out, frustratingly, to be Umayyad. The Mushattā debate became, in fact, something of a turning point, closely linked to the founding of the Berlin Islamic Museum.[22] At the same date another related conundrum occupied the same German Orientalist and art-historical circles, this time about the Umayyad bath house of Quṣayr ʿAmra quite near Mushattā. Was it fourth- or fifth-century, or Umayyad, or even later?[23] Disputes—and errors—such as these made scholars uncomfortably aware that the Islamic world was not as irrelevant to late Antiquity as they had assumed.

The passions Mushattā and Quṣayr ʿAmra aroused have to be understood in the light of a debate which, after simmering for some time, had taken off as recently as 1900 and 1901, especially in Vienna, and is often said to have inaugurated late antique studies. The debate was conducted within—indeed, at the very foundations of—the new discipline of art history, and revolved round the question of late antique style, touching on psychological issues at the heart of the period and its definition. Characteristic of this debate are four books representing a spectrum of positions from extreme Romanocentricity, via inclusive Romanocentricity, to emphasis on creative impulses sent out by the empire's eastern provinces, especially in Christian art. While none of these works dealt with the Islamic world, one of the scholars concerned had done so earlier in another book, to which I shall turn after examining the controversies of 1900 to 1901.

The Italian architectural historian Giovanni Rivoira (d. 1919) published his *Le origini dell'architettura lombarda* (translated into English, with revisions, as *Lombardic architecture: Its origin, development and derivatives*) in 1901–7 in the capital of the new Italian state, appropriately enough for this hymn to the creative genius of ancient Roman architects from the pen of a whole-hearted patriot. Given the strength of classical education in Europe, a considerable degree of Romanocentricity was taken for granted at this period; but Rivoira's version was particularly rabid. For him, both East Roman ("Byzantine") architecture and Islamic architecture were entirely derivative from Roman, their creators effeminate and/or depraved. With his Viennese opponents in mind (see below), Rivoira wrote disparagingly of "these days when Schools of Art are being discovered all over the East, and theories run

22 V. Enderlein and M. Meinecke, "Graben—Forschen—Präsentieren. Probleme der Darstellung vergangener Kulturen am Beispiel der Mschatta-Fassade," *Jahrbuch der Berliner Museen* 34 (1992) 137–72.

23 Fowden, *Quṣayr ʿAmra* [1:32] 19–21, 24.

riot on the evidence of little else than jewellery, enamels, ivories, textiles, painting, and carving." For Rivoira only architecture counted—the manly buildings of the Romans. He rubbed in this antipathy to the Orient by publishing in 1914 an abusive treatise on *Architettura musulmana, sue origini e suo sviluppo* (likewise translated with alacrity into English: *Moslem architecture: Its origins and development*). Rivoira had no serious interest in Muslim architecture—he merely wanted to remove any possible competitors with Rome. But he saw Islamic civilization could not be ignored.[24]

A considerably diluted version of Rivoira's Romanocentrism was promoted, in a theoretically sophisticated framework, by the Austrian art historian and—from 1895—professor of art history at Vienna, Alois Riegl (d. 1905). Significantly for the subsequent development of his ideas, Riegl started out cataloguing Egyptian textiles and Oriental carpets in Viennese collections, in other words analyzing mainly ornament rather than images, and on anonymous everyday objects. He argued, though, that even the carpets' characteristic motifs could be traced back to "international Hellenistic-Roman art."[25] It was in Riegl's two early books on Egyptian textiles and Oriental carpets that occurred the usages of the term "late Antiquity" ("die spätantike Zeit," "die späte Antike," defined by him as the fourth to seventh centuries)[26] which are usually, inaccurately, quoted as the earliest.[27]

For the purposes of the present exposition, Riegl's next book, the *Stilfragen* of 1893, is best held over for slightly later discussion. In any case his fame today rests principally on his *Die spätrömische Kunstindustrie*, published in Vienna in 1901 (and translated into English as *Late Roman art industry*). Here, Riegl addresses himself to artistic production in a spectrum of media, architecture, sculpture, and painting, but also the decorative arts derided by Rivoira, even belt buckles, brooches, and other items of personal adornment archaeologists had been discovering in abundance throughout the Austro-Hungarian Empire. From these neglected products of the era whose aesthetic Burckhardt had forthrightly dismissed, Riegl spun an analysis of a distinctive and original "artistic will" ("Kunstwollen") that demands to be understood for its own sake, rather than as decline from an earlier, ideal state. Kunstwollen, although rather nebulous, has endlessly fertilized subsequent theoretical

24 Cf. A. J. Wharton, *Refiguring the post classical city* (Cambridge 1995) 3–12, comparing Rivoira with Josef Strzygowski (see below). The quotation is from *Architettura musulmana* 70–71 (tr. 69). Rivoira's attitudes endured under fascism, galvanized by patriotic revulsion against Strzygowski's *Orient oder Rom*: M. Bernabò, *Ossessioni bizantine e cultura artistica in Italia* (Naples 2003) 82–83, 96–107.

25 A. Riegl, *Altorientalische Teppiche* (Leipzig 1891) 146.

26 A. Riegl, *Die ägyptischen Textilfunde* (*Mitteilungen des Österreichischen Museums für Kunst und Industrie* 2) (Vienna 1889) XV–XVI, XIX–XX, XXIII; id., *Altorientalische Teppiche* [2:25], e.g., 122, 123, 149.

27 E.g., M. Ghilardi, "Alle origini del dibattito sulla nascita dell'arte tardoantico," *Mediterraneo antico* 5 (2002) 119–20, 126 n. 54; E. James, "The rise and function of the concept "late Antiquity," " *JLA* 1 (2008) 20–21.

debate. Its interest in the present context, though, is that it was created specifically in order to deal with the apparent paradox of late Antiquity, which so markedly departed from earlier Roman canons of taste, yet whose artistic vigor and productivity implied that it possessed some rationale of its own, beyond simple failure to measure up to past achievements. After all, how could Constantine have commissioned such debased sculptures for his Arch in Rome, and placed them alongside other reliefs borrowed from the best age of Roman imperial art, the second century, if the former were such self-evidently inept[28] imitations of the latter? Riegl defined the new rationale, or "will," by minutely analyzing the conventions of the Arch of Constantine, among many other artifacts, in terms of symmetricality, frontality, rigidity, refusal of illusionism, schematization, and symbolization—in other words, all the formalist terminology that is now our main tool for describing the distinctive late antique aesthetic.[29]

Riegl's *Kunstindustrie* has acquired enormous importance in attempts to define late Antiquity; and "die späte Antike" is a concept that crops up here and there in the book, especially in its last pages.[30] Nevertheless, in the title and throughout the book Riegl prefers to speak of "late Roman" art, and explains that this is because his subject is not just the city of Rome but the whole Roman Empire, in which the most creative artists continued to be the Greeks and Orientals.[31] What is more, in the second volume—never published because he died so young—Riegl planned to take the story up where he had left off, with Justinian, and pursue it as far as Charlemagne. Plainly the focus would have been on what we call early medieval Europe. The Orient, whether East Roman or Muslim, was to have been excluded. As we shall see, this is a major contrast with Riegl's earlier *Stilfragen* of 1893, and even with his *Historische Grammatik der bildenden Künste* (*Historical grammar of the visual arts*) of 1897–99.[32] That makes *Stilfragen* of great interest in the context of the present argument; but it is *Kunstindustrie* that has enjoyed most of the attention. That speaks volumes about the majority view of late Antiquity.

Our other two publications from the first two years of the twentieth century represent the Oriental side of the debate, but are concerned with Christian art, not Islamic. The first is the Russian scholar Dmitrii Ainalov's (d.

28 ". . . sciocchissime, senza arte o disegno alcuno buono": Raffaello Sanzio (ed. E. Camesasca), *Tutti gli scritti* (Milan 1956) 55 ("A Papa Leone X"). My thanks to Luca Giuliani for this.

29 On Kunstwollen see J. Elsner, "The birth of late Antiquity: Riegl and Strzygowski in 1901," *Art history* 25 (2002) 361–70, esp. 363 and 367 on terminology.

30 A. Riegl, *Die spätrömische Kunstindustrie nach den Funden in Österreich-Ungarn* (Vienna 1901, 1927² [with different pagination, used here]; tr. R. Winkes, *Late Roman art industry* [Rome 1985]) 2 (6), 16 (14), 400–405 (230–33).

31 Riegl, *Kunstindustrie* [2:30] 16–18 (13–15).

32 A. Riegl (ed. K. M. Swoboda and O. Pächt), *Historische Grammatik der bildenden Künste* (Graz 1966) 33–37, 181–85.

1939) doctoral thesis titled *Ellinisticheskie osnovy vizantiiskogo iskusstva*, published in Saint Petersburg in 1900–1901 (and translated into English as *The Hellenistic origins of Byzantine art*). In this book, Ainalov develops and systematizes the thought of his teacher Nikodim Kondakov (d. 1925), professor of art history at Saint Petersburg. Kondakov belonged to a generation of Russians that, in the closing decades of the nineteenth century, embarked on the rediscovery of Russia's Byzantine heritage after almost two centuries of forced Europeanization. The icon was central to this undertaking, and behind Russian icons lay the whole history of Christian painting in the East, from even before Constantine. In a sequence of expeditions throughout the East, Kondakov gathered materials.[33] What Ainalov made of them was a narrative of Christian art history that saw it as, to be sure, an outgrowth from Greek and Roman Antiquity, but modified by borrowings from Asia Minor, Syria, Egypt, Iran, and even Central Asia. In Ainalov's analysis, Alexandria plays a prominent role. And the whole is articulated in explicit opposition to the Roman, especially Catholic view that art produced in the provinces was merely a series of variations on models created in the imperial city on the Tiber, particular weight being assigned to the catacomb paintings. Naturally, the foundation of New Rome on the Bosphorus hugely increased the force of Greek and Oriental influence.[34]

Kondakov's far-flung travels in the East, and the intellectual perspectives he communicated to his pupil, have to be seen in the light of Russia's geographical position, its Orthodox and viscerally anti-Roman Church, and the abundance of conveniently sited religious institutions it possessed in many of the areas in question. Nothing came more naturally than to look to Constantinople and the Christian Levant and Caucasus which had in varying ways depended on it—the East Roman Commonwealth to be discussed in chapter 4, but also the later "Byzantine Commonwealth" in the Slavic lands, of which Russia itself was a leading member. For a West European Catholic or Protestant to achieve this perspective required much more imagination and application, qualities possessed in superabundance by the fourth member of our quartet of art historians, another Austrian and a contemporary and classmate of Riegl, namely Josef Strzygowski (d. 1941).[35]

33 C. Mango, "Editor's Preface," in D. V. Ainalov (revised tr. E. and S. Sobolevitch), *The Hellenistic origins of Byzantine art* (New Brunswick, N. J. 1961) viii–ix; W. E. Kleinbauer, "Nikodim Pavlovich Kondakov," in D. Mouriki and others (eds), *Byzantine East, Latin West* (Princeton 1995) 637–42; H. Belting, *Bild und Kult* (Munich 2004[6]) 30–32.

34 Ainalov, *Hellenistic origins* [2:33] 3–7.

35 On Strzygowski's life see A. Karasek-Langer, "Josef Strzygowski. Ein Lebensbild," *Schaffen und Schauen. Mitteilungsblatt für Kunst und Bildungspflege in der Wojewodschaft Schlesien* 8 (7/8) (1932) 36–46; H. Schödl, *Josef Strzygowski—Zur Entwicklung seines Denkens* (diss. Vienna 2011) 12–20; A. Zäh, "Josef Strzygowski als Initiator der christlich-kunsthistorischen Orientforschung", *Römische Quartalschrift* 107 (2012) 251–69; id., "Josef Rudolf Thomas Strzygowski," in S. Heid and M. Dennert (eds),

Published in 1901, while Strzygowski was still a professor at Graz (he moved to Vienna in 1909), *Orient oder Rom: Beiträge zur Geschichte der spätantiken und frühchristlichen Kunst* (*The Orient or Rome: Contributions to the history of late antique and early Christian art*) was designed to annoy, and not only Catholics or supporters of the Habsburg Empire. Strzygowski was aware of the confused loyalties and desires Rome inspired, even if he knew nothing of Sigmund Freud's love-hate dreams about the city described in *The interpretation of dreams* (1900 [1899]), of his identification with the Semite Hannibal who vanquished Rome but never saw it, or of the Viennese psychoanalyst's long postponed visit there in the very year *Orient oder Rom* appeared.[36] Where Riegl's *Kunstindustrie* addressed late *Roman* art, Strzygowski's subtitle makes clear that the subject is late Antiquity, downgrading Rome from the very outset.[37] Where Riegl conceded that much of what was most creative in Roman art came from Greece and the Orient, Strzygowski pushes the argument further. Presenting a series of detailed studies of individual objects in a manner no less empirical than Riegl's, he demonstrates the impact Hellenistic, Coptic, Alexandrian, Syrian, Mesopotamian, and even Iranian visual culture made on the emergence of Christian iconography and, by extension, European art. In Strzygowski's view it was from origins in many Oriental centers rather than a single, "ultramontane" Western center—i.e., Rome—that late antique art drew its distinctive symmetricality, frontality, and so forth.[38] The idea that artistic inspiration all ran from imperial Rome to the provinces no longer held, and Strzygowski asserted the East's claim to be considered the source of major developments in what was known—rather undiscriminatingly, Strzygowski thought—as "Roman imperial art."[39] With Ainalov and Strzygowski the Mediterranean paradigm that had hitherto dominated art history took a decisive eastward shift[40]—a geographical theme I shall develop further in chapter 4.

Personenlexikon zur christlichen Archäologie (Regensburg 2012) 1200–1205. My thanks to Ebba Koch and Suzanne Marchand for help with Strzygowski.

36 S. Timpanaro, *La "fobia romana" e altri scritti su Freud e Meringer* (Pisa 1992) 23–86.

37 On the bitterly combative relations between Riegl and Strzygowski see Ghilardi, *Mediterraneo antico* 5 (2002) [2:27] 125–27; Elsner, Art history 25 (2002) [2:29] 358–79; G. Vasold, "Riegl, Strzygowski and the development of art," in *Towards a science of art history: J. J. Tikkanen and art historical scholarship in Europe* (Helsinki 2009) 103–16.

38 J. Strzygowski, *Orient oder Rom* (Leipzig 1901) 8, 22–23 (Iran), 24; id., *Hellas in des Orients Umarmung* (Munich 1902) 5 ("ultramontane"). Both works are helpfully analyzed by Schödl, *Josef Strzygowski* [2:35] 186–248. E. Kitzinger, *Byzantine art in the making* (London 1977) 9–10, points out that the Oriental artistic traditions so influential in the late antique Roman world had already absorbed—and adapted—the Greco-Roman "koine" in earlier centuries.

39 Strzygowski, *Orient oder Rom* [2:38] 1–2, 8, 53.

40 Despite vigorous resistance from such ultramontanes as Joseph Wilpert, student of Roman catacombs and sarcophagi: see his *Erlebnisse und Ergebnisse im Dienste der christlichen Archäologie* (Freiburg 1930), e.g., 186, 191–92, 204–6 (brought to my attention by Peter Brown); cf. C. Jäggi, "Die Frage nach

THE ORIENT AND ISLAM: VIEWS FROM VIENNA

Reviewing *Orient oder Rom*, Ainalov observed that "the whole direction of [Strzygowski's] thinking, with the addition of much more to which he has not yet paid adequate attention, is already contained *in extenso* in Russian scholarship."[41] Whatever the truth of this as regards the Christian East, Ainalov had no more to say about Islamic art than, at this stage, Strzygowski did; and of the two men, it was to be Strzygowski who turned out to be more open-minded in this direction, however ambiguously or inconclusively. Strzygowski's intellectual progress is in fact so paradigmatic of the shift eastward and beyond late Antiquity for which I am arguing, that it is worth following it in more detail, both before and after *Orient oder Rom*. In the matter of Islam, there is more to be said about Riegl too.

When in his mid-twenties Strzygowski conventionally enough went to pursue further study in Rome, there were already some hints of his future orientation. His projects, on Cimabue and the illustrated Calendar of 354 produced in Rome, reflected a sensitivity to the East derived from study of post-Greco-Roman art in Berlin with Eduard Dobbert, who had strong Saint Petersburg connections. In Rome he encountered Nadina Schakowskoy, wife of the assistant director of the German Archaeological Institute, Wolfgang Helbig. In 1887 the Helbigs rented the stunningly elegant Renaissance Villa Lante on the Janiculum—now the Institutum Romanum Finlandiae. Strzygowski, mid-twenties and ambitious, enjoyed the villa's artistic society, acquiring a social polish (as he freely admitted) and helping "la principessa" with her pet project, to translate Kondakov's *Histoire de l'art byzantin* (Paris 1886–91).[42] Beyond the Villa Lante's view across the Tiber and the Eternal City, there now opened up a far wider Oriental prospect, a new Byzantine horizon still largely uncharted by Western Europeans.[43]

Then in 1888, taking advantage of growing ease of travel by sea and rail, and the improving security of the Balkans and the Ottoman Levant, Strzygowski embarked on a thoroughly Kondakovian journey into the Byzantine

---

dem Ursprung der christlichen Kunst," in S. Heid (ed.), *Giuseppe Wilpert, archeologo cristiano* (Vatican 2009) 231–46.

41 *Vizantijskij vremennik* 9 (1902) 138–52, quoted by Mango in his Preface to Ainalov, *Hellenistic origins* [2:33] x (and cp. 4).

42 J. Strzygowski, *Aufgang des Nordens: Lebenskampf eines Kunstforschers um ein deutsches Weltbild* (Leipzig 1936) 11; cf. U. von Wilamowitz-Moellendorff, *Erinnerungen, 1848–1914* (Leipzig 1928) 142–43; L. Pollak, *Römische Memoiren* (Rome 1994) 89–91.

43 On the wider tension between "Romandom and Germandom" at this time, and German scholars' and artists' feeling that Rome was no longer exotic enough, see S. L. Marchand, *Down from Olympus* (Princeton 1996) 178.

East.[44] Thessalonica and Mount Athos were his first stops, and then Athens, where he threw himself into collecting the fragments of the Christian Acropolis at a time when Byzantine studies were beginning to take shape and efforts were being made by the newly established Christian Archaeological Society to set up a museum. Then on to Constantinople itself, and into Asia Minor, where our scholar might still find himself able to travel, even between such relatively familiar places as Bursa and Iznik, only as a guest of local brigands. Strzygowski now made his first contact with Armenia, an ancient Christian civilization, but also a land closely linked to Iran and destined one day to fertilize wide-ranging theories in the Austrian's mind about contacts and compatibilities between Aryan and Germanic culture.[45] Thence it was but a step to Moscow in 1890, where Strzygowski plunged headlong into the discovery of the icon by publishing two encaustic images recently brought from Sinai and now among the star specimens of early icon art. Co-editor of the *Byzantinische Zeitschrift* in Munich from its outset in 1892, Strzygowski had become every inch the Byzantinist. Yet six months in Egypt in 1894–95 opened his eyes—as Armenia had not—to a whole Oriental world at heart not Roman either Old or New. With his extraordinary talent for being in at beginnings, Strzygowski witnessed the early days of Coptic archaeology and the excavation, in large quantities, of papyri and textiles. (Here his raw materials intersect Riegl's exactly.) Henceforth the reevaluation of Eastern art, against conventional Romanocentrism and Mediterraneanism, was to be Strzygowski's vocation—or one of them, considering the literally planetary breadth of his interests and teaching once he moved to Vienna.

This extraordinary intellectual reach is implied in the words Strzygowski himself later chose to describe Egypt's effect on him. "From Egypt the road opened up, which led behind the coastal lands of the Eastern Mediterranean, into Inner Asia."[46] A similar course was being set by Strzygowski's friend with whom he had once "rummaged around" in the Vatican Library, Richard Reitzenstein (d. 1931). Both abandoned the classical canon in favor of previously neglected Oriental, especially Egyptian and Iranian currents of creativity. Reitzenstein became an eminent representative of the religious-historical school, and exhumed Hermes Trismegistus from his post-Casaubon neglect (*Poimandres*, 1904).[47]

44 Strzygowski, *Aufgang* [2:42] 11–14, 16–17; G. Fowden, "The Parthenon between Antiquity, barbarism and Europe" (review of A. Kaldellis, *The Christian Parthenon* [Cambridge 2009]), *Journal of Roman archaeology* 23 (2010) 806–7.

45 C. Maranci, "Locating Armenia," *Medieval encounters* 17 (2011) 147–66; ead., "Armenian architecture and Josef Strzygowski", in Zäh, *Römische Quartalschrift* 107 (2012) [2:35] 289–92.

46 Strzygowski, *Aufgang* [2:42] 14.

47 Strzygowski, *Aufgang* [2:42] 11; Mazza, *Tra Roma e Costantinopoli* [2:19] 25–30; Marchand, *German Orientalism* [2:19] 282–84, 287.

There is something unexpectedly Gibbonian (though more than excursive) about Strzygowski's gradual progress from Rome toward the Orient. Just as the historian of Rome's decline had used East Rome mainly to access fateful evolutions in the East, so Strzygowski treated it as an escape hatch from what he derisively called "Mittelmeerglauben"—while I have politely referred to it as the Mediterranean paradigm—and as his "Durchgangspunkt" or point of transition to the Orient and eventually to Iran, Inner Asia, and even China, all linked by the Silk Road.[48] Although these latter regions figure very little in *Orient oder Rom*, Strzygowski saw this book as the beginning of his "struggle" to prove Iran's insemination of early Teutonic culture along the northern Eurasian arc, bypassing the decadent "hot-house" cultures of the Mediterranean and Levant.[49] This theory became an obsession that partly (along with his fanatical hostility to Rome) explains the disrepute and even oblivion in which Strzygowski still languishes,[50] compared at least to Riegl, the patron saint of formalist reaction to the Warburg School's pursuit of meaning.[51] But it left, as we shall see, a legacy.

Between the Mediterranean world, which Strzygowski abandoned, and Iran, which he adopted—or, in the terms he himself came to prefer, between the Teutonic and Iranian halves of the Aryan world—lay what he called the

48 Strzygowski, *Aufgang* [2:42] 13–14, 65–66. On China see id., "Seidenstoffe aus Ägypten," *Jahrbuch der Königlich Preussischen Kunstsammlungen* 24 (1903) 147–78.

49 J. Strzygowski, *Altai-Iran und Völkerwanderung* (Leipzig 1917) IX. Discussion of archaeological evidence for cultural transmission along the northern Euroasiatic arc in terms of ethnicity has recently revived after a quiet period post-1945: see, e.g., V. Bierbrauer, *Ethnos und Mobilität im 5. Jahrhundert aus archäologischer Sicht: Vom Kaukasus bis Niederösterreich* (Munich 2008), esp. 5–8.

50 On Strzygowski's reputation, see P. O. Scholz, "Wanderer zwischen den Welten," in W. Höflechner and G. Pochat (eds), *100 Jahre Kunstgeschichte an der Universität Graz* (Graz 1992) 243–65. C. Wood, "Strzygowski und Riegl in den Vereinigten Staaten," *Wiener Jahrbuch für Kunstgeschichte* 53 (2004) 217–33, contrasts Strzygowski's striking but transient success in the 1920s United States with Riegl's long wait for recognition. On the extreme opinions espoused by Strzygowski in old age, see E. Frodl-Kraft, "Eine Aporie und der Versuch ihrer Deutung: Josef Strzygowski—Julius v. Schlosser," *Wiener Jahrbuch für Kunstgeschichte* 42 (1989) 37–38. I prefer to treat his scholarly views in context and on their merits, rather than in light of the political and racial ideas he expressed most forcibly at the end of his long life. For the kind of attitudinizing that passes for scholarship on Strzygowski, see Vasold, in *Towards a science of art history* [2:37] 112: "[I]s there any real justification to view Strzygowski in a positive light, to describe him as a pioneer of global art history, and to make a distinction between the 'early,' supposedly interesting Strzygowski, and the 'later,' openly racist scholar? In every respect the answer is emphatically 'no!' Strzygowski was a scholar who, despite his many innovative approaches, had a life-long attachment to his prejudices. A deep-seated anti-Semitism, coupled with an irrational fear of mixed, hybridized cultural forms, hindered his serious engagement with the complex unfolding of European and non-European culture." During and after Strzygowski's lifetime, the nature (and our understanding) of "anti-Semitism" underwent precisely such a "complex unfolding." The conference on "Josef Strzygowski and the sciences of art" at Bielsko-Biala in 2012 showed that a more balanced approach to Strzygowski is now possible: http://strzygowski.umcs.lublin.pl/konferencja_en.html; cf. also Zäh, *Römische Quartalschrift* 107 (2012) [2.35] 249–92.

51 Cf. J. Elsner, "Alois Riegl and classical archaeology," in P. Noever and others (eds), *Alois Riegl revisited* (Vienna 2010) 45–57.

"Semitic wedge."[52] Here, despite his interest in the region's Christian art, Strzygowski never established the warm sympathies he achieved elsewhere. In particular, he failed to get substantially to grips with the genesis and complex development of Islamic art.[53] Not for want of trying, though, and partly in response to Riegl's *Stilfragen: Grundlegungen zu einer Geschichte der Ornamentik* (translated into English as *Problems of style: Foundations for a history of ornament*), published in 1893. This book is a neglected and remarkably early milestone in our progress toward an integrated understanding of late Antiquity and Islam. Something needs to be said of *Stilfragen* here, before we return to Strzygowski.

Extending his early interest in Egyptian textiles and Oriental carpets, Riegl had next turned to a more general concern with the construction and history of ornament. Unlike figural art or its self-conscious avoidance, both of which can give one a sense of direct access to "meaning," ornament has often seemed an unattractively formal subject of research. Yet it is capable of telling historians a lot about quieter yet still substantial contacts, continuities, or evolutions between civilizations. In this arcane field of study, Riegl's achievement in *Stilfragen* was to trace the "historical and genetic continuity" of vegetal and tendril ornament "in an unbroken sequence" through Egyptian, Mesopotamian, Phoenician, Iranian, and Greek art to the arabesque in late Antiquity and East Rome and, finally, in Islamic art right down to fifteenth-century Cairo.[54] In the Introduction to *Kunstindustrie*, Riegl summarized his earlier findings as follows:

> I believe I have demonstrated in the *Stilfragen* that the Byzantine and Saracen tendril ornament of the Middle Ages was developed directly from the classical tendril ornament of Antiquity, and that the connecting links are present in Hellenistic and Roman imperial art. Accordingly, at least for tendril ornament, the late Roman period does not mean decay, but rather progress, or at least an achievement of independent worth.[55]

52 J. Strzygowski (tr. O. M. Dalton and H. J. Braunholtz), *Origins of Christian Church art* (Oxford 1923) 2, 32.

53 For an overview, G. A. Reisenauer, *Josef Strzygowski und die islamische Kunst* (Diplomarbeit, Vienna University 2008, http://othes.univie.ac.at/917/1/2008-08-18_9105823.pdf).

54 A. Riegl, *Stilfragen* (Berlin 1893; tr. E. Kain [Princeton 1992], with abundant commentary), esp. 338 (298) and 346 (305) for the quotations; also 258, 273, 291 (228, 240, 256) for references to "late Antiquity." Cf. the lucid recapitulation and contextualization of Riegl's argument by J. Trilling, *The language of ornament* (London 2001) 113–25; also the discussion of arabesque scholarship before and after Riegl by G. Necipoğlu, *The Topkapı scroll* (Santa Monica, Calif. 1995) 61–87. New early Islamic materials in B. Finster, "Researches in 'Anjar II," *Bulletin d'archéologie et d'architecture libanaises* 11 (2007) 143–65.

55 Riegl, *Kunstindustrie* [2:30] 7 (9, modified). On Islamic art in Riegl's *Historische Grammatik der bildenden Künste* (1897–99) [2:32] see J.-P. Caillet, "Alois Riegl et le fait social dans l'art de l'antiquité tardive," *Antiquité tardive* 9 (2001) 50.

The understanding of art history Riegl purveyed in *Stilfragen* was, in other words, both "universalhistorisch"[56] and optimistic. "There is no regression or pause, but . . . constant progress," Riegl himself claimed;[57] "the history of the acanthus scroll is turned into an epic of vast dimensions," as Ernst Gombrich put it.[58] No echo here of Burckhardt's late Antiquity as an era of decay, despite the sincere homage Riegl pays the Swiss historian in his Introduction. In fact, *Stilfragen* went to the opposite extreme. It now seems an overly mechanistic marshalling of scientifically catalogued phenomena into a narrative of inevitable linear evolution, though within a geographically rather circumscribed region, namely the Mediterranean and the Levant, whose monuments were more familiar to Europeans than those of—say—Iran. No space was left for parallel or divergent developments; everything was made to tend toward the same goal. Note too that it was—and remains—much easier to write epic history through objects than texts. What was more, by Riegl's day Semitic studies had become an independent field distinct from both theology (patristics) and classics. Philologists no longer expected to master all the relevant languages. Even if they had, that would not have made them historians. The compartmentalization and specialization of scholarship was making it too easy to write epic based on only one type of evidence.

Nevertheless, Riegl deserves great credit not only for having insisted, in *Stilfragen*, on taking late Antiquity on its own terms, indeed highlighting it, but also for making the Islamic world part of an organic yet at the same time highly creative continuum with the earlier phases of Antiquity. "The difference between late antique and Islamic ornament seems," he stated, "to be merely a matter of degree rather than some deep-seated distinction."[59] If not already by the ninth century, when the Abbasids were building their vast, repetitively decorated palaces at Sāmarrā' north of Baghdad, then certainly by the time of the Mamluks, Timurids, Ottomans, and Safavids, in other words from roughly the early thirteenth century onward, the Islamic world evolved—it is true—distinctive art styles of its own, whose relationship to Antiquity does not leap out at one.[60] But even so, many of the conventions of earlier Islamic art can be grasped in terms of the progressive geometrization of naturalistic Greco-Roman forms already under way in the nets of finely carved acanthus spread over capitals, pilasters, and so forth in Justinian's Hagia Sophia (and soon imitated in the eastern provinces[61]), along with the

56 J. von Schlosser, "Die Wiener Schule der Kunstgeschichte," *Mitteilungen des Österreichichen Instituts für Geschichtsforschung, Ergänzungsband* 13(2) (1934) 183.

57 Riegl, *Kunstindustrie* [2:30] 18 (15).

58 E. H. Gombrich, *The sense of order* (London 1984²) viii.

59 Riegl, *Stilfragen* [2:54] XVI–XVIII (11–12), 306 (271).

60 Riegl, *Stilfragen* [2:54] 326 (288).

61 Museum für Byzantinische Kunst, Staatliche Museen zu Berlin, nr. 6159: Bawit (?), sixth century.

infinite unbroken extension of designs thus generated, in any direction—what Riegl calls the arabesque's "infinite rapport."[62]

This continuum Riegl posited between Roman and Islamic art was anathema to Strzygowski, who in the aftermath of *Orient oder Rom* increasingly saw Muslim style as an outflow from Iran.[63] When Kaiser Wilhelm II first saw photos of the Mushattā facade, he observed that their carving resembled Sasanian textiles.[64] Since scholars had thought of Mushattā as Iranian ever since its discovery in 1872,[65] the idea may not have been the Kaiser's own; but it certainly became the perpetual Leitmotif of Strzygowski's involvement with Mushattā, even before it arrived in Berlin in 1903. Since those who maintained it was Umayyad had already carried the day by 1910,[66] we can see that in matters Islamic Strzygowski got himself on the wrong track from the very outset—and he was not one to retract. On the contrary, he dug himself in ever deeper, and in the twenties and thirties proclaimed Mushattā "Parthian" to any who would listen.[67]

This is not the place to pursue Strzygowski's subsequent contribution to Islamic art history, except to note that it was dominated by pursuit of Iranian and denial of Mediterranean roots, an attitude more appropriate to Turkish-Mongolian than to Umayyad and Abbasid Islam.[68] It is rewarding, though, to glance at a couple of recent statements on the field once dominated by Riegl and Strzygowski, to see how their influence now stands. On the question of ornament, Terry Allen offers the following general conclusion:

> Islamic art is an extension of, not a radical change of course from, the aesthetic trends of Late Antiquity (the fourth through sixth centuries A.D.).... Early Islamic art, while it naturally grows away from its sources, is still a branch of the art of Late Antiquity, coordinate in its aesthetic logic with Byzantine art and with Western medieval art from the Merovingians to the Gothic age.... Byzantine art, and Western medieval art too, had the same potential as Islamic art but took different courses. A parallel assimilation of vegetation to geometry hap-

62 Riegl, *Stilfragen* [2:54] 308 (273); cf. C. Vanderheyde, "Motifs et compositions géométriques des sculptures architecturales byzantines," *Ktèma* 35 (2010) 273–84, noting the reciprocal influence of geometrized Kufic decoration on Middle Byzantine architecture.

63 J. Strzygowski, *Die Stellung des Islam zum geistigen Aufbau Europas* (Acta Academiae Aboensis, Humaniora 3:3 [Åbo 1922]) 16.

64 W. von Bode, *Mein Leben* (Berlin 1930) 2.155–56.

65 Enderlein and Meinecke, *Jahrbuch der Berliner Museen* 34 (1992) [2:22] 146; also A. Gayet, *L'art persan* (Paris 1895) 113; G. Bell, www.gerty.ncl.ac.uk, letter 22.3.1900.

66 E. Herzfeld, "Die Genesis der islamischen Kunst und das Mshatta-Problem," *Der Islam* 1 (1910) 27–63, 105–44.

67 Strzygowski, *Stellung des Islam* [2:63] 25; id., Aufgang [2:42] 18.

68 Reisenauer, *Josef Strzygowski* [2:53]. For a sympathetic and entertaining judgment, see R. Hillenbrand, "Creswell and contemporary Central European scholarship," *Muqarnas* 8 (1991) 27–28.

> pened entirely separately in Ireland: the designs in the Book of Kells are very much like arabesques based on a different set of geometric constructions and using different motifs.[69]

It is not just the technical art-historical analysis of the arabesque, but also the universalist perspective reaching as far as Ireland, that puts us in mind here of Riegl. At the same time, Allen's recognition that there was a mutual openness between Roman and Eastern art, and insistence that the motifs in East Roman art, which foreshadowed the arabesque, were themselves of Eastern, especially Sasanian origin,[70] betrays the enduring but often (as here) unacknowledged influence of Strzygowski.

In her recent book on the architecture of Alexandria and Egypt, Judith McKenzie has adopted a fully Ainalovian/Strzygowskian reading of Alexandrian influence on the art of Constantinople, Armenia, and even Ravenna.[71] Strzygowski is acknowledged. McKenzie also pursues Alexandrian influence into the arts of the early Islamic world, so bringing about a timely synthesis of Riegl and Strzygowski. And by emphasizing the role of Alexandria's schools of mathematics both theoretical and applied (to engineering and architecture), as well as its workshops, McKenzie draws out not just the artistic but also the intellectual continuities underlying the First Millennium, to which we shall turn in chapter 5.

On the eve of the First World War, we can say that the concept of a distinctive, not merely transitional period known as late Antiquity had come to stay. Riegl even claimed that "the problem of late Antiquity [he meant its art] is the most important and radical one in the entire history of mankind so far."[72] In some minds this period was associated particularly with Rome and the West on the eve of the barbarian invasions and the Middle Ages, while others looked to the dynamic cultures of the Christian East and Iran. In other words the whole extended geographical zone from the Mediterranean to Afghanistan, which I shall sketch in chapter 4, had already been brought

69 T. Allen, "The arabesque, the beveled style, and the mirage of an early Islamic art," in F. M. Clover and R. S. Humphreys (eds), *Tradition and innovation in late Antiquity* (Madison 1989) 210, 230. Cf. Necipoğlu, *Topkapı scroll* [2:54] 95: "a concern with rupturing the classical ideal of mimesis . . . direct translations or reinterpretations of classical prototypes, reflecting a programmatic process of abstraction whose rationale has so far escaped explanation" (she proceeds to offer a philosophical one).

70 Allen, in Clover and Humphreys (eds), *Tradition and innovation* [2:69] 226–28; and cf. M. P. Canepa, *The two eyes of the earth: Art and ritual of kingship between Rome and Sasanian Iran* (Berkeley 2009) 330 n. 82, on S. Polyeuctus in Constantinople.

71 J. McKenzie, *The architecture of Alexandria and Egypt c.300 BC to AD 700* (New Haven 2007) 329–75.

72 A. Riegl, "Spätrömisch oder orientalisch?," *Beilage zur Allgemeine Zeitung München* 93 (23.4.1902) 153–56, 162–65, ad init. Cf. Herzog, *"Wir leben in der Spätantike"* [2:21] 26: "In der Tat . . . ist die Eroberung der Spätantike die letzte grosse Epochenkonstitution, die letzte grosse historische Aneignung der Antike gewesen."

into play. Finally, in the last forty pages of *Stilfragen* Riegl had put the Islamic development of late antique artistic tropes and "Kunstwollen"—in other words, of the whole late antique cast of mind—firmly on the agenda.

Strzygowski kicked against this, but could not deny the Islamic world's importance, or of course the fundamental role played by the study of art in establishing it. Meanwhile the more inclusive approach to the Islamic sphere found an eloquent advocate in Carl Becker (d. 1933), a combination of Semitic philologist and social theorist who made his academic career at Hamburg and then Bonn before going into politics.[73] Becker wanted to embrace Islam in a broader narrative of history, partly because he recognized the role it played in his own day. Early Islam he treated as neither Iranian nor just a self-generated, unique Qur'anic religion, but as a culture and polity together, standing on the shoulders of Greece and Rome—an Antiquity understood, though, in its full diversity, in the light of the religious-historical school. "Without Alexander the Great, no Islamic civilization!" was Becker's motto, even if that civilization was a reaction against Antiquity as well as its consummation.[74] This acceptance of Islam's relatedness to Antiquity broadly conceived had consequences, too, for how Becker viewed the contemporary Islamic world, which was of increasing concern to Europeans, especially colonial authorities. Becker encouraged the Kaiser's cultivation of an Ottoman-German alliance, and once war broke out backed the proposal that the Ottoman Empire declare jihād against the Entente powers. At least in some minds, Islam and Christendom had never drawn closer; nor had the prospects for integrated study of them been better.

PIRENNE TO THE PRESENT

The destruction of the German and Ottoman Empires, not to mention the Austro-Hungarian and Russian, along with deep disillusionment over the peace settlement throughout the Muslim world, created a blasted intellectual and political landscape without prospects for rapprochement between the Islamic world and Europe, despite Becker's continuing pleas. Historians of the period in which Islam first emerged found nothing in their new milieu to stimulate them to an inclusive or universalistic approach. As for students of the fifth-century West, they could hardly fail to notice that then, too, Roman civilization—in Gaul, for example—had faced Germanic barbarism or, in more modern terms, Teutonist ideology and rejection of Romanocentricity, in the manner of Strzygowski.[75] After 1918, French and other scholars

73 Marchand, *German Orientalism* [2:19] 361–67, and 438–46 on jihād.

74 C. H. Becker, *Islamstudien* (Leipzig 1924–32) 1.16.

75 On the background to this, see Marchand, *Down from Olympus* [2:43] 156–62.

dreamed of rebuilding Rome's frontiers to keep the barbarians out.[76] Scholars from the former Central Powers found themselves disinvited to international gatherings—though the charismatic and well-connected Strzygowski spent much of 1920 to 1922 lecturing in England, Holland, and the United States.[77] Some attempt to get to grips with the issues, at least as regards the earlier confrontation between civilization and barbarism—which in so many ways recalled both the recent past (1814–15, 1870–71) and the present[78]—was made at the International Congress of Historical Sciences held at Brussels in 1923. One of the questions agitated there was whether the Germanic invaders could have been bearers of any sort of culture worth talking about, with a predictable division of opinion between French and German scholars.[79]

It almost had to be a Belgian—and one for whom, in contrast to Strzygowski, "race and language were infinitely plastic"[80]—who found the perfect resolution to these Franco-German tensions. It was Henri Pirenne's (d. 1935) genial idea, first propounded in 1922 but fully published posthumously in 1937, to leave 410 and all that on one side, and blame the end of Antiquity on the Arabs.[81] For Pirenne, a low-level Romanity survived parallel to the establishment of the Germanic kingdoms, mainly because the basic patterns of commercial exchange also persisted (Pirenne's famous Syrian merchants in Gaul). It was only with the Arab invasions in the seventh century, especially when they spread across North Africa, that Mediterranean unity broke. Thereafter the Latin world turned in on itself, and substituted Frankish roughness for the old Mediterranean sheen. Just as for Becker Islamic civilization could not have come into being without Alexander, so for Pirenne Charlemagne was inconceivable without Muḥammad.[82] The difference was that for Becker (reading the Arabic sources) the Arabs' role was laudable, while for Pirenne (dependent on the Byzantinist Vasiliev) it brought about a permanent rupture.[83] But in the end both scholars were interested in one thing: the genealogy of Europe, not the development of a complex cultural tradition up to and *through* Islam.

76 On what follows, see C. Violante, *La fine della 'grande illusione': Uno storico europeo tra guerra e dopoguerra, Henri Pirenne (1914–1923)* (Bologna 1997) 147–279; K. D. Erdmann (tr. A. Nothnagle), *Toward a global community of historians: The International Historical Congresses and the International Committee of Historical Sciences 1898–2000* (New York 2005) 68–100.

77 Karasek-Langer, *Schaffen und Schauen* 8(7/8) (1932) [2:35] 43–44; Schödl, *Josef Strzygowski* [2:35] 17–19.

78 Herzog, *"Wir leben in der Spätantike"* [2:21] 12–13.

79 A. Marcone, "Un treno per Ravenna," in L. Polverini (ed.), *Arnaldo Momigliano nella storiografia del novecento* (Rome 2006) 228–29.

80 P. Brown, *Society and the holy in late Antiquity* (London 1982) 71.

81 Cf. P. Delogu, "Reading Pirenne again," in R. Hodges and W. Bowden (eds), *The sixth century* (Leiden 1998) 15–40, emphasizing how Pirenne managed to moderate his dislike of Germans.

82 H. Pirenne, *Mahomet et Charlemagne* (Paris 1937) 210.

83 Pirenne, *Mahomet et Charlemagne* [2:82] 132, 143.

Current scholarship maintains, in the light of a great deal of archaeology done since Pirenne's day, that there was less commercial continuity than he supposed, and that things had been coming adrift ever since the third century. Trade gradually got more and more localized; Pirenne concentrated too much on literary sources that focused on exotic long-distance exchanges and the luxury goods favored by the elites they wrote about. On the other hand, it continues to be held that there was indeed a further relaxation of Mediterranean-wide communications and commerce, reaching its nadir c. 700.[84] Our concern here, though, is not so much the economic realities of late Antiquity as the historiographical trends of the twentieth. Not only was Pirenne's thesis widely debated, and indeed adopted by many; it was also perceived to have moral justice on its side. Who better than the Muslim Arabs, doubly alien, to assume the role of Antiquity's executioner? Hence the still widespread conviction that late Antiquity lasts until c. 600 rather than ending in 410, or 476 with the last Western emperor, Romulus Augustulus, or in 529. After Pirenne, a student of late *Antiquity* might elect to include the Germanic successor states on formerly Roman soil, while a student of late *Roman* history might exclude them, as did A. H. M. Jones in what remains the standard reference work,[85] *The later Roman Empire 284–602: A social, economic and administrative survey* (1964). But all were agreed that the Arabs and Islam were not relevant. Their coming marked an entirely new epoch not just in religion but in society, economy, and administration—not to mention the language of the sources.

Given that my purpose is not to write the history of late antique studies, but to point out that the birth and early development of Islam has long been perceived, at least by some, as an integral part of the story, and that this should be our model, there is little to detain us in the post-Pirenne period. In Germany Albert von Le Coq, publishing his spectacular pre–Great War, often eighth- and ninth-century Buddhist and Manichean finds from the Silk Road oases of the Tarim Basin (especially Turfan) under the title *Die buddhistische Spätantike in Mittelasien* (1922–33), was pushing far beyond the bounds, both geographical and chronological, of what anybody else meant by late Antiquity. Hans Lietzmann, tackling the general cultural identity of late Antiquity, broadly followed Strzygowski in his positive evaluation of the Orient, yet saw Islam as a step too far. Riegl's art-historical analysis he found far too divorced from its general historical context.[86]

84 M. McCormick, *Origins of the European economy* (Cambridge 2001) 117–19, 576.

85 Or "the greatest intellectual achievement of twentieth-century ancient history": F. Millar, *A Greek Roman Empire* (Berkeley 2006) 4. Jones offered several dates for the end of the ancient world, none of them very convincingly argued: Av. Cameron, "A. H. M. Jones and the end of the ancient world," in D. M. Gwynn (ed.), *A. H. M. Jones and the later Roman Empire* (Leiden 2008) 241–43.

86 H. Lietzmann, "Das Problem der Spätantike," *Sitzungsberichte der preussischen Akademie der Wissenschaften, Philosophisch-historische Klasse* (1927) 345–46, 358 (= id., *Kleine Schriften* [Berlin 1958–62] 1.7–8, 24).

The leading French student of late Antiquity, Henri-Irénée Marrou, was a Catholic intellectual who stood in the tradition of patristic scholarship. Like Lietzmann he came to reject the decline diagnosis (having first espoused it, in his study of Augustine), and this rejection deeply influenced subsequent scholarship.[87] Yet he pointedly ignored Strzygowski[88] and barely touched on the Islamic world. In a few pages written at the very end of his life, he evoked what he called "entrelacs," interlace decoration either continuous or knotted, and dwelt with special warmth and admiration on its development in the Book of Kells, while dismissing the Muslim arabesque as too rigidly rational.[89]

As for the Italian Santo Mazzarino's famous notion that late antique culture underwent a "democratization,"[90] he understood that as a symptom of vigor and change not sclerosis, so one might take him as broadly sympathetic to Strzygowski's position, Oriental influences being a surge from "below." Mazzarino was mainly concerned with the third century, though, and had little to say about Islam. Ernst Stein's *Geschichte des spätrömischen Reiches/ Histoire du Bas-Empire* (1928–59) and Jones's *Later Roman Empire* were major achievements, but firmly Romanocentric (the empire not the city). They ended in 565 and 602, respectively, and eschewed the wider horizons that might have been accommodated under the rubric "late Antiquity."

On a quite different wavelength, closer to that of von Le Coq, the Tübingen Romanist Joseph Vogt was advocating a kind of UNESCO-style approach to ancient history, proclaiming in the year 1957:

> It is our generation's desire, after political catastrophes and spiritual debacles, to regain our bearings in a historical world that embraces all of mankind. In this situation, the problem of the ancient world's contacts

87 Cf. Mazza, *Tra Roma e Costantinopoli* [2:19] 36–50.

88 H.-I. Marrou, *Décadence romaine ou antiquité tardive? IIIe-VIe siècle* (Paris 1977) 12; id., *Christiana tempora* (Rome 1978) 69.

89 Marrou, *Décadence romaine* [2:88] 163–67 (and contrast T. Allen's observations quoted above pp. 35–36). In the long run, a much more fertile contribution to the study of Islam in relation to late Antiquity was made by the French sociologist Maurice Halbwachs in his *La topographie légendaire des évangiles en Terre Sainte: Étude de mémoire collective* (Paris 1941). Halbwachs began his investigation of the Palestinian holy places with the Bordeaux Pilgrim, who was already in 333 expounding a thoroughly Christianized vision of Roman geography (J. Elsner, "The *Itinerarium Burdigalense*: Politics and salvation in the geography of Constantine's empire," *Journal of Roman studies* 90 [2000] 194–95). Halbwachs's pursuit of his theme down to early modern times requires him to touch on the sociopolitical consequences of Muslim rule; but Islam also had its own literary take on the life of Christ, as now demonstrated, with copious acknowledgment to Halbwachs, by L. Valensi, *La fuite en Égypte: Histoires d'Orient et d'Occident* (Paris 2002). The development of Halbwachs's study of cultural or collective memory by J. Assmann, *Das kulturelle Gedächtnis* (Munich 1992), has already had some impact on study of Islam; see, e.g., the articles gathered in *Numen* 58 nos. 2–3 (2011). On Halbwachs, see recently D. Iogna-Prat, "Maurice Halbwachs ou la mnémotopie," *Annales: Histoire, sciences sociales* 66 (2011) 821–37.

90 S. Mazzarino, [*Il basso impero:*] *Antico, tardoantico ed èra costantiniana* (Bari 1974–80) 1.74–98.

with neighbouring cultural areas has become a problem of singular significance.[91]

A tremendous contribution to the opening up of those wider horizons was soon to be made by a Protestant scholar from Dublin whose failure in later life to embrace Romanocentricity had not a little to do with his upbringing—just as Strzygowski's Germanized Polish ancestry and education in first a Catholic and then a Protestant school presumably contributed to his pathological inability to think in the foreordained boxes.[92] It was while lecturing on Augustine in Oxford in 1964, and preparing a book on the great bishop of Hippo worthy to be set beside the Catholic Marrou's, that Peter Brown began to use the concept "late Antiquity,"[93] which had been trickling into English from German since the 1940s.[94] The context was once again cultural rather than political history, the fourth and fifth centuries' "haunting mixture of classical reticence and new religiosity." When he introduced the whole *World of late Antiquity* to a wider audience in 1971, what had hitherto been regarded as the catastrophe of 410 was given short shrift, as also were the fifth-century Germanic successor states. By contrast, gradual cultural transformations in the Roman East were highlighted. The book's last two sections were devoted to "Byzantium" and then the Islamic world, just as in Riegl's *Stilfragen*. The concluding chapter is subtitled "The late antique world under Islam, 632–809."[95]

91 Quoted by Marchand, *Down from Olympus* [2:43] 359.

92 Brown, *SODebate* 7–9 (note the comment on Haghia Sophia perceived "from the countries of the Middle East rather than from Rome"). On Strzygowski, see above, n. 35.

93 P. Brown, "What's in a name?," www.ocla.ox.ac.uk/pdf/brown_what_in_name.pdf p. 1; cf. id., *SODebate* 17–18, and M. Vessey, *Latin Christian writers in late Antiquity and their texts* (Aldershot 2005) XI.393–94.

94 James, *JLA* 1 (2008) [2:27] 21. A measure of Brown's achievement is the assumption that before him all was a "black hole" (or, one might say, jāhilīya). For choice expressions of this perspective, see Carrié, in Carrié and Rousselle, *Empire romain en mutation* [1:26] 20; P. Heather, *The fall of the Roman Empire* (London 2005) xii; C. Ando, "Narrating decline and fall," in Rousseau (ed.), *Late Antiquity* [2:9] 59; J. Osterhammel, *Die Verwandlung der Welt: Eine Geschichte des 19. Jahrhunderts* (Munich 2009) 88. One hundred ten French university teachers and researchers attended a Rencontre sur l'Antiquité tardive at Chantilly in 1972: A. Solignac, "Rencontre sur l'Antiquité tardive," *Revue des études augustiniennes* 18 (1972) 373–87. On Marrou's research seminar at the Sorbonne, 1950–75, and the foundation of the Centre de recherche sur l'Antiquité tardive Lenain de Tillemont in 1972, see http://henrimarrou.org/historien/directeur-recherches.htm. For a more personal view of the French scene, see E. Patlagean, "Sorting out late antique poverty in Paris around the '60s," in C. Straw and R. Lim (eds), *The past before us* (Turnhout 2004) 79–87. Even confining oneself largely to English-language publications, one can assemble an impressive late *Roman* bibliography from the 1920s up to Jones: Cameron, in Gwynn (ed.), *A. H. M. Jones* [2:85] 231–38.

95 P. Brown, *The world of late Antiquity from Marcus Aurelius to Muhammad* (London 1971; repr. as *The world of late Antiquity AD 150–750*, with revised Bibliography [New York 1989]). The cutoff point is notoriously hazy: apart from 809 we have 750 in the reprint title, 700 on the first page of the Preface, and "Muhammad" in the original title. P. Brown, "Late Antiquity and Islam: Parallels and con-

Although, for Brown, the rise of Islam was undeniably a crisis, it was a crisis in the religious history of late Antiquity not of some alien world, and it started in Mecca, which was linked to commercial and cultural centers in the Iranian-Roman sphere to the north. The Qur'ān alluded to both Judaism and Christianity as practiced in Syria and Mesopotamia. And although the Arabs' military and political successes turned inside out the old order centered on Ctesiphon and Constantinople, there was a substantial cultural continuity, still to this day visible in the Umayyad monuments of Greater Syria. Where Rome both Greek and Latin underwent deep transformations under the impact—however gradual in the West—of German and Arab conquests, the new Islamic empire preserved at least the late antique forms, Iranian as well as Roman. Indeed, the Iranian world got the upper hand after the Abbasid revolution that expelled the Umayyads in 750.

Besides its narrative text, *The world of late Antiquity* is also a visual feast. The last photograph of all shows figural carving from the Umayyad palace at Khirbat al-Mafjar, closely related in both space and time to Mushattā. The caption speaks of "this revival of Persian tastes and artistic traditions . . . that smothered the Late Antique forms of representational art." The adjacent, concluding pages of text dilate on the triumph of the Persianized Abbasids:

> Thus, in the end, it was the traditions of Khusro I Anoshirwan which won over those of Justinian I. . . . And, in Persian hands, the eternal lure of Further Asia reasserted itself. . . . Just before he was crowned Roman emperor of the West in 800, Charlemagne received from Harun al-Rashid a great cloak and a pet elephant called Abul Abaz. Little did the Frankish monarch know it, but in this gift the calif had merely repeated the time-honoured gesture of Khusro I Anoshirwan when, at the great Spring festival, the king of kings had lavished gifts of animals and cast-off clothing on his humble servants.[96]

Now Peter Brown, like Marrou and many others, is no admirer of Strzygowski, having deplored his "erratic and, to a modern reader, highly unpleasant tone,"[97] and pointedly excluded him (but not Riegl or—see below—Rostovtzeff) from a list of scholars who excelled where Strzygowski had shown the way, in the analysis of nonelite late antique culture.[98] Nonetheless, beyond certain similarities of style between two men both eager to offend the Establishment and replace traditional Romanocentricities with astonish-

---

trasts," in B. D. Metcalf (ed.), *Moral conduct and authority: The place of adab in South Asian Islam* (Berkeley 1984) 23–37, confines itself to reflecting on moral authority and deportment among educated men and monks in late Antiquity, and the Muslim elites.

96 Brown, *World of late Antiquity* [2:95] 200, 202, 203.

97 P. Brown, *Art bulletin* 77 (1995) 500, on T. F. Mathews, *The clash of gods* (Princeton 1993).

98 P. Brown, "Images as a substitute for writing," in E. Chrysos and I. Wood (eds), *East and West: Modes of communication* (Leiden 1999) 16.

ing new analogies and combinations,[99] there is also an undeniable congruence of historical analysis in the passage just quoted; and it is worth asking how this arose. Again, a crucial link is provided by a pupil of Kondakov, and the fertile Russian tradition of interest in the material culture of the East. Brown has described how at the age of sixteen he first encountered Mikhail Rostovtzeff's "heavy, olive-green volume," *The social and economic history of the Roman Empire* (1926), in the library of the Royal Dublin Society.[100] Especially its "superb illustrations"—chronologically and thematically arranged, incorporated in the text, and each accompanied by an extensive legend—introduced him to the material evidence for Roman civilization; and if Rostovtzeff's account of Rome did not reach beyond the catastrophic third century, his melancholic judgment on its aftermath caught the attention of a young man bent on studying medieval history. Was not Brown too a member of a "beleaguered elite" like that of late Rome, or prerevolutionary Russia?

Through Rostovtzeff, Brown and many others drank from the same Russian spring that had also nourished Strzygowski, who translated Rostovtzeff's beloved teacher Kondakov and like Rostovtzeff counted as one of his closest friends another Kondakov pupil, Yakov Smirnov, who starved to death in the winter of 1918.[101] Rostovtzeff in turn excavated the Euphrates trading town of Dura Europus, whose frescoes triumphantly vindicated Strzygowski's insistence on an independent and fertilizing artistic tradition in the eastern provinces.[102] But Brown's debt to the Vienna School, not just Strzygowski but also Riegl, is in fact still more direct. He himself concedes that, in writing *The world of late Antiquity*,

> art historians, for whom the concept of *Spätantike* had already achieved a definite profile, could teach me more about the pace and logic of the slow transformations of certain aspects of the classical tradition [Riegl] and about the rise of exotic forms [Strzygowski] than did the brisk, imperial narratives of a Rostovtzeff or a Piganiol.[103]

99 Compare the assessments of Brown by P. Rousseau, *SODebate* 53, or L. Cracco Ruggini, "All'ombra di Momigliano," *Rivista storica italiana* 100 (1988) 767; and of Strzygowski quoted by S. L. Marchand, "The rhetoric of artifacts and the decline of classical humanism: The case of Josef Strzygowski," *History and theory*, theme issue 33 (1994) 120. Also Brown himself on his "dogged guerilla," *SODebate* 9–10.

100 Brown, *SODebate* 5–7. On Rostovtzeff and Kondakov, see M. A. Wes, *Michael Rostovtzeff, historian in exile* (Stuttgart 1990) XIII, 3, 6–7, 73.

101 Strzygowski, *Aufgang* [2:42] 5; Wes, *Michael Rostovtzeff* [2:100] XIII n. 1.

102 As pointed out in G. Millet's "Introduction" to R. du Mesnil du Buisson, *Les peintures de la synagogue de Doura-Europus* (Rome 1939) VII, XVI; cf. Wharton, *Refiguring* [2:24] 15–23.

103 Brown, *SODebate* 17. But on Strzygowski's antipathy to "art history" and ahistorical, formalistic approach, unconcerned with either texts or contexts, see O. Pancaroğlu, "Formalism and the academic foundation of Turkish art in the early twentieth century," *Muqarnas* 24 (2007) 68–72. Brown also acknowledges ("The field of late Antiquity," in D. Hernández della Fuente [ed.], *New perspectives on late Antiquity* [Newcastle upon Tyne 2011] 11) Ugo Monneret de Villard's probing of continuities between

This catalytic role of art, architectural history, and archaeology in the "slow transformations" of the late antique world cannot be exaggerated. Appreciation of late Antiquity as a distinct period emerged in the second half of the nineteenth century in tandem with the rise of archaeology. The most powerful analysis of the Islamic world's continuation of late antique developments came from an art historian, Riegl. And just two years after *The world of late Antiquity*, Oleg Grabar published *The formation of Islamic art*, which stimulated the growth of Islamic art history in North America, and stirred interest in how Umayyad and early Abbasid buildings created "a monumental setting for the new culture, that is, a consistent body of forms different from other contemporary ones while utilizing in large part the same elements."[104] Abandoning the earlier "intercultural" view of Umayyad art as outsiders' imitation of ill-assimilated elements from Iran and Rome, Grabar and his pupils emphasized the first Islamic dynasty's "intracultural" and self-assured playing around with and development of vocabularies they and other inhabitants of Arabia had known even before the rise of Islam.[105]

Oddly, art and architecture play no part in the (nonetheless powerful) rationale advanced by the editor of volume 1 of the *New Cambridge history of Islam* for setting the rise of Islam against its Iranian and Roman as well as Arabian background.[106] At the same time, it is from historians deeply concerned with material culture that pressure has come, over the past decade and a half, for a reassessment of Peter Brown's wide-angle, culturally oriented and progressive, optimistic view of late Antiquity. Although in 1999 Jean-Michel Carrié could still observe with relief that late Antiquity was no longer seen as an era of decadence,[107] there had already in 1996 been an outburst of anguished neo-Rostovtzeffian rhetoric from Florence, with Aldo Schiavone demanding to know, "Why did the historical course of the West contain within itself the greatest catastrophe ever experienced in the history of civilization—a rupture of incalculable proportions . . . ?" For Schiavone, late Antiquity was "an entirely new universe" rather than an age of gradual transfor-

pre-Islamic and Umayyad materials: *Introduzione allo studio dell' archeologia islamica: Le origini e il periodo omayyade*, written in the early 1940s, published posthumously in 1966, immediately destroyed in the Florence floods, reprinted in Venice in 1968.

104 O. Grabar, *The formation of Islamic art* (New Haven 1973; revised and enlarged edition 1987) 200; more differentiated in revised edition, 208.

105 N. Rabbat, "Umayyad architecture: A spectacular intra-cultural synthesis in Bilad al-Sham," in K. Bartl and A. al-R. Moaz (eds), *Residences, castles and settlements: Transformation processes from late Antiquity to early Islam in Bilad al-Sham* (Rahden 2008) 13–18; cf. Fowden, *Quṣayr ʿAmra* [1:32].

106 C. F. Robinson, "Introduction," in *The new Cambridge history of Islam* (Cambridge 2010) 1.1–15.

107 Carrié, in Carrié and Rousselle, *Empire romain en mutation* [1:26] 20: "l'intérêt pour l'Antiquité tardive, aujourd'hui, ne relève plus d'un goût "décadentiste.""

mation.[108] Soon after this, Andrea Giardina in Rome complained that Brown's ambitious portrait had led to an "explosion" or "elephantiasis" of late Antiquity as it sprawled unmanageably across the centuries. Giardina tidy-mindedly insisted that each historical period must have a political, institutional, and economic structure plainly distinct from those that precede and follow it, and pronounced that the Lombard invasions of northern Italy from 568 marked a clear break, likewise the Arab conquests.[109] Then in 2005 came two books that took an even more radically conservative line: Peter Heather, *The fall of the Roman Empire*, and Bryan Ward-Perkins, *The fall of Rome and the end of civilization*. Both are too preoccupied with the West—in other words the origins of Europe—to engage effectively with the Oriental prospects opened up by Brown. For Heather and Ward-Perkins, 410 is once more a deeply significant date—as it was for Augustine too, except he knew how to conceptualize it, discerning its meaning amid the broader history of Christianized Rome.[110] Ward-Perkins, in particular, could not be remoter from this view of history. By emphasizing the destruction of physical infrastructures and the decline of material well-being, he attempts to compel acknowledgment of a major breakdown—"the end of civilization"—in the fifth century. Those who accept his values may or may not be inclined to accept his historical analysis. But a materialist and archaeological orientation, while evidently consistent with indifference to the achievements of art history, need not in itself be an obstacle to longer periodizations. I shall return to this point in chapter 3.

More interesting is Wolf Liebeschuetz's *Decline and fall of the Roman city* (2001), synthesizing a mass of archaeological material to reaffirm the view that the high imperial Roman city (urban core with monumental secular as well as religious architecture, rural territory, town council) declined and was well on the way to collapse by c. 600—at the latest—in the West, the Balkans, and Anatolia. But in the East Liebeschuetz sees a different scene: a higher level of prosperity in the later sixth to early seventh centuries, and maintenance of that prosperity ("paradoxically") into the early Caliphate, so that late Antiquity ends c. 750, in line with Brown's view.[111] Admittedly, where Brown reveled in the new, even exotic images and ideas flooding the

108 A. Schiavone, *La storia spezzata* (Rome 1996) (English tr. M. J. Schneider, *The end of the past* [Cambridge, Mass. 2000] 2, 22–29).

109 A. Giardina, "Esplosione di tardoantico," *Studi storici* 40 (1999) 157–80, esp. 176. In response, articles by various hands in *Studi storici* 45 (2004), and G. W. Bowersock, "Centrifugal force in late antique historiography," in Straw and Lim (eds), *The past before us* [2:94] 19–23.

110 Greek Christians were less likely to see 410 as a major event: A. Momigliano, *The classical foundations of modern historiography* (Berkeley 1990) 144.

111 G. Avni, ""From polis to madina" revisited—Urban change in Byzantine and early Islamic Palestine," *Journal of the Royal Asiatic Society* 21 (2011) 301–29, questions whether abandonment of monu-

senses and thoughts of late antique people, Liebeschuetz chronicles with ill-disguised regret or puzzlement—echoes of Burckhardt!—the fading not only of ancient urbanism but of Greco-Roman (especially mythological) literature and art, and the Christianization he perversely equates with "decline."[112] His acceptance, though, that in the immediately pre- and post-Muḥammad East things were otherwise, at least on the material level, shows a different story might have been told, if his cultural preferences had been less Greco-Roman (not even Syriac) and anti-Christian/Muslim, and his understanding of the polis less political/Aristotelian and more economic.[113]

Chris Wickham, in two major recent books, *Framing the early Middle Ages* (2005) and *The inheritance of Rome* (2009), succeeds up to a point in establishing a middle ground. He takes the early Caliphate quite generously into account, albeit always from a European perspective. His approach is materialist and Marxist, focused on the economy; yet he questions the easy correlation between a less monumental, more private environment and "decline"; and he (grudgingly) acknowledges that cultural factors cannot be ignored.[114] Culture to him, though, means education and the Church, as socially enmeshed and even socially controlled forces. He does not involve himself with the history of ideas as such, and when debates about the nature of Christ or the Qur'ān impinge on politics, he registers surprise at "the ap-

---

mental architecture implies socioeconomic decline, and stresses evidence for prosperity even after the Umayyads.

112 J. H. W. G. Liebeschuetz, *Decline and fall of the Roman city* (Oxford 2001), esp. 295–317, 414–16, and 11 for the Islamophobic lapse; id., "Transformation and decline," in J.-U. Krause and C. Witschel (eds), *Die Stadt in der Spätantike—Niedergang oder Wandel?* (Stuttgart 2006) 476 (Christianization = decline). On the danger of direct equations between abstract or dematerialized artistic style and "spirituality," see J. Trilling, "Late antique and sub-antique, or the "decline of form" reconsidered," *Dumbarton Oaks papers* 41 (1987) 469–76. Naturally, diverging views of the same developments are available in the ancient sources too. It was easy for traditionally minded intellectuals, anyway a minority, to be pessimistic (e.g., Damascius, *Life of Isidore* [ed. C. Zintzen (Hildesheim 1967); ed. and tr. P. Athanassiadi, *Damascius: The philosophical history* (Athens 1999)] 118 (Epitoma Photiana); John Lydus, *On the magistracies* [ed. and tr. (French) M. Dubuisson and J. Schamp (Paris 2006)] 3.11, and *On the months* [ed. R. Wuensch (Leipzig 1898)] 4.2 (and cf. A. Kaldellis, "The religion of Ioannes Lydos," *Phoenix* 57 [2003] 305–6); while one and the same writer might strike contradictory poses (Procopius of Caesarea).

113 For indications of economic resilience in seventh- to eighth-century East Rome as well as the Caliphate, and even in the West, see articles by C. S. Lightfoot, G. Varinlioğlu, and A. Walmsley in *Dumbarton Oaks papers* 61 (2007); M. Whittow, "Early medieval Byzantium and the end of the ancient world," *Journal of agrarian archaeology* 9 (2009) 141–47; L. Zavagno, *Cities in transition* (Oxford 2009); R. Alston, "Urban transformation in the East from Byzantium to Islam," *Acta Byzantina Fennica* 3 (2010) 9–45, esp. 34–35 on East Rome and 40–41 on Liebeschuetz; articles by J. Koder and C. Lightfoot in C. Morrisson (ed.), *Trade and markets in Byzantium* (Washington, D.C. 2012). In the early caliphal East, material decline is easiest to document in cities exposed to East Roman counterattack, such as those on the coast: M. Levy-Rubin, "Changes in the settlement pattern of Palestine following the Arab conquest," in K. G. Holum and H. Lapin (eds), *Shaping the Middle East* (Bethesda, Md. 2011) 155–72.

114 C. Wickham, *Framing the early Middle Ages* (Oxford 2005) 7, 258, 595, 672–74, 825; id., *Inheritance* [1:26] 9, 10.

parent obscurity of the religious issue at stake"!—and assumes it is all just power games.[115]

Given, though, that the two chief movements late Antiquity gave birth to—Christianity and Islam—were not in their origins economic doctrines, or primarily indebted to the Greco-Roman world, Liebeschuetz's "Klassizismus" and the others' materialism are both alike impediments, in the end, to grasping why one needs to study the period. One must also add that Giardina's—and many other historians'—privileging of political and military events and measurable economic data over cultural climates skews historical periodization toward the concerns of privileged, landed, documented but often transient social groupings (whatever the broader structural continuities of the societies in question) to an extent that favors change, or even rupture, over continuity, the short term over the long term.[116] It also—quite simply—neglects the conceptual dimension of human experience, and so falls short of providing adequate documentation for the writing of history in its full sense. By the conceptual dimension of human experience I mean not just, to quote Björn Wittrock, "ideological epiphenomena," but

> new conceptualizations of the location of human beings in time, [i.e.] historicity, and of the capacity of human beings to bring about changes in the world, [i.e.] agency. Such shifts made new forms of institutions and practices . . . meaningful and possible, and indeed conceivable.

The "new forms" Wittrock has in mind here are the modern nation-state and civil society. Just as these, and modernity generally, repose on new ways of thought, what we call the Enlightenment, rather than just (say) the Industrial Revolution, so too the emergence of the commonwealth of Christian states, the Papacy, and the community of Islam, the umma, presupposed "a deep epistemic and cultural shift," an intellectual and cosmological, not merely a social, revolution.[117]

Not surprisingly, it is to a historian of the Qur'anic text that we owe the most substantial contextualization, to date, of Islam in the flow of late Antiquity. The Berlin Corpus Coranicum project was already mentioned at the

115 Wickham, *Inheritance* [1:26] 329–30.

116 The halting emergence of new ideas about the meaning and disposition of economic wealth is of course another matter: P. Brown, *Through the eye of a needle: Wealth, the fall of Rome, and the making of Christianity in the West, 350–550 AD* (Princeton 2012). With this "cultural drag" on historical periodization, compare the distinction between "Antiquité tardive "littéraire"" and "Antiquité tardive "historique"" proposed by R. Martin, "Qu'est-ce que l'antiquité "tardive"?," in R. Chevallier (ed.), *Aiôn* (Paris 1976) 261–304. For an extreme example, see M. Heath, "Rhetoric in mid-antiquity," in T. P. Wiseman (ed.), *Classics in progress* (Oxford 2002) 419–39, on Greek rhetorical technique from Homer to Manuel II Palaeologus (1391–1425), and classifying the fourth-century CE rhetor Libanius as "mid-antique."

117 B. Wittrock, "The meaning of the Axial Age," in J. P. Arnason and others (eds), *Axial civilizations and world history* (Leiden 2005) 60, 64.

beginning of this book. Angelika Neuwirth's *Der Koran als Text der Spätantike: Ein europäischer Zugang* (2010) offers an extended reflection on the Qur'ān not as an off-the-peg canonical text but in its becoming ("Entstehungsgeschichte"), against the background of a Near East whose immediately pre-Islamic phase has been the object of intensive research in recent decades. Neuwirth presents the Qur'ān not as a spontaneously generated "Muslim" monologue composed by a single author, but as an ongoing conversation (during the Prophet's lifetime) with rabbinic Jews, patristic Christians, and others. The Muslim scripture becomes a voice in a late antique debate usually seen as part of Europe's origins. In this way, Neuwirth draws the Qur'ān closer to the European tradition, at the precise moment (now) when large and increasingly self-confident Muslim communities are establishing themselves at the heart of Europe.[118]

European civilization makes little sense without the religious and philosophical developments that occurred during the long late Antiquity. The refusal of many in the Islamic world to acknowledge the late antique pluralism to which the Qur'ān responds undermines their grasp on history and their access to the context and contacts which are Islam's birthright. Clearly, then, the attempt to understand the pre-Islamic world of ideas offers a profoundly serious, nonantiquarian reason—and one relevant to developments today—for taking the period into consideration. The question remains, though, whether even the long late Antiquity is a sufficiently broad stage for the investigation proposed. Is something "beyond late Antiquity" required? As we shall see, Peter Brown's apparently generous terminus at c. 800 ends up treating Islam as merely an extension of late Antiquity, rather than allowing it to reach a stage of intellectual and institutional maturation comparable with fully developed patristic Christianity, or capable of being used as an approach to the Islamic world we know today. If, then, we are to have the full benefit of studying early Christianity and Islam comparatively but not ahistorically, in other words within a firm sociohistorical framework, we need an alternative to the late antique paradigm. This is what I shall provide in the next chapter.

118 Neuwirth, *Koran als Text* [1:6] 14–15, 21–22, 62–63, 66–67, 76–80, 727, 730, 767–68.

3

A NEW PERIODIZATION

THE FIRST MILLENNIUM

When Augustus reigned alone upon earth, the many kingdoms (polyarchia) of men came to an end; and when Thou wast made man of the pure Virgin, the many gods (polytheïa) of idolatry were destroyed. The cities passed under one worldly dominion; and the nations believed in the lordship of one God.

—Kassia (b. c. 810), "Hymn on the birth of Christ," sung at Orthodox Vespers of the Nativity (25 December)

Once on a time—Year of Grace One, I think—
Thus spake the Sibyl, drunk without drink:
'Alas, how ill things go!
Decline! Decline! Ne'er sank the world so low!
Rome hath turned harlot and brothel too,
Rome's Caesar a beast, and God himself a Jew!

—F. Nietzsche, *Thus spake Zarathustra* (1885) Part 4 ("Gespräch mit den Königen")

DECLINE VERSUS TRANSFORMATION

In 1999, the same year Andrea Giardina denounced late Antiquity's elephantiasis, was also published what still stands as the most recent and authoritative statement of the maximalist position, namely Harvard's *Late Antiquity: A guide to the postclassical world*, edited by Glen Bowersock, Peter Brown and Oleg Grabar.[1] By taking as its cutoff point approximately the year 800, this weighty tome espouses—and up to a point exemplifies—the view that the early Islamic world shows significant continuities with late Antiquity. But at

1 This chapter supersedes G. Fowden, "Contextualizing late Antiquity: The First Millennium," in J. P. Arnason and K. A. Raaflaub (eds), *The Roman Empire in context* (Chichester 2011) 148–76.

the same time it places the Islamic synthesis achieved in ninth- to tenth-century Baghdad outside its remit, despite the important role played there by, for example, translation into Arabic of Greek scientific and philosophical literature.

Although I agree that a long late Antiquity is more useful than a short one, I assign more of a role to religion. Rather than joining the editors of the Harvard *Guide* in viewing the centuries after 250 as primarily an Age of Empires (as if the ancient world had not been full of them, while after 800 they were hardly in short supply), I foreground pre-600 the two major monotheistic traditions, rabbinic Judaism and Christianity, as they move toward a mature form still readily recognizable today. Then I add the third, closely related revelation, Islam, gradually emergent from soon after 600. All three of these major, seminal developments are unique to their period, without parallel in any other. Furthermore, I consider them in relation to each other, rather than separately as is so often the case. On closer inspection of the period in question, I also see other major intellectual developments, as for example the formulation of classical syntheses of Greek philosophy and Roman law. The combined effect of all these more or less interrelated evolutions justifies a new periodization running, as I shall shortly explain, from the lifetime of Jesus of Nazareth (c. 4 BCE–c. 30 CE) and the reign of Augustus (31 BCE–14 CE) to about the end of the First Millennium. During this period the ancient world was gradually transformed and there came into being, across Europe and West Asia, a triad of sibling civilizations, successors of Rome and Iran, whose commitment to revealed monotheism either Biblical in Greek and Latin Christendom, or Qur'anic in the Muslim world, was to varying degrees tempered by the rational principles derived from Greek and Roman Antiquity.

Put in terms of current historiographical convention, what we are talking about is a recontextualization of late Antiquity, however this period may be defined. The aim is to expand late Antiquity both backward and forward in time—exactly what Giardina objected to. (In chapter 4 we will expand late Antiquity—or rather its Mediterranean focus—in space as well.) The duration of the period in question—which will of course admit the possibility of, among much else, a narrative of political, military, and other events—will primarily be determined by cultural, conceptual, and literary developments. This recontextualization needs to take account of what can realistically be aspired to in university courses and textbooks. Nonetheless, if we are to make the most of what late Antiquity can contribute to our understanding of our own world, what is often anyway seen as a transitional or transformational zone, a subperiodization derived from Antiquity, needs to be reset within a new major periodization, the First Millennium. This new period is of roughly comparable length to Antiquity (Homer to Justinian, 1,200 years) or the Middle Ages (Boethius to Luther, 1,000 years).

Before we ask why the First Millennium makes a coherent and useful periodization, note the principal shortcoming of the division—devised as early as Petrarch and conventional since the sixteenth or at latest the seventeenth century—into Antiquity, Middle Ages, and Modernity. The point of this periodization was to present the Italian Renaissance and the Modernity that flows—ultimately—from it, as a return to the pure Grecian sources after the barbarism of the Christian Middle Ages.[2] Among contemporary historians of late Antiquity, Wolf Liebeschuetz is—we already saw—a prominent representative of this binary and polarizing approach, identifying Christianization and a fortiori Islamization with the setting aside or even destruction of the "classical" heritage and with decline, the Verfall Nietzsche's drunken Sibyl laments.

It would be no less simplistic to respond to this attitude of contempt for the Middle Ages by pointing out how much of Antiquity was preserved by Greek, Syriac, Armenian, Latin, and other Christianities. Texts were laboriously written out and carefully preserved—one thinks of the famous Paris Plato (Parisinus graecus 1807) copied in Constantinople c. 850, taken to Armenia c. 1045 and partly translated there, then transported in the thirteenth century to the West where by c. 1350 it became the first Greek manuscript to enter a humanist library, Petrarch's. It was finally removed to Paris in 1594.[3] Whole buildings were preserved, in at least one instance—the Athens Parthenon—complete with their "pagan" sculptures. A recent student of the Christian Parthenon has concluded that its holiness was more regarded in this phase than when it was a temple of Athena.[4]

More interesting than this swallowing-whole approach to the Greco-Roman heritage, whose motives and techniques are so complex, is the gradual digestion of, for instance, Roman law as it passed through the distillations of the high imperial, especially Severan jurists, the Diocletianic codifications of the 290s, then the *Theodosian code*, the *Justinianic code*, and the aptly named *Digest* (on all of which see chapter 6), to become a handbook of Christian imperium and society. One could copy the works of Virgil out just as he had written them, and illustrate them, even in the Christianized empire, with scenes of ritual addressed to the old gods.[5] Or one might take Virgil to bits line by line or half line by half line, and make him recount something quite different—the Bible story in the hands of the mid-fourth-century poetess Proba, or a pornographic wedding night in Ausoni-

2 Gibbon 2: 1.84; cf. F. Graus, "Epochenbewusstsein im Spätmittelalter," and K. Schreiner, ""Diversitas temporum": Zeiterfahrung und Epochengliederung im späten Mittelalter," in Herzog and Koselleck (ed.), *Epochenschwelle* [2:21] 153–66, 381–428.

3 H. D. Saffrey, "Retour sur le Parisinus graecus 1807," in C. D'Ancona (ed.), *The libraries of the Neoplatonists* (Leiden 2007) 3–28.

4 Kaldellis, *Christian Parthenon* [2:44].

5 Al. Cameron, *The last pagans of Rome* (New York 2011) 706–12.

us's (d. c. 395) *Nuptial cento*.[6] With similar ingenuity, Homer might be transmuted—with minor but cunning adjustments—into a life of Christ.[7] Aristotle did not lend himself to this particular form of perversion; but Porphyry's (d. c. 305) *Introduction* (*Isagoge*) made his logic universally applicable, to audiences Christian or—eventually—Muslim too, and was one of the most read books over the thousand years following its composition. It and related commentaries were still being laboriously copied out in Syriac in the monasteries of Kurdistan—and used—into the first decades of the twentieth century.[8] Aristotle's own writings also possessed much of this passe-partout quality, as I shall show in chapter 5. And then there was that great ocean of necessary knowledge, the Bible, which besides its salvific message conveyed all one needed to know about the ancient Near East, plus—in its Vulgate version largely by Jerome—a model of Latinity for those not up to Cicero.

In the face of this and—as we saw in discussing Liebeschuetz on eastern urbanism—much other evidence for gradual, discriminating transformation of the ancient world,[9] those who emphasize decline have to be selective and either (1) classicist/purist, or (2) antimonotheist in their orientation, or (3) materialist in their choice of evidence. Classicists and purists deplore the coarsening of an ancient and paradigmatic aesthetic. Antimonotheists see Christianity and Islam as offending the Greco-Roman tradition's essential rationalism (though the aggressive vigor of patristic Christianity hardly suggests decline). As for materialists, even those who grant that aqueducts and drains were but a means to a more comfortable and possibly reflective life do not necessarily show much interest in ideas—at least not ancient ones (such as Aristotle's notion, revived at the end of the First Millennium by the Arabic philosopher Fārābī, that city life is essential to the development of the human intellect).[10] All are so sure of their priorities that they miss a great deal else that was going on. But at least they have a clear vision of how the world ought

6 M. Bažil, *'Centones christiani'* (Turnhout 2009); S. McGill, "Virgil, Christianity, and the *Cento Probae*," in J. H. D. Scourfield (ed.), *Texts and culture in late Antiquity* (Swansea 2007) 173–93; Ausonius, *Nuptial cento* [ed. R. P. H. Green, *Decimi Magni Ausonii opera* (Oxford 1999) 145–54; English version D. R. Slavitt, *Ausonius: Three amusements* (Philadelphia 1998) 41–75].

7 R. Schembra, *Homerocentones* (Turnhout 2007); Mary Whitby, "The Bible Hellenized," in Scourfield (ed.), *Texts and culture* [3:6] 195–231.

8 H. Hugonnard-Roche, *La Logique d'Aristote du grec au syriaque* (Paris 2004) 95, 187 (on ms. Mingana syr. 606); H. Takahashi, *Aristotelian meteorology in Syriac* (Leiden 2004) 68.

9 On the tendency in modern discourse to regard transformation as gradual not sudden, see R. Markus, "Between Marrou and Brown: Transformations of late antique Christianity," in P. Rousseau and M. Papoutsakis (eds), *Transformations of late Antiquity* (Farnham 2009) 3.

10 Of course, materialism too is a concept, and D. Graeber goes so far as to argue that money, specifically debt, has molded civilizations and even theologies: *Debt: The first 5000 years* (New York 2011) (I was alerted to this by Anthony Kaldellis). For criticism of decline analysis from a materialist perspective see Wickham, *Framing* [2:114] 672–74.

(not) to be, which makes qualitative (or even moral) judgment and periodization relatively straightforward matters. It also allows for the possibility of sudden decline, or collapse, which 410 is still sometimes understood to have been.

For those, by contrast, who see humankind constantly, across the ages, adjusting bit by bit not to decline, either slow or precipitate, but to gradual transformations, drawing lines of demarcation is harder. For them, longer periodizations have undeniable appeal—but not so long as to become meaningless, and certainly not in association with "decline," which as a hermeneutic tool becomes more useless the further it is stretched out over time. Even Gibbon came to recognize this, at the end of his immense narrative of East Rome's "one thousand and fifty-eight years . . . of premature and perpetual decay" from 395 to 1453, and subtly recast it as "the triumph of barbarism and religion."[11] His heirs, rather than face the whole second millennium of Rome—and into its third—under the sign of decline, followed his example and called it "Byzantium" with its own distinctive rises and falls.[12] Ottomanists have likewise rejected the old view that Ottoman history from 1600 onward was an unremitting story of decline. Instead they prefer "to analyse the notion of decline, to study this concept as a phenomenon in intellectual history, and thereby to limit its wholesale and tendentious application."[13]

MATURATIONS

The First Millennium has the basic advantage of embracing the "long" late Antiquity advocated by Peter Brown, in other words the formation of Chris-

11 Gibbon 32: 2.237, 71: 3.1068; Pocock 1.2–3; and cf. Ghosh, *Journal of Roman studies* 73 (1983) [1:29] 5 nn. 24, 26, on the centrality of "decline" to the emotional and tragic appeal of Gibbon's book as a work of literature.

12 J. K. J. Thomson, *Decline in history: The European experience* (Cambridge 1998) 63–96. Cf. N. Baynes, *The Byzantine Empire* (London 1925) 7: "An empire to endure a death agony of a thousand years must possess considerable powers of recuperation." On Gibbon's use of the term "Byzantine," see above, p. 11 n. 33.

13 S. Faroqhi, "In search of Ottoman history," in H. Berktay and S. Faroqhi (eds), *New approaches to state and peasant in Ottoman history* (London 1992) 232–33; cf. A. Mikhail and C. M. Philliou, "The Ottoman Empire and the imperial turn," *Comparative studies in society and history* 54 (2012) 725–34. On Ottoman decline or at least uninventiveness as a Eurocentric construct, see C. Finkel, " 'The treacherous cleverness of hindsight': Myths of Ottoman decay," in G. MacLean (ed.), *Re-orienting the Renaissance* (Basingstoke 2005) 148–74; J. Goody, *The theft of history* (Cambridge 2006) 99–118. On the other hand, there is such a thing as congenital weakness. Cf. R. Matthee, *Persia in crisis: Safavid decline and the fall of Isfahan* (London 2012) xxvii: "In today's academic climate, skeptical about (non-Western) decline and especially averse to decline as a moral category, one is almost forced to reject this type of interpretation out of hand and to focus on manifestations of continued vitality in the form of artistic expression, religious disputation, or overlooked provincial initiative. But to do so [in the case of the Safavids] would be to ignore the many unmistakable signs of trouble."

tianity and the birth of Islam, while recognizing first that Christianity was already a movement with an almost three-century-long history when Constantine became emperor (306), and second that Islam did not begin to reach any sort of maturation comparable with Christianity's post-Nicaean (i.e., post-Constantinian) patristic era until the tenth century. One might also argue, from a more political perspective, that Constantine's achievement is hard to fathom in isolation from earlier Roman imperial history, especially the third century, while both the Umayyad and the Abbasid phases of the Caliphate need to be understood in the context of other great ancient empires—notably Rome and Iran—that preceded Islam in the lands it conquered.

What, then, makes the First Millennium a plausible major periodization? The short answer is that it provides the best framework in which to respond to our basic question about Islam's relation to its historical context "before and after Muḥammad," especially the Jewish and Christian traditions. At the beginning of the First Millennium there was no Christianity or rabbinic Judaism; but during the first century these began to form. Long before 1000, both had matured intellectually and institutionally to the point where one recognizes in them the doctrines and structures their mainstream adherents are familiar with today (and their fundamentalists often reject). We can observe a similar maturation of Greek philosophy in the schools of Alexandria, as I already noted in passing when discussing the significance of 529; for Roman law in Justinian's wide-ranging codification;[14] and we may add two parallels from the Sasanian Empire. First there was the national Mazdean or Zoroastrian religion of Iran, whose orally transmitted "scripture," the Avesta, was finally turned into hard copy at some point under the Sasanians, probably in the sixth century, but in a form that apparently embraced a lot of other material, even of Greek or Indian provenance.[15] Second, as already noted in chapter 2, there was the new religion preached by the Prophet Mani, who arose in third-century Mesopotamia and bequeathed his followers a rich body of doctrine, scripture, and art drawing on Judaism and Christianity, which they spread both in Iran and beyond, westward into the Roman Empire but also eastward to India and through Central Asia as far as China. Until the tenth century, Manicheism remained a subtle and adaptable if limited presence in the Caliphate and a threat to the orthodox, or so they chose to present it, even if just as a name to tar Muslims of a more liberal cast of mind.[16]

14 Conventional usage places the "classical" phase of Greek philosophy in the fifth to fourth centuries BCE, and of Roman law in the first to second centuries CE, much earlier than the fuller maturations of which I here speak.

15 S. Shaked, *Dualism in transformation* (London 1994) 99–119; see below, pp. 201–2.

16 F. de Blois, "Zindīk," *EIs*² 11.510–13.

But what truly holds the First Millennium together is the question of Islam's relation to the deeply rooted cultural traditions that dominated the world it was born into. It was a precondition of Islam that rabbinic Judaism and patristic Christianity should have matured (though in Christianity's case that also meant fully ventilating its doctrinal inconsistencies and improbabilities) before it appeared; but this does not mean that the First Millennium falls into two separate, independent halves. It is only the dialogue of continuing Judaism and Christianity—especially continuing Syriac Christianity[17]—with Qur'anic, then maturing Islam that generates the potent synthesis we find in tenth-century Baghdad.

What exactly do I mean by the "maturation" of a tradition?[18] In any tradition there will be conservatives and progressives. The former will believe enough has already been said, and maturity attained, even if the founder or the founding event is still a fresh memory and a potential stimulus to further development. If we give heavy weighting to the perspective of contemporaries, we will find the concept of maturation too controversial to be helpful. From the historian's viewpoint, though, a tradition may reasonably be called mature if it has—first and most fundamentally—acquired a clear sense (or senses) of what it is *and what it is not*.[19] Notions of "orthodoxy" and "heresy" may already be invoked; but that stage may come quite early on. A mature tradition needs also to have built up enough of its institutions and doctrines that it seems to correspond to what *we* perceive, now, to be its broadly characteristic articulation, however self-contradictory. I do not intend any necessary rigidification in the "mature" tradition, but rather its arrival at a point viewed by a widely influential sector of posterity as paradigmatic, worthy of imitation (or "classical").[20] After all, "decline" does not necessarily follow immediately upon maturation. Often we see diversification into channels less obviously "classical," but no less vigorous.

17 On the crucial connecting role played by the Syriac world see now Tannous, *Syria* [1:10].

18 With J. Brown, *The canonization of al-Bukhārī and Muslim: The formation and function of the Sunnī ḥadīth canon* (Leiden 2007) 18–19, I apply the biological term to cultural traditions because each of these is made up of individual human actors conscious of contributing to its incremental development. For further reflections on the relationship between intentionality and the use of biological metaphor, see R. Wisnovsky, "Towards a natural-history model of philosophical change," in R. Wisnovsky and others (eds), *Vehicles of transmission, translation, and transformation in medieval textual culture* (Turnhout 2012) 143–57.

19 For a courageous if controversial attempt to trace the earliest stages of this process in Islam, see Donner, *Muhammad and the believers* [1:2].

20 I distinguish popularly received understandings of historical periods or themes from those advanced by historians, who may be either more or less committed to the prevailing consensus. Those influenced in choice of subject and interpretation by concerns current in their own society are likely to face accusations of "teleology"—not all of which need to be taken equally seriously: see my comments below, pages 86–87, 89–90.

For the time being, we are primarily concerned with the diachronic development and comparative study of the Jewish, Christian and Muslim monotheisms. This is what underlies the periodization proposed, and mainly justifies the effort invested, given that all three are important to how we understand our past and our own times. (So, of course, are Greek philosophy and Roman law.) Is there, then, something characteristic, perhaps even distinctive, about the process of maturation undergone by rabbinic Judaism, Christianity, and Islam that encourages and facilitates our comparative effort and confirms the justness of the periodization?

As a first move, both Christianity and Islam had to disentangle themselves from Judaism (and even rabbinic Judaism had to emerge from Temple Judaism). Arguably, in the case of Christianity, this was not fully achieved until the late fourth century.[21] For Islam, as in many other things, the process of growing up was hugely accelerated—the Prophet already separated himself from the Jews at Medina, as we can see in the evolving tone of the Qur'ān's references to them.[22] But even once all three monotheisms stand completely alone, and often in opposition, it is possible to see that each arrives at its independence, and eventually its mature form, by a roughly comparable set of steps, three stages of development that are noted here not because they necessarily have any wider typological application (the application they already have is quite wide enough), but simply because they work for the traditions in question and the period proposed.

The three stages may be called the prophetic, the scriptural, and the exegetical.[23] The first of these is a brief but intense, transformative (perceived) encounter between God and a human being. This prophet, as he is called, may or may not record his encounters with God in durable form. He is more likely to communicate them to certain intimates, as a result of which he is accepted as their teacher and may come to be seen as the leader of a social or even political group. The scriptural phase follows, more commonly—but not necessarily—after the prophet's demise, and may last just a few years, or centuries. During this period, disciples write down the prophet's experiences

21 N. Koltun-Fromm, "Defining sacred boundaries," in Rousseau (ed.), *Late Antiquity* [2:9] 556–71.

22 N. A. Stillman, "Yahūd," *EI*s^2 11.240.

23 Or "patristic" as I had it in the article mentioned in n. 1 above. M. Weber (ed. H. E. Kippenberg), *Wirtschaft und Gesellschaft* Teilband 2: *Religiöse Gemeinschaften* (Tübingen 2001) 177–218, distinguishes the prophet and his revelation, canonical scriptures, and "dogmas," emphasizing credal formulations over the process of exegesis (with little understanding of Islam and almost no knowledge of Eastern Christianity). Assmann, *Kulturelle Gedächtnis* [2:89] 65, 93–97, 163–64, 175–76, 276, 295–96, has Prophetie, Kanonisierung, Auslegung; Hodgson, *Venture of Islam* [1:1] 1.80–81, creative action/revelation, group commitment thereto/institutionalization, cumulative interaction within the group/dialogue. Schiavone, *Invention of law* [1:37] 35–37, detects a similar Weberian tripartition in F. Schulz, *History of Roman legal science* (Oxford 1946). On the transition from prophecy via scripturalization to preaching in the specifically Christian context, see A. Stewart-Sykes, *From prophecy to preaching* (Leiden 2001).

and revelations and organize them into some form of book in order to delimit the canon—an agreed collection of texts inspired by this intervention of God in human affairs and now circulated, though with exclusions potentially controversial and capable of giving rise to countercanons. Not in Judaism, Christianity, or Islam did these texts add up to anything remotely resembling an ordered theology or systematic creed—the prophetic experience usually resists systematization.[24] But speculation, debate, and teaching, both concurrent with and subsequent to the scriptural phase, do gradually elicit and nurture a doctrine, typically through composition of commentaries on the canonical texts. Once this doctrine, or theology, has been expounded fully enough to permit brief presentation in handbooks or even as a creed, the tradition in question attains a consensus and a relatively mature formulation, for which reference can more conveniently be made to the writings of the tradition's outstandingly wise and pious representatives, than directly to its foundation texts. All of this, together, is what I call the "exegetical" phase.[25]

Objections to or modifications of such a generalizing analysis spring readily to mind. For example it has been argued that in the earliest decades of Islam neither the prophet nor the scripture were much emphasized as touchstones of identity until the reign of the Caliph ʿAbd al-Malik (685–705), who drew the community's boundaries more tightly.[26] It must also be admitted that the monotheist associations of terminology such as "prophetic" and "scriptural" seem less appropriate in fields such as philosophy and law. Yet the writings of Plato and Aristotle did come to enjoy semiscriptural status, and there was a revelatory element in some Greek philosophy, for instance Parmenides or the *Chaldaean oracles*;[27] while the formulation of law, though an ongoing process, could be presented by Justinian (to say nothing of Moses) as an act of divine inspiration.[28] The prophecy-scripture-exegesis schema can help us make at least preliminary sense of the welter of new doctrines emerging during the First Millennium. At this point it may be helpful to tabulate some of the evolutionary milestones of the main cultural traditions that matured during the First Millennium, in order to convey an impression of how they developed in relationship to each other.

24 Mani aspired to be an exception: see below pp. 188–89. On Islam, see A. Wensinck, *The Muslim creed* (Cambridge 1932) chap. 1.

25 Compare the "deuteronomic" phase—of harmonizing, standardizing, systematizing, and gap filling rather than addressing single, unique problems in a competitive and polemical spirit—detected by R. Netz, *The transformation of mathematics in the early Mediterranean world* (Cambridge 2004) 8, 121–23, 126–27, 133, in late Greek and Arabic mathematicians' treatment of Archimedes. For further discussion of Netz's thesis, see K. Tybjerg, "The point of Archimedes," *Early science and medicine* 10 (2005) 574–76.

26 Donner, *Muhammad and the believers* [1:2] 202–11.

27 P. Hadot, "Théologie, exégèse, révélation, écriture, dans la philosophie grecque," in M. Tardieu (ed.), *Les règles de l'interprétation* (Paris 1987) 23–34.

28 Humfress [1:37], in Maas (ed.), *Age of Justinian* [1:34] 167–68.

First Millennium cultural traditions: Prophetic, scriptural, and exegetical phases

GREEK PHILOSOPHY (ARISTOTELIANISM)	CHRISTIANITY	JUDAISM
SCRIPTURAL		**SCRIPTURAL**
after 86 BCE Aristotle's "esoteric" works become known at Rome. **c. 30 BCE** Andronicus of Rhodes's edition of Aristotle.		
	PROPHETIC **c. 4 BCE–c. 30** Jesus of Nazareth.	
	SCRIPTURAL **c. 50–c. 120** Composition of New Testament writings.	**c. 70** Destruction of Jerusalem Temple. **c. 100 or later** Contents of Jewish Bible finally fixed.
		EXEGETICAL
	c. 130 Emergence (as yet incomplete) of N.T. proto-canon.	**c. 80–c. 180** Mishnaic sages.
EXEGETICAL **c. 200** Alexander of Aphrodisias, Aristotle's earliest surviving major commentator.		**c. 200** Compilation of Mishnah.
	EXEGETICAL **c. 215** Death of Clement of Alexandria, theologian.	**c. 220–c. 375** Jerusalem Talmud sages.
270 Death of Plotinus, eminent Platonist but also student of Aristotle.	**c. 254** Death of Origen, leading Alexandrian exegete.	**c. 220–c. 500** Babylonian Talmud sages.

MANICHEISM	ISLAM	ROMAN LAW	MAZDAISM
		EXEGETICAL **c. 150** Gaius, jurist, author of *Institutes*, an influential textbook.	
PROPHETIC **216–76/77** Mani—unlike other founders—writes own scriptures and intends them to be definitive.		Severan jurists: **fl. c. 210** Paul. **212** Death of Papinian. **223** Death of Ulpian.	**SCRIPTURAL** **224–651** Sasanian dynasty.
SCRIPTURAL-EXEGETICAL Mani's writings passed through successive acculturated versions in a range of languages from Latin to Chinese, whose discreet development of the original teaching represents, to a limited extent, an exegetical phase.			**c. 240–72** Shapur I, traditionally credited with having Mazdeans' oral scripture, the *Avesta*, written down. This is more probably to be dated in the sixth century.
302 Diocletian's rescript against Manicheans.		**292** Gregorian Code. **295** Hermogenian Code.	

First Millennium cultural traditions: Prophetic, scriptural, and exegetical phases

GREEK PHILOSOPHY (ARISTOTELIANISM)	CHRISTIANITY	JUDAISM
c. 305 Death of Porphyry, pupil of Plotinus, advocate of harmony of Aristotle with Plato.	**306–37** Emperor Constantine I.	
	325 First Oecumenical Council at Nicaea: formulation of creed. **339** Death of Eusebius of Caesarea, historian of the Church under Rome. **367** Earliest exact witness (Athanasius of Alexandria, d. 373) to full N.T. canon. **373** Death of Ephrem of Nisibis, Syriac Church Father. **later 4th century** Cappadocian Fathers (Basil of Caesarea, Gregory of Nazianzus, Gregory of Nyssa).	
5th to 6th centuries Flourishing of Alexandrian schools.	**407** Death of John Chrysostom, Antiochene exegete. **419** Death of Jerome, Latin exegete and Hebrew scholar. **430** Death of Augustine, Latin theologian. **444** Death of Cyril of Alexandria, theologian. **451** Fourth Oecumenical Council at Chalcedon: decisive definition of Christ's nature. Death of Nestorius, theologian.	**c. 400** Completion of Jerusalem Talmud.
485 Death of Proclus, Athenian Platonist.	**c. 489** School of the Persians (Church of the East) expelled from Edessa to Sasanian territory.	
	fl. c. 500 Ps.-Dionysius the Areopagite, Platonizing theologian.	**c. 500** "Closure" of Babylonian Talmud.
c. 525 Death of Boethius, translator of Aristotle into Latin. **529** Justinian closes Athens philosophy schools.	**525** Dionysius Exiguus invents era of the Incarnation.	

MANICHEISM	ISLAM	ROMAN LAW	MAZDAISM
310–14 Pope Miltiades finds Manicheans at Rome.			
		390s *Comparison of Mosaic and Roman law.*	
		438 *Theodosian code.*	
		480s *Laws of Constantine, Theodosius and Leo* compiled in Greek. **506** Breviary of Alaric (*Lex Romana Visigothorum*).	
		529, 534 *Justinianic code,* first and revised editions.	

First Millennium cultural traditions: Prophetic, scriptural, and exegetical phases

GREEK PHILOSOPHY (ARISTOTELIANISM)	CHRISTIANITY	JUDAISM
536 Death of Sergius of Resh‘aina, Syriac commentator on Aristotle.	**543, 553** Condemnation of Origen.	
560 Death of Simplicius, Aristotle's last comprehensive commentator in Greek.		
570 Death of John Philoponus, last major Alexandrian Aristotelian, first major Christian Aristotelian.		
	after 594 Death of Evagrius, last of the Church historians in direct succession from Eusebius.	
	c. 630 Last Greek secular classicizing history (Theophylact Simocatta) and chronicle (*Paschal chronicle*).	
	636 Death of Isidore of Seville, encyclopedist; conventional closure of Latin patristic age.	
c. 650–700 Demise of Alexandrian schools.		
680–81 Sixth Oecumenical Council at Constantinople: anathematization of John Philoponus.	**680–81** Sixth Oecumenical Council at Constantinople: condemnation of Monotheletism.	
	685 Death of Ananias of Shirak, Armenian encyclopedist.	
708 Death of Jacob of Edessa, Syriac Aristotelian and chronicler.		
	740s Death of John of Damascus; conventional closure of Greek patristic age.	

MANICHEISM	ISLAM	ROMAN LAW	MAZDAISM
		533 *Institutes, Digest.*	
	PROPHETIC **c. 610** Beginning of Muḥammad's prophetic career. **622** Muḥammad's flight from Mecca; start of hijra era. **632** Death of Muḥammad.		
			c. 635–37 Sasanians defeated by Arabs at Qādisīya.
after 650 Arrival of first Manicheans in China.	**SCRIPTURAL** **c. 650** Caliph 'Uthmān's edition of Qur'ān.		
	685–705 Caliph 'Abd al-Malik. **694–714** Hajjāj, governor of Iraq, refines 'Uthmanic text of Qur'ān.		
		741 Leo III's *Ecloga.*	

First Millennium cultural traditions: Prophetic, scriptural, and exegetical phases

GREEK PHILOSOPHY (ARISTOTELIANISM)	CHRISTIANITY	JUDAISM
750s Earliest Arabic versions of Aristotle (Ibn al-Muqaffaʿ).		
c. 782 Caliph Mahdī commissions translation of Aristotle's *Topics* from Patriarch Timothy.	**787** Seventh (and last) Oecumenical Council at Nicaea: restoration of icons.	**c. 800** Latest additions to Babylonian Talmud.
		early 9th century Dāwūd al-Muqammaṣ, philosopher.
830s Partial Arabic translation of Plotinus and Proclus as *Theology of Aristotle.*	**c. 830** Death of Theodore Abū Qurra, Arabic Chalcedonian theologian.	
c. 870 Death of Kindī, first major Arabic philosopher.		**later 9th century** Rise of Karaite critics of rabbinism.

MANICHEISM	ISLAM	ROMAN LAW	MAZDAISM
	EXEGETICAL (see note below) **767** Death of (1) Abū Ḥanīfa, eponym of the Hanafi legal community; (2) Ibn Isḥāq, biographer of Prophet. **795** Death of Mālik, eponym of the Maliki legal community.		
			EXEGETICAL **9th century** Composition of *Denkard* and other compilations of tradition, the last major monuments of Mazdaism.
	820 Death of Shāfiʿī, eponym of the Shafiʿi legal community. **833** Caliph Ma'mūn officially espouses doctrine that the Qur'ān is created. **855** Death of Ibn Ḥanbal, eponym of the Hanbali legal community and opponent of rational theology. **later 9th century** Ascendancy of Muʿtazilism.		

Note: Despite its semiscriptural status in Islam, I classify the development of Prophetic tradition (ḥadīth) as exegetical because of the amount of fraud and controversy involved, and because a ḥadīth is not God's word like the Qur'ān. Also, Sunnis and Shiites read the same Qur'ān but not the same ḥadīth.

First Millennium cultural traditions: Prophetic, scriptural, and exegetical phases

GREEK PHILOSOPHY (ARISTOTELIANISM)	CHRISTIANITY	JUDAISM
		942 Death of Saadia Gaon, rabbi and philosopher.
948 Death of Fārābī, heir of Alexandrian philosophical commentary tradition.		**955** Death of Isḥāq al-Isrāʾīlī, philosopher.
c. 1000–1037 Ibn Sīnā moves Arabic philosophy into a new synthesis. **c. 1001** Ibn Sīnā, *Philosophy for ʿArūḍī.*		
	1046 Death of Elias bar Shenaya, Syro-Arabic chronicler dependent on Eusebius and Ṭabarī.	

MANICHEISM	ISLAM	ROMAN LAW	MAZDAISM
10th century Latest evidence for Manicheans in Caliphate.	**c. 900** Classical collections of traditions about the Prophet (ḥadīth) by Bukhārī (d. 870) and Muslim (d. 875) already in circulation. **923** Death of Ṭabarī, Qur'ān commentator and historian of pre-Islam and Islam. **935** Death of Ash'arī, theologian who reconciled rational and traditional theology. **940–41** Occlusion of the last of the Twelve Shiite Imams.	**c. 900** Leo VI's *Basilics*.	
	970s/980s Brethren of Purity, Baṣra.		
	c. 1000 Sunni-Shiite divide fully consolidated.		**1010** Completion of Ferdowsi's *Shahnameh*, a treasury of Iranian tradition but (intentionally) with minimal religious content.
before 1035 Deposit of Chinese Manichean texts in Dunhuang cave temple on the Silk Road; rediscovery initiates modern Manichean studies in early 20th century.	**1048** Death of Bīrūnī, polymath.		

From this rough tabulation emerges an especially intensive exegetical activity in the major spheres of Greek philosophy, Christianity, Judaism, and Roman law during the core period of the third to sixth centuries, what we conventionally call late Antiquity. Mazdaism thanks to Sasanian support, and Manicheism thanks to its missions, also attained a peak of influence at this time. The Christian scriptures were composed and largely canonized before the core period but still within the First Millennium. The Mazdean and Jewish scriptures, the origins of Greek philosophy, and a great deal of Roman law (from the Twelve Tables c. 450 BCE onward) belong to the previous millennium; but even so the Jewish Bible was not firmly fixed nor the rabbinic tradition evolved, the Avesta not written down, philosophy not matured through the harmonizing of Plato and Aristotle, and Roman law not finally codified, until the First Millennium CE. The development of Islam came just after the core period, but was well on its way by the end of the First Millennium, even if the completest reconciliation of the conflicts between theology, Sufi mysticism and philosophy was not achieved until Ghazālī, who died in 1111. Whatever their variations, though, all seven traditions attained an intellectual and institutional maturation, and became (those that survived) the recognizable forerunners of what they are today, during the First Millennium.

MONOTHEIST HISTORIOGRAPHY

No previous historian has used the First Millennium as a historical periodization in the way suggested here. Nevertheless, significant parts of the concept are foreshadowed in writings that belong to the First Millennium itself. The first step was to get away from the hitherto prevalent idea of empire as simply political and cultural dominion. Hellenistic historians had already developed the model of the succession of Oriental monarchies; some even included the Celts.[29] Polybius (d. 118 BCE) showed how all history, conceived as a "corporate whole," culminated with the establishment of Roman imperium.[30] Diodorus of Sicily (d. after 36 BCE) depicted a universal Roman Empire that reincarnated an earlier, mythical universality, realized by Dionysus in the East and Heracles in the West.[31] But while few doubted that the gods had favored and indeed participated in these developments, and it was henceforth taken for granted that human history was somehow fulfilled with the establishment of Rome's dominion over land and

29 A. Momigliano, *On pagans, Jews, and Christians* (Middletown, Conn. 1987) 31–57.

30 K. Clarke, *Between geography and history: Hellenistic constructions of the Roman world* (Oxford 1999) 77–128.

31 H. Inglebert, *Interpretatio Christiana* (Paris 2001) 468–70.

sea, one lacks the sense of a whole divine reality waiting to be revealed through history. It is to the Christian Eusebius of Caesarea (d. 339) that we owe the major advance. First he compiled a *Chronicle* in which the main events in the story of the principal ancient peoples were set out in parallel columns down to Constantine's embrace of Christianity. Then he wrote a history of the Church, to contextualize its intellectual and institutional evolution against the background of the Roman Empire. In other words, Eusebius stood at the dawn of a new historiography in which the history of Rome was intertwined with that of the one God's self-revelation, while what had hitherto been the historian's staple, namely political narrative, was for the first time systematically conjoined with cultural and especially religious developments.[32] Greek, Latin, and Syriac continuators of Eusebius carried the new genre of "ecclesiastical history" on into modern times.[33]

This Christian narrative overlaps somewhat with the account of the sixth-century Arabian background to the Qur'anic revelation provided by Muḥammad Ibn Isḥāq (d. 767) in his biography of the Prophet—he is the earliest Arabic historian of whose work substantial parts survive. And Ibn Isḥāq's book was drawn on in turn by the greatest of all Arabic historians, Ṭabarī (d. 923), when he compiled his *History of the prophets and kings*. (Ibn Isḥāq and Ṭabarī are here chosen as two outstandingly significant exemplars of a rich tradition of Arabic historical writing about pre-Islam, about which no more can be said here.[34]) Like Ibn Isḥāq, Ṭabarī began his narrative in Biblical times far past; but he did this only in order to provide a full account of monotheist prophecy designed to culminate with Muḥammad, and then continue down to his own day.

Putting all this together, we may create a contemporary narrative of the First Millennium from a clearly monotheist standpoint. That there were such forerunners cannot be a matter of indifference to us. We need not adopt their teleologies, which are conspicuous; but the tools and fashions of our own historiography lose nothing by being checked against the impressions entertained by informed contemporaries. Still more encouraging, though, is the fact that Syriac Church historiography, from its distinctive standpoint neither East Roman nor caliphal yet aware of both, produced works that drew on both the ecclesiastical and the Muslim versions of monotheist history. For example Elias bar Shenaya, Church of the East metropolitan of Nisibis (d. 1046), drew explicitly in his *Chronicle* on both Eusebius and Ṭabarī so as to sketch the whole First Millennium from his vantage point at the exact center of the Fertile Crescent, the old Abrahamic road that had linked the two em-

32 Momigliano, *On pagans* [3:29] 39.

33 See Momigliano, *Classical foundations* [2:110] 132–52, for a brief survey.

34 M. Springberg-Hinsen, *Die Zeit vor dem Islam in arabischen Universalgeschichten des 9. bis 12. Jahrhunderts* (Würzburg 1989).

pires of Iran and Rome and now joined the caliphal capitals of Damascus and Baghdad.

Eusebius was not simply the first to write an extensive and politically contextualized history of the Church from Augustus to the twentieth year of Constantine (325).[35] His greatest contribution was to see the coincidence in time of Augustus and Christ not as an accident but as providential. This opened up a powerful, totalizing vision of history in which Rome facilitated Christianity's rise and dissemination, not of course because it desired this outcome—after all, some emperors were persecutors—but because it was in the right place at the right time. Eusebius's view of this as divine design we may reject, but scarcely either the synchronicity or the relationship of empire and Church, let alone the impact of Eusebius's vision on contemporaries and posterity.

Eusebius's view that there was—at the very least—a connection between Christ and Augustus had been anticipated in the Gospels' careful allusions to both Roman imperial history and the local Herodian dynasty.[36] And from quite early on, Christian leaders had to persuade the authorities not to persecute. Common ground, a shared history, had to be established, if Church and empire were to coexist.[37] In an address to the Emperor Marcus Aurelius (161–80) we find Melito, bishop of Sardis (d. c. 190), pleading for an end to persecution and asserting that, although a barbarian "philosophy" in its first origins, Christianity flowered under Augustus and was of good omen given the empire's prosperity from that time. After Augustus, only Nero (54–68) and Domitian (81–96) had shown Christians serious hostility, while Hadrian (117–38), notably, had protected them.[38] In the following century Origen (d. c. 254) observed how

> Jesus was born during the reign of Augustus, the one who reduced to uniformity, so to speak, the many kingdoms on earth so that he had a single empire. It would have hindered Jesus's teaching from being spread through the whole world if there had been many kingdoms.[39]

Next we find the Emperor Constantine himself, in his *Oration to the saints* (variously dated between 313 and 327), reading a prophecy of Christ's coming into Virgil's reference in his fourth or "Messianic" *Eclogue*, probably

35 Eusebius, *Ecclesiastical history* [ed. E. Schwartz and T. Mommsen, *Eusebius Werke* 2.1–3 (Berlin 1903–9); tr. K. Lake and J. E. L. Oulton (Cambridge, Mass. 1926–32)].

36 Matthew 2; Luke 3:1.

37 In general, see Inglebert, *Interpretatio Christiana* [3:31] 365–69.

38 Melito of Sardis in Eusebius, *Ecclesiastical history* [3:35] 4.26.5–11.

39 Origen, *Against Celsus* [ed. and tr. (French) M. Borret (Paris 1967–76); English tr. H. Chadwick (Cambridge 1965, corrected reprint)] 2.30.

composed in 40 BCE, to the birth of a child who will usher in a golden age.[40] And in the inscription on the Arch of Constantine (315) we find allusions not only to the emperor's monotheism ("instinctu divinitatis"—unless this is Constantine himself), but also to his liberation of the state from a tyrannical faction, surely an implicit self-comparison to Augustus.[41]

As for Bishop Eusebius, through persecution, toleration, and then imperial favor he pondered Rome's role in the Christian dispensation, in varying moods and for different audiences.[42] But by 335–36, in his *In praise of Constantine*, he had come to see Rome as well as the Church as providential and beneficial. Admittedly he was speaking in Constantine's presence; but even so he insists that the empire's role is still secondary to Christ's.[43] Eusebius recalls how there had once been many states and constant warfare. The root of these evils was the worship of many gods, polytheism. But Christ came, undid the demons and proclaimed One God.

> At the same time, one single empire flowered for all people, the Roman, and the eternally implacable and irreconcilable enmity of nations was completely resolved. . . . Together, at the same moment, as if at a single divine sign, two beneficial shoots grew up for mankind: the empire of the Romans and the pious teaching. . . . Two great powers—the Roman Empire, which became a monarchy at that time, and the teaching of Christ—proceeding as if from a single starting point, and both together flourishing at the same moment, tamed and reconciled all to friendship. For while the power of our Saviour destroyed the polyarchies (polyarchiai) and polytheisms (polytheïai) of the demons and heralded the one kingdom of God to all men, Greeks and barbarians, to the furthest ends of the earth, the Roman Empire, now that the causes of polyarchy had been abolished, subdued the visible governments, zealous to combine the entire race into one unity and concord. Already it has united most of the various peoples, and it is further destined to attain as soon as possible all the others, right up to the very limits of the inhabited world.[44]

40 Constantine, *Oration to the saints* [ed. I. A. Heikel, *Eusebius Werke* 1 (Leipzig 1902) 149–92; tr. M. Edwards, *Constantine and Christendom* (Liverpool 2003) 1–62] 19–21; cf. S. MacCormack, *The shadows of poetry: Vergil in the mind of Augustine* (Berkeley 1998) 22–31.

41 H. Prückner, "Kaiser Konstantins Bilderbogen," *Thetis* 15 (2008) 59–75, esp. 63; M. Clauss, "*Instinctu divinitatis*", *Zeitschrift für Papyrologie und Epigraphik* 185 (2013) 294–96.

42 H. Inglebert, *Les romains chrétiens face à l'histoire de Rome* (Paris 1996) 165–68.

43 A. P. Johnson, *Ethnicity and argument in Eusebius' Praeparatio Evangelica* (Oxford 2006) 174–97.

44 Eusebius, *In praise of Constantine* [ed. Heikel [3:40] 193–259; tr. (adjusted) H. A. Drake, *In praise of Constantine* (Berkeley 1976)] 16.4–7. Circumstances and date of delivery: P. Maraval, *Eusèbe de Césarée, La théologie politique de l'empire chrétien* (Paris 2001) 29–34 (with a better translation).

Perhaps at this date or later, the Syriac poet-theologian Ephrem of Nisibis (d. 373) elaborated similar conceits in his *Hymns on the Nativity*:

> In the days of the king who enrolled people
> For the poll tax, our Saviour descended
> And enrolled people in the Book of Life.[45]

Whatever his reservations about Rome, though, Eusebius was not so naïve as to regard the happy conjunction of Augustus and Christ as the pure fruit of providential fiat, in no need of historical explanation or at least contextualization. As a student of the Old as well as the New Testament, and as bishop of Caesarea on the Mediterranean coast of Palestine, a city with numerous polytheist, Jewish and Samaritan inhabitants, Eusebius was well aware of Rome's diversity but also of its being the heir—and indeed (in the case of Iran) still the neighbor—of prestigious earlier civilizations. Furthermore, he understood that, if his account of Christ's life as the universal redemptive event was to convince, he had to locate Jesus of Nazareth not just in a remote Roman province (as Tacitus had[46]), but at the culmination, and in some sense as the resolution, of previous history. In this way Eusebius became a historian of civilizations, and necessarily a periodizer as well.[47] This is not his concern in the *Ecclesiastical history*, which begins with the life of Christ and goes on to trace the rise of the major sees, the course of the persecutions, the progress of Christian letters, the formation of the scriptural canon, and the lives of the most eminent Church leaders, through to the reign of Constantine. The ancient civilizations are surveyed in another work, quite different in form, namely the *Chronicle*. This became so fundamental to Greek Christian chronography that it was superseded and lost. The surviving Latin and Armenian translations/versions show the breadth of its influence, from the Sasanian frontier lands to far-away Ireland.[48]

If in the *Ecclesiastical history* Eusebius intertwined the story of Rome and the Church over three centuries in a continuous prose narrative, the *Chronicle* had far more stories to tell over a much longer period. In parallel columns across each opening of his book, Eusebius coordinated the year numbers

45 Ephrem of Nisibis, *Hymns on the Nativity* [ed. and tr. (German) E. Beck (Louvain 1959); English tr. K. E. McVey, *Ephrem the Syrian, Hymns* (New York 1989) 61–217] 18.2.

46 Tacitus, *Annals* [ed. S. Borzsák and K. Wellesley (Leipzig 1986–92); tr. M. Grant (London 1996, revised reprint)] 15.44.

47 It is harder to separate Eusebius's theological motivation from his historiographical performance than P. Van Nuffelen would like: "Theology versus genre? The universalism of Christian historiography in late Antiquity," in P. Liddel and A. Fear (eds), *Historiae mundi* (London 2010) 162–75 (correctly pointing out, though, that Eusebius's coverage gets less universal as he approaches his own day).

48 Eusebius, *Chronicle* [ed. R. Helm, *Eusebius Werke* 7 (Berlin 1984^3); cf. M. Wallraff (ed.), *Iulius Africanus Chronographiae* (Berlin 2007) XXXII nn. 76–77]; A. A. Mosshammer, *The Chronicle of Eusebius and Greek historiographical tradition* (Lewisburg 1979); B. Croke, "The origins of the Christian world chronicle," in id., *Christian chronicles and Byzantine history, 5th–6th centuries* (London 1992) iii.

(regnal or otherwise) of each people's history, assigning primacy to the era of Abraham (Abraham's birth = year 1) and Olympiads. In a broad spatium historicum in the middle of the page he made brief notes of salient events. In this way he made clear at a glance the shape of world history and the relations of its constituent parts. In his *Hexapla* the Christian scholar Origen, working again in Caesarea but a couple of generations earlier, had already used a six-column format in order to set out the relationship between the Hebrew scriptures and their Greek versions. Both Origen and Eusebius deployed this innovative layout, together with the flexible new book format known as the codex,[49] in order to respond to a fresh intellectual need, the coordination of Greek and non-Greek ("barbarian") history and thought. At an increasingly complex historical and cultural conjuncture—reflected in the Caesarea library's extensive holdings of Greek books both pre-Christian and Christian, along with the Hebrew scriptures—the codex and the columnar formatting of the page proved ideal tools for Eusebius's bold reorganization of historical knowledge.[50]

At his most expansive, Eusebius has columns for the Medes, Hebrews (divided into Judah and Israel), Athenians, Latins, Spartans, Macedonians, Corinthians/Lydians, and Egyptians.[51] Gradually the number of columns decreases, the Oriental empires fade away, and history revolves round the heirs of Alexander (notably the Ptolemies), the Romans, and the Jews. From the beginning of Augustus's rule, only the Romans and Jews remain, and after Titus's providential holocaust in the year 70 (sescenta milia uirorum interfecit[52]), the Jewish column disappears. Thereafter, Eusebius's understanding of history centers exclusively on Rome and the Church. (It is the same idea conveyed in the quotation from *In praise of Constantine*, above.) The rise of Sasanian Iran in the 220s remains offstage despite Caesarea's position at the western end of the Fertile Crescent, despite the Sasanians' ability to challenge Rome militarily, and despite their numerous Christian subjects. The Peace of the Church—or its "Liberty," according to a recent attempt to retrieve Eusebius's original Greek[53]—is recorded under the year 313. The

49 See below, p. 168.

50 A. Grafton and M. Williams, *Christianity and the transformation of the book* (Cambridge, Mass. 2006). For a newly discovered, perhaps Christian chronicle of ancient polities dated as early as the first quarter of the second century, on a papyrus arranged in columns meant to be read consecutively, see D. Colomo and others, "Die älteste Weltchronik," and A. Weiss, "Die Leipziger Weltchronik—die älteste christliche Weltchronik?," *Archiv für Papyrusforschung* 56 (2010) 1–37. Historians and archaeologists still struggle to produce a reliable relative and absolute chronology of the Near East based on synchronization of regional chronologies: www.arcane.uni-tuebingen.de.

51 Eusebius, *Chronicle* [3:48] 83–86.

52 Eusebius, *Chronicle* [3:48] 187. For other inflated figures, see *Ecclesiastical history* [3:35] 3.5.5, 7.2.

53 R. W. Burgess, *Studies in Eusebian and post-Eusebian chronography* (Stuttgart 1999) 56, 62, 97, 102.

Chronicle ends on a high point, with Constantine's twentieth anniversary celebrations in 325.

In one sense, Eusebius was both late and antique to his fingertips. Late, because while he looked forward to the spread of Christianity "to the very limits of the inhabited world" under Constantine's dynasty extending "to unaging time,"[54] and rejected his predecessor Sextus Julius Africanus's (d. c. 250) overprecise eschatology, still he believed history was gradually heading toward its end, the Second Coming.[55] Antique, because although he saw in Antiquity an abundance of empires, while his own age was dominated only by Rome, still Rome had grown organically out of the earlier narrative. We should not, though, underplay the uniqueness of Christianity and Rome—especially their combination—in Eusebius's vision of things. And the God-willed coming together of Christian monotheism and Roman monarchy he no doubt expected to endure as long into the future as was necessary.

In the century after Eusebius, it is true, the compromises and ambiguities of Christianization, especially the spread of Arianism, caused some to take a less rosy view. So too did a lingering awareness that imperial Rome had destroyed the more virtuous (but inconveniently pre-Christian) Republic. There were mounting pressures on the Rhine and Danube frontiers. Then came the sack of Rome in 410.[56] In Antioch, Bishop John Chrysostom (d. 407) was acutely aware of the gap between the reality of life in a nominally Christian empire and city, and the ascetic ideal he exhorted his flock to live by. Bishop Augustine of Hippo (d. 430), who gladly used Eusebius's chronology, nevertheless turned his gaze toward the City of God and away from Rome/Babylon and the triumphalist alignment of Church and empire under Augustus and his successors. Blame for Rome's humiliation he deflected away from Christianity by drawing attention to the disasters of its pagan past starting with the sack of Troy.[57] He toyed, true enough, with polemical applications of Virgil's Fourth *Eclogue*; while his intense boyhood to old age dialogue with the poet's whole oeuvre bridged the four centuries from Augustus to Alaric and is among the notable spiritual and literary experiences which bind the First Millennium's phases together. Yet Virgil, however admired (already in his own day) as the touchstone of Romanitas, was not the Scripture, and remained deeply ambivalent in Christian eyes.[58]

54 Eusebius, *In praise of Constantine*, as quoted above, p. 71; id., *Life of Constantine* [ed. F. Winkelmann (Berlin 1991^2); tr. Av. Cameron and S. G. Hall (Oxford 1999)] 1.9.2.

55 Inglebert, *Romains chrétiens* [3:42] 169–70; Grafton and Williams, *Christianity* [3:50] 148–54.

56 Inglebert, *Romains chrétiens* [3:42] 177–502.

57 I. Sandwell, "Christian self-definition in the fourth century AD," in I. Sandwell and J. Huskinson (eds), *Culture and society in later Roman Antioch* (Oxford 2004) 35–58 (reference courtesy of Myrto Malouta), with some ambivalences noted by MacCormack, *Shadows of poetry* [3:40] 212–14.

58 MacCormack, *Shadows of poetry* [3:40] 29–31 (*Ecl.* 4) and passim, esp. 7–38, 138–39, 225–31.

But if Eusebius's link between the Church and a Rome now defeated not triumphant meant for some that the last days were at hand, others were more optimistic about the durability of the Eusebian model.[59] One such was the historian Orosius (d. 418), who went so far as to make Christ a Roman citizen (because of the census), while his *Histories against the pagans* did much to form the Latin West's view of its past.[60] In the Greek East, Eusebius's *Ecclesiastical history* found a string of continuators down to Evagrius (d. after 594), as long as the Constantinian model seemed to work at least in the East. All of them interwove the Church's affairs with the fortunes of empire, viewed of course from varying ecclesiastical standpoints[61]—which has undoubtedly skewed our whole view of late Antiquity, but on the other hand legitimately reflects the concerns of then influential bodies of opinion. Those who expected the world to end in 500 were disappointed; yet ecclesiastical historians continued to adapt.[62] What had started with Eusebius as a thoroughly "late antique" genre was gradually stretched into something less expectant, to cope with the all too gradual unfolding of time.

The Arab conquests and the rise of Islam put such a question mark over this view of history—or at least gave East Rome such a jolt—that Evagrius found no continuator in Greek. Greek secular historiography likewise came to an end with Theophylact Simocatta, and—for a time—Greek chronicle writing too, with the *Paschal chronicle*; both works were produced c. 630. In the Muslim world, though, things were different. Here most Christians, whether Church of the East, Chalcedonian, or anti-Chalcedonian (miaphysite), preferred to write in Syriac. Eusebius's *Ecclesiastical history* and his *Chronicle* had been translated,[63] and miaphysite historians in particular went on compiling, either more or less under Eusebius's influence, chronicles such as that of Jacob of Edessa (d. 708)—a tradition that culminated in the great syntheses by Michael the Syrian (d. 1199) and Gregory Bar Hebraeus (d. 1286), attending to East Rome and the Caliphate as well as their own Church. This resolutely anti-Chalcedonian communion modeled itself, though, on the persecuted Jews of Old Testament times—which is why old-style ecclesiastical histories proved harder to write than chronicles.[64]

59 Inglebert, *Romains chrétiens* [3:42] 505–681.

60 Orosius, *Histories against the pagans* [ed. and tr. (French) M.-P. Arnaud-Lindet (Paris 1990–91)], esp. 6.22.4–9.

61 On divergences from and criticisms of Eusebius's model, see Inglebert, *Interpretatio Christiana* [3:31] 332, 535–36.

62 M. Meier, *Das andere Zeitalter Justinians* (Göttingen 2003) 11–22.

63 M. Debié, "L'héritage de l'historiographie grecque," in M. Debié (ed.), *L'historiographie syriaque* (Paris 2009) 11, 21–24; cf. K. Pinggéra, "Nestorianische Weltchronistik: Johannes Bar Penkāyē und Elias von Nisibis," in M. Wallraff (ed.), *Julius Africanus und die christliche Weltchronistik* (Berlin 2006) 277 n. 69.

64 Debié, in Debié (ed.), *L'historiographie syriaque* [3:63] 24–27; A. Palmer, "Les chroniques brèves syriaques," in the same volume, 71, 83. Even Momigliano, *Classical foundations* [2:110] 145, was unaware of any Eusebian tradition in Syriac after John of Ephesus (d. c. 585).

Muslim historians, by contrast, enjoyed the privilege of making a fresh start. Yet when we turn to Ibn Isḥāq in the mid-eighth century, we find that they too could see important continuities with the pre-Islamic past. Ibn Isḥāq prefaced his massive and much-read *Life of the Prophet of God*[65]—which survives only in an abridged edition prepared by Ibn Hishām (d. 828/33)—with the *Book of the beginning*, an account of history, especially the earlier prophets, from creation to the eve of Islam. Its latter parts concentrated on South Arabia and increasingly on Mecca, to prepare for Muḥammad's life-story.[66] Ibn Isḥāq recognized South Arabia to be a remote region in which neither Ctesiphon nor Constantinople was willing, or most of the time able, to intervene directly.[67] Rome nonetheless acted through its Christian proxy Aksum (Ethiopia) and the local Christian Churches, while Iran did eventually conquer and for a time control the region.[68] In this sense, Ibn Isḥāq manages to provide an imperial—Sasanian as well as Roman—backdrop for the birth of Islam,[69] just as Eusebius had linked Christ to Augustus.[70] But there is no denying that religious communities—notably the Christians of Najrān—or even individuals play the leading part in his narrative, rather than empires. Ibn Isḥāq delineates the circumstances under which Judaism and Christianity became established in South Arabia.[71] He also tells at length the story of Salmān from Iṣfahān, who abandoned Mazdaism for Christianity and Christianity for the Prophet after a long search. Ibn Isḥāq builds an atmosphere of expectancy before the appearance of Muḥammad,

65 Ibn Isḥāq, *Life of the Prophet of God* (*Sīrat rasūl Allāh*) (recension of Ibn Hishām, d. 828/33) [ed. M. al-Saqqā, I. al-Abyārī, ʿA. Shalabī (Cairo 1936; reprint Beirut 1994); tr. A. Guillaume, *The life of Muhammad* (London 1955), with marginal references to F. Wüstenfeld's edition (Göttingen 1858–60), here cited for convenience; passages excluded by Ibn Hishām have come to light in Fez and Damascus manuscripts: M. Ḥamīdullāh, *Sīrat Ibn Isḥāq* (Rabat 1396/1976), summarized by A. Guillaume, *New light on the life of Muhammad* (Manchester n.d.)]. See also R. Sellheim, "Prophet, Chalif und Geschichte," *Oriens* 18–19 (1967) 33–91.

66 On the fragmentarily preserved *Kitāb al-mubtadaʾ*, see J. Horovitz (ed. L. I. Conrad), *The earliest biographies of the Prophet and their authors* (Princeton 2002) 80–83; L. Conrad, "Recovering lost texts," *Journal of the American Oriental Society* 113 (1993) 258–63, many of whose strictures on the reconstruction by G. D. Newby, *The making of the last Prophet* (Columbia, S.C. 1989), also apply to that by M. K. al-Kawwāz, *Muḥammad ibn Isḥāq: Al-Mubtadaʾ fī qiṣaṣ al-anbiyāʾ* (Beirut 2006).

67 Ibn Isḥāq, *Life* [3:65] 25–26, 41–42.

68 Ibn Isḥāq, *Life* [3:65] 26, 42–47.

69 For a modern perspective see J. Retsö, "Arabia and the heritage of the Axial Age," in Arnason and others (eds), *Axial civilizations* [2:117] 337–58.

70 For the possibility Ibn Isḥāq was familiar with the genre, or at least the assumptions, of ecclesiastical history, see J. Wansbrough, *The sectarian milieu* (Oxford 1978) 98, 116, 117, 123, 125; cf. C. F. Robinson, *Islamic historiography* (Cambridge 2003) 135, and more generally M. Di Branco, "A rose in the desert? Late antique and early Byzantine chronicles and the formation of Islamic universal historiography," in Liddel and Fear (eds), *Historiae mundi* [3:47] 189–206. But there are no Arabic translations of Greek ecclesiastical historians to compare to that of the Latin Orosius (with continuation) done in tenth-century Spain: M. Penelas (ed.), *Kitāb Hurūšiyūš* (Madrid 2001).

71 Ibn Isḥāq, *Life* [3:65] 17, 22.

touching on many of the religious currents in the sixth-century Near East, and sketching portraits of sensitive souls like Salmān, who either simply waited or wandered from place to place looking for clues as to where the longed-for messenger might appear.[72] Such individuals were few, and Muḥammad's coming was undoubtedly a revolution; but still Ibn Isḥāq's emphasis is on this expectancy and on the chain of prophecy, not on the break between an old world and a new one coming to birth.

This generous historical contextualization of Islam, making Muḥammad "the pivot of world history,"[73] can be related to other roughly contemporary statements, either positive or negative, such as the fresco of the six kings at the late Umayyad bath house of Quṣayr 'Amra in Jordan, which implies a wide political and cultural context for the Caliphate by portraying the rulers of Rome, Iran, Aksum, and Visigothic Spain,[74] or John of Damascus's treatment of Islam as the hundredth of the Christian heresies. Indeed, Ibn Isḥāq himself made the transition from prophetic to subsequent caliphal history, and hence a better embedding of Islam in the flow of history, by compiling toward the end of his life a *History of the caliphs*. This work proved much less popular than the *Life*; only a few fragments survive.[75] Its significance for us, though, is that, like Eusebius, Ibn Isḥāq did not confine himself to the initial revelatory and prophetic events in the history of his religion, but saw virtue in pursuing the story almost down to his own time. He could have restricted himself to the first four, "rightly guided" caliphs, the rashidūn as they came to be called; yet he dared to embark on the controversial and divisive Umayyads. He got at least as far as the first Umayyad caliph, Mu'āwiya (661–80), and in the light of his suspected Shiite leanings one wonders whether he broached the reign of Mu'āwiya's son Yazīd and the brutal slaying of Muḥammad's grandson and 'Alī's son Huṣayn at Karbala in 681, a crisis of political and religious legitimacy at the root of the eventual Sunni-Shiite schism. In any event, Ibn Isḥāq was aware of the significance of the community's post-Prophetic and indeed postscriptural development, in the same way Eusebius was committed to writing the history of the Church. Both stories were indefinitely extendable.

But if the ecclesiastical historians gave up writing sequels to Eusebius once a more or less triumphalist narrative became unsustainable, the universalist (in both time and space) tradition in Arabic historiography—the progeny in other words of Ibn Isḥāq—suffered from a more insidious weakness: it came

72 Ibn Isḥāq, *Life* [3:65] 115–17, 130, 133–49.

73 W. Raven, "Sīra," *EIs*² 9.661a.

74 Fowden, *Quṣayr 'Amra* [1:32] 197–226; id., "The Umayyad horizon," *Journal of Roman archaeology* 25 (2012) 980–82.

75 *Ta'rīkh al-khulafā'*: N. Abbott, *Studies in Arabic literary papyri* (Chicago 1957–72) 1.80–99; F. Sezgin, *Geschichte des arabischen Schrifttums* (Leiden 1967–) 1.289–90. Ibn Isḥāq probably also wrote a history of the Arab conquests.

to see Islam as entirely self-sufficient. Already Ibn Hishām excised from his abridged edition whole tracts of Ibn Isḥāq's account of pre-Islamic history, fostering the illusion of an "empty Ḥijāz" and contributing to the oblivion of South Arabia/Ḥimyar's flourishing urban civilization, from which subsequent historical understanding has so deeply suffered.[76] Contextualizing Islam did not mesh with the growing conviction that it was unique and God-given and had no need to be related to anything else. Among Ibn Hishām's major criteria for deciding whether to keep Ibn Isḥāq's materials was their direct relevance to the Qur'ān, as he states at the outset of his edition. In the course of time, Islam came to see its origins as a case of spontaneous generation. It labeled the pre-Islamic world jāhilīya, "ignorance" or "barbarism" or "lawlessness" (at least from the religious perspective; pre-Islamic poetry was another matter[77]). As early as the Umayyad period, it is true, Muslim scholars worked out a framework narrative of pre-Islamic prophets and kings. They even calculated how many years passed between each of its main figures from Adam to Muḥammad[78]—in other words, an incipient "before hijra" chronology. But nothing came of it (and bare frameworks of kings and prophets anyway lacked the attractive texture of Ibn Isḥāq's pre-Islamic narrative). An early chronographer went so far as to call AH 1 "the first year of history."[79] Muslims still cannot narrate with any precision what happened before the hijra except by using BC/AD dates.[80] The insidious concept of jāhilīya remains to this day their answer to "late Antiquity": two exclusivist doctrines, two sides of the same coin.[81]

Despite Ibn Hishām, and others,[82] there were still for a time Muslims who dared take a wider view of the past. Notable ninth-century universal histories include those by Ya'qūbī and Dīnawarī, and culminate with Ṭabarī's monumental *History of the prophets and kings*, completed in the 920s and indebted to otherwise lost sections of Ibn Isḥāq for whole tracts of its account of pre-

76 J. E. Montgomery, "The empty Ḥijāz," in id. (ed.), *Arabic theology, Arabic philosophy* (Leuven 2006) 37–97, and I. Gajda, *Le royaume de Ḥimyar à l'époque monothéiste* (Paris 2009), attempt to fill this void by paying attention to pre-Islamic poetry and epigraphy, respectively.

77 Cf. Neuwirth, *Koran als Text* [1:6] 332–33.

78 A. el-R. Tayyara, "Prophethood and kingship in early Islamic historical thought," *Der Islam* 84 (2008) 1–30.

79 A. Borrut, *Entre mémoire et pouvoir: L'espace syrien sous les derniers Omeyyades et les premiers Abbassides (v. 72–193/692–809)* (Leiden 2011) 32.

80 The conventional Arabic formulae are explicitly Christian: qabla 'l-mīlād, "before the Nativity," and ba'da 'l-mīlād/sana mīlādīya, "after the Nativity." Cf. F. Rosenthal, *A history of Muslim historiography* (Leiden 1968²) 90. Even in Europe BC dating caught on slowly, becoming somewhat frequent only in the late thirteenth century: A.-D. von den Brincken, "Beobachtungen zum Aufkommen der retrospektiven Inkarnationsära," *Archiv für Diplomatik* 25 (1979) 1–20.

81 Neuwirth, *Koran als Text* [1:6] 39–42.

82 See, e.g., T. Khalidi, *Arabic historical thought in the classical period* (Cambridge 1994) 48, on the ninth-century historian Wāqidī.

Islamic times.[83] Being an Iranian, Ṭabarī provides an exhaustive account of the Sasanians (he was also aware that only Iranian and Jewish history was well enough documented to provide the rudiments of a pre-hijra chronology[84]). Admittedly he cares as little for Rome as Eusebius does for Iran, providing only a fleeting account of its rulers from Augustus to Heraclius based on Christian sources and focused almost exclusively on its involvement with Syria-Palestine and the Gospel story. He substitutes a history of prophets for Eusebius's ecclesiastical history; and elsewhere, when his sacred heroes lived on Roman soil (the Seven Sleepers of Ephesus, S. George) he prefers Muslim to Christian narratives.[85] But this is all in the cause of a monotheist perspective on history; and if there is one providential God there can, in the end, be only one history of mankind. After Ṭabarī, biographical and local histories—or at the most universal histories with a more and more local focus the nearer one got to the present—held the field.[86] Still, the *History of the prophets and kings* continued to provide a reference-narrative for the Caliphate's early history.[87]

It was in the tenth-century Syriac Christian world that prospects of producing a comprehensive monotheist historical narrative were brightest. Most East Romans did not want to fit Islam into their Eusebian narrative of Rome as the sole empire willed by God. Muslim historians were less and less interested in the pre-Islamic world. But Syriac Christians under the Caliphate, mostly miaphysite or Church of the East, could neither ignore Islam without losing contact with reality, nor efface the pre-Islamic past without losing their identity. This put them in a strong position—despite their Maccabean obsession[88] with suffering and struggle—to see things as they actually were. It is no coincidence that our best witness, the chronicler Elias bar Shenaya, occupied—starting in the year 1008—the Church of the East episcopal throne in Nisibis, a city situated exactly in the middle of the Fertile Crescent, at the very center of the First Millennium world.[89]

83 L. E. Goodman, *Islamic humanism* (New York 2003) 180–86.

84 Michael Whitby, "Tabari: The period before Jesus," in H. Börm and J. Wiesehöfer (eds), *Commutatio et contentio* (Düsseldorf 2010) 401.

85 Al-Ṭabarī, *History of the prophets and kings* (*Ta'rīkh al-rusul wa'l-mulūk*) [ed. M. J. de Goeje and others (Leiden 1879–1901); tr. ed. E. Yarshater (Albany 1985–)] 1.703–4, 740–44, 775–82, 795–812.

86 Robinson, *Islamic historiography* [3:70] 134–42, esp. 139; Goodman, *Islamic humanism* [3:83] 201–2. For a similar tendency among ecclesiastical historians in the medieval West, see Momigliano, *Classical foundations* [2:110] 146–49.

87 F. M. Donner, *Narratives of Islamic origins* (Princeton 1998) 291–92.

88 Cf. M. Detoraki (ed.), *Le martyre de Saint Aréthas* (Paris 2007) 64–77.

89 Elias bar Shenaya, *Chronicle* [ed. and tr. (Latin) E. W. Brooks and J.-B. Chabot, *Eliae metropolitae Nisibeni opus chronologicum* (Paris, Rome 1909–10)]; cf. Pinggéra, in Wallraff (ed.), *Julius Africanus* [3:63] 273–83 (note 269, 273, 281 on the Church of the East's view of itself as having always lived under rulers with other beliefs); A. Borrut, "La circulation de l'information historique entre les sources arabo-musulmanes et syriaques: Élie de Nisibe et ses sources," in Debié (ed.), *L'historiographie syriaque* [3:63]

That Elias, an experienced ecclesiastical writer preeminent in the Church of the East of his day, was also thoroughly embedded in the Arab world is already apparent from his provision of a parallel Arabic as well as Syriac version of his chronicle, and his deployment from 622 CE of the hijra dating system. Up to that point he used Olympiads (!) and the Seleucid era; Jacob of Edessa had employed a mixture of eras; Evagrius had favored the Antiochene era and regnal years. The era of the Incarnation had been invented by Dionysius Exiguus at Rome in 525, but was not widely disseminated even in the West before the eighth century.[90] One can imagine Elias turning with relief to the Muslim dates, which had rapidly been accepted over such an expanse of the earth's surface.

For pre-Islamic history, though, the Arabs could offer no dating system of their own, and only very partial historiographical content focused on the background to Muḥammad. Here, Elias's models were exclusively Christian, notably Eusebius. Little Church of the East historical writing has survived from before Elias's time,[91] and he himself was perfectly happy to adopt the miaphysite Jacob of Edessa's *Chronicle* as a model, including its Olympiads.[92] Jacob in turn was based on Eusebius's *Chronicle*. Elias begins with Adam, and covers all the ancient empires. But where Eusebius loses interest in Iran after the Achaemenids, and ignores the Sasanians completely, Elias (like Jacob of Edessa, again) records the Sasanian emperors just after their Roman colleagues, and eventually the caliphs too, for whom one of his sources (acknowledged, as is Elias's custom) turns out to be the great Ṭabarī. In space, the perspective is no longer Mediterranean, as was Eusebius's on the coast at Caesarea, but embraces the wider horizons to be explored in the next chapter. In time, Elias's chronicle highlights the First Millennium. The first part of the work confines itself to lists of Biblical figures, dynasts, and bishops, along with passages of chronological computation. Next comes a lacuna that ap-

---

137–59; H. Teule, "The Syriac Renaissance," in H. G. B. Teule and others (eds), *The Syriac Renaissance* (Leuven 2010) 3–5, 24, situating Elias symbolically at the turn of the millennium and the beginning of the era of absolute Muslim cultural dominance.

90 G. Declercq, *Anno Domini* (Turnhout 2000) 44–48, 97–101, 149–79 (my thanks to Anthony Kaldellis for this reference). On the hijra era and its possible encouragement of AD dating (attributed by Declercq 177–79 merely to confusion induced by too many regnal systems, which however went on being used alongside AD: 179–88), see below, pp. 84–85. Andrew Palmer informs me that the era of the Incarnation may not have been employed in Christian Syria before the onset of European missionizing.

91 Note though the tenth-century Arabic *Chronicle of Seert*, mainly on the Church of the East but mentioning events in Iranian, Roman, and Arab history too, probably (in its original state) from Christ to at least the late ninth century: J. Howard-Johnston, *Witnesses to a world crisis* (Oxford 2010) 324–31. On Ḥunayn ibn Isḥāq's lost world history, see S. Griffith, "Syrian Christian intellectuals in the world of Islam," *Journal of the Canadian Society for Syriac Studies* 7 (2007) 59.

92 Pinggéra, in Wallraff (ed.), *Julius Africanus* [3:63] 282; W. Witakowski, "The Chronicle of Jacob of Edessa," in B. ter Haar Romeny (ed.), *Jacob of Edessa and the Syriac culture of his day* (Leiden 2008) 37, 44.

parently does not indicate loss of text. (The sole surviving manuscript, in the British Library, may be Elias's own copy.[93]) Then the chronicle proper begins with King Abgar of Edessa, Tiberius, Pontius Pilate, and Christ, initiating a sequence extending down to the year 1018. And if this account of the monotheist First Millennium—featuring Rome and the Caliphate on a roughly equal footing, and Iran too albeit more summarily—had not actually been produced by a Church of the East prelate living in Nisibis soon after the year 1000, the modern student could still have collaged it together from the Greek ecclesiastical historians plus Ibn Isḥāq and Ṭabarī, by appealing to the example of Evagrius who adumbrated—even if he did not execute—just such a composite and, indeed, potentially universal history based on the works of a catholic selection of his predecessors.[94]

One can see now why Theophanes, the only East Roman historian who provided a serious narrative of the Umayyad and early Abbasid Caliphates, got it from a Syriac source—apparently the early Abbasid Chalcedonian polymath Theophilus of Edessa, whose chronicle recorded events in both the East Roman Empire and the Caliphate.[95] One ought in fairness, though, to underline that Elias was a simple chronicler not an ecclesiastical historian, far less an historian of religions. Therefore he was happily free of the need to offer a coherent account of the working of divine providence through the prophets. Not that it would have been easy for a bishop under Islam to write such a book, and not just because of Muḥammad. The task was made even harder because unlike Eusebius, who had before him in the Gospels and Acts a detailed narrative of beginnings to build on, Muslims like Ibn Isḥāq and in his wake Ṭabarī had to fit an almost entirely nonnarrative scripture round a massive, ahistorically organized stock of traditions about the events of Muḥammad's life. On the other hand, Ibn Isḥāq was writing much closer in time to Muḥammad's life than Eusebius was to Jesus's, and could feel surer of his sources, some of which were no doubt oral. Eusebius had to reconstruct the whole transmission of narrative and authority—a process beset by error and heresy—from the crucifixion to his own day, three whole centuries.

Thanks not least, though, to their respect for scriptural issues—the New Testament canon for Eusebius, the historicity of the Qur'ān for Ibn Isḥāq, and commentary on the Qur'ān for Ṭabarī—these historians managed to produce narratives that became authoritative in their communities and were therefore preserved. The separation and hostility of the communities has meant not only that their different versions of prophetic history have never been reconciled, but also that even their either more or less "secular" historians have scarcely been compared. In the present, programmatic book all that

93 Pinggéra, in Wallraff (ed.), *Julius Africanus* [3:63] 276, 282.

94 Van Nuffelen in Liddel and Fears (eds), *Historiae mundi* [3:47] 168–70.

95 R. G. Hoyland, *Theophilus of Edessa's Chronicle* (Liverpool 2011).

can be risked is some indication of the common denominators of their respective maturations, along with that of rabbinic Judaism and certain other traditions. At a not too far distant date I intend to produce a secular historical narrative of all these experiences, within the framework of the First Millennium.

FOR AND AGAINST THE FIRST MILLENNIUM

Carl Becker prophesied a century ago that "a time will come when late Hellenism will be appreciated retrospectively from the Islamic tradition."[96] If we accept the First Millennium as our primary framework (it does not exclude parallel use of late Antiquity either long or short, political, socioeconomic, or conceptual), we are indeed enabled to analyze certain major historical phenomena, which stand out better once the time frame is expanded in this way. "Before Muḥammad" appears in a different light when viewed from "after Muḥammad," and vice versa. For example, Christianity and the experience of Christianization are relativized when studied in the perspective of Islam, which saw itself as a corrective to Christianity's failures—but also succumbed to some of its vices. The uniqueness of Christian monarchy and priesthood, and of their interaction, are better seen when we examine the failure of the monarchical caliphate to endure effectively in Islam, and the success of a scholarly, nonsacramental form of religious leadership. And we more clearly appreciate the remarkable durability and influence of both Rome and Iran, whether as state or civilization or both, when we read the Umayyads in the light of East Rome, or the Abbasids in that of the Sasanids. These are all developments that continue to resound today;[97] and students of the First Millennium are better placed to address them than historians who act as if North Africa, Arabia, the Levant, and Iran just dropped off the map c. 640.

It has been well said that

> the rediscovery of late antiquity as a historical epoch with distinctive characteristics and of major importance for later developments is indisputably one of the major results of historical research during the last decades, and its implications for comparative history have yet to be explored in detail.[98]

96 Becker, *Islamstudien* [2:74] 1.201.

97 Others, which do not, may still be historiographically important. Note, e.g., R. Alston's "reading back" from early caliphal Syria in order to question the decline analysis of East Roman urbanism and economy: *Acta Byzantina Fennica* 3 (2010) [2:113] 14–15.

98 Arnason and others (eds), *Axial civilizations* [2:117] 287.

Yet if we try to facilitate this comparative effort by defining the period generously, the obvious comparandum for Christianity is Islam, we soon have a bigger "esplosione" on our hands than even Giardina imagined, and late Antiquity bursts any reasonable bounds. Nothing called "Antiquity" can convincingly be extended far enough into the "Middle Ages" to explain Islam's tenth-century maturation; while if we embrace Christianity's birth and growth, we must annex too that whole process's imperial Roman context, and in so doing stray far from any acceptable backward extension of the epithet "late." We have to face the fact that Giardina's diagnosis was right but his cure was excessively conservative, failing to rise to the challenge presented by the conjunction of late antique and Islamic studies.[99]

Apart from its inherent advantages for understanding the traditions and societies in question according to their own rhythms of development, and contextually, the First Millennium is also relevant to Europe's task of assimilating its Muslim populations, as I already hinted in chapter 1. Inclusive social attitudes and policies are more likely to be fostered by inclusive histories propagated through the school syllabus, than by any periodization of Antiquity or definition of the Middle Ages framed to exclude the world of Islam. It has been argued that specific "optimistic" conjunctures such as the collapse of communism and the scrapping of certain political boundaries during the 1990s helped, for a time, to make the relatively frontier-free long late Antiquity fashionable; that the strategic balance will one day shift again; and that longer periodizations are therefore destined to be a passing fashion.[100] Yet the population movements that have brought Islam to Europe have deep roots in decolonization and globalization; they are largely irreversible once grandchildren and by now even great-grandchildren are born to the original migrants, for whom Europe is their only home; and they will most likely intensify, given the pressures on Middle Eastern and African societies from climate change and water shortage, wars, popular unrest, and economic stagnation. For all these reasons, pressures for a more inclusive view of the past will not go away.

What other arguments can be offered, either more or less directly, against the First Millennium? Starting from general considerations, it may for example be objected that periodization is something we impose on history after it has happened, from a specific viewing point with unavoidable bias, and ought not to be assigned excessive importance, unavoidable though it is

99 Compare and contrast F. Millar's courageous proposal, *Rome, the Greek world, and the East* [2:3] 3.505–8, for a Judeo-Christianized ancient history syllabus concentrating on Greek and Hebrew at the expense of Latin, but still excluding Islam, not seen as part of ""our" (Western) conceptual origins."

100 Av. Cameron, "The 'long' late antiquity," in Wiseman (ed.), *Classics in progress* [2:116] 175–76, 190–91.

for purposes of coherent exposition and teaching. The historian will ideally be in a position to survey history as a continuum, breaking it down into microperiods for purposes of research, then expanding it again in order to achieve synthesis. One can only agree. But few are in practice able to achieve much of an overview, given the habit and necessity of specialization. If this situation is to be palliated, we can begin by promoting (or returning to) longer periodizations in usum scholarum, so that the ideal, at least, is inculcated at an early age. At the same time, there is no reason why complementary periodizations should not run simultaneously—in which case a major argument for the First Millennium would be that it helps clarify and contextualize late Antiquity, about whose definition it is proving so hard to reach agreement. (And it will not get easier: future Muslim participants in the debate will certainly want to know why late Antiquity is so much about Christianization, but not at all about Islamization.)

Another objection to our First Millennium is that it is not the only possible one: for example, the Romans celebrated the thousandth birthday of their city in 248 with wild animal displays in the Colosseum. Our First Millennium is a Christian formulation calculated from the birth of Jesus, an event of essentially theological significance and only to Christians; while the period culminates in the rather different religion of Islam, which plays down the significance of pre-Islamic history. To make a point of singling out the first Christian millennium may therefore seem Christianocentric or even Eurocentric to some, or just plain confused. As Arnaldo Momigliano put it in a lecture delivered almost fifty years ago,

> The modern notion of historical periods selected according to the intrinsic importance of the facts and according to the reliability of the evidence is quite clearly part of our pagan inheritance. Experience seems to show that it can somehow be reconciled with the Jewish idea of a history from the creation of the world. The reconciliation with the Christian notion of a history divided into two by Incarnation is a more difficult problem.[101]

Yet the point of the First Millennium as a *useful* historical periodization as well as one rooted in reliably attested (though less reliably interpreted) events is that by definition it embraces the formation of Christianity (not to mention rabbinic Judaism) *as well as* Islam, whose initial concept had not a little to do with the perceived shortcomings of Christianity. And the issues between Christianity and Islam, which gave such vigor and interest to their encounter, were—among much else—theological issues. Had they been purely military, political, or economic, we would not still be discussing them today. What is more, the spread of the AD dating system on which the First

101 A. Momigliano, *Essays in ancient and modern historiography* (Oxford 1977) 196–97.

Millennium is based may also have owed something to the rise of Islam. It did not catch on in the Latin world until Bede c. 731 (even more tardily among nonscholars), or in the Greek world until late Byzantine times. In both situations there was acute awareness of mounting pressure from Islam, so perhaps adopting the Christian era was a conscious—if delayed—reaction to the quick-off-the-mark formulation of the simple and uniform hijra era, which is first attested on a papyrus receipt as early as AH 22.[102] (The Church of the East, being on the front line, adopted hijra dating as early as 676.[103])

The aspect of the First Millennium which (experto credite!) attracts most criticism is, nevertheless, its suspiciously Eusebian inception with Augustus and Christ. Although nobody can deny Christianity begins and Roman imperium matures, or enters a new phase, with the millennium, the fact that the Christian historian Eusebius declares this coincidence providential is enough to make it taboo. Against this capital charge of Christianocentrism, various pleas may be entered, starting with the fact that I propose the First Millennium as a frame for not just one but several long-term cultural trends, with round-figure termini that are approximate and symbolic of course, but—apart from their Christian significance—happen also to correspond to various non-Christian processes of cultural maturation outlined in this chapter and elaborated in chapters 5 and 6. As for Eusebius, far from weaving private fantasies, he induced much of his posterity to think as he had about Rome and the Church,[104] and thus encouraged further convergence, for example in numerous bishops warmly committed to the Roman Empire's authority and prepared to act on that loyalty, assuming civic as well as ecclesiastical leadership in both East and West. Eusebius's vision, however theological in its origins, became an active force in history.

A more creative aspect of this debate is that it encourages thought about the nature of historical periodizations. These may emerge effortlessly from the phenomena (an empire or dynasty rises and falls); or they may respond, with greater or lesser appropriateness and accuracy, to a question the historian poses, as here: How do Judaism, Christianity, and Islam interact in their youth and early maturity, with each other or with more secular currents such as Greek philosophy or Roman law? Do these interactions speak to our own cultural conjuncture? I have explained how such preoccupations might lead one to find the First Millennium a rational and functional periodization, on

102 AD: V. Grumel, *La chronologie* (Paris 1958) 222–24; Declercq, *Anno Domini* [3:90]. Bede and the Saracens: R. G. Hoyland, *Seeing Islam as others saw it* (Princeton 1997) 226–27; K. S. Beckett, *Anglo-Saxon perceptions of the Islamic world* (Cambridge 2003) 18, 123–24. Hijra: A. Ghabban, "The inscription of Zuhayr," *Arabian archaeology and epigraphy* 19 (2008) 216; cf. Donner, *Narratives* [3:87] 237; and Pourshariati, *Decline and fall* [1:22] 167–71, 465, for some qualifications.

103 Pinggéra, in Wallraff (ed.), *Julius Africanus* [3:63] 281.

104 Note also Mann, *Sources of social power* [1:4] 1.306–10: "Christianity as the solution to the contradictions of empire" (insisting at 308 that Christianity spread continuously from the Crucifixion).

grounds of research convenience, not theological and providential arrière-pensée. In chapter 4 I will make some further comments about how the imperial regimes of Iran, Rome, and the Caliphate also fit into this framework. But since one way of making our analysis more convincing is by varying our vantage points, while periodizations that repose like an arch on a fixed support at each terminus offer irresistible provocation to the literal-minded ("Why Augustus/Jesus?", "Why Ibn Sīnā?"), I have also noted another approach. Starting as it were from the arch's keystone, that is to say from some pivotal event, from which one reads both backward and forward until one has sufficiently illuminated its causes and consequences, one may construct one's periodization around that focus rather than between a start and a finish.[105] The pivot here proposed is already announced in the book's title: *Before and after Muḥammad*. This could have been interpreted narrowly, the "before" being the religious and political turmoil of sixth-century Arabia, the "after" in terms of the rapid expansion of the Arab Empire in the century following Muḥammad's death. But I have chosen to take a wider view, making Muḥammad stand for a whole religious culture in dialogue with others from its inception, then maturing and in due course exercising its own gravitational pull. There is, in other words, much to be gained from using both arch and pivot together.[106] One of the most rewarding things about the resulting First Millennium periodization is its appropriateness to the study of philosophy and law as well as the monotheist religions from which its initial definition is derived.

A further objection to the First Millennium, particularly as a field of study partly designed to illuminate our contemporary clash of civilizations, is that it seems perilously teleological. Here we must acknowledge that there is both appropriate and inappropriate teleology. Viewing, for instance, Constantine primarily as the founder of Western civilization is inappropriate teleology because he also stood at the dawn of East Rome or "Byzantium," which was often in conflict with Latin Christendom; while the relationship between monotheism and monarchy he grappled with was likewise to be fundamental to the Islamic world, which was directly continuous and contiguous with East Rome, and at different times in conflict with both Eastern and Western Christendom. Nobody today could deny that the rise of Christianity and that of Islam are the fundamental events of the First Millennium, with crucial impact on our own era. The First Millennium can reasonably therefore be treated not just in its own right, but also as a prime source of (but not leading inevitably to) the present conjuncture.

105 Osterhammel, *Verwandlung* [2:94] 99.

106 Those who dislike supposedly Christianocentric periodizations might be expected to be allergic to Islamocentric ones too; but in practice this is not always the case, Islam being—apparently—less of a threat to the intelligentsia, for the time being, than Christianity.

A related issue is the study of intellectual systems over long periods, which also provokes charges of "teleology," especially if some later phase is presented as "orthodox" or "classical." That constructs popularly viewed as orthodox/classical do exist, it would be fatuous to deny. Part of the historian's job is to trace what produced such consensus and the sense of identity that derives from it. At the same time, though, one has to be careful about viewing cultural constructs at a given point in time mainly as "tendencies" on the way to a "classical crystallization" visible only to us, retrospectively. Just one example: ninth- and tenth-century Arabic philosophy has often been studied as a phase on the way to the formation of Latin scholastic philosophy and then the Renaissance. This is a particularly shameless teleology because it validates one culture only in terms of another. In the present book, Arabic philosophy is acknowledged to have had its own independent story right down to the present day. Among my objectives is to describe the formation of what came—and in different ways continues—to be regarded as a distinctively "Islamic" spectrum of ways of thinking. Therefore, in selecting my ninth- and tenth-century materials, I have an eye to what proved durable and influential. That is indeed "teleological," but it allows that there are various possible outcomes, not just one, namely Latin Europe. (Of course, "The Golden Age of Baghdad" may also turn out to be Euro-teleological, if it is used as a yardstick by which to "prove" that Muslims then spent the whole Second Millennium "declining.")

Finally, some reflections on the First Millennium in contemporary usage. So far the concept has not attracted narrative historians. Its debut may have been in 1985 in Paul Veyne's *Histoire de la vie privée* 1: *De l'Empire romain à l'an mil*; but the millennial aspect of this enterprise was so underwhelming that the English translation was titled *From pagan Rome to Byzantium*. The First Millennium mainly attracts archaeologists and historians interested in the material culture and economy of the Latin and Germanic worlds. They do not want to tie their subject down chronologically because they have so much difficulty dating their materials; they are also not usually prime suspects for promoting a Christian or Muslim interpretation of history. The proceedings of the Bradford University First Millennium Symposium, also held in 1985, provocatively proposed termini that have absolutely nothing to do with each other (wide distribution of Arretine/Samian pottery; adoption of Romanesque architecture), proclaimed the autonomy of material evidence from written sources, and accepted labels like "Roman," "German," "Saxon," or "medieval" only as necessary "myths" to ease communication with the outside world.[107] Such communication was achieved more successfully by Klaus Randsborg's *The first millennium AD in Europe and the Medi-*

107 R. Reece, "How to study the millennium," in R. F. J. Jones and others (eds), *First Millennium papers: Western Europe in the First Millennium AD* (Oxford 1988) 3–9.

terranean (1991) and Peter Heather's *Empires and barbarians* (2009), deploying the First Millennium because it embraces not only the flourishing and the fall of the Roman Empire in the West, but also the emergence of Europe, roughly as it is still configured, by about 1000. The major Silk Road exhibition at the British Library in 2004, which demonstrated with unusual clarity the interactive vitality of civilizations along the Central Asiatic trade routes, rather than just transmission of goods from one end to the other, also took the First Millennium as its frame of reference, invoking the fall of Khotan to the Turkish Karakhanids in 1006[108]—although no reference was made to the Karakhanids' high cultural level, or explanation offered why their arrival, after that of so many other invaders, should constitute such a defining break. (Perhaps it helped that they were Muslims?)

Among investigations of religion, only Peter Brown's *The rise of Western Christendom: Triumph and diversity, A.D. 200–1000* (2003[2]) gets close to exploiting the full chronological range of the First Millennium. But the focus here is on Christendom and only secondarily the world of Islam, mainly as perceived by Christians.

There are also, especially in the last decade, works that, while adopting periodizations other than the First Millennium, nonetheless call in question the idea of a major caesura c. 600–650, which is the main obstacle to the First Millennium. Peregrine Horden and Nicholas Purcell, in *The corrupting sea* (2000), argue for the great continuities of Mediterranean life such as economic diversification in the face of an unpredictable climate, irrespective of the ancient/medieval distinction.[109] In his *Origins of the European economy: Communications and commerce, A.D. 300–900* (2001), Michael McCormick rejects the notion that the seventh century has to be turned into an insuperable obstacle to research. His example is followed by Chris Wickham in his two books, *Framing the early Middle Ages: Europe and the Mediterranean 400–800* (2005), and *The inheritance of Rome: A history of Europe from 400 to 1000* (2009), albeit with reservations about the extremer forms of "continuitism."[110] The focus of all these works is European and/or Mediterranean, but they embrace the Arab-Islamic world as well.[111] They are sensitive to the material evidence. They also suggest that pressures to conform to

108 S. Whitfield (ed.), *The Silk Road* (Chicago 2004), e.g., 16, 287.

109 Their neglect of this distinction is chided by W. V. Harris, "The Mediterranean and ancient history," in id. (ed.), *Rethinking the Mediterranean* (Oxford 2005) 36.

110 E.g., Wickham, *Inheritance* [1:26] 8–9, 75, 216–17. Note the preference for starting c. 300/400, even in works that explicitly adopt the First Millennium as their frame: M. McCormick, "Movements and markets in the First Millennium," in Morrisson (ed.), *Trade and markets* [2:113] 51–98. But where noninstitutional aspects of Christianity are in play, as in the present work, this is a less attractive option.

111 On Iran see now Pourshariati, *Decline and fall* [1:22], e.g., 464.

an exclusively Latin and Greek perspective weigh less heavily on medievalists than on classicists.

The books by McCormick and Wickham, both economic historians mainly interested in early medieval Latin Europe, bear some further comment. They show admirable broad-mindedness not just in their chronological sweep, but also in taking on board the East Roman and Arab-Islamic worlds as well. Nonetheless, their perspective is quite different from that offered here. McCormick is perfectly aware that, after what he sees as the demise of the ancient Mediterranean economy in the seventh century, the eastern, southern, and western shores conquered by the Arabs continued more peaceful and prosperous than the northern shores, which remained in Christian hands.[112] Yet he is not really much concerned with this difference, in its own right, until the economic dynamism of the Abbasid economy becomes so irresistible that it begins, very slowly in the closing decades of the eighth century, to drag Latin Europe back into the light. And since, even then, his search is for the earliest signs of "the decisive advance of the European commercial economy,"[113] McCormick describes the influence of the Abbasid economy rather than the beast itself. One is constantly aware, reading his book, that a general history of the Eurasian economy from 750 to 900, free of anachronistic concern with a region not fully on stream until "several centuries"[114] later, would have to place Abbasid Iraq center stage. That admission, coming from such an accomplished historian of Europe, is an important gain; yet it remains only an *implicit* admission.

A similar viewpoint is adopted in Wickham's two books. By framing his narrative of the period up to 1000 not (it is true) in order to explain teleologically the origins of "Europe," but still from a firmly Latin and Roman perspective,[115] Wickham privileges a part of the world which was, as he himself admits,[116] distinctly peripheral to the great centers of power, wealth, and creativity: Constantinople, Cairo, Baghdad. There is an arbitrariness here, whose dependence on a modern European sense of identity we need to recognize more explicitly. (Wickham berates teleological approaches in others.) By contrast, the historian who passes by Baghdad rather than Aachen en route to the year 1000 and then into the Second Millennium follows the organic, mainstream development of the most vigorous elements in the late antique synthesis, those Greco-Roman, Sasanian, Syriac, and then Muslim currents that I have chosen as the focus of my account, and not arbitrarily,

112 McCormick, *Origins* [2:84] 115–19, 149, 782–84.
113 McCormick, *Origins* [2:84] 794.
114 McCormick, *Origins* [2:84] 793.
115 Cf. especially Wickham, *Inheritance* [1:26] 282, 333.
116 Wickham, *Inheritance* [1:26] 4, 281–82, 425.

but because these sent out the creative impulses which were dominant at the beginning of the Second Millennium, and then went on, in association with the Latin world but with a much greater time lag there, to mold what we call Modernity.

McCormick's and Wickham's choices on the one hand, and mine on the other, all in a sense represent teleological readings of the First Millennium. How would I describe the difference between mine and theirs? To put it crudely, my choice places the telos at the very end of the First Millennium itself, building to an account of the maturation of Islam presented as an essentialized construct for purposes of exposition, but recognizing too its growing diversity—the Sunni-Shiite schism, the political fragmentation of the caliphate, the role of philosophy and Sufi mysticism—as well as its continuing evolution after 1000. Those who wish to go on and use this picture in order to achieve a deeper understanding of our present situation and its potentialities are encouraged to do so. Indeed, it was from *current* stresses on Europe's sense of identity that I began this investigation, at the start of chapter 1. But I do not invoke the direct genetic link implied by McCormick's talk of origins, or by Wickham's choice to privilege a rather obscure region of the First Millennium world—Latin Europe—over others more powerful and creative, inevitably in part (whatever the disclaimers) because of its preeminence at a much later date. The goal of the Eurocentric historian ("Modernity") is remote from, yet conceived of as standing in a relationship of dependence toward, the First Millennium. To depict so chronologically extended a relationship convincingly is a very difficult enterprise in itself; and it is also the case that other, quite different traditions believe they too have a stake in the same past. The views of history on offer today in the schools and universities of, for example, the Sunni Muslim world, or in those of Iran or for that matter the United States, differ very largely—in emphasis if not necessarily in broad periodization[117]—from what is purveyed in Europe. Yet all find that much of what is important to them matured during the First Millennium—which must therefore be depicted in such a way as to explain all the roads that lead out of it.

If that is not an unrealistic goal, then we may look forward, sooner or later, to a new Eusebian moment when Islam this time, instead of the Church, will finally be woven into the fabric of world history.[118] Only the viewpoint

117 Cf. Blankinship, *American journal of Islamic social sciences* 8 (1991) [1:21] 438–39, on Muslim curricula.

118 Marshall Hodgson's *The venture of Islam* [1:1], however flawed, was a major step in this direction (complete with numerous chronological tables aligning events in the Islamic world and other regions). Cf., on a much less ambitious scale, T. Ansary, *Destiny disrupted: A history of the world through Islamic eyes* (New York 2009). The author, an American raised in Afghanistan, exemplifies traditional Islamic historiographical values in his neglect of history before the hijra, his emphasis on the determining

will not be Muslim, as Eusebius's was Christian. Nor will it be Eurocentric. Rather it will reflect a global world in which Islam, after long eclipse, once more moves closer to the heart of things.

---

significance of the careers of Muḥammad and the first caliphs, and his Islamocentric take on everything else. Nonetheless, in his account of the modern period he acknowledges the existence of a "Western narrative" increasingly impinging on the "Muslim narrative" (318, 351). And his goal is "a single shared history" (357). Blankinship, *American journal of Islamic social sciences* 8 (1991) [1:21] 442–51, proposes to divide world history into before and after Muḥammad. Whereas the deployment of this concept in the title of the present book points to the unity of the First Millennium, Blankinship's usage of the c. 600 caesura may reinforce the isolation of Islam from the earlier, cumulative development of monotheism.

4

SPACE

AN EASTWARD SHIFT

The distinction of North and South is real and intelligible; and our pursuit is terminated on either side by the poles of the Earth. But the difference of East and West is arbitrary, and shifts round the globe.

—E. Gibbon (ed. D. Womersley), *The history of the decline and fall of the Roman Empire* (1994) 3.1095 (marginal note added to one of Gibbon's own copies in 1790/91)

DISCOVERING THE MEDITERRANEAN

If we are to weave Islam into the fabric of our history, we must go beyond its scripture's dialogue with rabbinic Judaism and Syriac Christianity, or the caliphate's reminiscences of imperial style in Iran and East Rome. Islam's development of late antique artistic forms offers a strong hint in this direction. If Islam eventually touched everything, it is likely that everything touched Islam. To be serious about contextualizing its early history, we must pay attention to its physical, that is, geographical, as well as its mental and aesthetic environment. The geography is not just a stage for historical events to be played out on, it is a series of opportunities and contexts that mold events. But it takes effort to be as sensitive to the position of Arabia, and the various influences that played upon it, as we are—instinctively—to the Mediterranean paradigm.

Reaching his Italian tour in his memoirs, Gibbon affected indifference to once more recounting "scenes which have been viewed by thousands, and described by hundreds of our modern travelers."[1] "Discovering" the Mediterranean was already a commonplace, whatever its impact on individuals, not least Gibbon himself once he saw Rome. Coming down from Mont Cenis

1 Murray (ed.), *Autobiographies of Edward Gibbon* [1:23] 265–66.

into the plain of Piedmont, "not on the back of an Elephant," Gibbon was characteristically eager to ironize (not analyze) his own experience with a classical allusion; but the reference also serves to remind us in what a long and dominant tradition he stood, of men descending on Italy from the North. Nevertheless, the earliest surviving accounts in Eurasian literature of coming to and beholding the Mediterranean were written, not by Northerners, but by men from the East, from Mesopotamia.

As early as c. 2300 BCE, more than two millennia before Hannibal, we find King Sargon of Akkad conquering Lagash and washing his weapons in the Persian Gulf (where his kingdom came in contact with a trading system that already reached as far as India[2]). He also subdued the Upper Land as far as the Mediterranean shore, the Cedar Forest, and the Silver Mountains.[3] We may compare the Old Babylonian Akkadian *Epic of Gilgamesh*, which seems to have crystallized in the eighteenth century but was based on Sumerian poems of the third millennium. The epic has its hero and his friend Enkidu make their way from Gilgamesh's kingdom of Uruk in Southern Babylonia all the way to the Cedar Forest (Mount Lebanon) in order to cut down a giant tree for the door of the temple of Enlil at Nippur.[4] This may reflect Sargon's exploits and claims:[5] apparently Gilgamesh was a literary construct not a historical personality. We reach firmer ground about the year 1800 with King Iahdun-Lim of Mari on the Euphrates, who marched his army to the Mediterranean coast, "and made a great offering (befitting) his kingship to the sea; his troops bathed themselves in the sea." Then he ascended "the great mountains," cut down cedar, cypress, and other trees, and erected a monument to attest his might. He loudly proclaimed himself the first king of Mari to reach the sea, the mountains, and their forests.[6]

Almost a millennium later, when the coast dwellers of Phoenicia had already begun to explore even the furthest occidental reaches of the Mediterranean (see below), we find the great inland kings of Assyria, Ashurnasirpal II (883–59) and his son Shalmaneser III (858–24), following closely in Iahdun-Lim's footsteps toward the western horizon, and erecting vast, repetitive inscriptions to boast about it. In the sea Ashurnasirpal washed his weap-

2 M. R. Bhacker, "The cultural unity of the Gulf and the Indian Ocean," in L. G. Potter (ed.), *The Persian Gulf in history* (New York 2009) 167.

3 D. Frayne, *The royal inscriptions of Mesopotamia: Early periods* 2. *Sargonic and Gutian periods (2334–2113 BC)* (Toronto 1993) 11, 14, 17, 28–29, 30. For an archaeological perspective on cedar and silver supplies in early Syria, Mesopotamia, and Egypt, see L. Marfoe, "Cedar forest to silver mountain: Social change and the development of long-distance trade in early Near Eastern societies," in M. Rowlands and others (eds), *Centre and periphery in the ancient world* (Cambridge 1987) 25–35.

4 *Epic of Gilgamesh* [ed. and tr. A. R. George, *The Babylonian Gilgamesh Epic* (Oxford 2003)], tablets 2–5, 7.

5 As suggested by George, *Babylonian Gilgamesh Epic* [4:4] 20.

6 D. Frayne, *The royal inscriptions of Mesopotamia: Early periods* 4. *Old Babylonian period (2003–1595 BC)* (Toronto 1990) 604–8.

ons, soaked in the blood of countless foes, and sacrificed to his gods. He enjoyed subduing wild animals as well as felling trees in the forests of Amanus. He formulaically defines his kingdom as stretching "from the opposite bank of the Tigris to Mount Lebanon and the Great Sea," so the prominence of the Mediterranean in his imagination and propaganda is self-explanatory.[7] Shalmaneser kept his father's tireless momentum going, and his propaganda too, with frequent allusions to putting up images of himself by the seaside. After conquering various Syrian kings, washing his weapons, sacrificing and ascending Amanus, he even "boarded boats (and) went out upon the sea."[8] Jumping on almost another millennium and a half, we observe how another Oriental monarch, the Sasanid Khosrow I, after capturing Antioch in 540, bathed alone in the Mediterranean at Seleuceia and—in the heart of Justinian's most Christian empire!—sacrificed to the gods, especially the Sun, in other words Mithra.[9] Again, when the Seljuk Sultan Malik-Shāh (1072–92) formally took possession of Antioch in 1086, he rode his horse to the sea to drink, and rendered thanks to Allāh for granting him a kingdom from the Eastern Sea to the Western.[10]

The ritual repetition of actions such as these on the same stretch of Eastern Mediterranean coastline during three-and-a-half millennia, starting with Sargon, suggests the presence of some quite simple motives capable of serving as common denominators over this immense stretch of time and in such different cultural and political contexts. Practical considerations like resource extraction and control of coastal trade played their part. What is more, the Mediterranean coast below Lebanon and Amanus, especially by Seleuceia, had a dual significance. It was where the successful Oriental invader of Syria ended up willy-nilly once he secured the glittering prize of Antioch. İskenderun (Alexandretta) in particular enjoys rare, diachronic strategic and economic sensitivity as the passageway from the Mediterranean to Syria, Mesopotamia, and the Persian Gulf, a role comparable to that of

7 A. K. Grayson, *The royal inscriptions of Mesopotamia: Assyrian periods* 2. *Assyrian rulers of the early first millennium BC* 1 *(1114–859 BC)* (Toronto 1991) 218–19, 226, 298, etc.

8 A. K. Grayson, *The royal inscriptions of Mesopotamia: Assyrian periods* 3. *Assyrian rulers of the early first millennium BC* 2 *(858–745 BC)* (Toronto 1996) 17, 25, 34, 45, 51, 64, 74, 103. Exhaustive analysis in S. Yamada, *The construction of the Assyrian Empire* (Leiden 2000). Cf. R. Da Riva, "Desde la muralla de Media a los cedros del Líbano," *Geographia antiqua* 18 (2009) 217–26, on Nebuchadnezzar II of Babylon.

9 Procopius, *Wars* [ed. J. Haury; revised reprint ed. G. Wirth (Leipzig 1962–63); tr. H. B. Dewing (London 1914–28)] 2.11.1. On Mithra as the Sun, and the specifically Sasanian background, see H.-P. Schmidt, "Mithra I," *E.Ir.*, www.iranicaonline.org; Pourshariati, *Decline and fall* [1:22], Index s.v. "Mithra, as the sun."

10 C. Cahen, *Turcobyzantina et Oriens Christianus* (London 1974) I.48–49 and n. 1; cf. Gibbon 57:3.542. The reference to an "Eastern Sea" is no doubt rhetorical: cf., e.g., S. S. Blair, *The monumental inscriptions from early Islamic Iran and Transoxiana* (Leiden 1992) 158–59, for Malik-Shāh, "[King of the] East and the West," in an inscription from Ani.

Alexandria on the way to Arabia and India, Byzantium/Constantinople at the entrance to the Black Sea, Venice as gateway to Central Europe, or Marseille as point of access to Western Europe. It was not out of lack of something else to do that Kemal Atatürk spent his last illness forcing France to cede the sancak of Hatay (İskenderun, Antakya) to Turkey (1939).[11] But beyond these mundane considerations, Seleuceia had been founded after a divine sign given when Seleucus Nicator (d. 281 BCE) sacrificed to Zeus Kasios on Jabal Aqra—Mount Cassius as the Greeks and Romans called it—on the coast just south of the city. Later rulers who climbed this holy mountain and honored its patron included three Roman emperors—Trajan, Hadrian, and Julian.[12] Already in Hittite texts Cassius is closely associated with both divine supremacy and human kingship.[13]

In the present context, though, it is sufficient to retain one point, namely that according to the written record the Mediterranean was first discovered from the East. It provided, from the perspective of successive Oriental monarchies, no more than a watery and variously suggestive, but alien, western horizon for the world of the Fertile Crescent, at whose heart lay vast plains and deserts ringed about by mountains. The Mediterranean paradigm's hold over the European mind is still so strong that it is essential to relativize it in this way, before we tackle it directly.[14] Malik-Shāh reminds us that the Oriental perspective is that of the Islamic world too.

As it happens, reconceiving the Mediterranean as not merely a westerly horizon, but a whole world in its own right, was likewise the achievement of men from the Fertile Crescent, at least its western coastlands. It was one thing to survey the sea from a mountain eminence, to bathe in it or even sail along the shore; another to cross it and take its full measure. The Mediterranean first came into focus as an autonomous space in its full East-West extent[15] thanks to the voyages of Phoenician merchants and their establishment, from the ninth century BCE onward, of trading posts in Cyprus, Crete, North Africa, Italy, Sicily, Malta, Sardinia and Spain (already in the ninth century). They even ventured out into the Atlantic. And as we have seen, about the beginning of the first millennium BCE we find the name "Great Sea" applied to the Mediterranean—whether all of it is not clear—in

11 A. Mango, *Atatürk* (London 1999) 506–9.

12 R. Lane Fox, *Travelling heroes* (London 2008) 256–64.

13 Lane Fox, *Travelling heroes* [4:12] 273–75, 281. Emphasizing the ritual aspect of the texts discussed in the previous pages, see R. Rollinger, "From Sargon of Agade and the Assyrian kings to Khusrau I and beyond," in G. B. Lanfranchi and others (eds), *Leggo!* (Wiesbaden 2012) 725–43.

14 For other criticisms of "Mediterraneanism," see S. Stroumsa, *Maimonides in his world: Portrait of a Mediterranean thinker* (Princeton 2009) 3–5; S. Schwartz, *Were the Jews a Mediterranean society?* (Princeton 2010) 21–25.

15 D. Abulafia, *The Great Sea* (London 2011) 63–99; cf. M. Koch, "Von Tarschisch bis nach Indien," *Palaeohispanica* 10 (2010) 567–78.

several Semitic languages.[16] Greek colonists, led by the Euboeans of Eretria and Chalcis, and the Corinthians, followed the Phoenicians from about the year 800. Soon, the coastal lands round the Black Sea were also being settled by Greeks. But with the sole exception of this region directly accessible by sea, the colonization movement stuck to the Mediterranean; and the Mediterranean world remained one of shore dwellers (often in cities) and seamen, along with peasant populations in the fairly restricted plains that abutted on or were directly accessible from the sea. The mountains were an almost constant horizon, but a quite different world. Widely separate coastal regions now had far more in common, in terms of way of life, than any coastal region had with its own mountain hinterland.

This sense of "our" Mediterranean, "mare nostrum," is conveyed in the famous remark Plato puts in the mouth of Socrates, to the effect that the earth

> is vast in size, and we live around the sea in a small portion of it, from Phasis [the river that flows into the south-eastern corner of the Black Sea] as far as the Pillars of Hercules, like ants or frogs around a pond. And there are many other peoples living elsewhere, in many similar regions.[17]

Note Plato's awareness—anticipated by, among others, Hecataeus c. 500 BCE[18]—that there is much more to the world than just the Mediterranean. Given the Greeks' and Romans' contribution to the concept of Europe, and Rome's creation of an empire which embraced—for the only time in history—the whole Mediterranean, and remained thoroughly Italocentric until the third century, it is hardly surprising that Europe the geographical region should long have retained the Mediterranean alone as its southern base. West of the Mediterranean there was anyway only the Atlantic, perceived as a desert at the world's end.[19] Eastward, though, it was harder to draw a line that was not artificial. In fact it was to the East that most of Plato's "other peoples" dwelt.

DISCOVERING THE EAST

The Jewish and Christian holy places, in the low hills behind the Palestinian coastal plain, fit easily into the conventional map of the Mediterranean. Including the Ḥijāz and the holy places of Islam enlarges the frame; but while

16 "Great Sea": J. Elayi, "Terminologie de la Mer Méditerranée dans les *annales* assyriennes," *Oriens antiquus* 23 (1984) 75–92; Harris, in id. (ed.), *Rethinking the Mediterranean* [3:109] 15; and see above, p. 94.

17 Plato [ed. J. Burnet (Oxford 1900–1907); vol. 1^2, ed. E. A. Duke and others, 1995; tr. J. M. Cooper (ed.) (Indianapolis 1997)], *Phaedo* 109ab.

18 J. B. Harley and D. Woodward, "The foundations of theoretical cartography in archaic and classical Greece," in J. B. Harley and D. Woodward (eds), *The history of cartography* (Chicago 1987–) 1.134–35.

19 *Expositio totius mundi et gentium* [ed. and tr. (French) J. Rougé (Paris 1966)] 59.

Greeks and Romans mostly ignored the Arabs, the geographer sees Palestine and the Ḥijāz as related to the same vast Rift Valley geology, communicating easily both by land and via the Red Sea. Adding the origins of Judaism, Christianity, and Islam to the Mediterranean framework is no challenge, certainly not to the cartographer. The historian too can relate them easily to what was already familiar.

The Mediterranean paradigm begins to reveal its inadequacies, though, once we look at the dissemination of these religions, and the regions where they matured as cultural forms. Babylonian exile in the early sixth century BCE had established a major non-Palestinian focus for Jewish culture in Mesopotamia/Iraq, which endured two and a half millennia. So the Jews became entangled with the Iranian world, which also produced its own religions: Mazdaism, never much at home anywhere except the Iranian heartlands, or wherever in Iraq Iranians had settled; and Manicheism, which from third-century Iraq spread far to the East as well as the West.

As for Christianity, its early missions took it to the Greek cities of Syria, Asia Minor, and Greece itself, much the same places in which Greek philosophy and Roman law thrived. Also to Rome, which by this time could not but be a major objective for any new idea. West of Rome, it would be hard to rank Latin North Africa, or Spain, or Gaul, among the most creative regions of pre-Constantinian Christianity, even allowing for occasional charismatic or learned figures such as Irenaeus of Lyons (d. 200; actually a Greek-speaker from Smyrna), or Tertullian of Carthage (d. c. 225). Latin Christianity before Augustine of Hippo had little to offer the Greeks; and by Augustine's death in 430 the two worlds were drifting slowly apart. But in the East there was Syriac Christianity to be taken into account, already from the second century. Beyond the Hellenized regions of Syria, but also interwoven with them, strands of Syriac-speaking Christianity focused especially on Edessa in Mesopotamia, near to Rome's eastern frontier. Although to begin with Syriac Christianity was very much a translation culture from the Greek, it developed its own style and terms of reference, and as early as Ephrem of Nisibis (d. 373) produced a liturgical poet so distinctive he was translated into Greek, Latin, and various Oriental languages, and attracted a hive of imitators. The interest Syriac monastic milieus developed in Aristotle, from the mid-sixth century onward, turned out—as we shall see in chapter 5—to be a major channel by which Greek thought reached and fertilized the Muslim world. (The tenth-century Muslim writers who trace the exile of Greek learning from Alexandria round the Fertile Crescent to Baghdad oddly echo the sixth-century story according to which the philosophers expelled from Athens took refuge at Ctesiphon.[20])

Already by Constantine's day there were communities of Syriac Christians in Iran as well. Occasional Sasanian persecution reinforced their iden-

20 See above p. 11 n. 34, and below p.150.

tity; so did Rome's growing doctrinal intolerance, especially the expulsion of the so-called School of the Persians from Edessa c. 489. The members of this School followed the one-time Patriarch of Constantinople Nestorius (d. 451) and his (alleged) doctrine that the incarnate Christ existed "in" two separate natures, divine and human, so that God might not be said to have died on the cross, or Mary to be "Mother of God."[21] What eventually became the East Roman Church's official view was enunciated at the Council of Chalcedon in 451: Christ as perfect God inseparably united in one person to perfect man, like us in everything except our sin. With this "dyophysite" (two-nature) line the arch-heretic Nestorius declared himself reasonably content, to the delight of Chalcedon's miaphysite or henophysite (as contemporary scholarship calls them) opponents. Miaphysites preached one incarnate nature of the Word, "out of two natures" but not "in two natures," aspiring to underline the real unity of Christ's person but in so doing obscuring, so their critics felt, Christ's full humanity. In Iran, both "Nestorian"[22] or Church of the East Christians, and miaphysite communities, flourished mightily. By 635 a Church of the East mission had reached the court of the emperor of China,[23] and this branch of Christianity was to remain active in China until the mid-ninth century. It was reintroduced by the Mongols for a time in the thirteenth and fourteenth centuries. In Central Asia it enjoyed a more continuous history, but succumbed to Islam in the fourteenth century.[24]

Despite its eastward extent and creativity, the Syriac world is treated as an appendix to mainstream histories of Christianity, and the story as conventionally told (following Eusebius's bad example) is about the Greek and Latin traditions of the West.[25] In general—by secular as well as ecclesiastical historians, but with recent exceptions noted at the end of the previous chapter—it is only with the rise of Islam that the Mediterranean paradigm is finally felt to buckle and break; or rather, at this point ancient historians switch off so as

21 God also had to endure "wives" and even "mothers-in-law" (those whose daughters became nuns): Jerome, *letters* [ed. and tr. (French) J. Labourt (Paris 1949–63)] 22.16, 20. For a brief, lucid explanation of the issues at stake at Chalcedon, see H. Chadwick, "Philoponus the Christian theologian," in R. Sorabji (ed.), *Philoponus and the rejection of Aristotelian science* (London 2010²) 86–87.

22 On the misnomer, see al-Masʿūdī, *Meadows of gold* (*Murūj al-dhahab*) [ed. and tr. (French) C. Barbier de Meynard and J.-B. Pavet de Courteille (Paris 1861–77); revised C. Pellat (Beirut 1966–79, text; 1962–, translation)] 749.

23 P. Pelliot (ed. A. Forte), *L'inscription nestorienne de Si-ngan-fou* (Kyoto 1996).

24 H.-J. Klimkeit, *Die Seidenstrasse* (Cologne 1990²) 83–87; S. N. C. Lieu, *Manichaeism in the later Roman Empire and medieval China* (Tübingen 1992²) 232–33, 261; L. Tang, *A study of the history of Nestorian Christianity in China and its literature in Chinese* (Frankfurt 2004²). On the Church of the East generally, see C. Baumer, *The Church of the East* (London 2006); J. Walker, "From Nisibis to Xi'an: The Church of the East in late antique Eurasia," in Johnson (ed.), *Late Antiquity* [1:12] 994–1052.

25 A. Y. Reed, "Beyond the Land of Nod: Syriac images of Asia and the historiography of "the West,"" *History of religions* 49 (2009) 48–87.

not to have to venture beyond the Mediterranean paradigm.[26] It was not that some previous unity was now violently ruptured with disastrous results, as Pirenne held.[27] East-West communications and trade in the Mediterranean had already been battered by the Vandal fleet installed in North Africa and the Slav invasions of the Balkans. And then to a substantial degree the Caliphate actually resuscitated the single Mediterranean by engrossing not only the Levant but the whole African coast and the Iberian too, while persistently harassing and partly annexing the still Christian northern coast (Crete, Sicily; and note the mid-ninth-century Emirate of Bari). The Latin and Slavic worlds were significant to the Muslim world as a source of slaves, while trade networks based in the lands of Islam—Cairo, most notably—were active throughout the entire Mediterranean.[28] It was just that the Mediterranean could not be the epicenter of a Caliphate whose eastern frontiers lay in Sogdia and Afghanistan and on the Indus.[29] The new world's emergent power centers, Aachen as well as Baghdad, lay far from the inland sea, its peripheralization sealed by the Umayyads' destruction of the Visigothic kingdom in the Iberian Peninsula in 711, and Charlemagne's elimination of the powerful Lombard kingdom in Italy in 774.

The Qur'ān too, by repeatedly calling upon earlier prophetic traditions, provokes us to reread Judaism and Christianity and appreciate non-Mediterranean strands of their story that were intimately relevant to the seventh-century Ḥijāz—for example the rabbinic Judaism of Mesopotamia as well as Palestine,[30] or Syriac Christianity. Islam's maturation, incomplete but well under way by c. 1000, was brought about by a constellation of theologians, legal scholars, philosophers, and indeed artists and architects, that shone especially brightly in Iraq—above all Baghdad—and Iran, however great the contribution made by Mediterranean lands such as Egypt or Spain.

26 Or they rebaptize Iraq and Iran as the Mediterranean, e.g., Netz, *Transformation of mathematics* [3:25], much of which concerns mathematicians active in those regions. Cf. S. Stroumsa, *Maimonides* [4:14], on a thinker steeped in the Babylonian as well as the Palestinian Talmud, and in the Khurasanian Ibn Sīnā.

27 Cf. above, pp. 38–39.

28 S. D. Goitein, *A Mediterranean society* (Berkeley 1967–93) 1.59–70; Abulafia, *Great Sea* [4:15] 246–70.

29 Note Carl Becker's debate with Ernst Troeltsch about whether Islam belongs to Asia or Europe: Becker, *Islamstudien* [2:74] 1.24–32.

30 See, e.g., the contributions by D. Hartwig and R. Leicht to Hartwig and others (eds), *"Im vollen Licht der Geschichte"* [1:6], 191–221; also T. Power, *The Red Sea from Byzantium to the Caliphate AD 500–1000* (Cairo 2012) 27–28. Traditional accounts saw the Jews of Ḥimyar as descendants of refugees from the destruction of Jerusalem by Titus: *Martyrdom of Arethas*, Ethiopic version [ed. and tr. (Italian) A. Bausi and A. Gori, *Tradizioni orientali del "Martirio di Areta"* (Florence 2006)] p. 121; S. Krauss, "Talmudische Nachrichten über Arabien," *Zeitschrift der Deutschen Morgenländischen Gesellschaft* 70 (1916) 330–31. Archaeology offers some support to links with Palestine: Gajda, *Royaume de Ḥimyar* [3:76] 245–47. Palestinian origins are also favored by C. Robin, "Quel judaïsme en Arabie?" (forthcoming), §K. 4 ad fin.

To resume: Given, first, that our concern is chiefly with Judaism, Christianity and Islam, not just in their origins but in their spread and maturation, with the geographical emphases just noted; and second that our interest in ancient Greek thought is focused on its latest phases in Alexandria and then in Syriac and Arabic translation; it follows that the geographical space we are concerned with is not primarily the Greco-Romanists' and Europeanists' Mediterranean.[31] Nor is it Fernand Braudel's "Greater Mediterranean," which still focuses on the inland sea. Rather it is the region that extends from the easternmost reaches of the Iranian world to the Mediterranean in the West—a Mediterranean sometimes single and safe as under Rome at its zenith; sometimes weighted toward the East as in the fifth and sixth centuries when the West was disrupted and divided; and then eventually under substantial but not exclusive Muslim sway from the Levant to Andalus. This vast expanse is almost identical (more generous west of Epirus) to Alexander the Great's empire. More generally, it is the map familiar from histories of the ancient Near East. In proposing this eastward shift of emphasis, I take no side in the debate about whether the Mediterranean world has some intrinsic unity beyond having once been all controlled by Rome. I simply draw attention to the fact that the current inquiry, principally about the history of Greek and Arabic culture and ideas, favors a geographical framework whose western part is the Mediterranean variously weighted as the First Millennium proceeds, and whose center is Syria-Mesopotamia, while its eastern edge is the Hindū Kush mountains of Afghanistan. (For pre-Islamic Arabic poets, "Turk wa-Kābul" was the equivalent of "Ultima Thule."[32])

Neither the Latin end of the Mediterranean, nor Central Asia and China, is *by definition* excluded from this scheme. An Augustan official, L. Sestius Quirinalis, might erect altars to his master on Cape Finisterre in the Atlantic to mirror those of Alexander on the Central Asian Jaxartes and the Indian Hyphasis[33] and express a Roman dream of world empire over "our part of the earth" ("pars nostra terrarum").[34] The mental horizon of an Edessene intellectual c. 200 or of an Armenian c. 630 might stretch from China to Britain

31 And note how, rereading the myth of Dionysus in fifth-century Egypt, one might be led to recenter it on the Near East: F. Hadjittofi, "Nonnus' unclassical epic: Imaginary geography in the Dionysiaca," in C. Kelly and others (eds), *Unclassical traditions* (Cambridge 2010–11) 2.29–42.

32 C. E. Bosworth, "Kābul," *EIs*^{2} 4.356.

33 A. Grüner, "Die Altäre des L. Sestius Quirinalis bei Kap Finisterre," *Madrider Mitteilungen* 46 (2005) 247–66; and cf. Orosius, *Histories* [3:60] 6.21.19–20, on Indian and Scythian ambassadors visiting Augustus at Tarragona and hailing him as another Alexander, who had received a Spanish embassy at Babylon. It was a natural thought that once the Romans reached the ocean in the West, they would turn against the East: Sallust [ed. L. D. Reynolds (Oxford 1991); tr. J. C. Rolfe (London 1921)], *Histories* 4 fr. 69 (Letter of Mithridates) 17.

34 Pliny, *Natural history* [ed. C. Mayhoff (Leipzig 1899–1906); tr. H. Rackham and others (Cambridge, Mass. 1938–63)] 2.112.242.

or even Thule.[35] The Iberian Peninsula played an early and distinctive role in the story of the Caliphate, whose conquest of it actually realized Quirinalis's dream. But just as the Mediterranean paradigm takes Greece and Rome as its points of reference, so our story chiefly unfolds along the coasts and deep into the hinterlands of the Levant, in Mesopotamia and Arabia, and in Iran. If historians of Europe find this hard to swallow, they had better reflect on the merely ride-on part played in most accounts of this period by the steppe peoples of Central Asia such as the Huns, Hephthalites, Avars, and Turks.[36] Yet these held the fate of Iran, and often of Rome too, in their hands. The Turks bordered simultaneously on East Rome, Iran, and China. No Latin power ever even dreamed of such a role. My choice here is to deal with the central lands just now delineated and justified, and to touch on the Latin world and Central Asia only when required by this already wide perspective. The more one adopts the Eurasian perspective in its widest sense, from Japan or at least China to Britain, and makes Rome's eastern peripheries the center of one's world, the less surprising the framework I here propose will seem.[37]

EMPIRES AND COMMONWEALTHS

Because the emphasis this book gives to intellectual and religious traditions is historically motivated, some historical context has to be provided for them. However briefly, we need to acknowledge the political frameworks in which they became implicated or indeed to which—in the case of Christianity and especially Islam—they directly gave rise. During the period from Christ up to about 1000 the three fundamentally important states are Iran, formerly Achaemenid, then Arsacid, and finally Sasanian; the Roman Empire; and the Caliphate. Iran and Rome between them just managed to embrace an East-West territory comparable to the unified Caliphate in its greatest extension under the Umayyads, from Afghanistan to the Atlantic, or Farghānā to Andalus as they themselves put it.[38] (The Umayyads had Arabia too, but nothing permanent on the Mediterranean's northern shore.) When Iran and Rome interacted, they did so in Mesopotamia, Syria, and (somewhat less) Arabia. This is the same region we have identified as of prime importance to the three monotheisms, in their origins but also in their dissemination.

35 Philippus (Bardaisan), *The book of the laws of countries* [ed. and tr. (Italian) I. Ramelli, *Bardesane di Edessa: Contro il fato* (Rome 2009)] 174–206; Ananias of Shirak, *Geography* [tr. R. H. Hewsen, *The Geography of Ananias of Širak* (Wiesbaden 1992)] 2.4–5.

36 C. I. Beckwith, *Empires of the Silk Road: A history of Central Eurasia from the Bronze Age to the present* (Princeton 2009).

37 Sasanians would have been a lot less surprised than Romans, since the North Mesopotamian frontier was so close to their (winter) capital at Ctesiphon.

38 H. Kennedy (ed.), *An historical atlas of Islam* (Leiden 2002[2]) maps 6 and 9.

Not of course that we can understand Rome by looking at her eastern provinces alone; but these were nevertheless of great strategic, economic, and cultural importance, ever more so after the foundation of Constantinople and the permanent division of the empire into western and eastern halves from 395, not to mention the invigoration of Iran by the ambitious new Sasanid dynasty from 224. This period seems to have witnessed a distinct southward and eastward shift of Rome's center of economic gravity.[39] That will in turn have intensified her relationship with Iran, and Iran's appetite for her wealth. This was manifest especially during the fifth century in often extravagant Sasanian demands for financial assistance in defending their northern frontier, in particular the fortified passes through the Caucasus thanks to which the settled, civilized lands of the South were protected against the barbarians of the North.[40] Constantinople equivocated when she could; but her continued albeit episodic involvement in the western Mediterranean as well, especially in conflict with the Vandals, did not always leave her a free hand in the East.

Traditional scholarly neglect of the Sasanians is now being overcome;[41] but it is still hard to estimate how realistic was their propaganda about making Rome their vassal. Could the Sasanians really have forced her to "cease to be a Mediterranean power, and turn into a tribute-paying state in an empire whose centre of gravity would be the Fertile Crescent"?[42] (Mesopotamia was already the economic powerhouse and administrative hub of the Sasanid state.) Perhaps, in the first flush of Sasanid self-assertion, Shapur I (241–72) dreamed of this; after all, in his official propaganda he was able to claim victory over Gordian III and depict Philip the Arab as a suppliant, and Valerian as a prisoner of war.[43] What is certain, though, is that the Syro-Mesopotamian theater was of immense concern to fifth- and sixth-century Roman strategists; they were constantly obliged to consider the aspirations of their eastern neighbor; they were never, after 395, in a position to offer the Western Empire consistent and effective aid, so that it disappeared in 476; and in that sense there was no longer a Roman Empire that saw itself as pan-Mediterranean. And while what is best henceforth called the *Eastern* Roman Empire saw, in the fifth century, a rare combination of economic prosperity with peace on

39 B. Ward-Perkins, "Specialized production and exchange," in *CAH* 14.346–91.

40 Al-Masʿūdī, *Meadows of gold* [4:22] 504; Z. Rubin, "The Mediterranean and the dilemma of the Roman Empire in late Antiquity," *Mediterranean historical review* 1 (1986) 38–46.

41 M. G. Morony, "Should Sasanian Iran be included in late Antiquity?," *e-Sasanika* 6 (2008) 1–8; Pourshariati, *Decline and fall* [1:22] 453–54.

42 Rubin, *Mediterranean historical review* 1 (1986) [4:40] 46; cf. Sebeos (attributed), *Armenian history* [1:30] 122–23, with J. Howard-Johnston's commentary in Thomson's translation, 211–12; P. Sarris, *Empires of faith* (Oxford 2011) 249: "The shah's decision to reject even the most self-abasing of Roman overtures signalled his absolute determination to destroy the Roman state once and for all."

43 Canepa, *Two eyes of the earth* [2:70] 58–75.

the Sasanian front, still it was forced to duel diplomatically with Iran and pay—or, at its own risk, not pay—subsidies. At the dawn of the sixth century this situation turned to war again, an imbroglio from which Justinian's western reconquests in North Africa and Italy could not long distract him. Constantinople's insistence on adherence to the Council of Chalcedon's two-nature Christology was, it is true, closely linked to a desire for theological and ecclesiological harmony with Rome and its bishop; while the Emperors Maurice (582–602) and Heraclius (610–41) both believed strongly in Rome's Mediterranean destiny, and Constans II (641–69) went so far, in the 660s, as to move his capital to Syracuse in Sicily. But the Constantinopolitan elite's resistance was intense and successful, culminating in the emperor's assassination; while the fall of the whole of North Africa to the Arabs was now imminent.[44] The eastern empire was never in serious danger, at least after Justinian, of readopting the old Mediterranean paradigm.

Through the clash of Iran with Rome in the "Last Great War of Antiquity" from 603 to 628, the two empires finally became so debilitated that the Arabs, with astonishing ease, took over the whole of Iran and all Rome's provinces south of the Taurus Mountains between 634 and 651 (the death of the last Sasanid monarch, Yazdegerd III, though at this point Iran was still only patchily subdued). By 710–11, with the fall of the Visigothic monarchy in Spain and the first appearance of the Arabs at Samarqand, the Caliphate controlled—with wildly fluctuating thoroughness—everything from (as already noted) Sogdia to the Atlantic. Until 750 it was ruled from Damascus, near the Mediterranean periphery; but the Abbasids moved the capital eastward to Baghdad in Iraq. If by c. 1000 alternative power centers had emerged in Iran (Buyids and Samanids) and Egypt (Fatimids), this only intensified the overall eastward and southward shift of power since the beginning of Islam, and indeed earlier. Other power centers in North Africa and Spain were not of sufficient weight to invalidate this generalization.

Considering, then, the main currents both intellectual and political of the First Millennium CE, we have "shifted" (to use Gibbon's word from my epigraph) our interest away from the Mediterranean paradigm toward a region that stretches from the Western Mediterranean to the Hindū Kush. The central sector of this region is what I call the "Mountain Arena," in other words the Arabian peninsula plus its northward projection the Syrian Desert, along with the historically influential regions flanking it, namely Mesopotamia and Syria, the whole surrounded by a great rim of mountains.[45] Closely linked in to this Mountain Arena are to the East the Iranian plateau and to the West the Eastern Mediterranean basin, including Egypt and Libya to the South,

44 W. E. Kaegi, *Muslim expansion and Byzantine collapse in North Africa* (Cambridge 2010) 166–99; Sarris, *Empires of faith* [4:42] 289–93.

45 See further below, pp. 116–26.

and Asia Minor, the Aegean, and the Balkans to the North. These three regions (the last variously extended westward, as noted above) constitute a vast triptych at the meeting of Asia and Europe.

I shall call this triptych of regions the "Eurasian Hinge." It displays some striking geographical features that define and articulate it (see further below). But we should be wary of positing serious geographical and even geopolitical lines of division or noncommunication. Iran and Iraq interact despite the Zagros Mountains between them; indeed Iraq was the Sasanian Empire's urban heartland.[46] Greater Syria communicates by land and sea with Egypt, a country so distinctive that neither "Mediterranean" nor "Middle Eastern" nor "African" does it justice.[47] Its role as granary for the ancient Mediterranean and Middle East derived from the Nile flood created by the East African monsoon regime over Ethiopia, independently of Mediterranean—but not Indian Ocean—climatic vagaries.[48] Again, the Persian Gulf is linked to the Mediterranean via the Tigris-Euphrates route: the Syrian desert is not really "a clear geographical divide," nor the Euphrates a "geographically imperative" frontier or "fatal limit".[49] Outsiders (and even Eusebius of Caesarea) may have seen things that way, and Euphrates or Tigris frontiers have even acquired considerable symbolic force.[50] But they have actually represented nothing more profound than a political and military stalemate, the inability or indisposition of the powers on either side—the Sasanians and Romans, who claimed to be "the world's two eyes,"[51] are the clearest instance—to eliminate the other and so realize the Fertile Crescent's inherent

46 W. Eilers, "Iran and Mesopotamia," in E. Yarshater (ed.), *The Cambridge history of Iran* 3(1) (Cambridge 1983) 481–504; Pourshariati, *Decline and fall* [1:22] 38–41.

47 R. Bagnall, "Egypt and the concept of the Mediterranean," in Harris (ed.), *Rethinking the Mediterranean* [3:109] 339–47.

48 R. Ellenblum, *The collapse of the Eastern Mediterranean* (Cambridge 2012) 24.

49 See respectively J. Haldon, "Framing transformation, transforming the framework," *Millennium* 5 (2008) 348–50; E. Frézouls, "Les fluctuations de la frontière orientale de l'empire romain," in *La géographie administrative et politique d'Alexandre à Mahomet* (Leiden 1981) 225; Gibbon 46: 2.880. M. Sommer, "Difference, diversity, diaspora: Locating the Middle Euphrates on imperial maps," *Mediterraneo antico* 9 (2006) 426–27, sees the Euphrates as a social, cultural, and economic frontier, but not as a geographical divide. Navigation on it was particularly easy when it still ran through forests full of timber for boatbuilding: Dio Cassius [ed. U. P. Boissevain (Berlin 1895–1931); tr. E. Cary (London 1914–27)] 76.9.3. It can also be thought of as the main artery between the Persian Gulf and the Mediterranean. Compare C. Noelle-Karimi, "Khurasan and its limits," in M. Ritter and others (eds), *Iran und iranisch geprägte Kulturen* (Wiesbaden 2008) 9–12, on the Oxus as boundary but not barrier.

50 Sommer, *Mediterraneo antico* 9 (2006) [4:49] 427; Borrut, *Entre mémoire et pouvoir* [3:79] 207–8, 227, 348.

51 G. Schmalzbauer, "Überlegungen zur Idee der Oikumene in Byzanz," in W. Hörandner and others (eds), *Wiener Byzantinistik und Neogräzistik* (Vienna 2004) 408–19; Michael Whitby, "Byzantine diplomacy," in P. de Souza and J. France (eds), *War and peace in ancient and medieval history* (Cambridge 2008) 127–29; Canepa, *Two eyes of the earth* [2:70] 123–25; cf. L. Mecella and U. Roberto, " Ἰσοτιμία", *Studi ellenistici* 27 (2013) 99–119.

unity. This unity was nevertheless briefly brought about—before the Arabs—by the last great Sasanian monarch Khosrow II in the second and third decades of the seventh century. By taking Asia Minor, Khosrow bid for control of the Eastern Mediterranean basin as well. As ruler of Iran too, he briefly restored the Achaemenid Empire "from Sind to Sardis"[52] as it had been at its apogee under Darius I (d. 486 BCE).

Such political arrangements were transitory compared to the durable trans-Euphratene contacts enjoyed by Jewish communities in Mesopotamia and Palestine, or the Syriac Christian Churches. To grasp the historical functioning of the Eurasian Hinge, we need to look at its cultural as well as political role. Grosso modo, the Iranian plateau can be associated with the successive Iranian empires, Achaemenid, Arsacid, and Sasanian. The East Mediterranean was Rome's for two-thirds of our First Millennium. And the Mountain Arena became the heartland of the Umayyad Caliphate and—on its Mesopotamian side—of the Abbasids too. We have already encountered these three imperial traditions; but it will help us appreciate the immense and diachronic cultural interactivity of the space they occupied if we consider that, as well as empires with their apparently firm frontiers, we also find human networks which may be political as well as cultural, but are markedly less inflexible than the vast and autocratic states from which they often derive. We may call these networks commonwealths. Each of the empires we are concerned with—Iran, Rome, and the Caliphate—came to be associated with one. Our empires could not necessarily embrace the whole of the Eurasian Hinge—Rome never subdued the Iranian plateau, nor did any Muslim state take root in Asia Minor before the Second Millennium. But the commonwealths were cultural, therefore more pervasive.

I have already noted the achievement of the early Achaemenid Empire in unifying virtually the whole Eurasian Hinge, excluding the Balkans, in the early fifth century BCE. Several Greek and Roman writers asserted that the Sasanians consciously and explicitly aimed to reinstate this vast Iranian dominion by force of arms. Whether they were right is debated in current scholarship.[53] One thing is certain, though, namely that the Sasanians came very close to achieving such a restoration during Shapur I's campaigns in the 250s, and actually did so in the 610s and 620s. The pre-Islamic world can, then, as instructively be viewed looking west from Fars or Khurāsān as east from Greece or Italy. And if Iran temporarily lost its political independence to the Arabs, it reemerged as a major force, both political and cultural, in the

52 R. G. Kent, *Old Persian* (New Haven 1953^2) 136–37 (a text of Darius I).

53 In favor: G. Fowden, *Empire to commonwealth* (Princeton 1993) 27–36. Against: K. Mosig-Walburg, *Römer und Perser vom 3. Jahrhundert bis zum Jahr 363 n. Chr.* (Gutenberg 2009) 12–13, 19–21, 326. Z. Rubin, "The Sasanid monarchy," in *CAH* 14.645–47, argues that glorification of the Achaemenids was more for foreign than internal consumption.

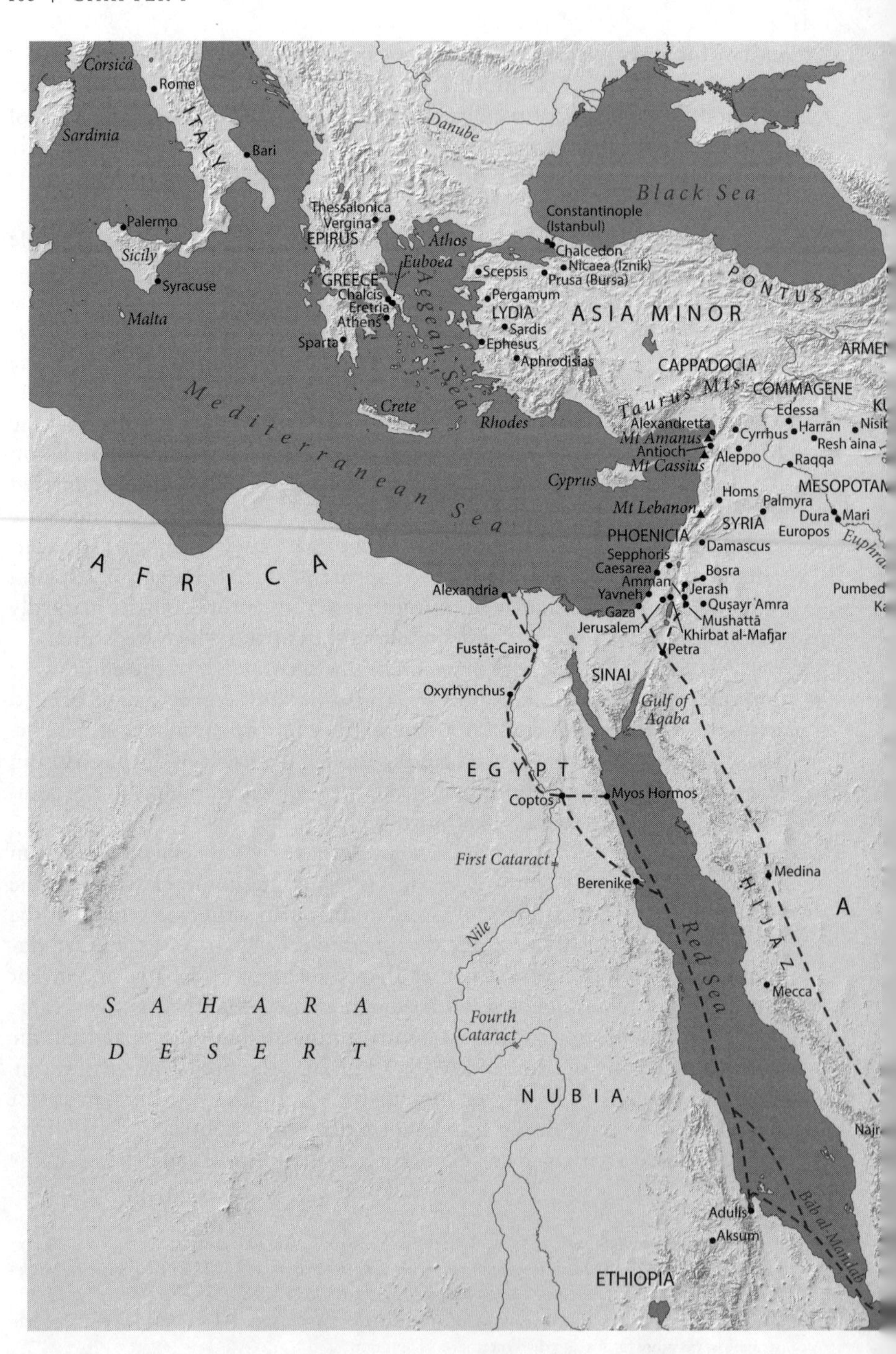

THE EURASIAN HINGE, WITH CIRCUM-ARABIAN TRADE ROUTES

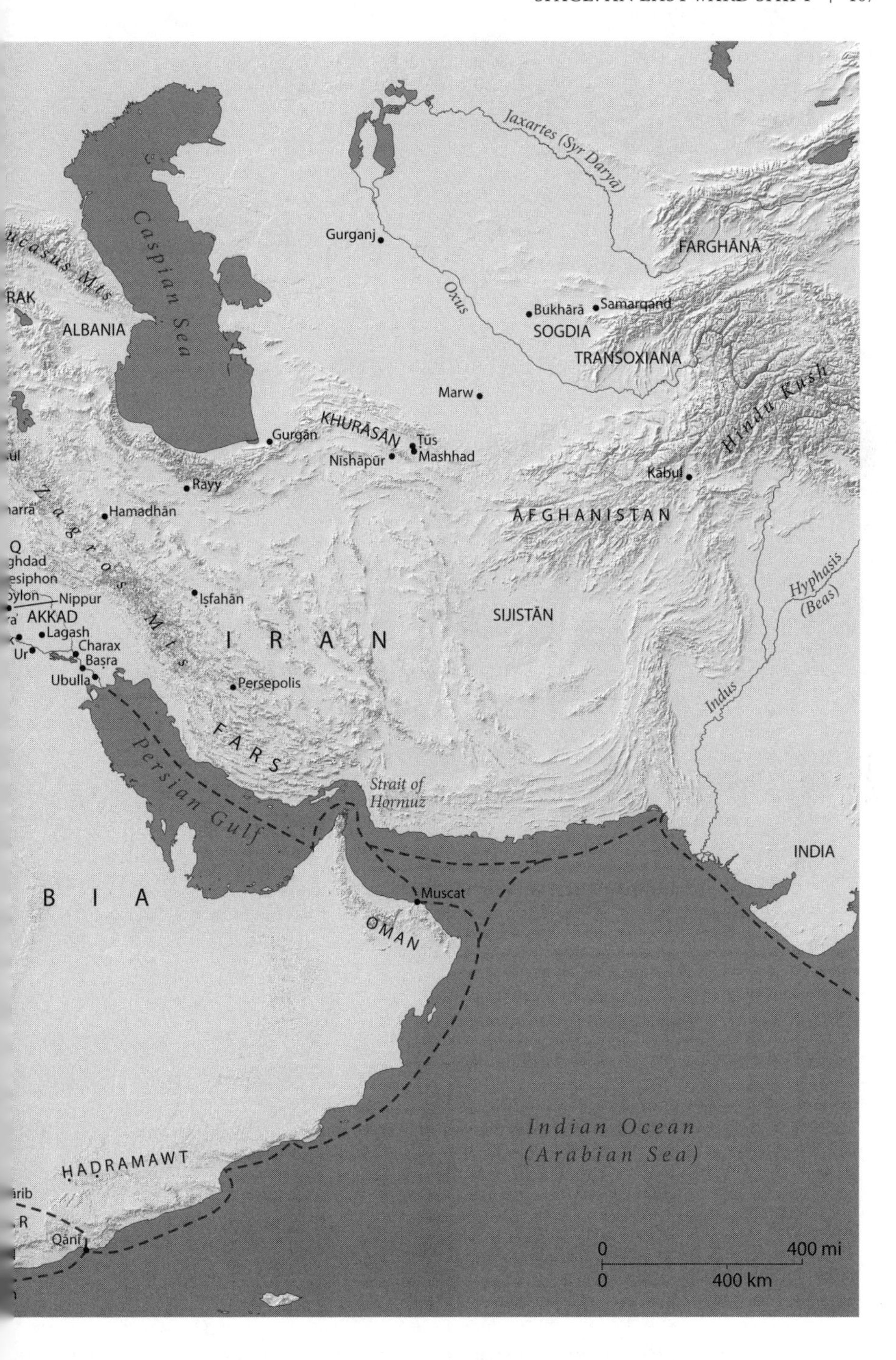
Jaxartes (Syr Daryā)
Caspian Sea
Gurganj
FARGHĀNA
Oxus
Bukhārā
Samarqand
SOGDIA
TRANSOXIANA
ALBANIA
Marw
Hindu Kush
KHURĀSĀN
Gurgān
Tūs
Nīshāpūr
Mashhad
Kābul
Rayy
Hamadhān
AFGHANISTAN
Zagros Mts
Nippur
Iṣfahān
AKKAD
SIJISTĀN
Hyphasis (Beas)
Lagash
Charax
Baṣra
Ur
I R A N
Ubulla
Persepolis
Indus
FARS
Persian Gulf
Strait of Hormuz
INDIA
B I A
Muscat
OMAN
Indian Ocean (Arabian Sea)
ḤAḌRAMAWT
Qāni'
0
400 mi
0
400 km

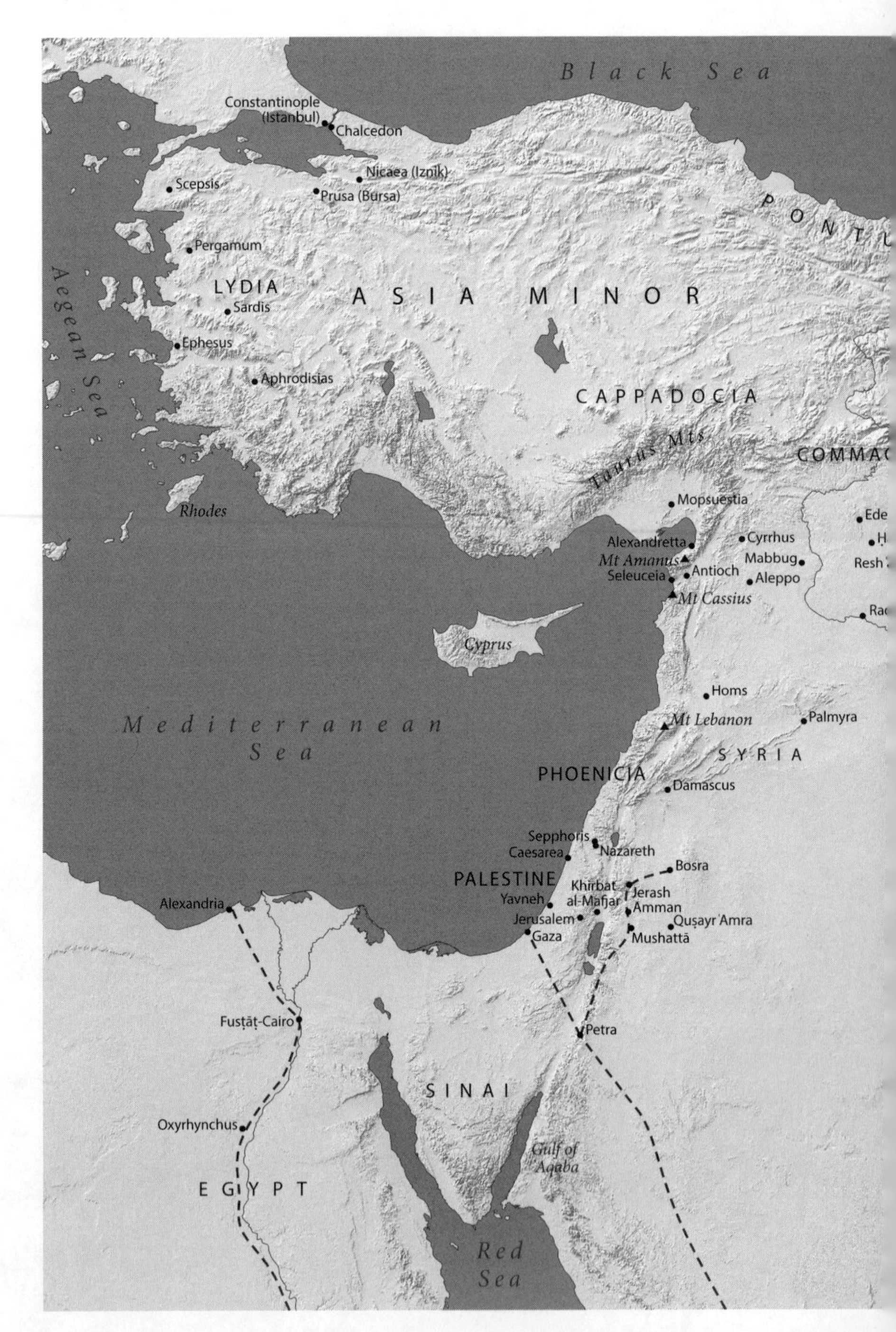

THE EURASIAN HINGE, WITH CIRCUM-ARABIAN TRADE ROUTES (DETAIL

Caucasus Mts
IBERIA
GEORGIA
SHIRAK
Ani
ALBANIA
Caspian Sea
ARMENIA
KURDISTAN
Nisibis
Mosul
SOPOTAMIA
Tigris
Dura Europos
Mari
Euphrates
Zagros Mts
Rayy
Hamadhān
Sāmarrā
IRAQ
IRAN
Pumbedita
Baghdad
Ctesiphon
Karbalā
Babylon
Iṣfahān
Kūfa
Nippur
Sūra
AKKAD
Uruk
Lagash
Ur
Charax
Baṣra
Ubulla
Persepolis
FARS
Persian Gulf
0
200 mi
0
200 km

maturing Islamic world.[54] There is a sense in which the Abbasid Caliphate was a revival of the Sasanid Empire.

Ancient Iran has traditionally been depicted as an administratively centralized empire on the model of Rome, and its dominant Iranian-Mazdean (or Zoroastrian) culture as an elite prerogative rather than something to be disseminated to other peoples—this in contrast to Rome or China.[55] It has begun to be recognized, though, that Sasanian Iran can also be seen as a decentralized confederacy of local dynasties,[56] and as a land of immense cultural including religious heterogeneity, in which Mazdean orthodoxy occupied a less hegemonic position than has been supposed,[57] while Judaism, Christianity, and Manicheism flourished. There is also growing appreciation of how, throughout history, Iran's language and culture has touched its neighbors beyond its fluctuating political frontiers, to different degrees depending on the period in question.[58] Among the more significant constituents of this Iranian Commonwealth were—in widely varying modes—those areas of Afghanistan not under direct rule, together with parts of India (or rather, Western Pakistan) from the Kushan period (first to mid-third centuries CE) onward;[59] tracts of Central Asia, until the rise of the Turks began, from the later sixth century onward, to erode Iranian influence;[60] certain areas of Asia Minor, notably Commagene, Cappadocia, and Pontus, during the Achaemenid and Hellenistic periods;[61] the Scythian, Sarmatian, and other inhabitants of the North Black Sea littoral;[62] also the Armenians, the Georgians, and other inhabitants of the Caucasus.[63] The Jews of Babylonia are still studied in such hermetic isolation from the culture of their Sasanid

54 Cf. J. Wiesehöfer, "'Randkultur' oder 'Nabel der Welt'? Das Sasanidenreich und der Westen," in J. Wiesehöfer and P. Huyse (eds), *Ērān ud Anērān* (Stuttgart 2006) 9–28.

55 X. de Planhol, "Iran i," *EIr* 13.205–12.

56 Pourshariati, *Decline and fall* [1:22] 33–160.

57 Pourshariati, *Decline and fall* [1:22] 321–95.

58 Yarshater (ed.), *Cambridge history of Iran* 3(1) [4:46] 479–624; cf. B. G. Fragner, *Die "Persophonie": Regionalität, Identität und Sprachkontakt in der Geschichte Asiens* (Berlin 1999), for a brilliant exposition of the role of the Persian language from the tenth to the twentieth centuries. For maximalist late Sasanian versions of Ērānšahr from Oxus to Nile, see T. Daryaee, "Ethnic and territorial boundaries in late antique and early medieval Persia", in F. Curta (ed.), *Borders, barriers, and ethnogenesis* (Turnhout 2005) 123–38. On the languages related to or influenced by Middle Persian, see R. Schmitt, *Die iranischen Sprachen in Geschichte und Gegenwart* (Wiesbaden 2000) 43–65.

59 On India, see P. Callieri, "India iv," *EIr* 13.13–16.

60 De Planhol, *EIr* 13.205–12 [4:55].

61 L. Raditsa, "Iranians in Asia Minor," in Yarshater (ed.), *Cambridge history of Iran* 3(1) [4:46] 100–15; and the relevant articles in *EIr*.

62 Y. Ustinova, "Orientalization: Once, twice, or more?," in C. Bonnet and others (eds), *Les religions orientales dans le monde grec et romain* (Brussels 2009) 311–24.

63 S. H. Rapp, "Chronology, crossroads, and commonwealths: World-regional schemes and the lessons of Caucasia," in J. H. Bentley and others (eds), *Interactions: Transregional perspectives on world history* (Honolulu 2005) 175–76, 185–86, 187–89 (my thanks to Anthony Kaldellis for this reference).

rulers that they too are envisaged as members of the Iranian Commonwealth.[64] At the opposite extreme of isolation, the Church of the East was for the first century of its presence in China perceived as Iranian rather than Roman.[65]

Each of the Commonwealth's constituents assimilated Iranism differently, but helped by the fact that, although Mazdaism played its part in the articulation of Iranian culture, religion was not the necessary constituent it was in the East Roman and Islamic Commonwealths. That was why Iranism could go on providing a cultural substrate for Armenia—for instance—even after it embraced Christianity;[66] also, to a remarkable extent, for the Abbasid Caliphate and its derivatives. Today the idea of the Iranian Commonwealth, or Greater Iran, continues to be propagated, especially by those who want Iran to compete with Turkey for influence in ex-Soviet Central Asia. It also underlies the major scholarly reference work on Iran, the *Encyclopaedia Iranica*, "covering a multi-lingual and multi-ethnic cultural continent." Through its numerous articles on regions and cities outside Iran proper (India, for example, or Asia Minor; Kabul or Jerusalem), the *EIr* rewrites, from the perspective of Iran, the history of its Roman and other peripheries.[67]

In these peripheries Rome had, ever since Augustus, competed with Iran for a role—in the Caucasus, for example, and in South Arabia, as we shall shortly see. But it was Constantine's genius to associate his empire with a force, namely Christianity, which would carry Roman influence into the whole region spread out between these poles. Between the fourth and sixth centuries a string of Christian communities or even states emerged, either close to or beyond Rome's eastern and southern borders: in Armenia and Georgia, among the Arab tribes in or beyond the Syrian and Arabian frontier zone, in South Arabia, Ethiopia, and Nubia, and even in South India. All these together constituted a cultural, spiritual, and to varying degrees political commonwealth associated with East Rome.[68] That Constantine also—in another stroke of genius—transferred the seat of his authority to Constantinople meant that henceforth Roman horizons, while still heavily influenced

64 C. Bakhos and M. R. Shayegan, "Introduction" to their *The Talmud in its Iranian context* (Tübingen 2010) XV.

65 T. H. Barrett, "Buddhism, Taoism and the eighth-century Chinese term for Christianity," *Bulletin of the School of Oriental and African Studies* 65 (2002) 555–60; S. N. C. Lieu, "The Luminous Religion (Ch'ing-chao, i.e. the Church of the East or Nestorianism) in China," in A. Mustafa and J. Tubach (eds), *Inkulturation des Christentums im Sasanidenreich* (Wiesbaden 2007) 315–16.

66 J. R. Russell, *Zoroastrianism in Armenia* (Cambridge, Mass. 1987); id., "Armenia and Iran iii," *EIr* 2.438–44.

67 See also the new *Journal of Persianate studies* (Leiden 2008–).

68 On this East Roman Commonwealth (or "First Byzantine Commonwealth"), see Fowden, *Empire to commonwealth* [4:53] 100–37. P. Wood, *"We have no king but Christ": Christian political thought in Greater Syria on the eve of the Arab conquest (c. 400–585)* (Oxford 2010) 209–64, prefers "Miaphysite Commonwealth," with reference to the period after 451.

by the empire's Mediterranean base, could open much more directly and self-confidently eastward. Viewed from the Constantinopolitan perspective of Justinian or Süleyman the Magnificent exactly a millennium later, whoever possessed Asia Minor was in a position to dominate or influence, culturally if not politically, the Eastern Mediterranean and the Aegean but also the Black Sea, the Caucasus, the Caspian and Syro-Mesopotamia, the Persian Gulf, Arabia, the Red Sea, and even the Indian Ocean. From roughly the same vantage point, the same horizons have now been revived by Turkey's neo-Ottomanist Foreign Minister (2009–), Ahmet Davutoğlu, whose book *Strategic depth* (2001) pays considerable attention to the historical as well as geographical factors that influence strategy.[69]

The theological and ecclesiastical crisis provoked by the Council of Chalcedon in 451 saw a strong anti-Chalcedonian movement emerge both in the Mountain Arena (Arabia, Palestine, Alexandria, Syria, Armenia) and beyond (Asia Minor as far as Constantinople)[70] by the early sixth century, and severe imperial repression of it. Our most useful source, the anti-Chalcedonian *Ecclesiastical history* by John of Ephesus (d. c. 588), emphasizes the role played by the Jafnid (Ghassanid) Arab dynasty in Syria—perhaps suggesting more of a political hypostasis than the movement really possessed,[71] though beyond the Roman frontier the kings of Aksum (Ethiopia) too were not unwilling to be called upon. On the theological front one of the leading anti-Chalcedonian missionaries, Simeon of Beth-Arsham (d. c. 540) "the invincible demon, the debater" as his opponents called him,[72] extracted statements of belief from the communities he tirelessly visited on both sides of the Sasanian-Roman frontier, and kept them together on "great linen cloths" specially treated to preserve them. "Above the [statement of] belief he affixed the seals of the king of that people and of the bishops of the same and of their chief men in lead upon these cloths, and thus confirmed it," lest anyone make alterations.[73]

69 A. Davutoğlu, *Stratejik derinlik: Türkiye'nin uluslararası konumu* (Istanbul 2001), tr. (Greek: the version used here) N. Raptopoulos, *Το στρατηγικό βάθος: Η διεθνής θέση της Τουρκίας* (Athens 2010) 193, 240, 253–54, 281, 335.

70 List of regions affected: John of Ephesus, *Lives of the eastern saints* [ed. and tr. E. W. Brooks in R. Graffin and F. Nau (eds), *Patrologia orientalis* (Paris 1907–) 17–19 (Paris 1923–26)] 50, p. 500. N. J. Andrade, "The Syriac Life of John of Tella and the frontier *politeia*," *Hugoye* 12 (2009) 199–234, discusses the application of the term "politeia" to anti-Chalcedonian clerical and ascetic networks.

71 John of Ephesus's line is adopted with gusto by I. Shahîd in his account of the Ghassanid phylarchate: *Byzantium and the Arabs in the sixth century* (Washington, D.C. 1995–2009) 1.398–406, 587–89, 774, 838, 859–60. If to one critic my East Roman Commonwealth seemed too much like a preview of the Muslim world (P. Blaudeau, *Alexandrie et Constantinople (451–491)* [Rome 2006] 88 n. 405), my attention to John's testimony is perhaps to blame.

72 John of Ephesus, *Lives of the eastern saints* [4:70] 10, p. 144. On Simeon, see A. Grillmeier, *Jesus der Christus im Glauben der Kirche* (Freiburg 1979–2002; 1^3, 1990; $2/1^2$, 1986) 2/3.263–65, 276–78 (T. Hainthaler), 2/4.315–16.

73 John of Ephesus, *Lives of the eastern saints* [4:70] 10, p. 156. Public display of late Roman imperial pronouncements on linen cloths: *Theodosian code* [ed. P. Krueger and T. Mommsen (Berlin 1905); tr. C. Pharr (Princeton 1952)] 11.27.1. The Romans and before them the Etruscans had long used linen for

Simeon's collection of cloth creeds must have seemed reassuring proof that the anti-Chalcedonian world both within and beyond Rome's frontiers was united round a defined doctrine. But it did not stop disputes such as the thirty-year schism between the Syrian and Egyptian hierarchies in the late sixth and early seventh centuries. Partly as a result of such internal differences, the distinction between Chalcedonians and anti-Chalcedonians was less clear-cut or widely understood than some modern students admit.[74] In any case, the East Roman Commonwealth cannot be identified solely with the opponents of Chalcedon. They were an important part of it, but they lived in a world where the imperial Chalcedonian Church, and in the Sasanian realm the Church of the East too, were likewise a presence. None of these theological and ecclesiastical distinctions and schisms seriously fragmented the state—that is why we can talk of an *East Roman* Commonwealth. Nevertheless, when the Arab believers in Muḥammad did finally come and shake the empire's foundations, it was with a scripture, the Qur'ān, that revealed God's deep displeasure at the Christians' internal dissensions (see below, p. 188), and valuably confirms not only the spiritually and socially fragmented nature of the East Roman Commonwealth, but also the role that world played in setting the scene for Islam.

Although the Church of the East in the Sasanian Empire, and its missions in Central Asia and China, eschewed political linkage to Rome (despite calling itself "Ta Ch'in," "East Roman" in Chinese), and except in Iraq can hardly be regarded as part of the East Roman Commonwealth however distantly,[75] still it too deserves mention in this context. The post-Roman Germanic kingdoms of Western Europe—Visigoths, Vandals, Burgundians, Franks, Ostrogoths, Anglo-Saxons, and others—provide a closer analogy to the East Roman Commonwealth, indeed a Latin equivalent; but they were not part of the same system.[76] They were geographically and politically remote from Constantinople, and espoused Arianism—a form of Christianity that came to be associated particularly with Germans, and marked political as well as religious distance. In the West, it was only the residual authority and prestige of Rome itself—especially its bishop—that really engaged the interest of the Greek Christian world. There was also the later "Byzantine" Commonwealth

---

sacred books: E. A. Meyer, *Legitimacy and law in the Roman world* (Cambridge 2004) 25, 54 (reference courtesy of Christina Kokkinia).

74 See, e.g., the anti-Chalcedonian John of Ephesus, *Ecclesiastical history*, Part 3 [ed. and tr. (Latin) E. W. Brooks (Louvain 1935–36)] 2.23; 3.12, 21. Also M. Whittow, *The making of Orthodox Byzantium, 600–1025* (Basingstoke 1996) 42–46; J. Shepard, "Byzantium's overlapping circles," *Proceedings of the 21st International Congress of Byzantine Studies* (Aldershot 2006) 1.28–29.

75 On the Church of the East remnant on East Roman territory even after the School of Edessa was closed, see John of Ephesus, *Lives of the eastern saints* [4:70] 10, p. 139.

76 I disagree, here, with A. Harris, *Byzantium, Britain & the West: The archaeology of cultural identity AD 400–650* (Stroud 2003), and Sarris, *Empires of faith* [4:42] 204, 226.

in the Slavic world, progressively Christianized from the sixth century onward. It merits notice here if only because Dimitri Obolensky's book about it was responsible for putting the concept of commonwealth on the First Millennium map.[77] Our third commonwealth, though, is none of these, for they are too remote from our central concern with the development of Jewish, Christian, and Muslim monotheism and Greco-Roman rationalism in their First Millennium heartlands. Instead we turn to the world of Islam in its early maturity, after the frenetic initial phase of empire building.

The Iranian and East Roman Commonwealths were at their most vigorous when running parallel to empire. When empire collapsed or contracted, the commonwealth dwindled or changed mode of operation—for example, Iranism, increasingly Islamized, under the Abbasids. The origins of the Islamic Commonwealth are more disputed. On one reading it already began to emerge as far back as the mass Berber revolt in 740 at the end of Umayyad rule, when Damascus lost direct control of everything west of Tunisia.[78] In other words, for a time it paralleled the Caliphate when that, now Abbasid, was still at the height of its power. But a more decidedly postimperial view[79] echoes the tenth-century historian Masʿūdī in emphasizing the administrative disarray and economic collapse of the 930s and 940s,[80] so that the steady decentralization of the Abbasid Caliphate and multiplication of competing centers of power and, by extension, culture too was the real genesis of commonwealth. (One might add the tenth/eleventh-century leveling out of the conversion curve—"religious homogeneity magnified the importance of other differences," especially regional identities.[81]) In Iran and North Africa new and vigorous shoots burst forth. The Samanid dynasty in Khurāsān and Transoxiana emerged c. 900 and lasted until 1005, while the Buyids dominated Iraq and parts of Iran, especially prosperous Fārs, from the 930s to the 1040s. As for the Fatimids, they established themselves at Qayrawān in 909. After the foundation of Cairo, which became the wealthiest city in the Eurasian world, their rule endured until 1171.

These were all substantial states, economically prosperous and the more culturally brilliant for their competing to maintain the efflorescence of Is-

77 D. Obolensky, *The Byzantine Commonwealth: Eastern Europe 500–1453* (London 1971); cf. Shepard, *Proceedings of the 21st International Congress of Byzantine Studies* [4:74] 1.17–28; also C. Raffensperger, *Reimagining Europe: Kievan Rus' in the medieval world* (Cambridge, Mass. 2012), positioning Rus' not just as part of a Byzantine Commonwealth, but within a pre-Crusades Europe, *all* of which looked to Constantinople for cultural models and Roman legitimacy.

78 Gibbon 51: 3.322; K. Y. Blankinship, *The end of the jihād state* (Albany, N.Y. 1994) 3, 203–4.

79 H. Kennedy, *The Prophet and the age of the Caliphates* (Harlow 2004^2) 187–88, 198–209.

80 Al-Masʿūdī, *Meadows of gold* [4:22] 395, 504; cf. H. Kennedy, "The decline and fall of the First Muslim Empire," *Der Islam* 81 (2004) 3–30.

81 Fowden, *Empire to commonwealth* [4:53] 163–65; E. L. Daniel, "The Islamic East," in *New Cambridge history of Islam* [2:106] 1.465–66 (whence the quotation).

lamic learning and art which occurred in eighth- to tenth-century Baghdad—with important contributions from the Jewish and Christian communities too. Among other significant centers were Saffarid Sijistān, Hamdanid Syria, and Umayyad Spain. From Bukhārā to Cordoba, teachers and students were ever on the move.[82] Examples of this peripatetic style of life were the philosophers Fārābī (d. 948), who moved between Baghdad, Damascus, Aleppo, and Egypt,[83] and Ibn Sīnā (d. 1037), who spent different parts of his career at the princely courts of Bukhārā, Gurganj on the Oxus, Gurgān near the Caspian, Rayy near Teheran, Hamadhān, and Iṣfahān.[84] The proximity of the last four illustrates especially well the Islamic Commonwealth's close-woven web of culture. Arabic, the language of the Qur'ān but also of administration and scholarship, provided a superb instrument of commonwealth in that it developed dialects but did not become a family of separate languages, as Latin did. The ḥajj ensured that the bonds of the Muslim world never relaxed as entirely as did those between the Christianities of the Latin and Oriental or, for that matter, Greek Churches.

This cultural strength in diversity of the Islamic Commonwealth allowed it to absorb and convert the Turkish invaders who arrived in such force during the eleventh century, and captured Baghdad in 1055. That the energy of the Turks was turned to the Islamic world's account was one of the decisive events in history. It ensured the East Roman Empire would eventually be eliminated and the Umayyads' goal achieved, of taking Constantinople and a large slice of the Mediterranean's northern coast. The Ottoman Empire fully reunited the East Mediterranean basin and the greater part of the Mountain Arena including Iraq and the Ḥijāz. If it never subdued Safavid Iran, it did control the old Sasanian heartland in Mesopotamia, so that the frontier ran along the natural geographical divider provided by the Zagros Mountains, and not the Euphrates.[85]

In other words, the evolution of empire into commonwealth was not a one-way street. New empires might emerge in ex-imperial territory whose cultural identity had been preserved by more flexible political arrangements. For the Ottomans possession of the Holy Cities in the Ḥijāz, whose value was religious but by extension political and legitimizing, became a major motive and pretext of politico-military expansion, and together with Yemen, likewise taken in 1517, reestablished a horizon in the Mountain

82 J. L. Kraemer, *Humanism in the renaissance of Islam* (Leiden 1992²), esp. 53, 233–34, 286; with a dose of statistical skepticism from M. Bernards, "*Ṭalab al-ʿilm* amongst the linguists of Arabic during the ʿAbbasid period," in J. E. Montgomery (ed.), *ʿAbbasid studies* (Leuven 2004) 33–46.

83 D. Gutas, "Fārābī," *EIr* 9.210.

84 A. Bertolacci, "Biblioteche e centri di cultura nell'Oriente musulmano tra il X e l'XI secolo," *SFIM* 495–521.

85 On the feebleness of the Safavids' attempts to control Iraq, see R. Matthee, "The Safavid-Ottoman frontier," *International journal of Turkish studies* 9 (2003) 157–73.

Arena well to the south of Syria-Mesopotamia, the traditional amphitheater of empire.

Our three commonwealths—Iranian, East Roman, and Islamic—have helped us, then, to analyze how empires and cultures, especially religious cultures, interacted and often reinforced or supplemented each other across the Eurasian Hinge zone, throughout the First Millennium and beyond. Bear in mind that the commonwealths overlap, so a given region may—perhaps because of the diversity of its populations, or the strategic character of its position—come under more than one commonwealth at once. The Caucasus, for example, belonged to the Iranian cultural zone, extensively adopted Christianity, and ended up—its more southerly regions—under Muslim rule. The same point may indeed be made about the entire Eurasian Hinge, in the sense that from the Sasanian world Mithraism and Manicheism (for example) entered the Roman Empire, while from Roman territory Christianity penetrated Iran. This large-scale cultural interaction between the two empires/commonwealths paved the way for the coming (or rather—recalling the Achaemenids—the return) of the "Near Eastern unitary state," namely the Caliphate.[86] In short, our "shift" from West to East, from the Mediterranean paradigm to the Eurasian Hinge, can hardly be called "arbitrary"—see again the epigraph to this chapter.

THE MOUNTAIN ARENA

The Caucasus is the northernmost tip of the central leaf of our East-West triptych. It is the point where the Mountain Arena's rim impinges on the alien nomadic world of the North, and it was one candidate for where Alexander built his great iron gate to keep the wild steppe tribes of Gog and Magog—in other words, the Huns—out of the settled world to the South.[87] (This was the forerunner of the Sasanians' elaborate defenses in the Caucasus.) Because the Mountain Arena is the focus of my shift away from the Mediterranean paradigm, it merits a more careful description at this point. This denotes no particular insistence that human life and thought was being "determined" by geography, beyond the responses any society of humans will make, given certain environmental pressures or opportunities. The most I would claim is that landscape and climate favor the evolution of distinctive cultural, economic, and social forms, which eventually may—or may not—constitute a basis for establishing a political entity.[88]

The arc from the Persian Gulf to Palestine, popularly known as the Fertile

86 Cf. Becker, *Islamstudien* [2:74] 1.18–19.

87 Van Bladel, in Reynolds (ed.), *Qurʾān in its historical context* [1:31] 186.

88 Cf. Haldon, *Millennium* 5 (2008) [4:49] 348–50.

Crescent, has been one of the traditional foci of Western as well as Eastern imagination and historiography. Following this ancient highway, we cannot but recall Abraham who went before us, from Ur of the Chaldees by way of Ḥarrān to the land of Canaan in Genesis, and on to Mecca according to Muslim tradition.[89] But the Fertile Crescent's unity, and by extension that of the Mountain Arena that contains it, has been obscured—as already noted—by the natural and political frontier which is deemed to separate its eastern from its western segment. I proposed a preliminary description of the Mountain Arena in my *Empire to commonwealth*.[90] Here I offer a new version of that account.

Speaking very generally, the Mountain Arena may be envisaged as "a rough parallelogram . . . as large as India,"[91] whose perimeter abuts on and interacts with, but does not embrace, the Black Sea in the North, the Iranian plateau in the East, the Indian Ocean in the South (with India itself beyond it), and in the West the Egyptian and Sahara Deserts and the Mediterranean Sea. Slightly more precisely, one might compare it to a Greek stadium, its square end the South Arabian coast and its half-circle end the Fertile Crescent in the North. I will loosely here call it an "arena," appealing for the general concept to the Younger Pliny's description of the Tuscan coast: "Picture to yourself a vast amphitheatre such as could only be a work of Nature. The great spreading plain is ringed round by mountains. . . ."[92] The geographer Ibn Ḥawqal, born and raised at Nisibis in the Jazīra (Upper Mesopotamia) and writing about the year 988 (therefore the chronicler Elias bar Shenaya's fellow townsman and elder contemporary), describes this heartland as like a bird, with Syria its head, the Jazīra its chest, Yemen its tail, and Baṣra (Iraq) and Egypt its wings.[93]

The arena in the strict sense, the great Syro-Arabian plain, is rimmed by an almost continuous line of mountains, Amanus and Taurus (and related ranges beyond[94]) in the North, Zagros to the East, then in the South the highlands of Oman, and of Yemen mirrored by Ethiopia's rugged plateau, "hard of access and covered in snow . . . where storms and cold are constant

89 R. Firestone, *Journeys in holy lands* (Albany, N.Y. 1990) 25–26, 63–71.

90 Fowden, *Empire to commonwealth* [4:53] 15–19, and the map following 205. For a superb panoramic representation of the Mountain Arena, see I. I. Nawwab and others, *Aramco and its world* (Washington, D.C. 1980) 6–7, and the map inserted at the end of the volume.

91 T. E. Lawrence, *The complete 1922 Seven pillars of wisdom: The 'Oxford' text* (Fordingbridge 2004) 12–13.

92 Pliny the Younger, *Letters* [ed. R. A. B. Mynors (Oxford 1963); tr. B. Radice (London 1963)] 5.6.7.

93 Ibn Ḥawqal, *The form of the earth* (*Ṣūrat al-arḍ*) [ed. J. H. Kramers (Leiden 1938–39^2); tr. (French) J. H. Kramers and G. Wiet, *Configuration de la terre* (Beirut 1964)] 209 (of the Arabic text, noted in the translation).

94 Ibn Ḥawqal, *Form of the earth* [4:93] 169; cf. C. E. Bosworth, "al- Ḳabḳ," *EIs*^{2} 4.342a.

and the snows so deep that men sink in up to their knees."[95] On its West the arena is bounded by the mountains flanking the Red Sea and backing the eastern Mediterranean littoral. The coherence of some, at least, of these ranges was perceived by the early Arabic geographers. For example, Ibn Khurradādhbih (d. c. 911) linked the mountains of Ḥijāz to Lebanon, Amanus, the Taurus, and the Caucasus, making the Holy Cities of Mecca and Medina, in pious conceit, the root of the whole system.[96] Later, Ibn Ḥawqal gave a more detailed description of the mountains bordering the Fertile Crescent, though conceived of as part of a far vaster chain stretching from China to the Atlantic.[97]

The mountains which rim our Arena are often of such extent that they constitute subregions independently interacting with as well as defining the edges of the immense expanse of Mesopotamian, Syrian and Arabian plain and desert (not without incident, of course) which forms the region's heart. Only in the northern hemicycle does a Fertile Crescent mediate between the mountains and the desert. In the South the transition is abrupt, and civilization is confined to the highlands (Yemen for example) and the valleys and oases bordering the desert: Najrān, Mārib, Ḥaḍramawt, and many others. The great Mārib dam nourished extensive agriculture and a markedly civilized urban society on runoff from the Yemen uplands until, in the lifetime of the Prophet Muḥammad, it finally broke without hope of repair, and the area reverted to wilderness.[98] As for the Nile Valley, strictly speaking it lies just beyond the great mountain rim. Yet it is pushed by the Sahara into the closest interaction with the whole Arena.

It is easy to raise objections to such a schematic geography. In the first place there are alternative, equally convincing—or not—schematic geographies available. Gibbon hints at one when he calls the North-South axis more "real and intelligible" than the East-West one. It was widely felt—the idea is attested in the early Arabic geographers for example—that the North stood for the barbarism of Gog and Magog, the South for civilization. The Huns had indisputably been much more of a threat to Iran and Rome than these were to each other. Like the Mountain Arena, the North-South divide could be articulated in terms of a vast mountain chain, this time the East-West range of Caucasus, Carpathians, Alps, and Pyrenees.[99] One might also see the North-South axis more interactively, and closer to the spirit of our present investigation, by emphasizing for instance how the Mountain Arena's

95 Cosmas Indicopleustes, *Christian topography* [ed. and tr. (French) W. Wolska-Conus (Paris 1968–73)] 2.60, quoting an Aksumite inscription probably of the late second or early third century.

96 Ibn Khurradādhbih, *The book of itineraries and kingdoms (Kitāb al-masālik wa-'l-mamālik)* [ed. and tr. (French) M. J. de Goeje (Leiden 1889)] 172–73.

97 Ibn Ḥawqal, *Form of the earth* [4:93] 168–70.

98 Gajda, *Royaume de Ḥimyar* [3:76] 128, 130–35, 200–203.

99 Bosworth, *EIs*² 4.341–42 [4:94].

northern rim draws into our picture the Caucasus and the seas which flank it, the Black Sea and the Caspian, in other words the sensitive northern frontier of the Irano-Roman world. By the same token, assigning due weight to the Mountain Arena's southern sector, Arabia, opens us up onto the Red Sea, the Persian Gulf and above all the Indian Ocean, another immense, autonomous, interconnected world,[100] a second "Great Sea"[101] quite as implicated in the symbolism of kingship[102] as was the Mediterranean. The sixteenth-century Ottoman Empire pursued a number of these possibilities, projecting naval power from its base in Istanbul right across the Mediterranean and, at the same time, into the Black Sea and even—briefly—the Caspian on its northern fringes, and southward into the Red Sea and, less successfully, the Persian Gulf and Indian Ocean (in which latter Portuguese competition was formidable).[103]

Against all this, though, we have to weigh the undeniable influence exerted by the East-West axis of the Mediterranean Sea,[104] by trade routes that are strongly impacted by geography, but also by the East-West spread of our three monotheisms, the Roman Empire, and the Caliphate, cultural and political developments that are much more loosely linked to geographical factors. We need to be frank: the refocusing of space I am proposing here is all to do with understanding the cultural and political developments of the First Millennium, and owes much less to geographical determinism, even though it acknowledges the force, at times, of such considerations.

The physical and geographical analysis of the Mountain Arena here offered is strengthened when we recall two things: first, that contemporary rulers and strategists saw things the same way, and acted accordingly; and

100 Bhacker, in Potter (ed.), *Persian Gulf* [4:2] 163–71.

101 S. P. Brock, "A Syriac life of John of Dailam," *Parole de l'Orient* 10 (1981–82) 173.

102 Apparently the Indian Ocean is intended when a Sasanid text exhorts the dynasty's founder, Ardashir I (224–42), to go and behold the sea with his own eyes, that he may never again fear an enemy. Iranian tradition held that the quintessence of kingly glory, or farr, was kept by the gods in the sea, at least when the throne had no legal occupant. See F. Grenet, "Lecture commentée du *Kârnâmag î Ardakhshêr î Pâbagân*," *Annuaire: École Pratique des Hautes Études, Section des sciences religieuses* 109 (2000–2001) 227–29; G. Gnoli, "Farr(ah)," *EIr* 9.314; A. Tafazzoli, "Frāxkard," *EIr* 10.201.

103 D. E. Pitcher, *An historical geography of the Ottoman Empire* (Leiden 1972) 116–23; S. Özbaran, "Ottoman naval policy in the South," in M. Kunt and C. Woodhead (eds), *Süleyman the Magnificent and his age* (London 1995) 55–70; S. Soucek, *Studies in Ottoman naval history and maritime geography* (Istanbul 2008) 7–29; D. R. Heedrick, *Power over peoples: Technology, environments, and Western imperialism, 1400 to the present* (Princeton 2010) 68–74; G. Casale, *The Ottoman age of exploration* (Oxford 2010) (this last reference kindly supplied by André Wink). Note how traditional Muslim including Ottoman cartographers placed the Indian Ocean at the top of their world maps, i.e., on a south-north rather than north-south axis, and in an overwhelmingly dominant posture vis-à-vis the Mediterranean: K. Pinto, "The maps are the message: Mehmet II's patronage of an 'Ottoman cluster,'" *Imago mundi* 63 (2011) 155–79.

104 Cf. G. W. Bowersock, "The East-West orientation of Mediterranean studies and the meaning of North and South in Antiquity," in Harris (ed.), *Rethinking the Mediterranean* [3:109] 167–78.

second that the Arena's rim of mountains was duplicated by a network of trade routes both terrestrial and maritime. Let us take the trade routes first.

The system[105] hinges on the head of the Persian Gulf—Seleucid Charax or Sasanian Ubulla, gradually succeeded from the seventh century by Baṣra—and the two Mediterranean cities of Alexandria and Gaza, from which Fusṭāṭ/Cairo took over in Islamic times. From Ubulla/Baṣra, the Persian Gulf funneled traffic through the Strait of Hormuz and then either along the bleak southern coast of Iran to India, or via the South Arabian coast to the Red Sea's exceedingly narrow opening at Bāb al-Mandab, where Arabia almost touches Africa. The Red Sea route, which took in Adulis near modern Massawa in Eritrea for the ivory and slaves of Aksum (Ethiopia), was shadowed beyond the coastal ranges to the east by the caravan route from South Arabia via the Ḥijāz to Petra and Gaza. Camels had not to hang around waiting for seasonal winds. As for the Nile Valley to the west, it became a usable route north of the First Cataract as it drew closer to the Red Sea. From the harbors of Berenike and Myos Hormos merchandise was carried overland to the relatively easy river route from Coptos down to Alexandria, avoiding persistent adverse winds at the northern end of the Red Sea.

Alexandria and Gaza keyed the—at least in Roman times—fantastically profitable Red Sea trade in spices, frankincense, and myrrh into the Mediterranean system of cabotage. As for Petra, it provided a jumping-off point for the inland Syrian emporia just east of the coastal mountains: cities such as Jerash, Bosra, and Damascus, leading on into North Syria. Here, Antioch offered another link to the Mediterranean, but also to Asia Minor beyond the Taurus Mountains. The Fertile Crescent highway also gave easy access to Mesopotamia, as did its more southerly desert variant via the oasis emporium of Palmyra to the Euphrates (until it succumbed to Roman-Sasanid tensions in the third century). Both the Euphrates and the Tigris served commerce, and were quicker and cheaper than the land routes. But all led down, via the Parthian-Sasanian capital at Seleuceia-Ctesiphon or later the Abbasid capital at Baghdad, to Charax/Ubulla/Baṣra and the Persian Gulf.

This Fertile Crescent route, linking Persian Gulf and Mediterranean much more efficiently than the Red Sea-Nile alternative, closed the circuit of trade, a humanly constructed mirror-image of the Mountain Arena and one to which the produce, harbors, prosperous southern regions (Oman, Yemen) and inland caravan routes of Arabia were integral. Iranians and Romans did not first notice Arabia thanks to Islam. Arabia was the point of contact and interchange between the two great maritime systems of the First Millennium, namely the Indian Ocean and the Mediterranean.[106] Archaeology and

105 Cf. M. Rostovtzeff (tr. D. and T. Talbot-Rice), *Caravan cities* (Oxford 1932) 1–35; N. Groom, "Trade, incense and perfume," in St J. Simpson (ed.), *Queen of Sheba* (London 2002) 88–101; R. McLaughlin, *Rome and the distant East* (London 2010) 23–33, 61–81, 92–103.

106 See the map in Hodgson, *Venture of Islam* [1:1] 1.122.

epigraphy are now revealing how, from the mid-fifth century, the South Arabian kingdom of Ḥimyar projected its authority into central and northern Arabia, anticipating the peninsula's unification under Islam. At the same time, both Iran and Rome were maneuvering for allies there.[107] When the Jewish ruler of Ḥimyar staged a revolting massacre of Christians at Najrān in 523, the news raced through the Mountain Arena provoking a flurry of letters and pamphlets in Syriac and Greek, and armed Aksumite intervention instigated by Constantinople.[108] Subsequently the kingdom passed under Sasanid control. Sixth-century Arabia was no mere periphery of the pre-Islamic world.

As for contemporary responses to the Mountain Arena we may begin, like the First Millennium itself, with the Emperor Augustus. Augustus was given to deep reflection on what a sustainable Roman Empire within defensible frontiers might look like, and was certainly no improvident expansionist. Even so, between 26 and 20 BCE he tried to strengthen Rome's position in both the immense, fortress-like blocks of mountains—the Caucasus and Transcaucasia (South Caucasus) to the North, and Yemen and Ethiopia to the South—which confined the Mountain Arena in their respective directions.[109] Despite their inaccessibility, he launched military expeditions into South Arabia as far as Mārib (perhaps to bring pressure on the Arsacids[110]), and to the upper Nile Valley as far as the fourth cataract, while making the first of a series of interventions in Armenia designed to impose rulers congenial to Rome's interests. Then again in 2 BCE Augustus sent his grandson Gaius Caesar to assert Rome's position first in Arabia (apparently in the Gulf of 'Aqaba) and then in Armenia. On this occasion, two historians contributed to the effort, Isidore of Charax with an account of the Arsacid Empire, and King Juba II of Mauritania with a book covering the southerly regions from West Africa via Egypt, Arabia and the Red Sea, Mesopotamia and parts of Iran, as far east as India, with special emphasis on Arabia's natural resources and trade routes.[111]

For six centuries after Augustus, Roman emperors pursued East-West equilibrium with Iran by strengthening their position in one or both of these

107 C. J. Robin, "Les arabes de Ḥimyar, des "romains" et des perses (IIIe-VIe siècles de l'ère chrétienne," *Semitica et classica* 1 (2008) 167–202; Gajda, *Royaume de Ḥimyar* [3:76] 43–58, 137–46; G. Fisher, *Between empires: Arabs, Romans, and Sasanians in late Antiquity* (Oxford 2011) 84–91; id., "Kingdoms or dynasties? Arabs, history, and identity before Islam," *JLA* 4 (2011) 254–58; G. W. Bowersock, *The throne of Adulis: Red Sea wars on the eve of Islam* (New York 2013).

108 Gajda, *Royaume de Ḥimyar* [3:76] 20–23, 97–109; J. Beaucamp and others (eds), *Juifs et chrétiens en Arabie aux Ve et VIe siècles* (Paris 2010).

109 Fowden, *Empire to commonwealth* [4:53] 103.

110 C. Marek, "Die Expedition des Aelius Gallus nach Arabien im Jahre 25 v.Chr.," *Chiron* 23 (1993) 121–56.

111 D. W. Roller, *The world of Juba II and Kleopatra Selene* (New York 2003) 212–43; A. Luther, "Zum Orientfeldzug des Gaius Caesar," *Gymnasium* 117 (2010) 103–27.

two same regions, Arabia in the South and Armenia (plus Iberia and Albania) in the North. The last decades of the sixth century and the first of the seventh saw the Sasanians, too, simultaneously on the offensive in both Armenia and South Arabia.[112] The story culminated with Heraclius delivering his knock-out blow against Khosrow II through the Armenian mountains rather than facing the Sasanian cavalry on their preferred terrain in Mesopotamia.[113] "This is virtually the only way to win, or at least it is the easiest," had observed a Latin historian already in the fourth century.[114]

Indisputably, the Armenians possessed a superb vantage point from which to survey the strategic issues between Iran and Rome, and to appreciate the natural arena in which they were played out. Procopius of Caesarea, the historian of Justinian's wars, brilliantly illustrates this by putting into the mouths of Armenian ambassadors to Khosrow I a threatening evocation of Justinian's all-consuming greed for power, with the Sasanians, by the late 530s, as inevitably the next in line. The ambassadors enumerate (how authentically, or with what insidious purpose, is here immaterial) the East Roman emperor's intrigues, interventions, and conquests across a vast front stretching from the northern and eastern shores of the Black Sea and the Huns who threatened Iran's northern frontiers, through the Caucasus, Syria, and Arabia as far as the Ethiopians ("of whom the Romans were completely ignorant"), while not omitting—in order to drive their point home—remoter regions such as North Africa and Italy.[115]

Our detailed literary sources for the Roman Empire enable us to decipher something of its policy makers' motives. But much else that was done in and around the Mountain Arena, by less documented but not necessarily less powerful actors, also serves to underline the region's dynamic centrality to our story. Let us glance at Iran and the Caliphate.

Despite the Roman elite's explicitly articulated appreciation of the Mountain Arena's importance, attacking Iran through Armenia was far easier in theory than practice. Heraclius's successful invasion of Iran from the North—in alliance with the Turks—was an exhibition of breathtaking generalship under extremely adverse conditions and with an army that enjoyed the unprecedented (for Rome) psychological advantage of fighting for the empire's very survival. Under the more usual conditions of warfare between the two empires, Rome might indulge the luxury of harrying urbanized Mesopota-

112 M. L. Chaumont, "Armenia and Iran ii," *EIr* 2.431–32; Gajda, *Royaume de Ḥimyar* [3:76] 152–67.

113 J. Howard-Johnston, *East Rome, Sasanian Persia and the end of Antiquity* (Aldershot 2006) VIII.16, 18, 23, 25 ,40, 42.

114 Aurelius Victor, *Caesars* [ed. and French tr. P. Dufraigne (Paris 1975)] 39.34. Cf. Theophanes, *Chronicle* [ed. C. de Boor (Leipzig 1883–85); tr. C. Mango and R. Scott (Oxford 1997)] 304, on Iranian fear of unexpected attack through Armenia.

115 Procopius, *Wars* [4:9] 2.3.37–48.

mia, but could not force the Zagros passes. Because, by contrast, the Mountain Arena's western side was open to the Mediterranean Sea, Iran enjoyed an advantage. It was possible for a strong Iranian empire—the Achaemenids or the Sasanians, but the Arsacids far less effectively—to project itself as far as the Mediterranean coast. The Sasanians managed this in the 250s, the 540s, and again in the 610s and 620s. Even the Safavids, who only rarely controlled parts of Mesopotamia, could still seriously distract the high-noon sixteenth-century Ottoman Empire if it was forced to fight on two fronts, against the Habsburgs as well, or the Russians.[116]

We may deduce as a rule of thumb, then, that strategic advantage within the Eurasian Hinge zone could be seized more easily from the East than the West. Alexander's conquests were too exceptional to disprove this.

Truth-loving Persians do not dwell upon
The trivial skirmish fought near Marathon.[117]

And by the same token, the Iranian Empire could not be ruled from Vergina. The Macedonian conquest had achieved little more than partial replacement of the Achaemenid elite by a Macedonian one, within very much the same imperial frontiers and structures.[118] The only two empires that ever gained simultaneous control of the three wings of our triptych and therefore the whole Eurasian Hinge zone—Iranian plateau, Mountain Arena, and Eastern Mediterranean—were the Achaemenids and then, a millennium after their demise, the early Caliphate. Achaemenid expansion peaked c. 559 to 486 under Cyrus, Cambyses, and Darius I,[119] and then again under Alexander, its natural continuator.[120] After the Battle of Salamis in 480, Iran no longer enjoyed natural dominance of the Eastern Mediterranean, but it did maintain a presence.[121] The Sasanians will have reestablished this only fleetingly, given the brevity of their three periods of conquest in the Roman East.[122] As for the Caliphate, the later Umayyads came to control the inland sea's eastern, southern, and western shores. The Abbasids lost the West but still enjoyed a substantial presence in the Mediterranean basin seconded by other Muslim

116 W. E. D. Allen, *Problems of Turkish power in the sixteenth century* (London 1963) 35, 38; Davutoğlu, *Στρατηγικό βάθος* [4:69] 296.

117 Robert Graves, "The Persian version."

118 P. Briant, *Histoire de l'Empire Perse de Cyrus à Alexandre* (Paris 1996) 895–96, 1077.

119 Plato [4:17], *Menexenus* 239d–240a.

120 Iranian tradition saw Alexander as either a demon who brought catastrophe, or a sage and hero: F. M. Kotwal and P. G. Kreyenbroek, "Alexander the Great ii," *EIr*, www.iranicaonline.org; W. L. Hanaway, "Eskandar-Nāma," *EIr* 8.609–12.

121 Briant, *Empire Perse* [4:118] 843–52; less sanguine, T. Kelly, "The Assyrians, the Persians, and the sea," *Mediterranean historical review* 7 (1992) 28.

122 C. Foss, *History and archaeology of Byzantine Asia Minor* (Aldershot 1990) I.724–25, on attacks on Cyprus and Rhodes in the late 610s and early 620s.

states, members of the Islamic Commonwealth, notably the Umayyads in Spain and later the Fatimids in Egypt, who both disposed of useful navies. But for Achaemenids, Sasanids, Umayyads, and Abbasids alike either the center of power or at the very least, in the case of the Umayyads, crucial resources of manpower and wealth for maintaining it, lay east of Syria. Their presence on—as distinct from around—the Mediterranean Sea was secondary in the sense of incomplete and/or transitory. For Muslims, the Indian Ocean felt much more theirs than the persistently Christian Mediterranean ever could.[123]

If we are to talk about "world empire" in Antiquity, it is to the Achaemenids and the early Caliphate that we must turn. For these there was no *direct competitor* on the world stage, India and China being too remote. Rome, by contrast, even though it bulks so large on the horizon of historians from the Atlantic world, was always twinned by Iran. And this was in fact the more usual situation: not for the Eurasian Hinge zone to form or focus world empire, but for the Mountain Arena to embroil the powers circumjacent to it. Syria-Mesopotamia, in particular, suffers from a crucial weakness—but also strength—that guarantees enmeshment in its affairs to whoever controls Iran or the Eastern Mediterranean. As the sometimes extensive but usually short-lived empires of Sargon of Akkad, the Assyrians, Babylonians, Seleucids, and—later and on a lesser scale—the Hamdānids of tenth-century Mosul and Aleppo demonstrated, the Fertile Crescent cannot maintain long-term political autonomy. It is too easily threatened from neighboring regions whose geography makes them natural fortresses and power centers: in the North and Northwest, Anatolia; in the East, as Herodotus recalls in the very last sentence of his *Histories*, the Iranian plateau;[124] in the South, Arabia; in the Southwest, Egypt, which was deeply involved in Syria during the Eighteenth Dynasty; and in the West, the Mediterranean. To confine ourselves to the First Millennium: before the Arab conquests, Anatolia and Egypt belonged to Rome's Mediterranean empire; Arabia was as yet quiescent. Therefore either Iran or Rome had to dominate the Fertile Crescent,[125] or they had to learn to coexist within it, ideally in an equilibrium of mutually recognized power, as "the world's two eyes."[126] The Umayyads and early Ab-

123 C. Picard, "La Méditerranée musulmane, un héritage omeyyade," in A. Borrut and P. M. Cobb (eds), *Umayyad legacies* (Leiden 2010) 365–402 ; id., "Espaces maritimes et polycentrisme dans l'Islam abbasside," *Annales islamologiques* 45 (2011) 23–46.

124 Cf. Dio Cassius [4:49] 40.28.4, on mid-first-century BCE Antiochenes viewing the Iranians as "neighbours and people of kindred ways."

125 See A. Kaldellis, *Procopius of Caesarea* (Philadelphia 2004) 119–28, esp. 126–27, for a subtle account of the interchangeability of Sasanian and Roman power in Syria in 540, according to Procopius; also H. Börm, "Der Perserkönig im Imperium Romanum," *Chiron* 36 (2006) 299–328.

126 Cf. D. Kennedy, "Parthia and Rome: Eastern perspectives," in D. L. Kennedy (ed.), *The Roman army in the East* (Ann Arbor 1996) 73–74.

basids, Arab dynasties that actually originated from the Mountain Arena, achieved world empire based at Damascus and Baghdad respectively. The first Umayyad caliph, Muʿāwiya (661–80), enjoyed paradigmatic success, manipulating with consummate dexterity his governors in Iraq and Egypt in order to maintain the balance of power within the Caliphate's Arabian-Mesopotamian-Syrian heartland,[127] while expanding or consolidating the Arab position in both Iran and the Eastern Mediterranean. But the Islamic Commonwealth that succeeded this brief heyday of Arab empire was composed for the most part of states based in Iran and others based in the Mountain Arena. The Buyids straddled the divide, but mainly just in Iraq and Fārs; the Seljuks embraced both great regions, but only fleetingly (in the late eleventh and early twelfth century).

Given this geopolitical reality, namely the Mountain Arena and particularly the Fertile Crescent as a vortex that pulls inward and fuses what lies around it, we are not in the least surprised to find—as already in our discussion of commonwealths—that cultural dissemination was another of its specialities. No doubt it performed this service best when it was united, especially when it formed part of a political-cultural continuum from the Iranian plateau into the East Mediterranean basin. But even when it was divided, its frontiers were always porous to commerce in both goods and ideas.

Earlier in this chapter, I already noted the pressures brought to bear on the Mediterranean paradigm by the spread of first Judaism, then Christianity, and finally Islam, beyond their places of origin along the western edge of the Mountain Arena. I made special reference to Syriac Christianity and its expansion into Iran, Central Asia, and even China. These three monotheisms are particularly prominent in our enquiry; but one ought also to mention, as another highly characteristic and dynamic product of the Mountain Arena, the missionary religion founded by the Mesopotamian prophet Mani. Mani may have failed to convert the Sasanid Shapur I, and he was done to death in 276/77. But his disciples carried exquisite scrolls and codices full of his writings across the Mediterranean and into Central Asia and China, anticipating the Christian missions in that direction.

As conductors of commerce and ideas, the Mountain Arena's plains, river valleys, and waterways offered superb lines of communication between the worlds of the Indian Ocean and the Mediterranean, via the Persian Gulf, the Tigris and Euphrates, and the Red Sea. For example, India sent spices to Antioch and Alexandria, but also ways of thought. The Syriac philosopher Bardaisan of Edessa discussed Brahmanism and Buddhism with Indian ambassadors on their way to the court of Elagabalus (218–22).[128] It is highly

127 Abbott, *Arabic literary papyri* [3:75] 3.52–53.

128 Bardaisan in (1) Jerome, *Against Jovinian* [ed. J. P. Migne, *Patrologia latina* (Paris 1844–64) 23.221–352] 2.14; (2) Porphyry, *On abstinence* [ed. and French tr. J. Bouffartigue et al. (Paris 1977–95)] 4.17.

probable that Edessene Christian traders implanted their faith on the Malabar coast where it flourishes to this day—if not in the time of the Apostle Thomas as tradition claims, then surely by the fourth century.[129] Mani both personally visited India and imagined himself in the prophetic company of Buddha and Zarathushtra as well as Jesus.[130]

Much later, the Muslim philosopher Fārābī (d. 948) and the historian Mas'ūdī (d. 956) drew a vivid if inaccurate picture of Greek medical science and Aristotelian logic being transmitted to the Arabs round the Fertile Crescent, from Alexandria to Baghdad (this will be discussed further in chapter 5). Once the Greek schools in the Egyptian metropolis closed and the teaching of medicine and Aristotle died out there, it was transferred to Antioch in the time of the Umayyad caliph 'Umar II (717–20). It persisted there until only one teacher remained, with two pupils who eventually left, "taking the books with them." One went to Ḥarrān in Northern Mesopotamia close to Edessa, and the other to Marw far away in what is today Turkmenistan. By these routes the erudition of the Greeks eventually reached Baghdad, where the scholarly Abbasid caliph Ma'mūn (813–33) especially favored it—as had several of his predecessors, but our narrative chooses to flatter Ma'mūn.

The history of Aristotelianism is in fact more than incidentally germane to my First Millennium thesis. I turn to it in the next chapter as a way of illustrating the period's cultural dynamic. Its strongly exegetical character is typical of the First Millennium's other main intellectual movements. In the next two chapters, I offer a more general account of First Millennium exegetical cultures.

129 S. Neil, *A history of Christianity in India* (Cambridge 1984–85) 1.26–34; Reed, *History of religions* 49 (2009) [4:25] 62–66; E. H. Seland, "Trade and Christianity in the Indian Ocean during late Antiquity," *JLA* 5 (2012) 72–86.

130 Fowden, *Empire to commonwealth* [4:53] 73; W. Sundermann, "Manicheism iv," *EIr*, www.iranicaonline.org.

5

EXEGETICAL CULTURES 1

ARISTOTELIANISM

Above all the Greeks is the wise Porphyry held in honour,
the master of all sciences, after the likeness of the godhead.
In all fields of knowledge did the great Plato too shine out,
and likewise subtle Democritus and the glorious Socrates,
the astute Epicurus and Pythagoras the wise
so too Hippocrates the great, and the wise Galen.
But exalted above these all is Aristotle,
surpassing all in his knowledge, both predecessors and successors:
entire wisdom did he contain in his books and writings,
making philosophy a single body, perfect and complete.
What was written concerning the wise Solomon found its fulfillment in him:
"none in any age was wise like he."

—David bar Paulos (later eighth century) (tr. S. Brock[1])

He bestrode antiquity like an intellectual colossus. No one before him had contributed so much to learning. No man after him might aspire to rival his achievements.

—J. Barnes, *Aristotle* (2000) 1

So far I have argued, rather theoretically, for the conceptual dimension of human experience as motivating our study of history; and I suggested this entails longer periodizations, especially in the case of the crucial millennium that saw the maturation of Greek philosophical thought and the emergence of rabbinic Judaism, Christianity and Islam. What is now needed is practical demonstration of how such a culturalist, ideas-oriented approach can help articulate our grasp of historical time. History is not just about ideas; it concerns polities and economies and social struggles and every aspect of human

1 S. Brock, *Syriac perspectives on late Antiquity* (London 1984) V.25.

society creative or destructive. Our First Millennium begins with Augustus as well as Christ, and any account of this period will of necessity be a story, like Ṭabarī's, of kings as well as prophets. Nevertheless, the conceptual dimension comes first, given that it has to do—I already quoted Björn Wittrock to this effect at the end of chapter 2—with

> the location of human beings in time, historicity, and . . . the capacity of human beings to bring about changes in the world, agency. [New conceptualizations] made new forms of institutions and practices . . . meaningful and possible, and indeed conceivable.

And if we ask who above all others gave Eurasians (in the sense defined in chapter 1) conceptual tools for ordering their impressions and their knowledge, and so made them more effective social and historical agents, the answer is: Aristotle. Before Aristotle there had been no shortage of effective agents, or of historians to analyze them. After Aristotle, humans were in possession of an exhaustive map showing what was known, and well-sharpened logical tools for improving and extending that map.[2]

This alone makes Aristotle a central figure on the prophetic side—no less than his pupil Alexander on the kingly side—in the history of the Greek world and all it impinged on. (Aristotle himself was skeptical about the possibility of prophecy,[3] but some of his Arabic admirers thought him "more deserving to be called an angel than a man"[4]). Eventually the rise of a new account of mankind's origin and destiny—the Christian revelation sprung from a Semitic, Jewish background—posed severe problems concerning its compatibility with the Greco-Roman thought worlds, problems that had to be solved in a variety of languages, not only Greek. Hence, parallel to the accelerated spread of Christianity after Constantine, Latin versions of Aristotle began to be made for the first time. The earliest Armenian translation appears to date from the later fifth century, and the first Syriac versions soon after (on all these, see below). These summaries and translations opened up new horizons for the dissemination of Hellenism, ultimately into Arabic as well. But the task more immediately at hand was to give the new Christian doctrine some basic expression in terms of the prevailing—and plainly irreplaceable—logical and philosophical language of Aristotle. Otherwise, it could hardly be expected to catch on among thinking people, in Greek or any other language. Arguing—which was what Christians of different stripes,

2 Encyclopedic knowledge allied to argumentation as the characteristic of Peripateticism: Agathias, *History* [ed. R. Keydell (Berlin 1967); tr. J. D. Frendo (Berlin 1976)] 2.28.5–29.1.

3 W. C. Streetman, ""If it were God who sent them . . . ": Aristotle and al-Fārābī on prophetic vision," *ASAP* 18 (2008) 211–20.

4 According to the tenth-century *Secret of secrets*: G. Fowden, "Pseudo-Aristotelian politics and theology in universal Islam," in P. F. Bang and D. Kołodziejczyk (eds), *Universal empire* (Cambridge 2012) 139–40.

and eventually Muslims too, often did when they got together, or encountered worshippers of the old gods—was based on Aristotle's logical works, the group of treatises known as his *Organon*, or *Instrument*. The First Millennium was chiefly remarkable for its generation of a Greek philosophical synthesis plus mature versions of Judaism, Christianity, and Islam. Much of this was done in the language of Aristotle. Hence the present sketch of how interest in Aristotle evolved across the whole of this extended period.[5]

By highlighting Aristotle it may be felt that I give short shrift to Hellenism more generally. The expected comparison for Judaism, Christianity, and Islam would be the whole of Greek philosophy, not just one representative. Nevertheless Aristotle was seen, as David bar Paulos puts it in the epigraph to this chapter, as having formulated "entire wisdom . . . making philosophy a single body." Not only was his doctrine deemed, as we shall see, compatible with that of his main competitor, but even the works of a late Platonist such as Plotinus (d. 270) might be circulated, at least in Arabic, as Aristotle's. Furthermore, emphasis on Aristotle has an expository advantage in a brief survey, in that it provides a single representative for a tradition that possessed powerful individual thinkers and schools, but no body of doctrine enshrined in scriptures comparable to those of the monotheist religions. It was a way of thinking, not a system of thought.[6] But since in Aristotle's mind it did prove susceptible to a degree of synthesis and systematization, he is the best choice to represent it, indeed "the most prominent (mubarriz) of the Greeks"[7]—also because his philosophy helped articulate Christian and Muslim thought too.

GREEK ARISTOTELIANISM

Aristotle was born in 384 BCE and died in 322. His relationship with Plato, his teaching career at the Lyceum in Athens, his tutoring the youthful Alexander, and his immense, innovative corpus of writings all guaranteed posthumous fame. The prophetic impetus both he and Plato gave philosophy led to major new developments in their own schools, such as Academic Skepticism, and to the emergence of new schools whether related (Stoicism) or reactive (Epicureanism). But around the start of the first century BCE a need was felt for a return to the sources, a canonization of classical masters such as had al-

5 Surveys of ancient Greek and Latin Aristotelianism in the same (collaborative) volume are not unknown, e.g., R. Sorabji (ed.), *Aristotle transformed* (London 1990). On the *Categories* (only) in Greek, Latin, and Arabic, see O. Bruun and L. Corti (eds), *Les Catégories et leur histoire* (Paris 2005). The Syriac and Armenian traditions are just starting to be incorporated: see below, pp. 140–46.

6 Cf. the parallel observations of A. Kaldellis, *Hellenism in Byzantium* (Cambridge 2007) 390.

7 Al-Kindī, *Letters* [ed. M. ʿA. H. Abū Rīda, *Al-Kindī: Rasāʾil al-falsafiya* (Cairo 1950–53)] 1.103.

ready occurred in literary studies, and a fresh engagement with the texts of Plato and Aristotle themselves.[8]

Aristotle had for the intervening two centuries been mainly known through his so-called exoteric compositions, a number of them cast in accessible dialogue form in the style of Plato. But in the first century BCE renewed interest in Aristotle led to the rediscovery of his "esoteric" writings too, the works by which he has mainly or exclusively been known ever since. These were treatises rather than dialogues, often in sketch or note form or even unfinished, and much closer to the original viva voce "prophetic" performance. A colorful but not demonstrably untrue story told how Aristotle's heirs hid his books at Scepsis in the Troad, "in a sort of tunnel, where they were damaged by mildew and worms," to stop the kings of Pergamum grabbing the collection for their library.[9] The manuscripts were discovered and taken to Athens, and thence to Rome by Sulla after his sack of the city in 86 BCE. Probably some decades later, they provided the basis for an edition of Aristotle's works devised by Andronicus of Rhodes. The importance of this edition is hard to judge: some of Aristotle's works had remained in circulation before it, and attracted at least a few readers.[10] Nonetheless Plutarch (d. c. 120) asserts that, before Andronicus, Aristotle's works had not been widely or accurately familiar, and implies that the new edition gave Peripateticism fresh impetus.[11] Another Platonist philosopher, Porphyry (d. c. 305), saw Andronicus as an important predecessor to, and paradigm for, his edition of the works of his teacher Plotinus, and says he undertook a serious remodeling of the damaged materials he worked with.[12] So Andronicus was to some degree responsible for the texture, perhaps even the shape, of the Aristotelian corpus as we have it today—still often indistinguishable from lecture notes, yet now of "scriptural" status.

8 M. Frede, "Epilogue," in K. Algra and others (eds), *The Cambridge history of Hellenistic philosophy* (Cambridge 1999) 772–76, 784; R. W. Sharples, *Peripatetic philosophy 200 BC to AD 200* (Cambridge 2010) viii; A. Falcon, *Aristotelianism in the first century BCE: Xenarchus of Seleucia* (Cambridge 2012) 17–21.

9 Strabo, *Geography* [ed. and (German) tr. S. Radt (Göttingen 2002–9)] 13.1.54; tr. and discussion by J. Barnes, "Roman Aristotle," in J. Barnes and M. Griffin (eds), *Philosophia togata* 2 (Oxford 1997) 1–8. For some reasons to believe Strabo, see J. Irigoin, "Les éditions de textes," in F. Montanari (ed.), *La philologie grecque à l'époque hellénistique et romaine* (Geneva 1994) 50–53.

10 For the thin evidence and divergent interpretations, see R. Goulet, "Andronicus de Rhodes," "Apellicon de Téos," "L'oeuvre d'Aristote," *DPA* 1.200–202, 266–67, 434–35; H. B. Gottschalk, "The earliest Aristotelian commentators," in Sorabji (ed.), *Aristotle transformed* [5:5] 55–81; Barnes, in Barnes and Griffin (eds), *Philosophia togata* 2 [5:9] 8–66 ("dispiritingly sceptical" by his own admission); M. Frede, in Algra and others (eds), *Hellenistic philosophy* [5:8] 772–76; G. Anagnostopoulos, "Aristotle's works and the development of his thought," in id. (ed.), *A companion to Aristotle* (Chichester 2009) 14–20.

11 Plutarch, *Sulla* [ed. and tr. (Italian) M. Manfredini and others (Milan 1997)] 26.1–3.

12 Porphyry, *Life of Plotinus* [ed. P. Henry and H.-R. Schwyzer, *Plotini opera* (*editio minor* Oxford 1964–83) 1.1–38; tr. A. H. Armstrong, *Plotinus* (London 1966–88) 1.3–85] 24.

Since Cicero (d. 43 BCE), who pretended to considerable knowledge of Peripateticism, does not mention Andronicus, his edition is to be located in the thirties or even later, close to the beginning of the First Millennium. After Andronicus, there was no lack of learned men interested in Aristotle, though it was perhaps not before the second century that it became at all usual to declare oneself unreservedly a Peripatetic.[13] This tendency culminated in Alexander of Aphrodisias, who flourished c. 200 CE, held a chair of philosophy at Athens (according to a recently disinterred inscription), and was the first to produce commentaries on Aristotle of sufficient weight to be not just preserved, but argued with, by posterity.[14] From our point of view and for most practical purposes, Alexander's commentaries on a very wide range of the master's works mark the beginning of Aristotelianism's exegetical phase. Indeed, Alexander came to be regarded as "the most authentic interpreter of Aristotle."[15] But at the same time he was the last significant thinker to owe *exclusive* allegiance to Aristotle, and to believe that his philosophy is not only a single, cohesive whole but also capable, from its own resources, of resolving any problem that may arise. After Alexander, Aristotelianism became part of a philosophical blend dominated by Platonism, rather than a freestanding school. Later thinkers went on dedicating whole commentaries to works of Aristotle, but in a more critical and contextualizing spirit, and with Plato looking over their shoulder.

> The worthy exegete of Aristotle's writings . . . should [not] obstinately persist in trying to demonstrate that [Aristotle] is always and everywhere infallible, as if he had enrolled himself in the Philosopher's school,

opined his last comprehensive commentator, Simplicius (d. 560).[16]

The great third-century Platonist Plotinus, for example, used Alexander's commentaries in his teaching and engaged—combatively but respectfully—with problems in Aristotle's philosophy. Porphyry says Plotinus's writings "are full of concealed Stoic and Peripatetic doctrines. Aristotle's *Metaphysics*,

13 A. Falcon, "Commentators on Aristotle," *SEP*, http://plato.stanford.edu/archives/fall2013/entries/aristotle-commentators/, §§2–3, but also (on a more cautious note) Barnes, in Barnes and Griffin (eds), *Philosophia togata* 2 [5:9] 45, and S. Fazzo, "Nicolas, l'auteur du Sommaire de la philosophie d'Aristote," *Revue des études grecques* 121 (2008) 99–126.

14 R. Goulet and M. Aouad, "Alexandros d'Aphrodisias," *DPA* 1.125–39; S. Fazzo, "Alexandros d'Aphrodisias," *DPA* Suppl. 61–70; id., in Adamson and others (eds), *Philosophy, science and exegesis* [1:35] 1.6–11; H. Baltussen, "From polemic to exegesis: The ancient philosophical commentary," *Poetics today* 28 (2007) 268–73; D. Frede, "Alexander of Aphrodisias," *SEP*, http://plato.stanford.edu/archives/sum2013/entries/alexander-aphrodisias/.

15 Simplicius, *Commentary on Aristotle's Physics* [ed. H. Diels (Berlin 1882–95)] 80.15–16.

16 Simplicius, *Commentary on Aristotle's Categories* [ed. K. Kalbfleisch (Berlin 1907); tr. (pp. 1–75) M. Chase (London 2003)] 7.23–29.

in particular, is concentrated in them."[17] An eminent twentieth-century student of Plotinus added that

> his originality showed itself, not in the discovery of a new philosophical method, or in the affirmation of a new attitude towards life, but in the constructive power which, starting from certain scattered hints in Plato, the most unsystematic of creators, and certain loose ends in Aristotle, the most inconclusive of systematisers, and utilising whatever seemed valuable in Stoicism and the later Academy, evolved a scheme of Reality at once more comprehensive and more closely knit than anything which had yet been attempted.[18]

Only we should not underestimate his pupil Porphyry's contribution to the task of reconciling, as Gibbon put it, "the strong and subtle sense of Aristotle with the devout contemplation and sublime fancy of Plato."[19] The assumption of Aristotle's essential compatibility, or "harmony," with Plato, despite his protestations to the contrary, was to become an article of faith, a characteristic expression of philosophy's exegetical phase. It is also one of the things that distinguish late Greek understanding of the philosophical tradition from the narrative espoused by most modern scholarship.[20]

Unacceptably for Platonists, Aristotle depicted God as the mover of the whole world, but not as its creator and sustainer.[21] He also identified God/the First Principle with Intellect, which is complex, whereas God must be simple.[22] But since Plato was the main authority on the world known by intellect, while Aristotle was seen as concentrating on the world as known through the senses,[23] it was possible to forgive Aristotle his misunderstandings of metaphysics, and go on treating him as a Platonist at heart. In the words of Simplicius again, Aristotle

> always refuses to deviate from nature; on the contrary, he considers even things which are above nature according to their relation to nature, just as, by contrast, the divine Plato . . . examines even natural things insofar as they participate in the things above nature.[24]

17 Porphyry, *Life of Plotinus* [5:12] 14.

18 E. R. Dodds, *Select passages illustrating Neoplatonism* (London 1923) 10.

19 Gibbon 39: 2.550; cf. G. E. Karamanolis, *Plato and Aristotle in agreement?* (Oxford 2006) 216–330.

20 R. Sorabji, *The philosophy of the commentators, 200–600 AD* (London 2004) 3.37–40; L. P. Gerson, *Aristotle and other Platonists* (Ithaca, N.Y. 2005) 1–16.

21 R. Sorabji, "Infinite power impressed: The transformation of Aristotle's physics and theology," in id. (ed.), *Aristotle transformed* [5:5] 181–98.

22 Plotinus [ed. P. Henry and H.-R. Schwyzer (editio minor Oxford 1964–83); tr. A. H. Armstrong (London 1966–88)] 5.1.9; Gerson, *Aristotle and other Platonists* [5:20] 10–11.

23 Damascius, *Life of Isidore* [2:112] 36 Zintzen, 34D Athanassiadi.

24 Simplicius, *Commentary on Aristotle's Categories* [5:16] 6.27–30.

One might put it another way: that Aristotle conveyed the "lesser mysteries," which opened the way to Plato's "mystagogy."[25] The upshot of reading Plato and Aristotle in this complementary spirit was a strong statement of the Greek philosophical world view, which left less room for damaging controversy than in earlier periods, when philosophers had been much mocked for their inability to agree. Simplicius argued for the harmony of virtually *all* Greek philosophers, against not only their own dissensions but also those Christians who gloated over them. Hence his habit of quoting extensively even from the pre-Socratics. Without Simplicius's eleventh-hour attempt to remold the more-than-millennial tradition of Greek thought, the earliest representatives of the tradition would be far less known to us.[26]

Which of Aristotle's treatises were most read, and how? There is a genre of introductions to philosophy in general and in particular to Plato or much more commonly Aristotle, several specimens of which survive from the time of the Alexandrian philosopher (and Simplicius's teacher) Ammonius son of Hermeias (d. c. 517/26) onward. The introductions to Aristotle strongly resemble each other.[27] They start by enumerating the schools of philosophy and the works of Aristotle. Then they divide philosophy into logic, ethics (and/or politics), physics, mathematics, and finally theology, since the goal is knowledge of the First Principle, God.[28] After animadverting on the qualities required in a student, the harmony of Aristotle with Plato, and Aristotle's use of obscurity to exclude the unworthy, the introductions then move on to the *Categories*, which were regarded as the portal to not only logic, but the whole of philosophy and indeed all human knowledge. Often the *Categories*, being hard to grasp, were prefaced by Porphyry's famous *Introduction* (*Isagoge*) to logic; and there were even introductions (*Prolegomena*) to the *Isagoge* and philosophy in general. After the *Categories* the next works to be read were *On interpretation*, *Prior analytics*, *Posterior analytics*, *Topics*, *Sophistical refutations*, *Rhetoric*, and *Poetics*.[29] These together made up the *Organon*, whose title underlined the strictly instrumental role of logic in the overall pursuit of philosophy.[30] Without logic under one's belt—*Prolegomena*, *Isagoge*, *Organon*—there was no progress to be had in ethics (except of the most practical sort), physics, mathematics, or theology.

25 Marinus, *Proclus, or On happiness* [ed. and tr. (French) H. D. Saffrey and A.-P. Segonds (Paris 2001)] 13.

26 H. Baltussen, *Philosophy and exegesis in Simplicius* (London 2008) 9–10, 62–64, 137–38, 203, 211–15.

27 L. G. Westerink and J. Trouillard, *Prolégomènes à la philosophie de Platon* (Paris 1990) XLIII–LVI; P. Hoffmann, "La fonction des prologues exégétiques dans la pensée pédagogique néoplatonicienne," in J.-D. Dubois and B. Roussel (eds), *Entrer en matière: Les prologues* (Paris 1998) 215–22.

28 See also Marinus, *Proclus* [5:25] 13, with n. 1 in the Saffrey-Segonds edition.

29 P. Hoffmann, "What was commentary in late Antiquity?," in M. L. Gill and P. Pellegrin (eds), *A companion to ancient philosophy* (Oxford 2006) 605–6.

30 J. Brunschwig, "L'*Organon*. Tradition grecque," *DPA* 1.482–91.

Though Plato, not Aristotle, had the last word in theology, the overwhelming bulk of the philosophical literature produced in fifth- and sixth-century Alexandria—which along with Athens was the main center of philosophical teaching at this period—consisted of commentaries on Aristotle's work, notably the *Categories* and the other logical treatises, but also the *Physics*, *On the soul*, the *Metaphysics*, and others.[31] Probably only few students got to Plato. Even Aristotle was perceived as anything but easy. The sixth-century Syriac scholar Paul the Persian estimated "ten to twenty years" for getting a grip on him, allowing for occasional refreshment.[32] But Aristotle was a gift to overachievers, allowing Augustine of Hippo (d. 430) a chance to mock his rhetoric teacher,[33] and Proclus of Athens (d. 485) to crow about how he had got it all done in "less than two years"—though he seems to have left no commentaries.[34]

Commentaries might be compiled from lecture notes, or inserted as marginalia in the teacher's commentary. In either case the pupil's work came to be regarded as his own rather than his teacher's, and knowledge achieved a seamless progression.[35] But alongside this conservative, accumulative approach to exegesis, commentaries also offered a flexible format that left room for innovation. The text could be analyzed as minutely as one liked, and Aristotle's coherence with both himself and Plato plainly demonstrated—on such matters the disjointed, allusive manner of Aristotle's esoteric works offered plenty of scope for exegesis. Old interpretations could be revisited and new ones propounded in the guise of open-ended discussion of possibilities. Fresh ideas were advanced cumulatively, with due reverence accorded both the author and earlier commentators—except that older commentaries were unlikely to be recopied unless outstanding like those of Alexander of Aphrodisias.

There was no question of investigating, in this line-by-line format, such modern concerns as Aristotle's personal intellectual development, in relation to either Plato or himself. It was assumed all his works purveyed the same monolithic teaching.[36] Moreover his prestige was such that he might still provide the conceptual and linguistic framework even when he was being

31 Catalogues of Greek commentaries on Aristotle: R. Goulet, "L'oeuvre d'Aristote," *DPA* 1.437–41; M. Chase, "Les commentaires grecs et byzantins," *DPA* Suppl. 113–21.

32 D. Gutas, *Greek philosophers in the Arabic tradition* (Aldershot 2000) IX.235.

33 Augustine, *Confessions* [ed. J. J. O'Donnell (Oxford 1992); tr. H. Chadwick (Oxford 1991)] 4.16.28–29.

34 Marinus, *Proclus* [5:25] 9, 13; cf. Proclus, *Commentary on the Cratylus of Plato* [ed. G. Pasquali (Leipzig 1908)] 2 (Peripatetic logic accessible to all but the most stupid); C. Hasnaoui, "La tradition des commentaires grecs sur le *De interpretatione* (*PH*) d'Aristote jusqu'au VII[e] s.," *DPA* Suppl. 156.

35 See, e.g., Marinus, *Proclus* [5:25] 12, 26, 27; R. Sorabji, "John Philoponus," in id. (ed.), *Philoponus* [4:21] 43–44. On commentaries generally, see I. Hadot, "Der fortlaufende philosophische Kommentar," in W. Geerlings and C. Schulze (eds), *Der Kommentar in Antike und Mittelalter* (Leiden 2002) 183–99; Fazzo, in Adamson and others (eds), *Philosophy, science and exegesis* [1:35] 1.1–19.

36 Elias, *Commentary on Aristotle's Categories* [ed. A. Busse (Berlin 1900)] 123.7–9.

attacked, as by the Christian John Philoponus (d. 570) in his *On the eternity of the world against Aristotle*, a polemical treatise in commentary form. Philoponus was the first to debate with Aristotle in terms of scriptural revelation as well as philosophical rationality;[37] for the Bible (and Philoponus) held the physical world was created and had a beginning, while for Aristotle it had always existed. His in-depth engagement with Aristotle on a front far wider than just the *Organon* provoked an attack from Simplicius the champion of the Greek tradition's unity and integrity, especially as regards the eternity of matter.[38] Simplicius rejected Philoponus's treatment of Aristotle, while Christian critics excoriated his view that Moses taught a Ptolemaic, spherical cosmology.[39] Yet the dialogue of revealed religion and philosophy could hardly be wished away. The Church of Constantinople anathematized Philoponus in 680 and Christians forgot him; but Muslim thinkers found in him just the arguments they needed on the beginnings of the universe.[40]

Even when strictly philosophical in content, late Greek commentaries might also partake of the nature of a prayer, a hymn, or a spiritual exercise, a map for the soul's ascent, especially if one of Plato's more theological dialogues, such as the *Timaeus*, was the subject.[41] That commentaries on Plato have survived from Athens more than Alexandria reflects not a fundamental difference in intellectual orientation between a cultic-theological Athens and a rational Alexandria, but rather a greater exposure of the Alexandrian schools to Christian students and the sensitivities of the city's powerful ecclesiastical Establishment. "An exegetical preference for Aristotle would be less likely to precipitate a sense of rivalry with Christian theology, whereas Proclus' detailed system of Platonic dogmatics easily appears as if it were almost intended as an alternative to Christian doctrine."[42] Compromises had to be made; and while Athens—especially Proclus—produced totalizing syntheses and summaries of ancient Platonism, Alexandria's flexibility fitted it to become the foundation not just for Christian (including Armenian and Syriac) philosophy, but eventually for Arabic Aristotelianism too, and the attempt to formulate a rational approach to reality capable of accommodating the Qur'ān. That commentary was the preferred vehicle, whatever revered foundational text—*Parmenides*, *Categories*, Gospels, or Qur'ān—one was dealing with, reflects the substantial common ground, and scriptural

37 C. Wildberg, "John Philoponus," *SEP*, http://plato.stanford.edu/archives/fall2008/entries/philoponus/.

38 Baltussen, *Philosophy and exegesis* [5:26] 176–88.

39 Grillmeier, *Jesus der Christus* [4:72] 2/4.153–54.

40 R. Wisnovsky, "Yaḥyā al-Naḥwī," *EIs^2* 11.251–53.

41 L. Brisson, "Le commentaire comme prière destinée à assurer le salut de l'âme," in M.-O. Goulet-Cazé (ed.), *Le commentaire entre tradition et innovation* (Paris 2000) 329–53; Baltussen, *Philosophy and exegesis* [5:26] 195; A. Fürst, "Origen: Exegesis and philosophy in early Christian Alexandria," *IBALA* 23.

42 H. Chadwick, *Boethius* (Oxford 1981) 18.

orientation, shared by learned exponents and systematizers of all these First Millennium traditions of thought, in what I here call the exegetical phase.

This is a quite different perspective from the one which sees Justinian's ban on philosophical teaching at Athens in 529 as the "end of Antiquity." As I already remarked in chapter 1, the prestige of Plato and Athens has imposed premature closure on a period now coming to be seen as one of continued intellectual activity and dissemination. Partly this reevaluation is based on recognition that the Aristotelian commentators were not so stuck to their texts that they were unable to think new thoughts. Partly it is a more general acknowledgment of late Platonism's ability to engage modern minds caught somewhere between reason and religion. In other words, a substantial region of later Greek thought is well on the way to getting over its inferiority complex vis-à-vis the "classical," in comparison with which both the commentaries stigmatized as "derivative" and the Platonists downgraded to "Neo-" have been deemed distinctly parasitic.[43] This development reinforces my argument for a First Millennium built on the power and legacy of ideas.

CHRISTIAN POLEMIC

Aristotelianism not only enjoyed its own almost millennial exegetical age between Alexander of Aphrodisias and Ibn Sīnā c. 1000; it also contributed vitally to Christian exegesis.

Aristotle would hardly have been rendered into Armenian and Syriac, or probably Arabic, had not Christians early on—centuries before Philoponus—felt a need for his logic in refining and propagating their faith, and developing a common terminology in which to argue. Philosophical opponents of Christianity like the second-century Platonist Celsus emphasized the rigor and sophistication of their way of thought compared to the simplicity—in content and style—of the Gospels. Answering Celsus, the learned third-century Alexandrian Christian Origen, already encountered in chapter 3, quoted Proverbs, Ecclesiasticus, and the Epistle of Titus to show that the scriptures likewise encourage study of dialectic (the art of arguing) because "proofs are friendly," as Plato put it, while preaching the Gospel involves "refuting the adversaries" too.[44] In his school at Caesarea, Origen took his pupils through dialectic and logic, physics including geometry and astronomy, and ethics, before getting to Christian theology and the study of scripture.[45]

It was notably in the schools of Alexandria that, in ensuing generations, Christian intellectuals sharpened their wits and deployed their eristic skills

43 Cf. Baltussen, *Poetics today* 28 (2007) [5:14], esp. 248, 262, 273–75.

44 Origen, *Against Celsus* [3:39] 6.7.

45 Gregory Thaumaturgus, *Address to Origen* [ed. and tr. (French) H. Crouzel (Paris 1969)] 7–15; Eusebius, *Ecclesiastical history* [3:35] 6.18.3–4.

on each other as well as their pagan critics. The teachings of Arius of Alexandria (d. 336) had a markedly Platonic tinge, presenting Christ as the created Son of an utterly transcendent God rather than a flesh-and-blood man who is also uncreated God. An appropriate scriptural formula eluded the bishops summoned to settle the dispute at the Council of Nicaea in 325, so resort was had to the philosophical term homoousios, "consubstantial."[46] Second-generation Arian controversialists like the Syrian Aetius (d. c. 366) or the Cappadocian Eunomius (d. 394) studied Aristotle in Alexandria and then displayed their mastery of the technical vocabulary in the *Categories*—so ideally suited to the discussion of the divine attributes—during their controversies with the proponents of Nicaea. In this way they might secure ecclesiastical patronage and even imperial favor. Some complained they had turned theologia into technologia, "logic-chopping" that could be mastered from a manual of withering, even sarcastic retorts such as Aetius's *Syntagmation*.[47] While patristic interest in Aristotle grew much less fast than in Plato, he was frequently invoked in the context of apologetic and polemic. It became a commonplace that his categories and syllogisms were at the root of all "heresy."[48]

The Carthaginian theologian Tertullian (d. c. 225) had already called down

> a plague on Aristotle, who taught them dialectic, the art which destroys as much as it builds, which changes its opinions like a coat, forces its conjectures, is stubborn in argument, works hard at being contentious and is a burden even to itself. For it reconsiders every point to make sure it never finishes a discussion.[49]

In the 370s and 380s Christian intellectuals began to pride themselves on thinking "as fishermen" rather than "as Aristotle."[50] Poses like this no doubt explain why some patristic writers drew on Aristotle without mentioning his name. But Nicaea had set the example of resort to philosophy. Later, both

46 M. Frede, "Les *Catégories* d'Aristote et les Pères de l'Église grecs," in Bruun and Corti (eds), *Catégories* [5:5] 157–58.

47 On Aetius and Eunomius and their critics: R. Lim, *Public disputation, power, and social order in late Antiquity* (Berkeley 1995) 112–38. Also L. R. Wickham, "The *Syntagmation* of Aetius the Anomean," *Journal of theological studies* 19 (1968) 532–69.

48 D. T. Runia, "Festugière revisited: Aristotle in the Greek Patres," *Vigiliae christianae* 43 (1989) 1–34; J. Barnes, "Les Catégories et les *Catégories*," and Frede, *"Catégories"* [5:46], in Bruun and Corti (eds), *Catégories* [5:5] 58–60, 151–55.

49 Tertullian, *The prescriptions against the heretics* [ed. and tr. (French) R.-F. Refoulé (Paris 1957); tr. S. L. Greenslade, *Early Latin theology* (London 1956) 31–64] 7.6–7.

50 Epiphanius, *Panarion* [ed. K. Holl (Leipzig 1915–33), revised J. Dümmer (Berlin 1980–), index (Berlin 2006); tr. H. F. Williams (Leiden 1987–94)] 76.37.16; Gregory of Nazianzus, *oration* 23 [ed. and tr. (French) J. Mossay (Paris 1980)] 12; E. Schwartz and others (eds), *Acta conciliorum oecumenicorum* (Strasbourg 1914–) 2.5, 84.2–3; cf. A. Grillmeier, ""Piscatorie"—"Aristotelice,"" in id., *Mit ihm und in ihm* (Freiburg 1978²) 283–300; G. Podskalsky (tr. G. D. Metallenos), *Ἡ ἑλληνικὴ θεολογία ἐπὶ Τουρκοκρατίας 1453–1821* (Athens 2005, revised edition) 44 n. 3.

supporters and opponents of Chalcedon mired themselves in Aristotelian logic and syllogistic and churned out collections of theological definitions, or Christological problems and their solutions, to rehearse their debates.[51] A rhetorical coup might more easily clinch a non-scholarly disputation than resort to logical subtlety. But the *Organon* became an accepted weapon in the polemicist's armory during the sixth century, even in the Syriac world.[52] While the Platonizing theology of Ps.-Dionysius the Areopagite (c. 500) had only gradual impact, even a Platonist like Maximus the Confessor (d. 662) resorted to Aristotle when he wanted to discuss Christology.[53] When Anastasius of Sinai (d. after 701) equates each of the ten horns of the Beast in Revelation with a noted anti-Chalcedonian heresiarch who derived his error from one of Aristotle's ten categories,[54] one notes not only the pot calling the kettle black, but also the ambiguity of Aristotle, so tempting to blame but also to mine.

Among the great questions the historian must pose is whether these conflicts of ideas undermined the social fabric and had political repercussions. A recent student of public disputation in late Antiquity concluded,

> Writings such as the *Categories* were considered dangerous because they furnished a precise, respected philosophical vocabulary for constructing propositions about the divine, which, in situations of open disputation, threatened to upset established patterns of social authority when appropriated by self-taught men [the likes of Aetius and Eunomius] who had not been socialized into an ethos subordinating individual advantage to "the common good."[55]

What was at issue was once more the interaction of ideas and social or political history—"new conceptualizations" giving rise to "new forms of institutions and practices," as Wittrock puts it. And as the new institution and new practice par excellence, namely the Church, spread through the nations, it desired to preach its Gospel and its doctrines in their own languages. Now as never before, the philosophical vocabulary in which Christian teaching was articulated had to be rendered and adapted for those who thought and communicated in Latin, Armenian, or Syriac as well as or—increasingly—instead of Greek.[56] It was to a polyglot but also intellectually riven world that the

51 Grillmeier, *Jesus der Christus* [4:72] 2/1.94–100.

52 D. King, *The earliest Syriac translation of Aristotle's Categories* (Leiden 2010) 5–8, id., "Why were the Syrians interested in Greek philosophy?", in P. Wood (ed.), *History and identity in the late antique Near East* (New York 2013) 61–81.

53 D. Krausmüller, "Aristotelianism and the disintegration of the late antique theological discourse," *IBALA* 151–64.

54 Anastasius of Sinai, *Guide* [ed. K.-H. Uthemann (Turnhout 1981)] 6.2, 100.

55 Lim, *Public disputation* [5:47] 232.

56 Coptic sources have so far yielded little philosophy and no Aristotle. The more philosophically inclined Greek Church Fathers are scantily represented in Coptic translation. If there was some interest

Qur'ān was vouchsafed, and whose divisions it vigorously condemned (below, p. 188).

ARISTOTLE IN LATIN, ARMENIAN, AND SYRIAC

While Justinian's closing the Athens schools in 529 reflected Christian suspicion of their Platonic philosophy, two scholars at opposite ends of the Roman world, Boethius in Italy and Sergius of Reshʿaina east of Ḥarrān in Syria, had recently produced work which helped guarantee Aristotle's hold on both Christian and—eventually—Muslim minds for centuries to come. Historians lavish attention on Justinian's ordinance of 529, but leave the rise of Aristotelian scholarship outside—or for that matter inside—the Greek world to historians of philosophy. The clash of paganism and Christianity, especially with an emperor involved, seems like real history. The less spectacular yet more durable dissemination and working out of ideas is harder to dramatize and evaluate, even though the particular ideas we are interested in here still mattered, and at the very heart of power. A stray text, recently recognized, apparently reveals that Menas, praetorian prefect in 528 to 529, was prepared to admire Plato for his literary style, but deemed Aristotle the master of thought. Nor was he alone.[57]

In Ostrogothic Italy the senatorial scholar Boethius, consul in 510 but imprisoned and executed by King Theodoric c. 525, planned to translate as much as he could find of both Plato and Aristotle,[58] hitherto known in Latin only for—respectively—half the *Timaeus* plus parts of the *Organon*, though there had been a well-established school tradition in logic since the mid-fourth-century translations by Marius Victorinus. What Boethius actually managed to finish before his premature death was translations of and commentaries on Porphyry's *Introduction* and Aristotle's *Categories* and *On interpretation*; translations of the *Prior analytics, Posterior analytics, Topics* and *Sophistical refutations*; several original works on Aristotelian logic; and some

---

in philosophy outside the Greek schools of Alexandria, it was in the cosmopolitan monasteries around the city, with their substantial contingent of learned Syrian monks. Cf. T. Orlandi, "Traduzioni dal greco al copto," in G. Fiaccadori (ed.), *Autori classici in lingue del vicino e medio oriente* (Rome 1990) 93–104; J. Gascou, "The Enaton," and K. H. Kuhn, "Philosophy," in A. S. Atiya (ed.), *The Coptic encyclopedia* (New York 1991) 954–58, 1958.

57 M. Rashed, *L'héritage aristotélicien* (Paris 2007) 293–302, editing verses found in ms. Paris gr. 1116, f.128r. Compare Agathias, *History* [5:2] 2.28.2–3 (Plato), 2.28.6–29.1 (Aristotle). Also Gibbon 42: 2.707: "If the reason of the Stagyrite might be equally dark, or equally intelligible in every tongue, the dramatic art and verbal argumentation of the disciple of Socrates, appear to be indissolubly mingled with the grace and perfection of his Attic style."

58 Chadwick, *Boethius* [5:42] 108–73, esp. 135–36 and 140 on Boethius's plan of work and translation style (also S. Ebbesen, "Boethius as a translator and Aristotelian commentator," *IBALA* 121–33), and 115–18 on Marius Victorinus; S. Gersh, "Boethius," *DPA* 2.117–22.

scholia, perhaps on the *Physics*. Among Boethius's motives for undertaking this project was his reverence for both Plato and Aristotle, and his wish to demonstrate their harmony in line with the teachings of Porphyry, for whom likewise he nourished the greatest respect. At the same time he was a Christian much involved in Church affairs. And while Aristotle was all too often set to work by Christian thinkers in the course of party strife, Boethius was convinced, to quote a scholar well versed in ecumenical negotiation,

> that a number of divisive problems in ecclesiastical communion are created simply by a fog of linguistic confusions. Among logicians he is one of that rare species who hopes, by drawing distinctions and looking for clear classification, to reconcile rather than to separate.[59]

In particular he set out to demonstrate, in the fifth of his theological tractates, how Chalcedonian Christology holds the via media between two-nature "Nestorianism" and the miaphysite view that Christ is one nature as well as one person.

For at least six centuries, Boethius's carefully literal versions, made with almost religious respect for the originals, served as the Latin world's sole direct access to the Stagirite's fundamental contribution to logic, and therefore theology. After the Lombard invasion of Italy in 568 there was little margin for learned leisure. Philosophy was not entirely done for in the Latin world—its orderly habits of thought still underlay the encyclopedism of Isidore of Seville (d. 636).[60] But where Boethius drew intellectual energy from Alexandria, while his far longer-lived contemporary and fellow-senatorial Cassiodorus (d. c. 580) aspired to upgrade the Christian schools of Rome on the model of the schools of Alexandria and Nisibis,[61] in the following generations it was only in the East that philosophy was still cultivated outside its Greek homelands—in Syria as we shall shortly see, but also in Armenia. Even here, though, philosophy meant, in practice, almost exclusively the *Organon*—in other words, it provided no more than the basic tools for thinking with.

The *Categories* were, it seems, already translated into Armenian in the fifth century.[62] There followed, apparently in the later sixth or seventh century,[63] various other Aristotelian translations, including commentaries by one or other of the two similar and sometimes hard-to-distinguish Alexandrian philosophers and pupils of Olympiodorus (d. after 565), namely Elias (fl. mid-sixth century) and David (fl. second half of sixth century), the latter

59 Chadwick, *Boethius* [5:42] 190, and the pages following, on the fifth theological tractate.

60 J. Fontaine, "Isidore de Séville," *DPA* 3.879–90.

61 Cassiodorus, *Institutions* [ed. R. A. B. Mynors (Oxford 1937); tr. L. W. Jones, *An introduction to divine and human readings* (New York 1946)] 1.pref.1.

62 R. Bodéüs (ed.), *Aristote* [*Catégories*] (Paris 2001) CLVII.

63 A. Terian, "The Hellenizing school," in N. G. Garsoïan and others (eds), *East of Byzantium* (Washington, D.C. 1982) 178–83; Inglebert, *Interpretatio Christiana* [3:31] 567 n. 30.

possibly himself an Armenian.[64] These translations tended, like Boethius's, toward the literal, full of calques both syntactical and lexical[65]—Armenian had acquired its own alphabet only c. 400. Building on these foundations, and especially on David's definition of the subdivisions of philosophy, Ananias of Shirak (d. 685), Isidore of Seville's younger contemporary and fellow spirit, was able to complete by the year 666 an encyclopedia of Greek science called the *K'nnikon* (from the Greek *Kanonikon* or *Chronikon*), covering the basic quadrivium of arithmetic, music, geometry (including geography), and astronomy, along with calendrical studies.[66] This compilation became one of the pillars of subsequent Armenian erudition. Yet, for all that he had pupils and influenced later Armenian thought, "Ananias appears to have been an isolated figure with no one comparable to him in Armenian intellectual history known to have been working before, during or after his time."[67] Whatever its intrinsic vigor and durability, the Armenian learned tradition did not feed into and nourish either the larger Christian world or the sphere of Islam. Its early interest in Aristotle ran along lines closely similar to those we observe in the Syriac sphere;[68] yet it was the Syriac tradition, through its linkage to the Arabic translation movement, which became not just a beneficiary of but a contributor to mainstream intellectual history.

While Ephrem of Nisibis (d. 373) still warned against the poisoned wisdom of the Greeks (yet deployed philosophical concepts in his work), the disputes arising from Chalcedon forced thinkers like Philoxenus of Mabbug (d. 523) to develop a more systematic Christology founded on Aristotelian metaphysics.[69] The *Organon* began to be translated into Syriac in the mid-sixth century, and with increasing impetus and literalness in the seventh, so that two or even three versions were made of the earlier, more frequented treatises. Some commentaries were translated too, or composed in Syriac.[70] In the preface to an exposition of the *Categories*, Sergius of Resh'aina

64 On both see J.-P. Mahé, "David l'Invincible dans la tradition arménienne," in I. Hadot (ed.), *Simplicius, Commentaire sur les Catégories* 1 (Leiden 1990) 189–207; R. Goulet, "Elias," *DPA* 3.57–66; and various contributions in V. Calzolari and J. Barnes (eds), *L'oeuvre de David l'Invincible et la transmission de la pensée grecque dans la tradition arménienne et syriaque* (Leiden 2009).

65 V. Calzolari, "Aux origines de la formation du corpus philosophique en Arménie," in D'Ancona (ed.), *Libraries* [3:3] 259–78.

66 J.-P. Mahé, "Quadrivium et cursus d'études au VIIe siècle en Arménie et dans le monde byzantin d'après le "K'nnikon" d'Anania Širakac'i," *Travaux et mémoires* (Collège de France, Centre de recherche d'histoire et civilisation de Byzance) 10 (1987) 159–206; Hewsen, *Geography* [4:35].

67 Hewsen, *Geography* [4:35] 14; T. Greenwood, "A reassessment of the life and mathematical problems of Anania Širakac'i," *Revue des etudes arméniennes* 33 (2011) 131–79.

68 M. Hugonnard-Roche, "La tradition gréco-syriaque des commentaries d'Aristote," in Calzolari and Barnes (eds), *David l'Invincible* [5:64] 166–73.

69 K. Pinggéra, "Syrische Christen als Vermittler antiker Bildung an den Islam," *Ostkirchliche Studien* 58 (2009) 36–56.

70 Hugonnard-Roche, *Logique d'Aristote* [3:8] 5–20 (and 29–33, 37, 83–86, on translation style); id., "Le corpus philosophique syriaque aux VIe-VIIe siècles," in D'Ancona (ed.), *Libraries* [3:3] 279–91; id. [5:68], in Calzolari and Barnes (eds), *David l'Invincible* [5:64] 153–73; King, *Earliest Syriac translation*

(d. 536) emphasized how Aristotle was the first to unite the scattered domains of human knowledge into a coherent whole, just as a wise doctor assembles the materials for his cures.[71] Although Sergius's surviving translations are mostly of medical works by Galen (d.c. 216) and include nothing authentic by Aristotle, he was aware that, without the theoretical framework of Aristotle's logic, medicine and philosophy and even the inner meaning of scripture would remain a closed book. He saw in the corpus of Aristotle's writings a survey of human knowledge and the best guide to its systematization and structure. He planned to write introductions to each of Aristotle's works in their proper sequence: practical philosophy, physics, mathematics, and finally theology. His project was not only contemporary with but also similar in scale to Boethius's, and as much influenced by the teaching traditions of his alma mater Alexandria, still the world leader in science, philosophy, *and* medicine.

Syriac literature is largely Christian. Sergius was a (Chalcedonian) Christian with, as we shall see, theological interests. Yet there were dissenters. In a treatise on Aristotelian logic addressed, originally in Syriac or Middle Persian, to the Iranian philosopher-king Khosrow I (531–78/79), and much influenced by—again—the Alexandrians Elias and/or David, Paul the Persian compared knowledge which addresses what is near, manifest and uncontroversial, with belief which deals with invisibles such as God, not exactly describable and therefore likely to spur doubt and dispute.[72] Therefore, Paul argued, knowledge—meaning philosophy and in particular logic—is better than belief; for knowledge is authoritative, gives access to all the world's beauty, and pacifies the soul by showing it the realm of Intellect. A story circulated that Paul was denied episcopal advancement and converted to Mazdaism. He represented the other extreme of Christian reaction to philosophy compared to Ephrem's or Anastasius of Sinai's view that it was the font of all evil. Between came Christian theologians and philosophers like Elias and David who, sometimes with misgivings, deployed Aristotle in defense of their faith, and accommodated non-Christian doctrines such as the eternity of matter.[73] Such, broadly speaking, was the position of Sergius too.

[5:52] 79. In general on the growing literalness of translation technique, see D. King, *The Syriac versions of the writings of Cyril of Alexandria* (Louvain 2008) 15–25, 358–60.

71 H. Hugonnard-Roche, "Aux origines de l'exégèse orientale de la logique d'Aristote," *Journal asiatique* 277 (1989) 8–13; id., *Logique d'Aristote* [3:8] 168, 175 n. 1, 182–85. For a bibliography of Sergius's works, see http://www.cardiff.ac.uk/share/research/centres/clarc/projects/latinandsyriac/list-of-serguis-works.html.

72 Gutas, *Greek philosophers* [5:32] IX, esp. 247–48; J. Teixidor, *Aristote en syriaque* (Paris 2003) 37–39; P. Bruns, "Paul der Perser," *Römische Quartalschrift* 104 (2009) 28–53, esp. 45–47. On Paul's debt to Alexandria: Gutas, *Greek philosophers* [5:32] IX.238–50. On Sasanian Aristotelianism generally: J. T. Walker, *The legend of Mar Qardagh* (Berkeley 2006) 180–90; D. Gutas, "Origins in Baghdad," in R. Pasnau (ed.), *The Cambridge history of medieval philosophy* (Cambridge 2010) 15–17, esp. n. 18.

73 Westerink and Trouillard, *Prolégomènes* [5:27] XXXVI, XXXVIII; cf. Chadwick, *Boethius* [5:42] 22. For the possibility Elias and David were still polytheists, see C. Wildberg, "Elias," *SEP*, http://

Whatever these modalities of Christian response to Aristotle, it was the Church that mainly patronized translation of Aristotle's logical works into Syriac from the sixth century onward, to facilitate its own priorities such as the debates around Chalcedon.[74] The existence of commentaries on Aristotle, as well as translations, implies there were schools where these texts were studied.[75] The outstanding center of Syriac scholarship, including Aristotelianism, was the monastery of Qenneshre on the Syrian Euphrates, the seat of the Syrian miaphysite patriarch for most of the seventh century.[76] Among its alumni were members of that notable group of intellectuals who, during the seventh and eighth centuries, ensured that Syria-Palestine, and in particular its Syriac speakers, stayed far ahead of Constantinople culturally.[77] At a time when East Roman intellectuals were focusing almost exclusively on theology, various figures associated with Qenneshre, most notably Severus Sebokht (d. 666/67) and his pupil Jacob of Edessa (d. 708), were *also* working on Aristotle, especially his logic,[78] and on cosmology, astronomy, the natural sciences, and the astrolabe.[79] Their achievements parallel those of Ananias of Shirak in Armenia, at the same period. Jacob perhaps did more than anyone else to ensure the survival of Greek learning in Syriac, and hence in Arabic too.

What we see, then, in the sixth to seventh centuries, is a Syriac scholarly elite at least part of which was eager to incorporate the whole of Aristotle, and all useful secular knowledge (such as Galen's medicine), into the Christian worldview. The tenth-century Muslim philosopher Fārābī, who studied with Syriac Christian teachers, claimed (with some support in the texts which survive to us) that Syriac commitment to logic extended no further than *Prior analytics* 1.7. This is the point where Aristotle passes from syllogistic (in which a pair of premises gives rise to an unavoidable conclusion, e.g., A = B, C = A, therefore C = B) to modal logic (where the truth of the premises, and therefore of the conclusion too, is qualified by "necessarily"/ "possibly"), which Christians supposedly regarded as inimical to their faith.

plato.stanford.edu/archives/fall2008/entries/elias; id., "David," *SEP*, http://plato.stanford.edu/archives/fall2008/entries/david/.

74 Walker, *Legend of Mar Qardagh* [5:72] 187–88.

75 H. Hugonnard-Roche, "Jacob of Edessa and the reception of Aristotle," in Romeny (ed.), *Jacob of Edessa* [3:92] 217, 218.

76 Tannous, *Syria* [1:10] 277–83, 344–46; M. Debié, "Livres et monastères en Syrie-Mésopotamie d'après les sources syriaques," in F. Jullien (ed.), *Le monachisme syrien* (Paris 2010) 142–43.

77 L. I. Conrad, "Varietas syriaca," in G. J. Reinink and A. C. Klugkist (eds), *After Bardaisan* (Leuven 1999) 85–105, esp. 90–91 on Severus and Jacob; Fowden, *Quṣayr ʿAmra* [1:32] 299; G. Cavallo, "Qualche riflessione sulla "collezione filosofica,"" in D'Ancona (ed.), *Libraries* [3:3] 164.

78 Severus Sebokht: Hugonnard-Roche, *Logique d'Aristote* [3:8] 18. Jacob of Edessa: id. [5:75], in Romeny (ed.), *Jacob of Edessa* [3:92] 205–22 (and 205–6 on Qenneshre generally); M. Wilks, "Jacob of Edessa's use of Greek philosophy in his Hexaemeron," in Romeny (ed.), *Jacob of Edessa* [3:92] 223–38. See also King, *Earliest Syriac translation* [5:52] 10–11, 36–37; J. W. Watt, "Von Alexandrien nach Baghdad," in A. Fürst (ed.), *Origenes und sein Erbe in Orient und Okzident* (Münster 2011) 213–26.

79 J. Teixidor (ed.), "La scienza siriaca," *Enciclopedia italiana: Storia della scienza* 4(1) (Rome 2001) 3–71.

But apart from (1) the difficulty of modal logic, which had caused it to be skirted by many Greek and Latin students too, and (2) the fact that many Syrians were bilingual so had no need of translations, we have evidence that the whole of the *Organon* was in fact known in Syriac.[80] Nor is this surprising: logic remained attractive because it could support ontological conclusions—about the very nature of being or reality—derived from Christian teaching and therefore quite different from those Aristotle himself had espoused. Porphyry's studious avoidance of ontology in presenting the *Categories* to his Platonist audience had already implied the same point, and in fact prepared the way for Christian exploitation of Aristotelian logic.[81] Among Syriac scholars, one might also find a Jacob of Edessa prepared to tackle even the *Metaphysics*, or at least the lexicon of philosophical terms in book 5, for the light it could throw on the Christian theological vocabulary of "nature," "substance," "hypostasis," "person."[82]

Another apparent limitation of Syriac philosophy in this phase was its neglect of Plato (though, as with all gaps in the Syriac bibliography, we must allow for the bilingual Syrian elite reading Plato, and indeed untranslated Aristotle, in the original). Where Alexandria saw Aristotle as ideally the prelude to Plato, Syriac scholars saw him as philosophy's consummation, to be approached with the same reverence late Platonists kept for his teacher.[83] (The parallel between Sergius and Boethius breaks down here.) Yet by more subterranean channels late Platonism did fertilize the Syriac mind, notably through Sergius of Resh'aina's translation of the Christian mystic Ps.-Dionysius the Areopagite, probably a Syrian pupil or reader of the Athenian Platonist Proclus. That Sergius translated Dionysius but not Aristotle may imply he saw Dionysius as directly accessible, without scholastic/logical preparation, to monks and others of ascetic disposition; or he assumed a bilingual audience. But as translation of Aristotle proceeded, this inconsistency dissolved. And another version of Dionysius followed in the eighth century.[84] Dionysius was to Sergius's Aristotle as Plato was to Alexandria's: the finest flower of divine contemplation. Together, Aristotle and Dionysius might provide a Syriac ascent comparable to the lesser and greater mysteries of Aristotle and Plato. Both ascents, but especially the Christian one, remind us that what all too easily seems like a history of books is a story of people, and that our exegetical cultures nourish communities, schools, and monas-

80 H. Daiber, "Die Aristotelesrezeption in der syrischen Literatur," in D. Kuhn and H. Stahl (eds), *Die Gegenwart des Altertums* (Heidelberg 2001) 331–35; King, *Earliest Syriac translation* [5:52] 11–12.

81 Hugonnard-Roche, *Logique d'Aristote* [3:8] 145–46.

82 Hugonnard-Roche, *Logique d'Aristote* [3:8] 51–53.

83 Hugonnard-Roche, *Logique d'Aristote* [3:8] 180–81, 185–86; id. [5:75], in Romeny (ed.), *Jacob of Edessa* [3:92] 219–21.

84 On Dionysius in Sergius and subsequently, see J. Watt, "From Sergius to Mattā: Pseudo-Dionysius in the Syriac tradition," *IBALA* 239–57.

teries made up of individuals who may never proceed to the "greater mysteries" but even so—to quote Wittrock once more—"bring about changes in the world . . . ma[k]e new forms of institutions and practices."

Sergius, Severus, and Jacob all had a vision of how Greek learning might inform and nourish a Christian worldview that extended far beyond logic and Christology to embrace not only theology but the whole material world through study of physics, cosmology, and also medicine. We glimpse more of this vision in a unique Syriac manuscript, British Library Add. 14658.[85] This is a seventh-century collection of mainly philosophical texts covering especially cosmology, rhetoric and logic by drawing on such as "Plato," Alexander of Aphrodisias and Porphyry, but also the *Categories* and works falsely attributed to Aristotle ("pseudo-Aristotle")—notably, in the latter case, Sergius of Resh'aina's translation of *On the universe*. There seems to be something here of Sergius's aspiration to make coherent the scattered domains of human knowledge and bring them together into a single whole, with Aristotle's aid. *On the universe* even assigns Aristotle the doctrine of a transcendent God. It has been suggested that this collection reflects the enduring influence of Sergius's interest in the cosmological and astrological teachings of the third-century Edessene thinker Bardaisan—in other words of a rational and natural-philosophy approach to reality, allied with Christian faith. No doubt it was this strand of "free-thinking" that got Sergius labeled an "Origenist"—too intellectual/speculative/Alexandrian, not a simple ascetic Christian. His taste for Ps.-Dionysius cannot have helped. Exegetical traditions disseminated philosophical ideas in society at large, but nothing obliged society to like them.

We also detect here symptoms of what we have seen is a recurring feature of sixth- to seventh-century intellectual life, namely its encyclopedism. This is a Renaissance term used here in the loose sense—the only one applicable to premodern times—of collecting or anthologizing and maybe organizing too, even if only alphabetically, in a single work or collection of works, materials either possessed of general interest or focused on a theme, but not necessarily achieving or even aiming at comprehensive or systematic coverage.[86] In Armenia Ananias of Shirak had a similar vision and put it into practice. In the Latin world there was Boethius and then Isidore of Seville, whose *Etymologies* served as the basic encyclopedia of useful knowledge for centuries to come throughout the West, and thanks to which Isidore is the patron saint of the internet.

None of these men was in a position to engage with the entire range of Aristotle's research, though Boethius at least dreamed of translating the

85 D. King, "Origenism in sixth century Syria," in Fürst (ed.), *Origenes* [5:78] 179–212.

86 See the debate about the usefulness of the term "encyclopedism" among P. Schreiner, P. Odorico, and P. Magdalino in P. van Deun and C. Macé (eds), *Encyclopedic trends in Byzantium?* (Leuven 2011) 3–25, 89–107, 143–59.

whole corpus (and Plato!). The father of encyclopedism, the catalogue of whose works served as a general classification of human knowledge,[87] remained a distant, awesome figure. Yet the encyclopedic ideal itself was embraced, perhaps because there was a widespread sense that civilization, learning and "orthodoxy" were threatened, while the new Christian dispensation imposed a revision of how inherited ancient knowledge was presented. Boethius belonged to the first generation of Catholic Christians who had only ever known Arian Ostrogothic rule, and saw how easily his world might lose touch with the Greek East. Isidore's family had fled North Africa and been forced to live as a Catholic under Arian Visigothic rule, at least until King Reccared's conversion to Catholicism in 589. He looked back to the example of Varro (d. 27 BCE), who had propounded another vastly influential encyclopedia at a time of civil strife and incipient Augustan transition. Both men felt a vocation to undertake an intellectual and moral renewal of Romanitas under a new monarchy, in Isidore's case that of the learned and Catholic Sisebut, who commissioned his *Etymologies*.[88] As for Ananias, he lived through the rise of Islam and the first Arab assaults on Armenia.

It is an open question whether Boethius, Isidore, and Ananias, who exercised literary influence but lacked posterity in the sense of imitators, self-consciously aspired to "build up local Christendoms" in competition with East Rome.[89] But they were certainly aware—as had been Eusebius—of the need to reformulate the encyclopedia for the needs of Christian societies under extraordinary pressures. And what underlay and made possible this whole effort was the Alexandrian philosophical curriculum, above all the organizing and logical genius of Aristotle.

ALEXANDRIA TO BAGHDAD

That there was something exceptional about the Syriac strand in all this, I have already suggested. In assessing the Syriac philosophical achievement we must bear in mind its direct contribution to the emergence of Muslim civilization. Given the familiarity with Syriac Christian language and arguably literature manifest in the Qur'ān,[90] and its animadversions on Christian dis-

87 Cf. D. Gutas, "The Greek and Persian background of early Arabic encyclopedism," in G. Endress (ed.), *Organizing knowledge* (Leiden 2006) 91–96. Encyclopedism is deemed a Roman not Greek invention, but so too was the Aristotelian*ism* we are here concerned with, and which conveniently appeared at Rome just as the encyclopedic habit was catching on: T. Murphy, *Pliny the Elder's Natural history: The empire in the encyclopedia* (Oxford 2004) 13, 194–97.

88 Fontaine, *DPA* [5:60] 3.882–83, 885, 887–89.

89 P. Brown, *The rise of Western Christendom* (Malden, Mass. 2003) 365.

90 See, e.g., S. Griffith, "Christian lore and the Arabic Qur'ān," in Reynolds (ed.), *Qur'ān in its historical context* [1:31] 109–16, 131.

putatiousness, the Prophet himself can be said to have lived near the fringes of Aristotle's sphere of influence.[91] It was also Syriac scholars who did the spadework of the Arabic translation movement, and gave Arabic speakers access to Greek learning and Muslims the possibility of articulating their faith philosophically like Christians. The story of how Greek philosophy survived the "end of Antiquity" is more of a piece than appears at first sight, or is acknowledged in much scholarship.[92] Syriac Aristotelianism was to be as closely related to the later but overlapping Arabic Aristotelianism of Baghdad as it had been to the earlier but overlapping Greek Aristotelianism of Alexandria. This point deserves further development. It is central to our understanding of the First Millennium as a periodization based on ideas and spiritual/intellectual movements.

Sergius of Resh'aina, who inaugurated Syriac Aristotelianism in the early sixth century, studied at Alexandria. Paul the Persian's writings reveal an intimate knowledge of the late Alexandrian curriculum. Jacob of Edessa, who was born c. 633 on the eve of the Arab conquest of Syria, and died in 708, was one of the last students who made his way to Alexandria. He acquired profound knowledge of Greek literature both philosophical and Christian, and on returning to Syria fell foul of monks who loathed the language and all it represented.[93] If there was at once such an admiration for things Greek—and for philosophy—among Syriac scholars, and a parallel anti-intellectualism (such as that deployed against Sergius) capable of distracting even men who now lived in the shadow of Islam,[94] we may doubt their conquerors remained unaware of such passions.[95] Greek learning's passage through the Syriac milieu into Arabic came to exercise a considerable fascination over at least some Arabic-speaking intellectuals, who formulated a schematic account of it.

According to what I shall call the Alexandria to Baghdad narrative[96] (already evoked at the end of the last chapter), Aristotle died at Alexandria—

91 While itself untouched by Aristotle, the Qur'ān was subjected to logical analysis as soon as Aristotle became known in Arabic: C. Schöck, *Koranexegese, Grammatik und Logik* (Leiden 2006); and cf. R. W. Gwynne, *Logic, rhetoric, and legal reasoning in the Qur'ān* (Abingdon 2004), esp. X, 98–105, 152–69.

92 D. Gutas, *Greek thought, Arabic culture* (London 1998), a superb account of the Arabic translation movement, seriously underplays the role of Syriac translators and translations: cf., e.g., Watt, in Fürst (ed.), *Origenes* [5:78] 222–23.

93 Michael the Syrian, *Chronicle* [ed. and tr. (French) J.-B. Chabot (Paris 1899–1924)] 11.15 (tr. 2.471–72).

94 Brock, *Syriac perpectives* [5:1] V.23–24; Hugonnard-Roche, *Logique d'Aristote* [3:8] 169, 173–75; A. H. Becker, *Fear of God and the beginning of wisdom: The School of Nisibis and Christian scholastic culture in late antique Mesopotamia* (Philadelphia 2006) 169–203.

95 Cf. Gutas, in Pasnau (ed.), *Cambridge history of medieval philosophy* [5:72] 19.

96 D. Gutas, "The 'Alexandria to Baghdad' complex of narratives," *Documenti e studi sulla tradizione filosofica medievale* 10 (1999) 155–93 (versions set out in parallel columns; I use Gutas's translations); C. D'Ancona, "La filosofia della tarda antichità e la formazione della "falsafa,"" *SFIM* 41–44.

false, but oblique acknowledgment of his influence on Alexandrian scholarship and the Museum.[97] Under the Ptolemies, instruction in philosophy thrived in that city. The last in a succession of twelve teachers during this period was Andronicus of Rhodes (mentioned as eleventh Peripatetic scholarch by the fifth-century Alexandrian Ammonius, whose account of Aristotle's philosophy much influenced the Arabs.[98]) In the story as purveyed by Fārābī, after the death of Cleopatra the Emperor Augustus

> inspected the libraries [in Alexandria] and the [dates of] production of the books, and found there manuscripts of Aristotle's works, copied in his lifetime and in that of Theophrastus. . . . He ordered copies to be made of the books copied in the lifetime of Aristotle and his pupils, and that the teaching be based on these, disregarding the rest. He appointed Andronicus to manage this task

and teach philosophy at Rome. With the coming of Christianity, instruction ceased at Rome[99] while continuing at Alexandria.

By attributing to Augustus the rediscovery of Aristotle's lost works, Fārābī and our other sources both sharpen the First Millennium trajectory of Aristotelianism, and recall Eusebius on Augustus and Christ. But Fārābī argues that Islam not Christianity seals the tradition, thus validating his own heritage and bringing us down—according to our reckoning, though not his—almost to the end of the First Millennium (he died in 948). He alleges that philosophical teaching in Alexandria was investigated by the "king of the Christians" and the bishops, who

> assembled and took counsel together. . . . They formed the opinion that the books on logic were to be taught up to the end of the existential figures,[100] but not what comes after it, since they thought that would harm Christianity, while that whose teaching they endorsed contained [material] that could be called upon for help in the [theological] defence of their religion. Of public teaching, then, this much remained, while whatever was examined of the rest remained private, until Islam came after a long period.

This restriction was, according to other versions of the Alexandria to Baghdad narrative, part of a more general decline of sixth- and seventh-century Alexandrian teaching in what we already saw, in the work of Sergius of Resh'aina, to be the closely interrelated subjects of medicine and logic. A

97 N. J. Richardson, "Aristotle and Hellenistic scholarship," in Montanari (ed.), *Philologie grecque* [5:9], esp. 12–14.

98 Goulet, *DPA* 1.201 [5:10].

99 I disagree with S. Stroumsa's notion, "Al-Fārābī and Maimonides on the Christian philosophical tradition," *Der Islam* 68 (1991) 267–68, that Constantinople or Athens is intended.

100 Aristotle [ed. I. Bekker (Berlin 1831; revised second edition O. Gigon, Berlin 1960–87); tr. J. Barnes (ed.) (Princeton 1984)], *Prior analytics* 1.7; cf. above, pp. 143–44.

main cause of this decline was said to be student laziness, thanks to which basic medical textbooks by Hippocrates and Galen had to be simplified and abridged. Curricular contraction is in fact well attested at this period;[101] and the cure will have hastened the progress of the disease, to judge from the mechanical aridity of the surviving Arabic *Summaries*, with their tedious division and subdivision of definitions.[102] What is more, the Alexandrian teaching tradition really did come to an end in the second half of the seventh century, judging by our scant literary evidence[103] and the recent discovery of a complex of auditoria buried immediately beneath an Umayyad cemetery—its extensiveness vividly illustrating how an exegetical tradition fed into everyday student life.[104] But the explicitly anti-Christian bias to the story, attributing the decline of secular studies to the malevolence of Christian rulers, is likely to have been introduced under the Abbasid Caliph Ma'mūn (813–33), who notoriously held that the caliphate rather than the East Roman Empire was the true heir of Greek scholarship and values. Dimitri Gutas dubbed this attitude "anti-Byzantinism as philhellenism";[105] and students of Byzantine philosophy are indeed hard put to find anything of interest going on in their field during the couple of centuries after Heraclius,[106] even allowing for the philosophically informed—at a fairly elementary level—theology of Maximus the Confessor (d. 662)[107] and John of Damascus (d. 740s), a Syrian subject of the Umayyads.[108] As I already pointed out, it was Syria that made the cultural running at this period, in Greek as well as Syriac. The loss of this region to the Arabs was not just a military and economic blow.

101 M. Roueché, "Did medical students study philosophy in Alexandria?," *Bulletin of the Institute of Classical Studies* 43 (1999) 153–69; E. Watts, "Where to live the philosophical life in the sixth century? Damascius, Simplicius, and the return from Persia," *Greek, Roman, and Byzantine studies* 45 (2005) 311–14. On Alexandrians' ignorance of basic philosophical concepts, see Anastasius of Sinai, *Guide* [5:54] 1.3, 18–19.

102 P. E. Pormann, "The *Alexandrian summary* (*Jawāmi'*) of Galen's *On the sects for beginners*," in Adamson and others (eds), *Philosophy, science and exegesis* [1:35] 2.27–28 (whose materials scarcely justify his upbeat conclusion); and compare Roueché, *Bulletin of the Institute of Classical Studies* 43 (1999) [5:101] 166–69.

103 M. Roueché, "The definitions of philosophy and a new fragment of Stephanus the Philosopher," *Jahrbuch der Österreichischen Byzantinistik* 40 (1990) 128; Hoyland, *Seeing Islam* [3:102] 234–35; Walker, *Legend of Mar Qardagh* [5:72] 183 and n. 68.

104 G. Majcherek, "The late Roman auditoria of Alexandria," and J. S. McKenzie, "The place in late antique Alexandria 'where alchemists and scholars sit (...) was like stairs,'" in T. Derda and others (eds), *Alexandria: Auditoria of Kom el-Dikka and late antique education* (Warsaw 2007) 11–50, 53–83.

105 Gutas, *Greek thought* [5:92] 83–95.

106 Conrad, in Reinink and Klugkist, *After Bardaisan* [5:77] 88–89.

107 B. Roosen and P. van Deun, "Les collections de définitions philosophico-théologiques appartenant à la tradition de Maxime le Confesseur," in M. Cacouros and M.-H. Congourdeau (eds), *Philosophie et sciences à Byzance de 1204 à 1453* (Leuven 2006) 53–76.

108 V. S. Conticello, "Jean Damascène," *DPA* 3.1008–12; M. Frede, "John of Damascus on human action, the will, and human freedom," in K. Ierodiakonou (ed.), *Byzantine philosophy and its ancient sources* (Oxford 2002) 63–95; id., "*Catégories*" [5:46], in Bruun and Corti (eds), *Catégories* [5:5] 166–73.

According to the Alexandria to Baghdad narrative, found in not only Fārābī but also the historian Masʿūdī (d. 956) and elsewhere, once the teaching of medicine and Aristotelian logic died out at Alexandria it was transferred to Antioch under the Umayyad caliph ʿUmar II (717–20). It persisted there until only one teacher remained, with two pupils who eventually left "taking the books with them." One went to Ḥarrān in northern Mesopotamia close to Edessa, and the other to Marw far away in what is today Turkmenistan. By these routes the erudition of the Greeks eventually reached Baghdad, where the scholarly caliph Ma'mūn especially favored it—as had several of his predecessors, but our narratives' common source was evidently well disposed to Ma'mūn. Fārābī's and Masʿūdī's accounts both highlight the role of Christian teachers in disseminating philosophy.[109] With one of them, Fārābī himself studied the fuller version of Aristotelian logic up to the end of the *Posterior analytics*.

In other words, Fārābī locates himself in a clearly articulated and reformed tradition of Aristotelian studies, ultimately derived from the master himself, but to whose purification and organization the Emperor Augustus had personally contributed almost exactly a millennium earlier. We need not take literally the historical data provided by this narrative. It would be pedantic to object that it neglects cities such as Nisibis[110] or Constantinople[111] which had also been favored by doctors and philosophers—not to mention monasteries on the Fertile Crescent highway, such as Qenneshre. What the narrative does accurately reflect is ninth- and tenth-century Baghdadi intellectuals' awareness that their books and teaching techniques derived either directly or indirectly from Alexandria,[112] and that this transmission had been effected by individual teachers and by books they carried with them. The discovery of neglected manuscripts in libraries is not excluded, and we know that such finds occurred. But here the ideal is the reception of learning from living sources, and specifically from Syriac scholars (as implied by the prominence assigned Antioch and Ḥarrān) whose intellectual genealogy could be traced through the Greek schools of Alexandria to Aristotle himself. The translation movement into Syriac is not evoked at all. But the centrality of Syria and

109 Cf. C. Ferrari, "La scuola aristotelica di Bagdad," *SFIM* 352–79.

110 Becker, *Fear of God* [5:94] 92–95, 126–54; S. Stroumsa, "Soul-searching at the dawn of Jewish philosophy: A hitherto lost fragment of al-Muqammaṣ's *Twenty chapters*," *Ginzei qedem* 3 (2007) 143*.

111 B. Bischoff and M. Lapidge (eds), *Biblical commentaries from the Canterbury School of Theodore and Hadrian* (Cambridge 1994) 50–64. M. Roueché, "Stephanus the Alexandrian philosopher, the *Kanon* and a seventh-century millennium," *Journal of the Warburg and Courtauld Institutes* 74 (2011) 1–30, and "Stephanus the Philosopher and Ps. Elias," *Byzantine and Modern Greek studies* 36 (2012) 120–38, questions Stephanus's removal from Alexandria to Constantinople, but upholds Ps.-Elias's presence there.

112 C. Hein, *Definition und Einteilung der Philosophie: Von der spätantiken Einleitungsliteratur zur arabischen Enzyklopädie* (Frankfurt am Main 1985); G. Schoeler (tr. U. Vagelpohl, ed. J. E. Montgomery), *The oral and the written in early Islam* (Abingdon 2006) 46–49.

of Syriac scholarship is unmistakable—and not unjustified, despite being imposed by a Baghdadi perspective that plays down the Alexandrian teaching model's simultaneous dissemination to a spectrum of other destinations from Canterbury via Italy and Constantinople to Armenia and, as we saw, northeast Iran.[113] From Constantinople we have a closely interlinked group of seventeen philosophical manuscripts copied c. 850–75, whose origin some seek in the removal perhaps of a single scholar and his books from seventh-century Alexandria.[114] Several of the texts derive from late Alexandrian circles, so this "philosophical collection" provides an interesting speculative parallel to the Alexandria to Baghdad narrative and its emphasis on individuals and their libraries. It may also reflect demand for Greek manuscripts triggered by the early Abbasid translation movement.[115]

Behind the Alexandria to Baghdad narrative's concern with familiar Syrian terrain and teachers there lurks anxiety about the status of the Greeks. Because Fārābī stands at the receiving end of a teaching tradition, it is hard for him to diminish its Christian phase. His own teacher was a Christian, as he concedes in the passage just summarized. But other Muslim writers were less reticent about hailing philosophy in its new, caliphal phase as something qualitatively different from what was on offer in rival East Rome.[116] The East Romans read and spoke Greek after a fashion, nobody denied that. But otherwise they were not to be compared with the true Greeks, the Ancients, men like Aristotle, Ptolemy, Euclid, Galen, Democritus, Hippocrates, or Plato. These, not the Christian Romans, are the Greeks, argued Jāḥiẓ, man of letters and Abbasid propagandist, who died in 868.

> Their religion was different from the religion of the East Romans, and their culture (adab) was different from the culture of the East Romans. They were scientists, while these people are artisans who appropriated the books of the Greeks on account of geographical proximity.[117]

Masʿūdī painted a similar picture, with more strongly contrasted colors:

> During the time of the ancient Greeks, and for a little time during the Roman Empire [probably he means the first two centuries of the First Millennium, up to the time of Galen], the philosophical sciences kept on growing and developing, and scholars and philosophers were respected and honoured. They developed their theories on natural sci-

113 Bischoff and Lapidge, *Biblical commentaries* [5:111] 255–59; Calzolari [5:65], in D'Ancona (ed.), *Libraries* [3:3] 262–63.

114 But see the articles by Roueché [5:111].

115 See various contributions to D'Ancona (ed.), *Libraries* [3:3], e.g., 54–57, 145–48, 155–65, 167–75; Gutas, *Greek thought* [5:92] 181–86.

116 Gutas, *Greek thought* [5:92] 85–90.

117 Al-Jāḥiẓ, *Letters* [ed. ʿA. M. Hārūn (Cairo 1964–79)] 3.315 (tr. Gutas, *Greek thought* [5:92] 87).

> ence—on the body, the intellect, the soul—and on the quadrivium, i.e. on arithmetic, . . . geometry, . . . astronomy, . . . and music. . . . The sciences continued to be in great demand and intensely cultivated . . . until the religion of Christianity appeared among the Romans. They then effaced the signs of philosophy, eliminated its traces, destroyed its paths, and changed and corrupted what the ancient Greeks had set forth in clear expositions.[118]

Jāhiz, Masʿūdī, and Fārābī too, up to a point, see the coming of Christianity as marking a change for the worse in human culture, at the very least a narrowing of interests, while the coming of Islam is a return to a more elevated culture that had been lost sight of. We know that the Muslim writers' schematic contrast between Greece and Christian Rome is a misrepresentation of history, because the Greek heritage went on developing under Rome: if late antique studies have taught us anything, this is it. Philosophy in particular reached its most sophisticated form in already substantially Christianized fifth- and sixth-century Alexandria. Likewise, Masʿūdī's contrasted picture of East Rome and Caliphate is inspired more by religious animus than any serious assessment of their relative cultural standing. (Jāḥiẓ at least admits the East Romans' superiority in art and architecture, and competence in arithmetic, astrology and calligraphy.) What we are dealing with is polemic not history, aimed at those in the Islamic world who rejected the learning of the Greeks. But whether Muslim civilization is read as developing—at least in part—from Christian civilization, or returning to the earlier Greek model from which Christian Rome had strayed, the First Millennium is still the chronological framework appealed to, since—as Masʿūdī recognizes—Hellenism had continued to be the dominant culture at the beginning of the Roman Empire.

Several of the points I have just touched on are resumed, and a transition to the world of the Arabic translators effected, in the person of Theodore Abū Qurra (c. 755–c. 830), a Syrian Christian who served as Chalcedonian bishop of Ḥarrān.[119] Theodore's theological writings place him in the tradition of John of Damascus, who constructed what was to remain the only comprehensive statement of Chalcedonian—in other words Greek Orthodox—doctrine using basic concepts of Aristotelian logic compiled from the *Isagoge* and the *Categories* mediated through their late Alexandrian commentators.[120] John proves that, at a low level, Greek as well as Syriac Aristotelianism was alive on Muslim territory up to the eve of the first Arabic translations. As for Theodore, he was familiar with both Aristotle and late Greek philosophy. He translated into Arabic a compendium of ps.-Aristotelian

118 Al-Masʿūdī, *Meadows of gold* [4:22] 741 (tr. Gutas, *Greek thought* [5:92] 89).

119 S. H. Griffith, *The Church in the shadow of the Mosque* (Princeton 2008) 60–61.

120 A. Louth, *St John Damascene* (Oxford 2002) 40–44.

texts *On the virtues of the soul.*[121] Evidently he knew Greek; as for his own books, they were in Syriac or—mainly—Arabic. They show he had absorbed the new Muslim theological language of kalām (on which more below), and knew how to use it to justify Christianity under the new dispensation,[122] as no doubt when he disputed with Muslim scholars before Ma'mūn during the latter's visit to Ḥarrān in 829.

Note, too, Theodore's association with the Edessa-Ḥarrān area athwart the Fertile Crescent highway from Alexandria to Baghdad. This location not only reminds us of other luminaries (Bardaisan, Ephrem of Nisibis, Sergius of Resh'aina, and two more Nisibenes, Ibn Ḥawqal and Elias bar Shenaya) we have encountered on these supposed East-West/North-South peripheries between Sasanids/caliphs and Rome, but really at the very center of the Eurasian Hinge. It also makes Theodore easy to integrate into the schematic Arabic narrative of how ancient learning passed to its Muslim heirs. Theodore fits well into the milieu of Christian Syrian translators of Greek texts, and as a bishop was the absolute insider who knew where to get his hands on the sought-after manuscripts of Aristotle and the other ancients. If he has yet to find his due place in modern versions of this story, we can put that down to Islamic scholars' continuing allergy to Christian Arabic.

ARABIC ARISTOTELIANISM

The Fertile Crescent was the most intellectually accessible and stimulating region for the new religion of Islam and its nascent Arabic culture to claim as its own. And if the Mountain Arena was the geographical hinge of the world which concerns us, the seventh and eighth centuries—essentially the Umayyad and early Abbasid period—were its narrative, political, and intellectual hinge, when the old Greek and Christian tradition entered an advanced stage of maturation, not least in the minds of Syriac scholars, while tremendous new forces from Arabia were brought to bear on that synthesis.[123] The durability of city life in early Islamic Syria has preoccupied recent scholarship, but not the period's intellectual dynamism. The distance be-

121 P. Vallat, *Farabi et l'École d'Alexandrie* (Paris 2004) 23 esp. n. 8; Griffith, *Church in the shadow of the Mosque* [5:119] 61. J. Lameer, *Al-Fārābī and Aristotelian syllogistics* (Leiden 1994) 3–4, rejects the theory that Theodore translated the *Prior analytics* into Arabic. See further S. K. Samir (tr. J. P. Monferrer Sala), *Abū Qurrah* (Cordoba 2005) 97–100, 110–11.

122 See below pp. 186–87; and compare S. T. Keating, *Defending the 'People of Truth' in the early Islamic period: The Christian apologies of Abū Rā'iṭah* (Leiden 2006), on a similarly oriented miaphysite contemporary of Theodore.

123 On the Umayyads' neglected contribution to the formation of Muslim identity, see F. M. Donner, "Umayyad efforts at legitimation," and C. Décobert, "Notule sur le patrimonialisme omeyyade," in Borrut and Cobb (eds), *Umayyad legacies* [4:123] 187–253.

tween the Greek and the Qur'anic mind is to blame, along with neglect of the Syriac intermediary.[124] From the First Millennium perspective, what now remains is to assess not so much the continuing and already well-known role of Syriac scholars in creating a Syro-Arabic philosophical vocabulary and translating Aristotle (and other Greeks) first into Syriac and then Arabic,[125] but rather the impact Aristotle made on the intellectual maturation of Islam up to Ibn Sīnā, who died in 1037.

The beginnings of this story lie in puzzlement experienced by thoughtful auditors or readers of the Qur'ān. For example, since the holy book expresses both views, it was reasonable to wonder whether God really has a face, hands, eyes and speech like a human being, and sits on a throne; or is he entirely transcendent?[126] Do the epithets the Qur'ān uses of Allāh, the ninety-nine "beautiful" names, correspond to distinct qualities such as are predicated of human beings? Or is God immune to verbal description?[127]

Admittedly the earliest Muslims' most pressing needs were to understand the exact meaning of the Qur'anic text, to decide how their community should be governed, to put together a body of laws. Hence grammarians, experts in the sayings or ḥadīth (the singular form is customarily used in English) of the Prophet, or jurists were more prominent than theoretical theologians. But there was also a need to answer the community's and its scripture's non-Muslim critics. The early apologists of Islam were known as mutakallimūn. Their aim was to corroborate the Qur'anic doctrines of divine unity, prophecy, and so forth by adducing arguments and proofs. They were not philosophers. They always started from revelation not reason; and that is what they returned to as well. But they were the first Muslims who deployed reasoned argument against doubt in order to define their faith in the service of the community, in a situation where Islam, far from putting an end to religious disputation, had given it new impetus. 'Ilm al-kalām, as this scholarly method

124 D. Gutas, "Geometry and the rebirth of philosophy in Arabic with al-Kindī," in R. Arnzen and J. Thielmann (eds), *Words, texts and concepts cruising the Mediterranean Sea* (Leuven 2004) 195–97, 209, and id., in Pasnau (ed.), *Cambridge history of medieval philosophy* [5:72] 14–15, holds philosophy was "dead" from c. 610 (Stephanus) to c. 830 (Kindī). While largely true of the Greek world, in the Syriac sphere this judgment depends on a prejudice in favor of philosophical "creativity"/"praxis" (in other words, research) and against teaching, also against philosophy turned to religious goals. By the former criterion, Greek philosophy died before 610. By the latter, its long-standing revealed element (e.g., the *Chaldaean oracles*) is disqualified. The project, whether Syriac or Greek, of expressing Christian doctrine in philosophical terms was both creative and challenging, while the skill of the Abbasids' Syriac translators into Syriac and Arabic suggests a mature relationship with the Greek legacy.

125 S. K. Samir, "Rôle des chrétiens dans la *nahḍa* abbasside en Irak et en Syrie (750–1050)," *Mélanges de l'Université Saint-Joseph* 58 (2005) 541–72; King, *Earliest Syriac translation* [5:52] 14–17.

126 Anthropomorphic attributes: Qur'ān 55.27, 5.64, 23.27, 2.253, 20.5 (respectively). Transcendence: 6.102–3, 42.11, 112.4.

127 G. Böwering, "God and his attributes," *EQ* 2.319–22; C. Gilliot, "Attributes of God," *EIs*[3] 2007–2.176–82; J. van Ess, "Tashbīh wa-tanzīh," *EIs*[2] 10.341–44.

was called, literally the science of discourse/controversy, owed a lot to earlier Christian apologetic against heretics, Jews and pagans—but also in turn influenced contemporary Christian controversialists such as Theodore Abū Qurra or Patriarch Timothy (see below).[128]

Theological debates might affect high politics. Take the question of how God deploys his power in relation to humans. Does he eavesdrop on their private conversations and determine their every wish, as the Qur'ān states?[129] Or does he allow a measure of free will, as is both clearly stated,[130] and implied by the scripture's numerous accounts of disbelief and sin (unless God determines that as well, as sometimes asserted[131])? If God determines all actions, neither rulers nor rebels can be blamed for their behavior.[132]

Notable among the mutakallimūn for their promotion of a more reasoned understanding of Muslim theology—indeed, for the view that scripture and reason cannot contradict each other—were the so-called Muʿtazilites.[133] Proclaiming God's absolute unity and justice, they espoused a theology as negative as could be reconciled with scripture, questioning whether God's nature can adequately be conveyed through the positive qualities enumerated in the ninety-nine beautiful names, which were already mentioned in one of the Umayyad inscriptions in the Dome of the Rock in Jerusalem c. 692. Although the first mutakallimūn, up to the reign of Ma'mūn, seem not to have been adepts of Greek philosophy, an early encounter between ancient and Qur'anic thought occurred when one of the first systematic Muʿtazilites, Ḍirār ibn ʿAmr of Kūfa (c. 728–96), composed a *Refutation of Aristotle on substances and accidents*.[134] This is lost, but Ḍirār had apparently got hold of some concepts from the *Categories*, probably among the first of Aristotle's works made available in Arabic—in summary, not full translation—by Ibn al-Muqaffaʿ in the 750s.[135] The *Categories* listed ten types of

128 J. van Ess, "The beginnings of Islamic theology," in J. E. Murdoch and E. D. Sylla (eds), *The cultural context of medieval learning* (Dordrecht 1975) 87–111; I. Zilio-Grandi, "Temi e figure dell' apologia musulmana," *SFIM* 137–42; also M. Abdel-Haleem, "Early *kalām*," in S. H. Nasr and O. Leaman (eds), *History of Islamic philosophy* (London 1996) 71–88, for criticism of current non-Muslim views. Christian debts: J. Tannous, "Between Christology and kalām?," in G. A. Kiraz (ed.), *Malphono w-Rabo d-Malphone* (Piscataway, N.J. 2008) 671–716.

129 Qur'ān 58.1, 76.30.

130 Qur'ān 18.29.

131 Qur'ān 2.6–7, 4.155.

132 P. Crone, *Medieval Islamic political thought* (Edinburgh 2004) 35; van Ess, in Murdoch and Sylla (eds), *Medieval learning* [5:128] 97.

133 On Muʿtazilism, see Wensinck, *Muslim creed* [3:24] 58–85; K. Blankinship, "The early creed," in T. Winter (ed.), *The Cambridge companion to classical Islamic theology* (Cambridge 2008) 47–51.

134 J. van Ess, *Theologie und Gesellschaft im 2. und 3. Jahrhundert Hidschra* (Berlin 1991–97) 3.37–38, 42; 5.229 no. 8, 240–41.

135 Van Ess, *Theologie und Gesellschaft* [5:134] 2.27; C. D'Ancona, "Le traduzioni di opere greche e la formazione del corpus filosofico arabo," *SFIM* 202 (reading "al-Manṣūr" for "al-Ma'mūn"); Gutas, in Pasnau (ed.), *Cambridge history of medieval philosophy* [5:72] 18–19.

predicate, among which those relating to quality were most relevant to discussion of Allāh's attributes. The *Categories* would have struck Ḍirār as useful for his passages of arms with Kūfan anthropomorphists. He had some fun with one of these by forcing him to admit he might bump into God in the street without even recognizing him. " 'It could be me,' " Ḍirār could not resist adding, only to be taken down a peg by his interlocutor: " 'You are ugly, (God) is beautiful.' " Such encounters between anthropomorphists and "Origenists" had been common in Alexandria c. 400. Bishop Theophilus had checkmated a mob of irate monks by saying he saw in them the face of God.[136]

As Aristotle gradually came out in full translations, Muslim readers applied the new methods and knowledge to interpreting the Qur'ān and other theological issues thrown up by the spread of Islam and the Caliphate. Questions of "orthodoxy" and "heresy" quickly emerged, hence the translation of the ancient world's basic guide to debating techniques, Aristotle's *Topics*, which the Caliph Mahdī commissioned c. 782 from the Church of the East Patriarch Timothy I. The two men put the rules to test in a disputation about the Trinity, the nature of Christ and the significance of Muḥammad and Islam.[137] We also find Timothy disputing with an Aristotelian philosopher he met at court, and showing familiarity, like Theodore Abū Qurra, with the conventions of kalām.[138] Another early translation, under the Caliph Hārūn al-Rashīd (786–803), was the *Physics*, designed to counteract physical theories based on atomistic attempts to explain the world as a bundle of parts "in a wholly mechanical way, without metaphysical principles, simply as a result of chance, with no creation and no God."[139] Unsurprisingly, the *Metaphysics* attracted particular attention. In whole or part it was translated seven or eight times during the ninth and tenth centuries.[140] Yet its inadequacies as a textbook had long been recognized;[141] it did not engage the issues that preoccupied the faithful; and its unmoved mover[142] was not the personal, providential God taught by religions of the Book.

Traditionally, scholarship has held that the Muʿtazilites gained serious, if short-lived, political influence when at the end of his reign the Caliph

136 Socrates, *Ecclesiastical history* [ed. G. C. Hansen, tr. (French) P. Périchon and P. Maraval (Paris 2004–7)] 6.7.

137 Gutas, *Greek thought* [5:92] 61–69; M. Heimgartner, "Die Disputatio des ostsyrischen Patriarchen Timotheos (780–823) mit dem Kalifen al-Mahdī," in M. Tamcke (ed.), *Christians and Muslims in dialogue in the Islamic Orient of the Middle Ages* (Beirut 2007) 41–56.

138 S. H. Griffith, "The Syriac letters of Patriarch Timothy I and the birth of Christian *kalām*," in W. J. van Bekkum and others (eds), *Syriac polemics* (Leuven 2007) 103–32.

139 Gutas, *Greek thought* [5:92] 69–74; J. van Ess (tr. J. M. Todd), *The flowering of Muslim theology* (Cambridge, Mass. 2006) 81 (for the quotation).

140 A. Bertolacci, "On the Arabic translations of Aristotle's *Metaphysics*," *ASAP* 15 (2005) 270–71.

141 Plutarch, *Alexander* [ed. K. Ziegler, Stuttgart 1994] 7.9.

142 Aristotle [5:100], *Metaphysics* 12.1072ab.

Ma'mūn (813–33) required the religious scholarly elite explicitly to accept their doctrine that the Qur'ān is created rather than being the ungenerated speech of God, as the pious maintained.[143] It now appears that the Mu'tazilites were just one of a constellation of rationalists and semirationalists who embraced this teaching, and that they gained prominence only toward the end of the century. It is also disputed, whether Ma'mūn's policy change should be taken as just an attempt to undermine the guardians of tradition and doctrine, the 'ulamā' (and resistance, conversely, as merely bolstering the scholars' authority), or was a full-blown doctrinal revolution aimed at opening up Qur'anic exegesis to rationalist methodologies.[144] It is striking that Ma'mūn chose a burning issue for all Muslims, not an "obscure" doctrinal point, out of which to make this political issue.[145] The main consequence of this policy (apart from discrediting the caliph as arbiter of orthodoxy) was the victory it handed those who believed scripture should be accepted just as it is, "without asking how" as later generations put it, and without reconciling its contradictions. Foremost among these believers was the unyielding Aḥmad ibn Ḥanbal (d. 855). By the beginning of the 850s the rationalists were forced to back down. Rather than being a passing political incident, this was—or, more crucially, came to be perceived as[146]—a defining moment in the emergence of Sunni Islam, with its exclusive insistence on the authority of Qur'ān and Prophetic tradition. Ibn Ḥanbal's example stands behind the legal community which later took his name, the Hanbalis, and some of the most vigorous—and rigorous—currents in the Muslim world today.

Nonetheless, Ma'mūn's support of the translation movement ensured philosophy would continue to sustain interest in rational thought and empirical science. It was said that Aristotle himself appeared to Ma'mūn in a dream, and bade him prefer "personal judgment," or intellect, above all else, evidently including scripture.[147] It was during his reign and that of his son Mu'taṣim (833–42) that Kindī (d. c. 870) emerged, at Baghdad, as the first noted Arabic (and indeed Arab) philosopher in the sense of one dedicated to

143 Van Ess, *Theologie und Gesellschaft* [5:134] 3.446–508; C. Melchert, "The adversaries of Aḥmad ibn Ḥanbal," *Arabica* 44 (1997) 234–53; L. Holtzmann, "Aḥmad b. Ḥanbal," *EIs*^{3} 2009-4.15–23.

144 Crone, *Medieval Islamic political thought* [5:132] 131.

145 Cf. Wickham, *Inheritance* [1:26] 330: "The apparent obscurity of the religious issue at stake is one element that reminds us of the Christological schisms of the late Roman empire. . . . Why al-Ma'mun chose the created Qur'an as the issue to make a stand on is, however, even less clear than the reasons for the Iconoclast controversy." A similar debate, pitting sociopolitical considerations against exclusive interest in texts and ideas, ebbs and flows round the Arabic translation movement. Fortunately it is not an either/or situation. Gutas's austerely sociopolitical hermeneutic in *Greek thought* brilliantly defuses the charge that periodizations based on religious or philosophical ideas—here, Aristotelianism—lack contact with everyday life.

146 Robinson, *Islamic historiography* [3:70] 63–64, 123.

147 Gutas, *Greek thought* [5:92] 96–104.

pursuit of philosophy in its own right as well as in relation to theology.[148] In addition to coordinating translation projects, especially on Aristotle, and writing commentaries on the *Organon*, Kindī immersed himself in the Aristotelian sciences, especially in the certainty provided by mathematical and geometrical rather than logical proofs of cosmological and metaphysical propositions.[149] Kindī's metaphysics also helps us locate him within the broader tendencies of early Islamic thought.[150] He read Aristotle's *Metaphysics* not so much as a philosophical approach to being-as-such, but for the light it threw on the central doctrines of Muslim theology (kalām): God's unicity, attributes and "beautiful names"! Kindī's conviction that obscurities in the Qur'ān could be resolved by resort to reasoning provided common ground between him and the Muʿtazilites.

During the 830s a member of Kindī's circle, a Christian from Homs in Syria named Ibn Nāʿima al-Ḥimṣī, produced a paraphrastic and expanded version of extracts from Plotinus's fourth to sixth *Enneads* and Proclus's *Elements of theology*, under the title *The theology of Aristotle*.[151] An introduction explains that the work supplements Aristotle's *Metaphysics*. It conveys what is best described as a scripture-compatible late Platonism, ascribing to the utterly transcendent, obliviously emanating Plotinian One a creative and providential activity often expressed in language Plotinus himself had used only of the next (lower) level of being, namely Mind or Intellect. It seems, moreover, that the *Theology*'s compiler concurred with the Muʿtazilites' denial that the Qur'anic names of God correspond to actual attributes, since attributes might be seen as separate from God, who is entirely simple. God must not be made multiple by predication.[152]

Through the *Theology*, Platonism made its debut in Arabic under the name of Aristotle. This was an extreme manifestation of late Greek harmonization of Plato and Aristotle even as regards the One,[153] and is all the more important because the translators neglected Plato and the Platonist tradition.[154] From the tenth century onward the *Theology of Aristotle* deeply influenced Muslim theology, at least in philosophical circles.[155] It attests with

148 C. D'Ancona, "Al-Kindī e la sua eredità," *SFIM* 282–351; P. Adamson, *Al-Kindī* (New York 2007); G. Endress and P. Adamson, "Abū Yūsuf al-Kindī," *PIW* 92–147.

149 Gutas, in Arnzen and Thielmann (eds), *Words, texts and concepts* [5:124] 195–209.

150 D. Gutas, *Avicenna and the Aristotelian tradition* (Leiden 1988) 243–49.

151 C. D'Ancona, "La teologia neoplatonica di "Aristotele" e gli inizi della filosofia arabo-musulmana," in *Entre Orient et Occident: La philosophie et la science gréco-romaines dans le monde arabe* (Geneva 2011) 135–95.

152 P. Adamson, *The Arabic Plotinus* (London 2002) 165–70.

153 I. Hadot, "Aristote dans l'enseignement philosophique néoplatonicien," *Revue de théologie et de philosophie* 124 (1992) 414–16.

154 D. De Smet, "L'héritage de Platon et de Pythagore: La "voie diffuse" de sa transmission en terre d'Islam," in *Entre Orient et Occident* [5:151] 87–126.

155 M. Aouad, "La *Théologie d'Aristote* et autres textes du *Plotinus arabus*," *DPA* 1.541–90.

unique eloquence the formation of an Islamic synthesis on Greek foundations, partly through creative pseudepigraphy. Unlike other Arabic translations, it does not aspire to exactitude. It transforms the target text by rereading it through Muslim eyes in the case of Kindī who edited the final version, but also Christian eyes in the case of Ḥimṣī who did the actual translation, with its echoes of Ps.-Dionysius's Christian Platonist vocabulary.[156] One could hardly imagine better testimony to Arabic civilization's successful connection to an immensely complex and at times contradictory cultural evolution rooted in the late Greek world, but also in the remoter reaches of Greek and Near Eastern Antiquity. At its heart stands Aristotle, understood no longer as primarily a logician, but as the author of a vast encyclopedia from which the Arabs omitted only the *Politics*. Through the *Theology*, they embraced too the mature Platonism of Plotinus and Proclus. If it could be made to speak with one voice, and to unify—as among certain of Kindī's pupils—the scientific traditions of Egypt, Babylon, Iran, and India into a single vision, then Greek philosophy might be accepted by Muslims as a worthy interlocutor, and even as a tool for expounding scripture.[157]

Second only after Aristotle himself, according to tradition, was Fārābī,[158] whose account of his own intellectual genealogy we have already seen, and who together with Kindī and Ibn Sīnā belongs to the trinity of names which dominate early Arabic philosophy or falsafa. Fārābī, perhaps from the East Iranian world and of Turkish origin, spent much of his adult life in Baghdad, Syria, and Egypt. His travels, and the prominence of Christians among both his teachers and his pupils, made him an ideal citizen of the cosmopolitan Islamic Commonwealth.

Fārābī's philosophy synthesized and systematized what had gone before, with special regard for the Alexandrian Aristotelianism he saw as his personal heritage. His extension of the Syriac logic curriculum beyond *Prior analytics* 1.7, to include not just the *Posterior analytics* but the entire *Organon*, on all of which he wrote commentaries or paraphrases or both, was highly characteristic of the role attributed to him as, after Aristotle, the "Second Master." Logic provided Fārābī with not just one possible expression of the world of concepts, but a description of the structure of reality itself, free from the constraints imposed by the particular language in which it is formu-

156 Gutas, *Greek thought* [5:92] 136–50, esp. 149; Adamson, *Arabic Plotinus* [5:152] 9–12, 165–77; D'Ancona, in *Entre Orient et Occident* [5:151] 194–95.

157 For a general assessment of Aristotle's role in Arabic philosophy from Kindī to Ibn Rushd, see G. Endress, "L'Aristote arabe. Réception, autorité et transformation du Premier Maître," *Medioevo* 23 (1997) 1–42.

158 D. Gutas and others, "Fārābī," *EIr* 9.208–29; C. Martini Bonadeo and C. Ferrari, "Al-Fārābī," *SFIM* 380–448; D. C. Reisman, "Al-Fārābī and the philosophical curriculum," in P. Adamson and R. C. Taylor (eds), *The Cambridge companion to Arabic philosophy* (Cambridge 2005) 52–71; U. Rudolph, "Abū Naṣr al-Fārābī," *PIW* 363–457.

lated. The possibility of rendering Greek accurately into Arabic, and the related issue of the primacy of grammar (favored by students of the Qur'ān) or logic, were much discussed at this time, in the context of a wider debate about the possible role of reason in thought informed by religious values and, in particular, by scriptural revelation. Fārābī espoused the view that, with the help of logic, philosophy can make true statements about everything, including God. This marked a distancing from kalām compared to Kindī, and therefore a less specifically Muslim reading of the *Metaphysics*;[159] but Fārābī was not thereby led into confrontation with the Qur'ān. Rather, he integrated the scripture into a previously unprecedented single hierarchy of knowledge, a synthesis of Aristotle with the revealed religious learning of Islam, but also with Plato and later Platonism as represented by the *Theology of Aristotle* in the place of Ps.-Dionysius still favored by Fārābī's Christian teachers.[160] Within such a synthesis, concessions had to be made, though they might be more apparent than real. The *Theology* had already compromised on the Plotinian One's utter transcendence. Aristotle's eternity of matter was saved, but veiled by obfuscatory language.

Alongside Aristotle's original works, a range of Greek commentaries had also been translated, by Alexander of Aphrodisias, Porphyry, Themistius and various Alexandrians such as Ammonius and Philoponus.[161] Part of Fārābī's contribution to philosophy lay in the composition—according to the Alexandrian tradition to which he felt he belonged, but also following the example of Kindī—of further original commentaries in Arabic. But the next great figure in Arabic philosophy, Ibn Sīnā (d. 1037), was largely an autodidact and is harder to subsume in an institutional narrative, though he warmly acknowledged his debt to Fārābī, above all to his commentary on the *Metaphysics*.[162] And if Fārābī's travels illustrate the Islamic Commonwealth's extent, Ibn Sīnā's life spent entirely in Khurāsān and other parts of the Iranian world without, so far as we know, even one visit to Baghdad stands for the growing autonomy of its constituent regions.

Ibn Sīnā's familiarity with both Aristotle, whom he praised as the first to define philosophy's parts and delineate their fundamental principles,[163] and

159 Gutas, *Avicenna* [5:150] 238–42, 248–50.

160 Watt [5:84], in *IBALA* 247–57. Fārābī did not seriously doubt the *Theology* was Aristotle's: C. D'Ancona (ed.), *Plotino: La discesa dell' anima nei corpi* (Padua 2003) 99 n. 258 (to be revised if the treatise *On the harmonization of the opinions of the two sages the divine Plato and Aristotle* is not by Fārābī: cf. Rudolph [5:158], *PIW* 402–3).

161 J. Jolivet, "Le commentaire philosophique arabe," in Goulet-Cazé (ed.), *Commentaire entre tradition et innovation* [5:41] 397–410; D. Gutas, "Die Wiedergeburt der Philosophie und die Übersetzungen ins Arabische," *PIW* 79–87.

162 The most useful account of Ibn Sīnā from my First Millennium and Aristotelian perspective is Gutas, *Avicenna* [5:150], with translations of the relevant sources. On Fārābī, see 28, 64. On Ibn Sīnā's autodidacticism, see 211, and R. Wisnovsky, "Avicenna and the Avicennian tradition," in Adamson and Taylor (eds), *Arabic philosophy* [5:158] 120.

163 Gutas, *Avicenna* [5:150] 45.

with the Aristotelian commentators, was profound. At Bukhārā, "the meeting-place of the most unique intellects of the age,"[164] in the Samanid library, he read so voraciously that by the age of eighteen or nineteen, by his own account, he had nothing more to learn—that was in or soon after the year 998, and recalls earlier overachievers, Augustine and Proclus.[165] Thereafter Ibn Sīnā took the well-trodden Alexandrian path of reconciling Aristotle both with himself (the "lesser harmony") and with Plato ("the greater harmony");[166] yet he came to offer certain solutions that were distinctive and might not have occurred to him had he received a conventional education. As he wrote to a pupil,

> I have neither the time nor the inclination to occupy myself with close textual analysis and commentary. But if you would be content with whatever I have readily in mind on my own, then I could write for you a comprehensive work arranged in the order which will occur to me.[167]

That is precisely what Ibn Sīnā already did in the early, Bukharan phase of his career, in the work known as *Philosophy for ʿArūḍī*, composed in the year 1001 at the request of a neighbor of that name, and still largely unpublished.[168] This is a systematic summation of the entire Alexandrian philosophical curriculum, and the first such summa to be produced in the Arabo-Islamic world. It would be hard to think of a document more appropriate to the end of our First Millennium.

In his maturer works, notably *The cure* (1020–27), Ibn Sīnā presented himself as an admirer but also reformer of Aristotle, who had no compunction about criticizing or diverging from him, or omitting material discussed by his predecessors simply because it was part of the Aristotelian corpus. Ibn Sīnā eschewed the writing of commentaries, in which (at least conventionally) the whole text had to be covered regardless of its relevance to one's own preoccupations.[169] Instead, he addressed Aristotle as an equal and propounded a system based on the corpus Aristotelicum and the commentary tradition with its marked Platonist coloring, but internalizing it and recasting it into a carefully argued, scientifically structured, coherent synthesis, almost a new edition of Aristotle a millennium after Andronicus.[170] Central to

164 Al-Thaʿālibī, *Yatīmat al-dahr*, tr. E. G. Browne, *A literary history of Persia* (London 1902–24) 1.365.

165 Gutas, *Avicenna* [5:150] 21, 24–29, 196–97 (drawing a parallel with late Greek biographies of Aristotle himself), 163, 173–76.

166 This distinction is concisely explained by Wisnovsky [5:162], in Adamson and Taylor (eds), *Arabic philosophy* [5:158] 97–98, who calls the combination of the two the "Ammonian synthesis," after the fifth-century Alexandrian philosopher Ammonius.

167 Quoted and tr. by Gutas, *Avicenna* [5:150] 41; cf. 101.

168 Gutas, *Avicenna* [5:150] 87–93.

169 Gutas, *Avicenna* [5:150] 47–48, 52–53, 111, 125–26, 175, 193, 223, 286–96.

170 Gutas, *Avicenna* [5:150] 199–200, 288–89; A. Bertolacci, "Il pensiero filosofico di Avicenna," *SFIM* 546–47.

this synthesis was the study of the rational soul and the related general questions of how one knows (epistemology) and what one knows (ontology), which together embrace the whole Aristotelian encyclopedia.[171] By taking the rational soul as common denominator, Ibn Sīnā unified philosophical discourses which, thanks to progressive adaptation of Greek philosophy by Christian and Muslim thinkers, had tended to go their separate ways.[172] We should also note how Ibn Sīnā appreciated the full philosophical range of the *Metaphysics*, with Fārābī, rather than treating it as an essentially theological treatise as Kindī had.[173]

In his later works Ibn Sīnā referred less, and more critically, to the ancient Greek philosophers, Arabized his vocabulary and became more systematic.[174] He emphasized this reorientation by calling his philosophy "Eastern," which in effect means "Khurasanian," and may be taken as repudiation of the old, "Western" exegetical tradition of Alexandria and Baghdad,[175] and a symptom of the eastward shift I proposed in chapter 4. For centuries to come, Arabic philosophy rejected, reformed or followed Ibn Sīnā, but could not ignore him.[176] Robert Wisnovsky was moved to write the following words in the Conclusion to his book *Avicenna's metaphysics in context*:

> Those scholars of late antiquity and of medieval Europe who ponder about when the late-antique era ended and the medieval began, can infer from my book that at least as far as the history of metaphysics is concerned, the decisive moment occurred around 1001, in the Sāmānid library in the city of Bukhārā in the Central Asian province of Transoxania, far outside their traditional area of focus.[177]

And the obverse of this is that, with Ibn Sīnā and the beginning of the Second Millennium, Arabic philosophy moves into a new phase of autonomous development, out of the shadow of the Greeks. This may encourage modern scholarship, too, to take a more "postcolonial" approach to the subject.[178]

Any overall judgment on Ibn Sīnā—and indeed more generally on the invigorating but socially constricted role of philosophy in the First Millen-

171 Gutas, *Avicenna* [5:150] 85–86.

172 Gutas, *Avicenna* [5:150] 260–61.

173 A. Bertolacci, "From al-Kindī to al-Fārābī: Avicenna's progressive knowledge of Aristotle's *Metaphysics*," *ASAP* 11 (2001) 257–95.

174 Gutas, *Avicenna* [5:150] 290–96.

175 Gutas, *Avicenna* [5:150] 115–30. For the Baghdad/Iraq-Khurāsān antithesis, see Kraemer, *Humanism* [4:82] 234–35.

176 C. Martini Bonadeo, "Seguaci e critici di Avicenna," *SFIM* 627–68.

177 R. Wisnovsky, *Avicenna's metaphysics in context* (London 2003) 266. (My thanks to Tony Street for this reference.) Ibn Sīnā himself was aware of being the heir to a philosophical tradition that had lasted almost 1,300 years: Gutas, *Avicenna* [5:150] 37.

178 Cf. H. Eichner, "Das Avicennische *Corpus Aristotelicum*," in *Entre Orient et Occident* [5:151] 197–203.

nium—must take account that he was a *Muslim* philosopher and a central figure in the growth of kalām, which touched a wide audience and continued to do so until the hold of madrasa education, established in the eleventh century, began to weaken in the late nineteenth.[179] The Muʿtazilite ascendancy, established in the latter half of the mid-ninth century, had fed into the compromise effected by Abū 'l-Ḥasan al-Ashʿarī (d. 935) and his followers.[180] The Ashʿarites insisted on Qur'ān and sunna and rejected clever allegorical readings of God's attributes—after all, we *will* see God at the Last Judgment. They accepted that the Qur'ān's sensible manifestations are created, but not its essence. They retained (incurring the odium of the Hanbalites) something of Muʿtazilite esteem for the role of reason in obtaining theological knowledge, and while cool toward philosophy, were open to Aristotelian logic. In the aftermath of Ibn Sīnā, they facilitated a surprisingly rapid fusion between his metaphysics (most problematically, his insistence on the eternity of the natural world) and kalām. And Ashʿarite Islam was gradually accepted as the voice of orthodoxy—a major symptom of Islam's tenth-century maturation. If there was something austere about it, that was alleviated by Ghazālī's critique of Ibn Sīnā's high claims for philosophy, and his further synthesis of it with not only kalām but also the more personal spiritual dimensions offered by Sufism.[181] As for the Muʿtazilites, they gradually faded away after the mid-eleventh century, and it was only thanks to the interest of Zaydi Shiites in Yemen, and Karaite Jews, that many of their works were preserved and finally published from the 1950s onward.[182]

Nonetheless, the significance of Arabic philosophy in the First Millennium context is most fully appreciated when we move outside the framework of strictly Muslim discourse to look at the Baghdadi circles of the ninth and tenth centuries, in which representatives of different religions, and of different sects within Islam itself, met and debated issues between and beyond the confines of confessional allegiance.[183] The declining Abbasid capital fostered a level of interaction and synthesis between the theological and philosophical currents of the First Millennium that has never since been rivaled. I shall return to this point in the last chapter, after we have first investigated some of the First Millennium's other exegetical cultures.

179 Wisnovsky [5:162], in Adamson and others (eds), *Philosophy, science and exegesis* [1:35] 152–58—note especially his comments on the penetration by philosophical terminology of a wide spectrum of works not conventionally regarded as philosophical.

180 Wensinck, *Muslim creed* [3:24] 86–94, 245–76.

181 Philosophy and kalām: F. Griffel, *Al-Ghazālī's philosophical theology* (New York 2009).

182 See the editorial Introduction to C. Adang and others (eds), *A common rationality: Muʿtazilism in Islam and Judaism* (Würzburg 2007) 11–18; G. Schwarb and others (eds), *Handbook of Muʿtazilite works and manuscripts* (forthcoming in the Handbuch der Orientalistik series, Leiden).

183 On the confessional mix in these circles, see Kraemer, *Humanism* [4:82] 53, 59–60, 115–16, and below, pp. 208–9.

6

EXEGETICAL CULTURES 2

LAW AND RELIGION

The oriental philosophy of the Gnostics, the dark abyss of predestination and grace, and the strange transformation of the Eucharist from the sign to the substance of Christ's body, I have purposely abandoned to the curiosity of speculative divines. But I have reviewed, with diligence and pleasure, the objects of ecclesiastical history, by which the decline and fall of the Roman empire were materially affected, the propagation of Christianity, the constitution of the Catholic church, the ruin of Paganism, and the sects that arose from the mysterious controversies concerning the Trinity and incarnation.

—E. Gibbon (ed. D. Womersley), *The history of the decline and fall of the Roman Empire* (1994) 3.86[1]

I ignore the two major intellectual achievements of the age, theology and law. . . .

—A. H. M. Jones, *The later Roman Empire 284–602* (1964), first paragraph of Preface

If we may call Aristotle the founding genius or prophet of his school, its scriptures were his writings both exoteric and esoteric. The latter were "published" as a corpus only some three centuries after his death, but then became a dominant presence in various strands of First Millennium thought. Being, many of them, little more than cryptic lecture notes, they drew exegetes and commentators eager to annotate, cross-reference, explain. Alexander of Aphrodisias c. 200 CE was the earliest durable representative of this exegetical phase, which culminated in fifth- and sixth-century Alexandria, and then again among the early Arabic philosophers. There was also a proliferation of short introductions to philosophy for teaching purposes, with Porphyry's

1 But cf. Theodor Mommsen, in a letter to Henry Pelham, 1894: "He [Gibbon] has taught us to combine Oriental with occidental lore; he has infused in history the essence of large doctrine, and of theology" (quoted by B. Croke, "Mommsen on Gibbon," *Quaderni di storia* 32 [1990] 56).

Isagoge especially influential.[2] Indissociable from this didactic emphasis was the spread of encyclopedic undertakings, which reflected the universal reach of Aristotle's project.

The dynamic role of secondary scholarship in the First Millennium, among philosophers but also in medicine,[3] law, and of course Judaism, Christianity and Islam, leads me to characterize the period as hospitable to "exegetical cultures." Exegetical cultures feed off earlier prophetic and scriptural phases, which provide them with materials for commentary and analysis. Their influence may then filter down, say through the medium of sermons, to less educated circles with little or no firsthand familiarity with the scriptures.[4] I already noted in chapter 1 the galvanizing effect on First Millennium scholarship of Richard Sorabji's *Ancient commentators on Aristotle* project. To be fully appreciated, though, this has to be seen against the background of previous generations' conviction that commentary, as a literary genre, is a symptom of unoriginality and (once more) *decline*.[5]

The writing of commentaries serves several purposes. A body of canonical writings or scriptures may emerge without, for a while, provoking commentary. But in practice commentary helps define the canon, and mold it by giving some scriptural texts more attention than others: note for example the prominence of Genesis and Psalms in Christian exegesis. Commentaries also embed scripture in a wider literary context, they make its meaning more accessible, and they establish its applicability in the sphere of public doctrine and often also law. In this last respect they contribute directly to shaping the boundaries of community, especially in situations where several exist in close proximity in a multicultural empire; and this is perhaps the main function of a canon as well.[6] Commentary is furthermore, as we saw in chapter 5, a necessary school activity. It provides a framework for teaching, and initiates the young into a defined curriculum based on scripture, earlier commentary, and the lessons of their immediate teachers, on which pupils may build new commentaries and so contribute to the sedimentation of tradition[7]—and the strength and influence of their own guild, a theme that will occasionally surface in the following pages.

2 On this genre of Introductions, already emergent by c. 200 BCE and routine in the late Alexandrian schools, see J. Mansfeld, *Prolegomena* (Leiden 1994); id., *Prolegomena mathematica* (Leiden 1998). On prologues, see Dubois and Roussel (eds), *Entrer en matière* [5:27].

3 On Hippocratic/Galenic exegesis and its relationship to Peripatetic exegesis, see Mansfeld, *Prolegomena* [6:2] 148–76.

4 See, e.g., R. Bagnall, *Livres chrétiens antiques d'Égypte* (Geneva 2009) 21–22.

5 Wisnovsky [1:36], in Adamson and others (eds), *Philosophy, science and exegesis* [1:35] 150–52.

6 Note the remarks of Brown, *Canonization* [3:18] 20–46.

7 Cf. also G. W. Most, "Preface," in id. (ed.), *Commentaries-Kommentare* (Göttingen 1999) VII–XI.

The exegetical process is measured compared to the energy burst required for prophecy and the production of scripture. But it is through exegesis that prophecy and scripture become socialized and consumable—and indeed historicized. This is why the First Millennium is so important, though several of its characteristic strands—Greek philosophy, Alexandrian philological scholarship,[8] Judaism, the Avesta—originated earlier. And it is in the everyday socialization of ideas and scholarly techniques, in the repercussions for example of scriptural exegesis on financial dealings or the marriage bed, that we come fully to appreciate the role of ideas in non-elite history as well.

We begin with another tradition rooted in pre-First Millennium, non-monotheistic Antiquity, namely Roman law, which from the first to third centuries CE produced an abundance of commentaries, and then a codification under Justinian. After that we turn to the three monotheisms: Judaism, Christianity, and Islam.

ROMAN LAW

Of the three towering textual monuments produced during the First Millennium, two are scriptures—the New Testament and the Qur'ān—while the third is Justinian's *Corpus of civil law* (*Corpus iuris civilis*).

> The vain titles of the victories of Justinian [wrote Gibbon] are crumbled into dust: but the name of the legislator is inscribed on a fair and everlasting monument. . . . [T]he public reason of the Romans has been silently or studiously transfused into the domestic institutions of Europe, and the laws of Justinian still command the respect or obedience of independent nations,[9]

though sadly not the attention of those who define a "declining" late Antiquity exclusively in terms of political and military events and economic cycles.

Roman law[10] began accumulating from the earliest code, the Twelve Tables drawn up by a special commission in 451–50 BCE without a hint—so far as we know—of Sinaitic theatricality, though with comparable consequence. Although rendered increasingly obsolete by the development of a more cosmopolitan society and the accretion of later laws, the Twelve Tables

8 P. M. Fraser, *Ptolemaic Alexandria* (Oxford 1972) 1.447–79.

9 Gibbon 44: 2.778. His final judgment was more nuanced: see the "Introduction" to Womersley's edition, lxxxi–lxxxiii.

10 F. Wieacker, *Römische Rechtsgeschichte* (Munich 1988–2006)—even in its unfinished state, the second volume, here relevant, is a mighty resource. For materials online, see www.ucl.ac.uk/history2/volterra/resource.htm.

remained valid throughout the millennium up to Justinian.[11] Cicero says schoolboys had it by heart. Interpretation of the law (lex) and its expansion to meet new needs was the task of the jurists, whose discipline (ius) emerged from roughly the beginning of the third century BCE, and acquired known (to us) representatives from the mid-second century, along with more than a dash of dialectical method derived from the latest Greek philosophy.[12] This imbued Roman law with a logical and theoretical dimension that enabled systematic analysis, and brought out the unity, of a tradition whose ad hoc, case-by-case procedures were strained by the rapid expansion of empire. Still, Roman law remained at heart pragmatic, loath to argue from general principles. In that lay its clarity and strength.

Roman law entered its classical phase approximately in the reign of Augustus. Especially through the writing of commentaries on earlier works, jurists sought to establish continuity with the past, thicken the web of legal precedent, and embed it in a rational framework indebted to Stoicism and Aristotle. About the year 150 one Gaius produced a beginners' textbook, the *Institutes*, later hugely influential, not least on Justinian's *Digest* (despite which, it is the only specimen of classical Roman legal writing to have been preserved almost intact, its material intensely subdivided following philosophical models). The classical period culminated with the jurists who served the Severan dynasty (193–235), gathering imperial rescripts (responses to individual petitions) and fashioning them into an impressive body of private law. Notable among these Severan jurists were that "man of superior genius"[13] but no great expository talent Papinian (d. 212), along with the more lucid, systematic, and incipiently encyclopedic Ulpian (d. 223), and Paul (fl. c. 210). These latter two, in their huge commentaries, saved most of what has survived from the wreck of republican and imperial law via the *Digest*, about half of whose contents they supplied. "The sharpness of focus is unmistakeable, the shortness of the period in which practically all of the surviving major legal writing of the Roman world was produced little short of astonishing."[14]

Ulpian defined jurisprudence as "knowledge of things divine and human, the science of what is just and unjust." It is the "true philosophy"; the jurists are her priests.[15] "The house of a great lawyer is assuredly the oracular seat of

11 M. Humbert (ed.), *Le Dodici Tavole* (Pavia 2005). For a skeptical view of their historicity, see M. T. Fögen, *Römische Rechtsgeschichten* (Göttingen 2002) 63–69 (reference courtesy of Luca Giuliani).

12 O. Behrends, "Die geistige Mitte des römischen Rechts," *ZRG* 125 (2008) 25–107.

13 *Theodosian code* [4:73] 1.4.3.2.

14 D. Ibbetson, "High classical law," *CAH* 12.186. On the importance of commentary see Schiavone, *Invention of law* [1:37] 356–57 and n. 64.

15 *Digest* [ed. T. Mommsen, revised P. Krueger, *Corpus iuris civilis* 1 (Berlin 1928[15]); tr. ed. A. Watson (Philadelphia 1998, revised ed.)] 1.1.1.1, 1.1.10.2; Ibbetson [6:14], *CAH* 12.192; Schiavone, *Invention of law* [1:37] 424–28.

the whole community," had declared Cicero; and to that oracle, even or especially when he ventured forth for a walk in the forum, all citizens had recourse on any conceivable business.[16] Although Roman law is more resistant than Aristotelianism to categories such as "prophecy" and "scripture," still the deposit of early laws, notably the Twelve Tables, attracted durable reverence and commentary, while the imperial Roman jurists can reasonably be labeled exegetes. But by the end of the third century, the emperor's growing absolutism and role as unique source of law was eclipsing the jurists, who gave way to codifiers and the compilers of anthologies and summaries, notably under Diocletian (284–305).[17] The two most important instantiations of this tendency were the *Gregorian code* (c. 292 with later additions) gathering imperial rescripts from Hadrian to 291, and the *Hermogenian code* (295 with later additions) assembling rescripts issued by Diocletian in 293–94.[18]

These at least semiofficial codes simplified the hunt for precedents in chronologically arranged archives on rolls; they were also symptomatic of Diocletian's wish to install a revised and rationalized Romanitas after the turbulence of the mid-third century. They deployed the now fashionable codex form,[19] a crucial First Millennium technology and index of Romanization, having originated in Rome in the first century CE.[20] We already saw Origen and Eusebius using it, again to facilitate scholarly compilations scanning broad conceptual horizons in an easily accessed format. No doubt the popularity of the codex also marks a significant shift away from oral transmission in the Roman legal tradition, perhaps in the Church too. But as we shall see, orality remained central to Judaism and, later, Islam. That strengthened the scholarly guild's monopoly compared to the less predictable and controllable circulation of books, but it also intensified the vividness of the tradition and the conviction it carried. It was rarely an either/or choice, though. Recitation and reading coexisted. "Qur'ān" means both.

Diocletian's project to revive Romanity was not unrealistic given the progress made by Augustus, Hadrian and, not least, the Severan jurists, in consolidating a sense of Roman identity, a "Romanocentric consensus."[21] Tensions had long been apparent, though, and they came out into the open

16 Cicero, *On the orator* [ed. A. S. Wilkins (Oxford 1902); tr. E. W. Sutton and H. Rackham (Cambridge, Mass. 1942)] 1.45.200, 3.33.133.

17 D. Johnston, "Epiclassical law," *CAH* 12.202–6.

18 S. Corcoran, *The empire of the Tetrarchs* (Oxford 2000, revised ed.) 25–42; S. Connolly, *Lives behind the laws: The world of the Codex Hermogenianus* (Bloomington, Ind. 2010) 39–45. Recently discovered Latin fragments of the *Gregorian code*: S. Corcoran and B. Salway, "*Fragmenta Londiniensia Anteiustiniana*", *Roman legal tradition* 8 (2012) 63-83. Syriac fragments of both codes, not always noticed in the scholarly literature: W. Selb, *Sententiae syriacae* (Vienna 1990) 189–96.

19 Wieacker, *Römische Rechtsgeschichte* [6:10] 1.135–37.

20 Bagnall, *Livres chrétiens* [6:4] 90–93; cf. M. Nicholls, "Parchment codices in a new text of Galen," *Greece and Rome* 57 (2010) 378–86.

21 Kaldellis, *Hellenism in Byzantium* [5:6] 45–61, 79.

when, less than a generation later, Constantine espoused Christianity. This provoked a double clash, between polytheistic Roman tradition and the Church, and different interpretations of Christianity struggling to attract imperial patronage. Even if the impulse toward codification had not been given, still the inherited body of law and procedure, and the writings of the authoritative imperial jurists, would have provided an indispensable touchstone of Romanitas in an age when the theoretical superstructures were questioned as never before. Despite earlier scholars' assumption that the story of late Roman law was one of codification equals petrification, therefore decline, it was in fact a vigorous and evolving organism.[22]

It is some measure of the durable pragmatism of Roman law and society that it was only a century after Constantine that a systematic statement of the legal basis of the new, Christianized society was attempted. The document known as the *Comparison of Mosaic and Roman laws* shows how some were seeking (Rome? 390s) to reassure themselves—in the manner of Eusebius of Caesarea—about the compatibility of the two traditions, and the feasibility of harmonizing Moses with the classical jurists and the two Diocletianic codes.[23] Then under Theodosius II (408–50) the need was finally recognized for a codification of laws—Christian laws—promulgated since Constantine, and for an attempt to digest and homogenize legal opinion both for practical reasons and in order to formulate reliable "guidance for life" (magisterium/ratio vitae).[24] But the *Theodosian code* promulgated at Constantinople in 438 did not resemble a philosophical treatise. It dispensed with "the exhortatory rhetoric in which imperial pronouncements were regularly clothed."[25] Far from encouraging rational reflection, it explicitly maintained the prestige of the imperial and especially Severan jurists (who had no equivalent under the Dominate); and it confined itself to making somewhat mechanical rules for establishing doctrine when the opinions expressed in their voluminous writings diverged.[26] Production of a digest of jurisprudence had to wait another century. The codex containing Theodosius's authoritative statement of orthodoxy was formally presented to and acclaimed by the Senate of Old Rome as well[27]—for similar treatment of the Bible, see below.

Note also the collection known as the *Laws of Constantine, Theodosius and Leo*, in Greek not Latin, which had been the language of the *Theodosian*

22 J. F. Matthews, *Laying down the law: A study of the Theodosian Code* (New Haven 2000) 10–30; C. Humfress, *Orthodoxy and the courts in late Antiquity* (Oxford 2007) 18–19.

23 R. M. Frakes, *Compiling the Collatio legum Mosaicarum et Romanarum in late Antiquity* (Oxford 2011).

24 *Theodosian code* [4:73] 1.1.5; cf. A. J. B. Sirks, *The Theodosian code* (Friedrichsdorf 2007) 36–53.

25 Matthews, *Laying down the law* [6:22] 20.

26 *Theodosian code* [4:73] 1.4.3 (the Law of citations, 426).

27 J. Harries, *Law and empire in late Antiquity* (Cambridge 1999) 64–66.

code and all legislation hitherto. The *Laws*, apparently compiled for school use shortly after the reign of Leo I (457–74), were translated into Syriac, the so-called *Syro-Roman law book*, before the end of the seventh century, and later into Armenian, Georgian, and Arabic. The demand for and durability of Christian Roman law were impressive, and this collection perhaps made its mark in the Church of the East and non-Chalcedonian (miaphysite) world by being *not* Justinian's code, and therefore less tainted by association with the repressive Chalcedonian Establishment.[28]

The first edition of Justinian's code of imperial law (lex) appeared in 529, and a revision in 534.[29] Where Theodosius had "appended Christian matters at the end, as a subject largely new to law,"[30] Justinian's code started out with a ringing declaration of Christian orthodoxy. It was accompanied by an immense *Digest* of the body of private law/legal opinion (ius) which had got so out of hand over the centuries—about 2,000 books, more than three million lines boiled down to roughly 150,000[31]—and a handbook aimed at law students, the *Institutes*. Both were published in 533. All these followed Diocletianic rather than Theodosian precedent by reaching back into pagan times, as far as Hadrian. Justinian could do this because he held that laws he decontextualized and repromulgated were baptized Christian even if originally issued by pagans (just as laws he omitted lost their force ipso facto). "To the emperor," he declared, "God has subjected the laws themselves by sending him to men as the living law (lex animata)."[32] Chapter 1 of the *Code* is titled "On the supreme Trinity and the Catholic Faith." Completion of the *Digest* is ascribed to the "inspiration of heaven and favour of the supreme Trinity."[33] On the writing of legal commentaries Justinian sought—not quite successfully—to place limitations,[34] signaling that the polyvocal exegetical period of Roman jurisprudence was not to be revived. It had been overtaken by—almost—a fresh revelation, under the emperor's auspices not those of private jurists.

The crisis precipitated by the Arab conquests did not destroy the legal tradition. It evolved, as did political and religious life. Justinian's *Corpus* con-

28 W. Selb and H. Kaufhold, *Das syrische-römische Rechtsbuch* (Vienna 2002).

29 C. Humfress, "Law and legal practice in the age of Justinian," and C. Pazdernik, "Justinianic ideology and the power of the past," in Maas (ed.), *Age of Justinian* [1:34] 161–212; S. Corcoran, "Justinian and his two codes," *Journal of juristic papyrology* 38 (2008) 73–111.

30 S. Corcoran, "The publication of law in the era of the Tetrarchs," in A. Demandt and others (eds), *Diokletian und die Tetrarchie* (Berlin 2004) 62.

31 Constitution *Tanta* (533), prefaced to the *Digest* [6:15], §1.

32 Justinian, *Novels* [ed. W. Kroll and R. Schoell, *Corpus iuris civilis* 3 (Berlin 1912^{4})] 105.2.4 (536); cf. J. H. A. Lokin, "The significance of law and legislation in the law books of the ninth to eleventh centuries," in A. E. Laiou and D. Simon (eds), *Law and society in Byzantium* (Washington, D.C. 1994) 72–76, 81–82.

33 Constitution *Tanta* (533), prefaced to the *Digest* [6:15], §1 and cf. Preface.

34 Wieacker, *Römische Rechtsgeschichte* [6:10] 2.300, 325–26; cf. J. F. Haldon, *Byzantium in the seventh century* (Cambridge 1990) 260 and n. 24.

tinued to be a massively authoritative presence, symbolic of Christian Roman imperium in its absolute God-given form.[35] But for just that reason it was liable to be subtly perverted in daily use, because unable to renew itself through debate and exegesis.[36] Though based on Justinian's *Corpus*, Leo III's *Ecloga* of 741 shows significant divergences from a work that it claims has become "unintelligible"—as any learned tradition does unless recast in current idiom. One notices both specific changes, for example in marital and penal law, such as the introduction (in the latter sphere) of bodily mutilation;[37] and more general evolutions, such as the notion that law comes direct from God, no longer from the emperor as lex animata.[38] The *Basilics*, compiled c. 900, gave the *Corpus* new life by purging the older Greek translations of their freight of Latinisms, and imposing a more thematic structure.[39] Later, the status of the *Corpus* again became controversial, hence a mid-eleventh-century writer's pointed preference for the original Justinianic sources over the *Basilics*.[40]

The new millennium signals no fresh developments or particular maturation in Roman law in the Greek East. In the Latin world, the story was different. Here, law was the fifth- and sixth-century Germanic successor kingdoms' principal borrowing from and link with Romanitas, though applied primarily to Roman subject peoples and perhaps more readily available in the Mediterranean lands of the Burgundians and Visigoths than in the North. The Gregorian, Hermogenian, and Theodosian codes were all known and used, for example in the *Breviary of Alaric* (*Lex Romana Visigothorum*) of 506. Law teaching continued in towns such as Narbonne and Lyons into the sixth century.[41] Gregory of Tours preserves a piquant tale about one Andarchius, a slave to a senator named Felix.

> He joined in the literary studies of Felix [apparently at Marseille] and distinguished himself by his learning. He became extremely well informed about the works of Virgil, the books of the Theodosian laws and the study of arithmetic.[42]

35 Haldon, *Byzantium in the seventh century* [6:34] 258–61.

36 B. Stolte, "Is Byzantine law Roman law?," *Acta Byzantina Fennica* 2 (2003–4) 122–26; Wieacker, *Römische Rechtsgeschichte* [6:10] 2.328.

37 Haldon, *Byzantium in the seventh century* [6:34] 85–86, 257, 262, 266–67.

38 Lokin, in Laiou and Simon (eds), *Law and society* [6:32] 76–80.

39 M. T. Fögen, "Reanimation of Roman law in the ninth century," in L. Brubaker (ed.), *Byzantium in the ninth century* (Aldershot 1998) 11–22.

40 *Essay on bare contracts* (*Meditatio de nudis pactis*) [ed. H. Monnier, *Études de droit byzantin* (London 1974) III.28–64] 6.25–27.

41 D. Liebs, "Roman law," *CAH* 14.254–56; T. M. Charles-Edwards, "Law in the Western kingdoms between the fifth and the seventh century," *CAH* 14.274, 277, 282–87; S. Lafferty, "Law and society in Ostrogothic Italy," *JLA* 3 (2010) 337–64.

42 Gregory of Tours, *History* [ed. B. Krusch and W. Levison (Hanover 1965^2); tr. L. Thorpe (Harmondsworth 1974)] 4.46 (tr. emended).

Andarchius contrived to parlay his learning into employment at the court of King Sigibert of the Franks (561–75), who used him in the public service until Andarchius overstepped the mark and came—but it's a long story—to a sad end.

After the sixth century the Roman and Germanic populations tended to merge, and so did their legal systems. Only the Church's canon law preserved recognizable elements of the Roman legal heritage. Just how Roman law was preserved and transmitted in the West between the sixth century and its eleventh-century revival—whether intact, in epitomes, or in re-expansions—is now becoming the subject of intensive research.[43] But transmission there was, especially—albeit indirectly—of the *Theodosian code*.[44] And this serves—better than anything in the history of Latin Aristotelianism—to underline how the West did not entirely lose sight of the Greco-Roman heritage after the sixth or seventh century. The Augustinian heritage sparked no debate remotely comparable to the reverberations set off by Chalcedon; nor was there any vigorous new shoot like Islam. Yet the postimperial Latin West cannot be written out of the First Millennium entirely; and the sphere of law is one of the areas of its life most susceptible to integration into the wider picture.

Unlike East Rome, the Latin West does see a new epoch at the beginning of the Second Millennium, with the rediscovery of the *Corpus* c. 1070 in Northern Italy. Thanks to teachers such as Pepo and Irnerius (c. 1050–after 1125), this now became the foundation text for the new law school in Bologna, which was destined for fame and influence. The *Corpus* was also crucial to the reform of the Papacy undertaken by Gregory VII. It has even been argued that, compared to East Roman lawyers' ingrained veneration for Justinian's work, Latin lawyers' more piecemeal and less obligatory use of it, alongside local law, was closer to the pragmatic, case-by-case methods of the imperial jurists—the *Digest* rather than the *Code*.[45] Certainly the *Digest*'s richness, and approachability compared to the *Code* and *Novels* or even the textbook manner of the *Institutes*, was fundamental to the revival of Roman law. But one should not underestimate the religious awe these early Western scholars felt for everything contained in Justinian's *Corpus*.[46]

As for the Caliphate, it was until recently deemed "out of the question . . . that the early Muslim specialists in religious law should consciously have ad-

43 M. H. Hoeflich and J. M. Grabherr, "The establishment of normative legal texts," in W. Hartmann and K. Pennington (eds), *The history of medieval canon law in the classical period, 1140–1234* (Washington, D.C. 2008) 2–3; W. Kaiser, "Nachvergleichungen von Novellen- und Codexzitaten," *ZRG* 125 (2008) 603–44; S. J. J. Corcoran, "New subscripts for old rescripts," *ZRG* 126 (2009) 401–3; http://www.ucl.ac.uk/history2/volterra/pv2.htm.

44 J. Harries and I. Wood (eds), *The Theodosian code* (Bristol 2010²) 159–216.

45 Stolte, *Acta Byzantina Fennica* 2 (2003–4) [6:36] 122–26.

46 P. Stein, *Roman law in European history* (Cambridge 1999) 43–47.

opted any principle of foreign law."[47] Christian communities in the Caliphate continued to regulate their internal affairs according to Roman law;[48] but Muslims took their law from the Qur'ān, eked out by the growing body of sayings attributed to the Prophet and other early figures. Yet in the Umayyad and early Abbasid Caliphates, religious scholars had not yet gained their later stranglehold on legal authority. Arguments, unfortunately very speculative, have recently been adduced, that under Hārūn al-Rashīd (786–803) a code of imperial law closely modeled on the *Corpus of civil law* was formulated, and remained effective for the half-century that also saw the flourishing of the philosophical translation project, until it was suppressed thanks to the efforts of the same religious circles that resisted rational theology and Mu'tazilism.[49] Whatever the outcome of this debate, it remains probable that elements of Roman law entered the early Muslim world through Syriac and Jewish intermediaries and the continuity of legal practice;[50] while a need for a corpus of secular or imperial law, known by the Greek name qānūn, was felt in later Muslim states, notably by the Ottomans.

RABBINIC JUDAISM

Jewish law demands attention in its own right.[51] Like Roman law, it began with a few brisk imperatives inscribed on tablets. But we need not deal here with the emergence of the Torah and the rest of the Jewish scriptural canon, still not quite complete c. 100 CE. The historian of the First Millennium is concerned with the rabbis, who slowly come into focus as a separate group during the second century, some time after the Jewish temple was destroyed in 70 CE and its priests dispersed.[52] The business of scriptural and legal commentary in Hebrew for which the rabbis were proverbial entered its most vigorous phase in third-century Palestine. The rabbis specialized in harmonizing discrepant scriptural texts and adducing them (they were not always ideally explicit) in support of rulings on religious, ethical, and social matters, for example Sabbath observance. In other words, they were engaged simulta-

47 J. Schacht, *An introduction to Islamic law* (Oxford 1964) 20–21.

48 W. Selb, *Orientalisches Kirchenrecht* 1 (Vienna 1981) 213–16.

49 B. Jokisch, *Islamic imperial law: Harun al-Rashid's codification project* (Berlin 2007); cf. the reviews by R. Peters, *Journal of the American Oriental Society* 129 (2009) 529–31; M. Tillier, *Revue des mondes musulmans et de la Méditerranée* 125 (2009), http://remmm.revues.org/6111.

50 A. S. Ahmedov, "On question of influence of Roman law on Islamic law," *Diritto@storia* 8 (2009), www.dirittoestoria.it; Jokisch, *Islamic imperial law* [6:49] 61–62, on possible relations between Roman and Jewish law.

51 S. T. Katz (ed.), *The Cambridge history of Judaism* 4 (Cambridge 2006) chaps. 12–14, 26–27, 33–35.

52 For a general account of this process up to the sixth century, see H. Lapin, *Rabbis as Romans: The rabbinic movement in Palestine, 100–400 C.E.* (New York 2012) 38–63, 77–83, 151–67.

neously in exegesis and legislation. No doubt their opinions were initially solicited informally like those of the old Roman jurists recalled by Cicero, and transmitted orally. The third century saw the production, just as the prestigious period of Roman jurisprudence was waning, of the Mishnah, designed to elaborate, clarify and supplement the commandments contained in the Torah, but with its own distinctive structure. Probably by the fourth century especially in Palestine, and more certainly by the sixth century even beyond Palestine, the rabbis were on their way to becoming communal/synagogal functionaries, with circles of pupils meeting in study houses, and inclined to promote norms of what they regarded as "orthodoxy."[53]

The "Jerusalem" or rather Palestinian Talmud (since it appears to have been finalized in late fourth- or early fifth-century Tiberias) offered commentary on the Mishnah, but neither comprehensively nor systematically. Rather, it foregrounds the opinions of five generations of Palestinian sages (amoraim) and three of Babylonian, discussing them for their own sake, not just for the light they throw on the Mishnah. The Babylonian Talmud adds later generations of Babylonians to the mix, and must have been nearing completion about when Justinian's corpus was promulgated, though additions accumulated into the eighth century.[54] It is more expansive, discursive, and associative in its interpretations than its Palestinian counterpart. The literary form is that of free-ranging debates, but if these preserve any record of actual historical discussions, they have been reworked and idealized. Down to the present day, the "Bavli" provides the most monumental statement of Jewish law.

In a remarkably explicit and political acknowledgment of the grip exegetical traditions can obtain on a community, Justinian's *Novel* 146 of 553 banned exposition of scripture during synagogue services because it is "not handed down from above by the prophets, but is merely the invention of men speaking from the earth alone and has nothing of the divine about it." The readers must stick to "ipsos codices" (actually scrolls) and not corrupt the uninstructed by adding extraneous commentary. All must be made aware of "the depravity of interpreters." One recalls the same emperor's restrictions on legal commentary. In the case of the Jews, Justinian hoped exposure to scripture on its own terms, preferably in the inspired (albeit translated!) Greek of the Septuagint and not just in Hebrew, would make them see the light.[55]

Shared areas of interest naturally occur in legal systems operative within the same society or at least state. There may or may not be conceptual kinship too. Almost contemporary Roman jurists and Jewish sages or rabbis pro-

53 S. Schwartz, "Rabbinization in the sixth century," in P. Schäfer (ed.), *The Talmud Yerushalmi and Graeco-Roman culture* (Tübingen 1998–2002) 3.55–69.

54 D. Goodblatt, "A generation of Talmudic studies," in Bakhos and Shayegan (eds), *Talmud in its Iranian context* [4:64] 3–4, 12–18 (reference courtesy of Daniel Boyarin).

55 Justinian, *Novels* [6:32] 146. The rabbinical milieu did not adopt the codex before the eighth century: Goodblatt [6:54], in Bakhos and Shayegan (eds), *Talmud in its Iranian context* [4:64] 3–4.

duced works which, once codified (rather earlier in the case of the rabbis), were massive, were inchoate yet harmonizing, were derivative yet inventive, and eventually became (whether or not this was originally intended) normative for their respective societies, with semiencyclopedic status.[56] They bear broad comparison—not least for their essentially nontheological character. But while the rabbis cannot have been completely ignorant of Roman law, while Roman legislators were certainly not unaware of the Jews, direct debts are hard to pin down. The Mishnah and Talmud are no less deficient in imperial law (and sponsorship) than the *Digest* (based on jurists' law and therefore the only directly comparable part of the *Corpus of civil law*) is in rules concerning cultic ritual. As for the Gospel, its spirit went plain against the legalism of the Torah, so there could be no Christian equivalent to rabbinics, and the Church contented itself with Christianizing Roman law.[57] Not surprisingly, rabbinic Judaism has often been represented as a world unto itself, not least by Zionist scholars seeking in the rabbinate a distillation of the Jewish national will. Nonetheless, rabbinics has of late benefited, especially in the United States, from a contextualizing historical approach, and incorporation into study of late Antiquity.[58] This has led to a realization that, while intimate interaction with Roman law or patristics is not to be expected, there was a more general cultural atmosphere that linked the Talmudic milieu with developments within the Church.

Here, the prophecy-scripture-exegesis analysis offers a securer base for comparison than in the case of Roman law. First came divine revelation to Moses in the Torah; then the rest of the Jewish Bible; and finally rabbinic tradition, exegesis not scripture and, in the case of the Mishnah, thematically arranged rather than following the Torah's divisions. Nevertheless, the rabbis' purpose was unmistakably exegesis of a scriptural canon, whose expression, precisely because fixed, was diverging more and more from current modes, and had to be recaptured by the efforts of a scholarly elite. At least, that is our academic way of seeing the process, and not just in Judaism.[59] But the rabbis themselves—especially those of Babylon as distinct from their

56 D. Stern, "On canonization in rabbinic Judaism," in M. Finkelberg and G. G. Stroumsa (eds), *Homer, the Bible, and beyond* (Leiden 2003) 227–52; C. Hezser, "The codification of legal knowledge in late Antiquity: The Talmud Yerushalmi and Roman law codes," in Schäfer (ed.), *Talmud Yerushalmi* [6:53] 1.581–641. If Middle Persian legal texts were more accessible to comparative scholarship, this would be the place to compare them with the Babylonian Talmud: cf. S. Secunda, "The Sasanian "Stam": Orality and the composition of Babylonian rabbinic and Zoroastrian legal literature," in Bakhos and Shayegan (eds), *Talmud in its Iranian context* [4:64] 140–60.

57 Early Muslims could be quite puzzled by the absence of systematic law from the gospels: A. Papaconstantinou, "Between *umma* and *dhimma*," *Annales islamologiques* 42 (2008) 148–49.

58 S. Schwartz, "The political geography of rabbinic texts," in C. E. Fonrobert and M. S. Jaffee (eds), *The Cambridge companion to the Talmud and rabbinic literature* (Cambridge 2007) 80–93; Bakhos and Shayegan (eds), *Talmud in its Iranian context* [4: 64].

59 J. Børtnes, "Canon formation and canon interpretation," in E. Thomassen (ed.), *Canon and canonicity* (Copenhagen 2010) 189–91, 197–98, invoking Jan Assmann.

cousins of Palestine—were inclined to see the whole tradition as Torah, and themselves rather as its culmination than its tail end.[60] An often-quoted story has Moses encounter God attaching little crowns to the letters of the alphabet. God explains that there will come a man destined to "expound upon each crownlet heaps and heaps of laws." Moses asks to see this paragon, and God tells him to turn round. He finds himself sitting in the back row of Rabbi Akiva's classroom—a notoriously imaginative exegete who died c. 135. Moses cannot understand what is being said. He feels weak, but then

> the disciples said to him [sc. Rabbi Akiva], "Rabbi, how do you know this?" He replied, "It is a law given to Moses at Sinai." And Moses was comforted.[61]

In other words the so-called "oral Torah" of the rabbis, which was eventually also written down, is in direct but unrecognizably evolved line of descent from God's revelation at Sinai. It covers the whole spectrum from revelation to exegesis, from curt mountain-top commands to involuted school-room hermeneutics. While ordinary Jews knew only the written Torah, the five books of the Pentateuch, the rabbis had their own Torah that was likewise revealed, but contained elements of human ratiocination, and indeed diversity and divergence of opinion, and therefore innovated in relation to the Sinaitic revelation, as Justinian pointed out. That meant multiple possible truths (or at least levels of truth, depending on each student's abilities), which is not what we associate with monotheist traditions.[62] It also meant an open-ended canon, unlike in Christianity, and constant debate aimed at a more refined understanding of God's word, analogous to the rationalist technique of the modern scientist who strives for ever closer approximation to truth rather than for exact truth, which is beyond human grasp.[63] The Babylonian Talmud codified this outlook, which was passed on to the newer Jewish communities in North Africa and Europe, and defined them until the rise of liberal, secularizing, and assimilationist forces in the nineteenth century.[64]

We must not overemphasize, then, the common denominators of our exegetical cultures. Like Christianity, rabbinic Judaism was a product mainly of

60 I. Gafni, "Rabbinic historiography and representations of the past," in Fonrobert and Jaffee (eds), *Talmud and rabbinic literature* [6:58] 303–4; D. Kraemer, "Fictions and formulations: The Talmud and the construction of Jewish identity," in H. Liss and M. Oeming (eds), *Literary construction of identity in the ancient world* (Winona Lake, Ind. 2010) 237–38.

61 Babylonian Talmud, Menahot 29b, quoted and discussed by E. S. Alexander, "The orality of rabbinic writing," and D. Boyarin, "Hellenism in Jewish Babylonia," in Fonrobert and Jaffee (eds), *Talmud and rabbinic literature* [6:58] 42–43, 348–49.

62 Cf. J. Howland, *Plato and the Talmud* (Cambridge 2011) 45–49.

63 Cf. M. Fisch, *Rational rabbis: Science and Talmudic culture* (Bloomington, Ind. 1997), discussing Menahot 29b at 192–96.

64 G. Stemberger, *Der Talmud* (Munich 1994^{3}) 286–316.

the earlier part of the First Millennium. A comparative approach is imposed by their partially shared scriptures, and by the fact that Islam drew on both. But there was considerable complexity, and we are not always as well informed as we would like. In discussing, for instance, the uses to which Aristotelian logic was put, I already mentioned the *Organon*-fueled disputatiousness of fourth-century Christianity and the reaction it sparked, the conceit among certain Christian intellectuals that they thought "like fishermen," not Aristotle. But beyond this affectation, and despite continuing interest in Aristotle, there was growing conviction in thinkers like Evagrius of Pontus (lived mainly in Constantinople and Egypt, d. 399), Ps.-Dionysius the Areopagite (c. 500), and Isaac of Nineveh (d. c. 700), that it was vain to speak about God. Better say as little as possible, or just what God is not, "apophaticism." "Competitive forms of knowledge such as Aristotelian dialectic were subordinated to an apophatic, mystical *theōria* that stressed the importance of a hierarchical status quo and the mediation of priests in the spiritual anagogy."[65] The more scholastic approach also persisted, though, and is well exemplified by the grammatical, historical, typological, antiallegorical, nonspeculative, and *Organon*-influenced Biblical exegesis practiced, especially from the late fifth century to the early seventh, by the school of Nisibis, and propagated among adherents of the Church of the East in Sasanid Mesopotamia.[66] Note once again the Syriac contribution to these interesting evolutions in "late" Hellenism.

There is no sign that the Nisibenes talked to the rabbis of Pumbedita (near or at Anbār, Iraq), or vice versa; but both circles belonged to the same region, era, and scripturalist, exegetical milieu.[67] Daniel Boyarin has detected shared ground between the rabbis and both the scholastic and the apophatic strands in Christian thought. On the one hand he compares the Babylonian Talmud's obsession with Torah for its own sake, and "the pure spiritual pleasure of . . . logic chopping," to the scholasticism of Nisibis. But we must also consider the fluctuating state of the Talmudic corpus, the slowness with which it reached the state we are now familiar with, and the later generations of Babylonian rabbis' joy in the multiplication of opinions and insistence on discussing even the most improbable of them, rather than pursuing certain

65 R. Lim, "Christian triumph and controversy," in G. W. Bowersock and others (eds), *Interpreting late Antiquity* (Cambridge, Mass. 2001) 205.

66 Grillmeier, *Jesus der Christus* [4:72] 2/3.252–56 (T. Hainthaler); P. Bruns, "Aristoteles-Rezeption und Entstehung einer syrischen Scholastik," in P. Bruns (ed.), *Von Athen nach Baghdad* (Bonn 2003) 32–34; Becker, *Fear of God* [5:94] 87–92. For the possibility Christians were still teaching the *Organon* at Nisibis in the early ninth century, see S. Stroumsa, *Ginzei qedem* 3 (2007) [5:110] 143*.

67 D. Boyarin, "Dialectic and divination in the Talmud," in S. Goldhill (ed.), *The end of dialogue in Antiquity* (Cambridge 2008) 239–41; Y. Arzhanov, "Zeugnisse über Kontakte zwischen Juden und Christen im vorislamischen Arabien," *Oriens Christianus* 92 (2008) 90–91. E. Narinskaya, *Ephrem, a "Jewish" sage* (Turnhout 2010), argues Ephrem of Nisibis was closely acquainted with rabbinical circles in that city.

knowledge.[68] In all this Boyarin sees a symptom of the impasse experienced in Greek Christianity too, as regards the possibility (still accepted by the earlier Palestinian Talmud) of adjudicating between different versions of the truth, and attaining unity of mind. Once that Nicaean aspiration was abandoned—to look on the bright side—the community was less likely to split over doctrine, and might allow pluralism of practice as well.[69]

Despite these similarities of spiritual and intellectual experience, there was a fundamental mistrust between Jews and Christians, which usually prevented productive conversations between their scholarly representatives. They belonged to the same First Millennium exegetical culture; yet their parallel and chronologically close rereadings of the Jewish Bible, respectively through the Mishnah's law and ritual and the New Testament's proclamation of faith,[70] set them at odds. The coming of Islam introduced another perspective. Already in the later suras of the Qur'ān there is marked hostility to both Jews and Christians; but there is also throughout the text recognition that the new revelation follows and reinforces the older ones, while correcting corruptions introduced by their exegetes. Not only is the Qur'ān full of allusions to Torah and Gospel, but the role of monks and rabbis is acknowledged, albeit at times critically: "They have taken their rabbis and monks as lords apart from God."[71] One senses, though, that the Jews were more of a presence to Muḥammad. The Qur'ān, like the Torah but not the Christian Bible, is full of law; and in its pronouncements the hand of the rabbis may on occasion be discerned.[72]

The establishment of the Caliphate united most of the world's Jews under one government more tolerant than East Rome had become by the seventh century. It offered the rabbis a chance to impose the moral hegemony of their new Talmudic orthodoxy from Central Asia to the setting sun—not implausibly, given the need to present a single front to the new ruler, his faith, and his tax collectors. To the Pumbedita and Sūra' academies (yeshivot), which moved to Baghdad in the course of the later ninth and tenth centuries, Jews

68 The best rabbi was the one who could devise most arguments for a manifestly absurd position: R. Kalmin, "The formation and character of the Babylonian Talmud," in Katz (ed.), *Cambridge history of Judaism* 4 [6:51] 872; and cf. D. Kraemer, *Reading the rabbis* (New York 1996) 60–70.

69 D. Boyarin, *Border lines: The partition of Judaeo-Christianity* (Philadelphia 2004) 151–201; id., in Goldhill (ed.), *End of dialogue* [6:67] 226–39; id. [6:61], in Fonrobert and Jaffee (eds), *Talmud and rabbinic literature* [6:58] 341, 349, 358. Cf. Kraemer, *Reading the rabbis* [6:68] 71–85 (pluralism of practice); C. Batsch, "Le(s) corpus rabbinique(s): Questions de clôture," *Cahiers Glotz* 21 (2010) 359–70 (anarchic formation of rabbinic literature); A. Becker, "The comparative study of "scholasticism" in late antique Mesopotamia: Rabbis and East Syrians," *AJS review* 34 (2010) 91–113.

70 G. G. Stroumsa (tr. S. Emanuel), *The end of sacrifice* (Chicago 2009) 47–48.

71 Qur'ān 5.82; 9.31 (whence the quotation, tr. A. Jones), 34.

72 Cf. R. Leicht, "The Qur'anic commandment of writing down loan agreements (Q 2:282)—Perspectives of a comparison with rabbinical law," in A. Neuwirth and others (eds), *The Qur'ān in context* (Leiden 2010) 593–614.

from all over did indeed appeal on disputed questions of belief and practice.[73] But just as resistances emerged to the assertive political and religious elites of the Muslim world, so by the late ninth century the rabbis confronted a rejectionist movement, the Karaites.[74] The Karaites espoused rational theology and ditched oral Torah in favor of scripture, and Aramaic/Hebrew for the new world-language Arabic. That exposed them to the latest currents in both Muslim and Christian thought, especially in Baghdad where the whole world flowed together. Until very recently the Karaites seemed obscure and peripheral, but thanks to the improved accessibility of Russian libraries they are now an exciting new frontier in scholarship. One result is realization that their intellectual choices were more typical of late First Millennium Judaism than had been appreciated.

Here again, scriptural exegesis is central, both as the channel through which the Karaites imbibed Christian and Muslim thought and as the cudgel with which they set about the rabbis. Already Dāwūd al-Muqammaṣ in the early ninth century[75] shows a taste for the more coherent exegetical style of Christian writers over the rabbis' competitive, contradictory, too-ingenious, punning, or off-the-wall interpretations arranged into loose structures. Growing up at Raqqa in Northern Syria, Dāwūd converted to Christianity and studied at Nisibis with a Christian philosopher who taught him some Aristotle.[76] (Besides the *Categories* and *Isagoge* he rather surprisingly, at this early date, invokes *On the soul* as well.) Reverting to Judaism, he wrote the first Jewish (and, as it happens, earliest surviving Arabic) summa theologica, titled *Twenty chapters*; refutations of Christianity; and translations into Arabic of Syriac commentaries on Genesis (the hexaemeron) and Ecclesiastes. Dāwūd is accounted a philosopher not a Karaite; but Karaites too—notably Daniel al-Qūmisī (late ninth century) in Hebrew, and later another member of the important Jerusalem community, Yefet ben ʿEli (d. after 1006) in Arabic[77]—espoused systematic, sequential, contextual commentary with a single authorial voice and attention to philological and historical issues, also to literal translation into Arabic (after al-Qūmisī). With these tools they aspired to show how, if taken at face value and assessed in the light of reason, the

73 D. E. Sklare, *Samuel ben Ḥofni Gaon and his cultural world* (Leiden 1996) 69–97, esp. 71–72.

74 M. Polliack (ed.), *Karaite Judaism* (Leiden 2003), esp. F. Astren's "Islamic contexts of medieval Karaism," H. Ben-Shammai's "Major trends in Karaite philosophy and polemics," and M. Polliack's "Major trends in Karaite Biblical exegesis"; D. Frank, *Search scripture well: Karaite exegetes and the origins of the Jewish Bible commentary in the Islamic East* (Leiden 2004) 1–32, 248–57.

75 S. Stroumsa (ed. and tr.), *Dāwūd ibn Marwān al-Muqammiṣ's Twenty chapters* (Leiden 1989) 15–35; id., "The impact of Syriac tradition on early Judaeo-Arabic Bible exegesis," *ARAM* 3 (1991) 83–89; id., *Ginzei qedem* 3 (2007) [5:110] 137*–161*.

76 H. G. B. Teule, "Nonnus of Nisibis," in D. Thomas and B. Roggema (eds), *Christian-Muslim relations: A bibliographical history* 1 (Leiden 2009) 743–45.

77 M. G. Wechsler (ed. and tr.), *The Arabic translation and commentary of Yefet ben ʿEli the Karaite on the Book of Esther* (Leiden 2008) 3–71 H. Ben-Shammai, "Daniel al-Qūmisī", *EIs*³ 2013–2.87–90.

Bible may often yield a *single* correct meaning. This incensed the Rabbanites (as scholars call them when they need to be contrasted with Karaites); but Karaite commentaries embraced, where appropriate, the midrashic heritage too, as also the Muʿtazilites' insistence on God's inner and essential—not just external—unity, and his justice. Indeed, we would know a lot less about Muʿtazilism today were it not for the preservation of their books by Karaite Jews. Nor was the Karaites' impact confined to the East. They were the First Millennium forerunners of the major exegetical achievements of Spanish Sephardic scholars in centuries to come.

Jews had taken no serious interest in philosophy since the profoundly Hellenized exposition of the scripture by Philo of Alexandria (d. 50 CE), even if, in the more quotidian aspects illuminated by archaeology, many Jewish communities had continued to be culturally Greek. The rabbis never allude to Philo.[78] But interest in (a very different sort of) philosophy revived in the ninth and tenth centuries thanks to Dāwūd al-Muqammaṣ and later to other pioneers such as Saadia Gaon (d. 942) and Isḥāq al-Isrā'īlī (d. 955), writing in Arabic of course, though often in Hebrew script.[79] Saadia is perhaps the one most central to Abbasid Jewry's rapid evolution. He was fully trained in rabbinic tradition, and became head of the Sūra' Academy. At the same time he was well read in Aristotle, who had by his day been almost entirely translated into Arabic, and in the Platonizing thought of the first Arabic philosopher, Kindī. His writings defended oral Torah against the Karaites, but also demonstrated the compatibility of both Jewish scriptural commentary and rabbinic erudition with the authority of reason, as exemplified by the Greeks and by Muslim theological discourse, including Muʿtazilism. The Bible's anthropomorphic language about God he was inclined to explain as metaphor.[80]

Saadia reveals a maturation in Jewish thought. He is still indebted methodologically to the Syriac Christian exegetical tradition,[81] but his manner is more specifically Jewish than Dāwūd al-Muqammaṣ's. At the end of the First

78 On the exiguous evidence for direct rabbinic engagement with Greco-Roman philosophy, see C. Hezser, "Interfaces between rabbinic literature and Graeco-Roman philosophy," in Schäfer (ed.), *Talmud Yerushalmi* [6:53] 2.161–87.

79 H. Ben-Shammai, "Kalām in medieval Jewish philosophy," and T. M. Rudavsky, "Medieval Jewish Neoplatonism," in D. H. Frank and O. Leaman (eds), *History of Jewish philosophy* (London 1997) 99–104, 120–23; S. Stroumsa, "The Muslim context," in S. Nadler and T. M. Rudavsky (eds), *The Cambridge history of Jewish philosophy* 1 (Cambridge 2009) 39–59. On Saadia, see further S. Stroumsa, "Saadya and Jewish *kalam*," in D. H. Frank and O. Leaman (eds), *The Cambridge companion to medieval Jewish philosophy* (Cambridge 2003) 69–90; E. Schweid (tr. L. Levin), *The classic Jewish philosophers* (Leiden 2008) 3–38.

80 H. Kreisel, "Philosophical interpretations of the Bible," in Nadler and Rudavsky (eds), *Cambridge history of Jewish philosophy* [6:79] 1.92–94.

81 S. Stroumsa, "Prolegomena as historical evidence: On Saadia's introductions to his commentaries on the Bible," in Wisnovsky and others (eds), *Vehicles of transmission* [3:18] 139–41.

Millennium, Saadia and a few others[82] were nudging Judaism back toward the mainstream of Arabic intellectual debate. They made the Jewish voice heard in that extraordinary milieu of ninth- to tenth-century Baghdad, where intellectuals could agree (as we shall see in the last chapter) to put aside quarrels about the authority of their respective scriptures and debate together using the tools of Greek logic and rationality as adjusted and refined in the schools of Alexandria, and then in Syriac and Arabic translation. Indeed, Saadia established rationalist theology as central to Judaism, whereas in Islam it was being diluted. Where Jews had played almost no part in translating Greek philosophy from Greek into Arabic, they were prominent in its next transition, from Arabic to Latin.[83] Thereafter Jewish philosophy did not disappear again as it had after Philo, but became an increasingly vigorous part of both the Latin and the Arabic thought worlds. One has only to think of the Aristotelianism of Maimonides (d. 1204)—one of the many good reasons we talk about Arabic not Islamic philosophy.

PATRISTIC CHRISTIANITY

Judaism and Islam resemble each other strikingly. The first Muslims' violent triumph over the old empires in the name of an uncompromisingly single God recalls Old Testament models, rather than Christianity's subtle penetration of Rome without recourse to arms or even to God-given law. Both religions precisely regulated personal conduct and family and community life; both came to be dominated by scholarly-exegetical and legal rather than sacramental elites.[84] Consider also the Qur'ān's dialogue with the Jewish Bible, especially the Psalms. And where Christians absorbed themselves in Christology, both Muslims and the later Jewish thinkers we have just been considering were markedly more concerned with prophetology. Jewish writers might even on occasion refer to their scriptures as "Qur'ān."[85]

Against this background, taking in Christianity on the way from rabbinic Judaism to Islam could seem a diversion.[86] Yet Christianity too was a major exegetical culture, which emerged parallel to rabbinism in response (partly) to the same scriptures,[87] and likewise figured prominently in early Islam's

82 E.g., a later head of the Sūra' yeshiva, Samuel ben Ḥofni Gaon (d. 1013). His rational, critical rabbinics and openness to Muʿtazilism is excellently discussed by Sklare [6:73] 37–67.

83 S. Stroumsa, in Nadler and Rudavsky (eds), *Cambridge history of Jewish philosophy* [6:79] 1.57–58.

84 J. Neusner and T. Sonn, *Comparing religions through law: Judaism and Islam* (London 1999).

85 S. Stroumsa, in Nadler and Rudavsky (eds), *Cambridge history of Jewish philosophy* [6:79] 1.52–53.

86 Pocock 2.108: "It was a problem for all would-be composers of treatises *de tribus impostoribus* that Jesus had not been a legislator. . . ."

87 The argument of G. Stroumsa, *End of sacrifice* [6:70]: see esp. 130.

field of reference. Its differences from these traditions, as well as its similarities, are instructive. Needless to say, patristics also became a prime influence on all subsequent Christian cultures and, as we saw in chapter 2, the field of late antique studies.

To speak of Jesus's ministry as Christianity's "prophetic" phase seems tendentious given the Gospels' presentation of him, already at his baptism, as the son of God. Whatever else this meant, it followed that his teaching carried greater authority than that of the prophets, who had gone before him and foretold his coming. Nonetheless, Jesus was regarded by some who encountered him as simply another in the line of prophets sent by God to warn Israel.[88] For us, recognizing his prophetic aspect underlines the crucial experience, that of the founder, which a number of religions share, and renders Christianity susceptible to a comparative approach, despite the unique claims derived from its doctrine of divine incarnation. And in Islam Jesus was revered, precisely, as a prophet. God could not have a son.

To this prophetic phase of Christianity Eusebius of Caesarea dedicates the first of the ten books of his *Ecclesiastical history*, starting with a firm, theological statement of Christ's divinity and underlining how, on the human level, his coming had deep roots in the ancient and honorable race (ethnos) of the Hebrews, whose prophets had foreshadowed it. Indeed, "the announcement to all the Gentiles, recently made through the teaching of Christ," is identical with "that first, most ancient and antique discovery of true religion by those lovers of God who followed Abraham"—precisely the same "primitive, unique and true" Abrahamic pedigree later claimed by Islam as well. Eusebius resists, for sound theological and historical reasons, any understanding of Christianity as spontaneously generated. But at the same time Christians are for him a "new race," whose founder was born—as we saw earlier—in the reign of Augustus the first Roman emperor, and just after the end of "the Egyptian dynasty of the Ptolemies."[89]

Eusebius situates Christianity's prophetic phase both in the broader flow of the history of empires, and at the outset of a fresh period inaugurated by a new "people." Later ecclesiastical historians assumed but did not restate this scheme of things, simply picking up where Eusebius, or one of his successors, had left off. The inestimable value of the *Ecclesiastical history*, though, is that besides the prophetic beginnings of the new religion, it also delineates the scriptural *and* exegetical/patristic phases. Into its basic framework of narrative history plus episcopal lists for the major sees, it inserts detailed accounts of the formation of the scriptural canon (a term Eusebius is the first to use in this context[90]), and of the major exegetical and other patristic writings pro-

88 Matthew 16:13-16, Mark 6:14-15; cf. Hebrews 1:1-2, 3:1-6.

89 Eusebius, *Ecclesiastical history* [3:35] 1.4.1–5.2.

90 Eusebius, *Ecclesiastical history* [3:35] 6.25.3; cf. L. M. McDonald and J. A. Sanders, "Introduction," in their *The canon debate* (Peabody, Mass. 2002) 12–13.

duced by leading ecclesiastical figures, especially in their constant warfare on heresy.[91] (Here, at least, Eusebius implicitly recognizes the polyvocality of a tradition he usually prefers to represent as a more or less seamless historical development culminating in the Constantinian Church of his own day.) The two phases, scriptural and exegetical, ran concurrently, because it took the Church until the end of the fourth century to finalize which books deserved canonical status, the Old Testament (Septuagint) presenting even thornier problems than the New.[92] The task was accomplished inclusively, therefore durably, thanks to lived experience of regional variety and of the nexus between liturgy and teaching on which Justinian was to put his finger in legislating about the synagogue services. Also without need of conciliar decrees—in fact it was discovered that the Gospel book, enthroned or placed on the altar to represent Christ's presence (just as the *Theodosian code* was displayed before the Roman Senate), was the best antidote to the precedence struggles between bishops that marred so many councils.[93] This scene, frequently depicted thereafter in Christian art, made clear on the symbolic level what the Diocletianic persecutors' demand for surrender of books[94] had already acknowledged in practice, namely that Christianity was a religion of the Book as well as of bishops—though bishops were indispensable for policing orthodox exegesis of all texts, creeds as well as scriptures.

The most prominent individual in Eusebius's account of early patristics is Origen (d. c. 254), who divided his career between Alexandria and Palestinian Caesarea.[95] In the latter city, Origen's intellectual heirs Pamphilus and Eusebius himself (Caesarea's bishop) continued to labor among the master's books.[96] Origen and Eusebius stand for one of the main threads of Christian self-awareness and self-definition—learned and Alexandrian—during the third and the first half of the fourth centuries. If Eusebius's principal contribution was to history, Origen's was to theology distilled from book-by-book

91 For an example, see, e.g., Eusebius, *Ecclesiastical history* [3:35] 7.24–25 on Dionysius of Alexandria. On the emergence of the concept of patristics, and Eusebius's role in it, see T. Graumann, "The conduct of theology and the "Fathers" of the Church," in Rousseau (ed.), *Late Antiquity* [2:9] 546–54.

92 Eusebius, *Ecclesiastical history* [3:35] 3.25 etc.; Athanasius of Alexandria, *Festal epistle* [ed. T. Zahn, *Grundriss der Geschichte des neutestamentlichen Kanons* (Leipzig 1904²) 86–92] 39, for the earliest complete list of twenty-seven books including Revelation; cf. B. M. Metzger, *The canon of the New Testament* (Oxford 1987) 210–12; C. Markschies, *Kaiserzeitliche christliche Theologie und ihre Institutionen* (Tübingen 2007) 215–335; M. W. Holmes, "The Biblical canon," in S. A. Harvey and D. G. Hunter (eds), *The Oxford handbook of early Christian studies* (Oxford 2008) 406–26; E. Thomassen, "Some notes on the development of Christian ideas about a canon," in id., *Canon and canonicity* [6:59] 9–28.

93 C. Walter, *L'iconographie des conciles dans la tradition byzantine* (Paris 1970) 34–37, 61 (with 62 fig. 28), 75–77, 147–48, 235–39.

94 Eusebius, *Ecclesiastical history* [3:35] 8.2.4.

95 Convenient accounts in T. D. Barnes, *Constantine and Eusebius* (Cambridge, Mass. 1981) 81–94; A. Le Boulluec, "L' "école" d'Alexandrie," in J.-M. Mayeur and others (eds), *Histoire du Christianisme* (Paris 1990–2000) 1.560–78.

96 A. Carriker, *The library of Eusebius of Caesarea* (Leiden 2003) 1–36.

exegesis of the Bible, then expounded in almost daily sermons as part of the Church's liturgical cycle,[97] and in teaching catechumens—not just a book learning to be dictated, copied, and distributed, but also an intensely practical and oral spirituality against a background of sporadic persecution and martyrdom, as for Origen's father and at least seven of his pupils. (Recall the martyr bearing cross and codex marching toward a gridiron beside a cabinet full of Gospel books, in a mosaic in the mausoleum of Galla Placidia at Ravenna.)

Origen was not the first Christian exegete: the Gospels themselves frequently allude to the Jewish scriptures, not to mention Paul. But Origen was the first to deploy the spectrum of available erudition on the Bible, and write systematic commentaries in the manner of the philosophers, exhibiting the scripture's underlying coherence and rationality—therefore also compatibility with philosophy.[98] Indeed, it is arguable that Eusebius sees in Origen an outstanding exemplar of the fact that Christianity is to be located, historically and intellectually, not only—as in chapter 3—against the backdrop of Rome (*Ecclesiastical history*) and earlier empires and civilizations (*Chronicle*), but also (*Preparation for the Gospel*) as a development from Greek philosophy, Plato in particular. And Greek philosophy derived, in its turn, from the wisdom traditions of the ancient Hebrews.[99]

Being so deeply versed in philosophy, especially Platonism, Origen found much in the Bible that escaped those who stayed on the text's surface. He keenly studied scripture's literal meaning, in Hebrew as well as Greek: on the Jewish Bible he consulted his Jewish or rabbinic contemporaries, and unlike them was much influenced by Philo. But behind the philology he always sought hidden, spiritual doctrine. Scripture's many obscurities, absurdities, or lapses of taste—God strolling in his garden, Lot lying with his daughters, Jesus viewing all the kingdoms of the world—made this allegorical style of exegesis (which had a long pedigree) seem defensible, and left Origen a free terrain on which to construct a philosophical, rationalizing Christianity. He was also much given to finding foreshadowings of the new, Christian dispensation in the Jewish scriptures—a "typological" approach that helped make sense of the difficult relationship between Judaism and the Church, while typifying the Christian tendency to see primarily history and prophecy in the Jewish Bible, where the parallel exegetical tradition saw primarily law, framed in history.

97 On recent growth of interest in homiletics, see W. Mayer, "Homiletics," in Harvey and Hunter (eds), *Early Christian studies* [6:92] 565–83. This will be intensified by the April 2012 discovery in the Bayerische Staatsbibliothek, Munich, of an eleventh/twelfth-century manuscript with the previously unknown Greek text of twenty-nine sermons on the Psalms by Origen: http://www.uni-muenster.de/FB2/origenes/spektakulaererfund.html.

98 Fürst [5:41], in *IBALA*.

99 C. Fraenkel, "Integrating Greek philosophy into Jewish and Christian contexts in Antiquity: The Alexandrian project," in Wisnovsky and others (eds), *Vehicles of transmission* [3:18] 23–47.

In Origen we see a confluence of Christianity, philosophy, and Judaism with a spiritualizing, symbolic allegorization that seemed beguiling in his relatively undogmatic age, but after Constantine—especially under Justinian—fell under suspicion of undermining Jesus's historical actuality. The council of the whole Church which Constantine summoned to Nicaea in 325 marked a new determination to formulate obligatory dogma and exclude dissenters. The fourth century saw growing awareness of "Hellenism," Judaism, and Christianity as distinct "religions," thanks not least to intellectuals like Eusebius and the Emperor Julian.[100] And with these better-defined horizons and borders, and the clearer historicization that came with them, there also emerged a less speculative, more philologically and historically contextualizing school of exegesis, prominently represented by John Chrysostom (d. 404). The Antiochenes concentrated on a text's narrative logic rather than treating it as a code to crack, though once the story line had been established a spiritual interpretation was licit, as for example of Abraham's sacrifice of Isaac prefiguring the Cross.[101] In other words, there was not quite so sharp a contrast between Antioch and Alexandria as was once supposed.[102]

When the Greek Church condemned Origen as a heretic in 543 and 553, most of his works perished, though Latin translations by Jerome (d. 419) preserved him for the West.[103] Like Eusebius, Jerome had worked in Origen's library at Caesarea. His own commentaries either directly translated Origen's or were much influenced, deploying Hebrew and rabbinic scholarship not only as regards canon and text, but even in matters of interpretation. (Some also see in him the compiler of the *Comparison of Mosaic and Roman laws.*[104]) Admittedly Jerome diluted allegory with literalism, and from the 390s went with the flow and waxed ever more bilious about Origenism. Just as in the philosophical world, though, commentaries provided the perfect context for the maturation of an orthodoxy layer by layer, century by century, egregious heresy excluded but useful earlier scholarship embraced albeit often (as in Jerome's use of Origen) unacknowledged.[105] It was Jerome who was the first

100 Boyarin, *Border lines* [6:69] 202–25.

101 Grillmeier, *Jesus der Christus* [4:72] 2/3.231–38 (T. Hainthaler). The Alexandrian and Antiochene schools are compared by Inglebert, *Interpretatio Christiana* [3:31] 240–46.

102 F. M Young, *Biblical exegesis and the formation of Christian culture* (Cambridge 1997) 186–212, 296–99.

103 On Jerome, Origen, Hebrew scholarship, and commentary: M. Hale Williams, *The monk and the Book* (Chicago 2006) 73–131; F. Millar, "Jerome and Palestine," *Scripta classica israelica* 29 (2010) 59–79.

104 S. Ratti, *Antiquus error* (Turnhout 2010) 149–54. This old idea does not attract Frakes, *Compiling the Collatio* [6:23].

105 Cf. especially Williams, *The monk and the Book* [6:103] 102–4, on Jerome's commentary technique.

nonbishop to be hailed a "Father," by Augustine;[106] and he came to symbolize the patristic endeavor for posterity, laboring at his writing desk amid massive codices, a skull reposing nearby, his friendly lion asleep at his feet.

It is absurd to end the exegetical or patristic phase in 451 as eminent students of the subject have done.[107] The Council of Chalcedon held in that year gave the starting signal for a new round, not just of the polyvocality that had characterized Christian debate in the fourth century, but of intense odium theologicum that cannot be said to have ended until the monothelete dispute, about whether Christ had one or two wills, was settled at the Council of Constantinople in 680–81. Many Christian intellectuals, it is true, abandoned the earlier free debate in favor of definitions and summaries and in general the scholasticism we already noted at the School of Nisibis.[108] Justinian was as determined to put down theological as legal dissent, condemning not only Origen but also the three "Nestorian" theologians Theodore of Mopsuestia, Theodoret of Cyrrhus, and Ibas of Edessa (the "Three Chapters"). But the Greek theological tradition was not formally summed up until John of Damascus compiled his *Fount of knowledge*, in conscious response to the new Qur'anic doctrine and its strictures on Christianity.[109] Even then, there was still to come the last of the seven "ecumenical" councils recognized by the Chalcedonian Orthodox Churches, that of Nicaea in 787, at which the use of icons was fully argued for and accepted. The deliberations of this council allow us a fascinating glimpse of a world of ambitious, frequently irate bishops and slanted scholarship based on the corruption or forgery of proof texts, in other words patristics in full cry, powered as much by testosterone as testimonia. But this too was necessary for the consolidation of the Church and the digestion of its doctrine. The acts and dogmatic definitions issued by the councils were the outcome of debate about scriptural exegesis no less than were the works of the fathers, on which the councils also drew extensively.

Among the fathers who contributed to the debate on icons and were invoked at Nicaea was again John of Damascus, from the safe distance of Umayyad Syria. But his successors in the Chalcedonian Church under Arab rule saw no point in writing Greek when their flock and their whole social and intellectual environment spoke Arabic. By the lifetime of the next major Chalcedonian thinker on this side of the frontier, Theodore Abū Qurra (d. c. 830) already encountered in chapter 5, part of that intellectual environment was a vigorous theological debate among Muslim scholars who had built on

106 J. Flamant and F. Monfrin, "Une culture "si ancienne et si nouvelle,"" in Mayeur and others (eds), *Histoire du Christianisme* [6:95] 633.

107 E.g., J. N. D. Kelly, *Early Christian doctrines* (London 1977^{5}); F. M. Young, *From Nicaea to Chalcedon* (London 2010^{2}); cf. Bruns, in Bruns (ed.), *Von Athen nach Baghdad* [6:66] 29–30.

108 Above, pp. 138, 177; cf. Lim, *Public disputation* [5:47] 227–29.

109 Griffith, *Church in the shadow of the Mosque* [5:119] 40–42.

the Qur'ān their own edifice of interpretation, expressed in a distinctive Arabic vocabulary. Recent research on Theodore and other eighth- and ninth-century writers has shown something unexpected, anticipating developments we already noticed among ninth- and tenth-century Jewish intellectuals: namely that Christian theologians came over time, not merely to offer a general response to the challenge presented by Islam, but actually to express even such distinctively Christian doctrines as Trinitarianism in the concepts and language of the Qur'ān and Qur'anic scholarship.[110] They did this in part simply because that was the air they breathed, but also to facilitate dialogue and polemic, for between "oneness" and "associating (partners with God)" (tawḥīd and shirk) the Qur'ān offered no room for maneuver, and three is not one. Note the attention they give to those parts of the Old Testament—the Prophets and Psalms—to which the Qur'ān also frequently alludes, and which had long been debated by Christian and Jewish exegetes from their own angles. There was no end to the fertility of what started out as the Jewish Bible.

Given the durability of Islam, and the alienation brought about by the failure of almost all the other Christian traditions to engage with it, in both East and West, it is perverse to ignore this evidence of patristic Arabic Christianity's (and Judaism's) adaptability under Muslim influence. It is germane to the periodization issue too, since it makes the full maturation of patristics in the light of Islam virtually coterminous with the First Millennium. The recognition by mainstream patristics of Muslim-influenced Arabic patristics as an authentic mode of expression for a Christian mind would be an example of late Antiquity taking on new dimensions when viewed through the First Millennium lens, from the multicultural and multiconfessional perspective of the Caliphate.[111] And finally it is germane to the present-day dialogue of religions, and the need to build on what Judaism, Christianity and Islam hold in common, most of all the oneness of God, mediated to mankind (but also tragically obscured) through the doctrines of the Trinity and the Incarnation.

This open-minded, even risk-taking aspect of Christianity's patristic phase can be observed earlier, in the willingness of Origen, or the fourth-century Cappadocian Fathers, or Ps.-Dionysius the Areopagite, to engage with Platonism.[112] But, as we have noticed, there were other, equally patristic tenden-

110 S. H. Griffith, "Faith and reason in Christian kalām," in S. K. Samir and J. S. Nielsen (eds), *Christian Arabic apologetics during the Abbasid period (750–1258)* (Leiden 1994) 1–43; Griffith, *Church in the shadow of the Mosque* [5:119] 53–57, 60–63, 93–99; R. G. Hoyland, "St Andrews MS. 14 and the earliest Arabic *Summa theologiae*," in van Bekkum and others (eds), *Syriac polemics* [5:138] 159–72; D. Bertaina, *Christian and Muslim dialogues* (Piscataway, N.J. 2011) 212-28.

111 Compare an interesting recent attempt to contextualize Maimonides (d. 1204) against an Islamic rather than an exclusively Jewish background: S. Stroumsa, *Maimonides* [4:14].

112 Thus betraying the "real essence" of Plato, complains N. Siniossoglou, "Plato Christianus: The colonization of Plato and identity formation in late Antiquity," in P. Hummel (ed.), *Pseudologie* (Paris 2010) 145–76. This is a diatribe against "the fanciful, dominant and convenient line of argument adopted

cies at work too, especially later on, toward suppression of philosophical speculation and imposition of orthodoxy, "correct opinion," consolidating Christian identity round a single creedal statement summarizing all necessary belief. The loss of the eastern provinces, where miaphysitism had concentrated, left supporters of Chalcedon in unchallenged control of the imperial Church. This rigidification of doctrine can be taken as diagnostic of the end of the patristic phase in pre-Reformation Church history (the Reform bred its own fathers), and may be dated (with the above reservations about Arabic patristics) after John of Damascus's summa, and the last of the ecumenical councils in 787. Not that rigidification meant an end to controversy. On the contrary, part of it was the perpetuation of controversy in the form of the same classic arguments, especially in the Caliphate, where Christians had to argue not only with Muslims but also with a wider spectrum of Christian allegiance—Chalcedonian, non-Chalcedonian, and Church of the East—than was available on the East Roman side of the frontier.[113]

Hence the Qur'ān's perception of Christianity as a self-defeatingly disputatious religion that corrupts and betrays its scriptures—an accusation it levels at the Jews too, and more frequently.[114] But it is legitimate to ask how Islam proposed to resolve the problems of doctrine and authority that had defeated the older revelations. This is a major part of the First Millennium story—one might indeed say, of the debate that constitutes the First Millennium.

ISLAM

The Qur'ān's debts to, but also criticism of, its forerunners were not unprecedented. In the second century Marcion had accused the Church of falsifying its Gospel, and retained only Luke (which of course encouraged adherence to the four-gospel model). The third-century Mesopotamian prophet Mani (d. 276/77), raised in a Judeo-Christian Baptist sect, had upbraided Jesus, Zarathushtra, and Buddha for not clearly stating their teaching in book form, with the result that their Churches were bound to pass away and their

---

by specialists in the history of late antiquity . . . that shifting Christian and Hellenic identities are little more than discursive constructs" (147), tantamount to demotion of the "reality" of Platonism to a cultural construct variously conditioned and manipulated. "The social and cultural history dominating the field of late antique and Byzantine studies progressively absorbs intellectual history and diverts [attention] from the underlying philosophical and theological incompatibility between the Judaeo-Christian world-view and the Hellenic world-view" (150). Certainly Christians used Plato according to their own doctrinal criteria, not searching for what Plato himself intended. But even philosophers who adhered to the old religion did not hesitate to "harmonize" Plato with Aristotle. Just like a chapel built with spolia from a temple, the new intellectual construct had its own meaning and viability. The historian's job is to elucidate that, not offer libations to shades of the ancients.

113 Griffith, *Church in the shadow of the Mosque* [5:119] 62.

114 Qur'ān 2.253, 3.19, 5.14, 19.34 on disputatiousness; 2.75, 4.46, and especially 5.12–15, on corruption of scripture.

teachings be adulterated.[115] Mani, Marcion, and the Qur'ān were all focusing on a problem inherent in scriptural religion, namely the gap between the prophetic and scriptural phases. Mani set out to innovate, by inventing a total religion from scratch. For the first time, the prophet-founder presented his own doctrine in both textual and visual form:

> This (immeasurable) wisdom I have written in the holy books, in the great *Gospel* and the other writings; so that it will not be changed after me. Also, the way that I have written it in the books: (this) also is how I have commanded it to be depicted . . . in the *Picture(-Book)*.[116]

Mani also demanded of his followers that they record the many oral traditions they had from him, which he himself had not written down.[117] He aspired to be remembered as prophet, evangelist, and exegete all in one. Such was his self-assurance that he convinced some modern scholars that Manicheism—despite its complexity, and regional variations in the canon—hardly went through an exegetical phase at all.[118] This is now beginning to seem doubtful, as evidence accumulates for his disciples' evolution away from Mani's Jesus-centered "moral instruction rather than elaborate schematisations."[119] Nevertheless, his polemics against orality may have provoked the rabbis to write their teachings down, and the Mazdeans to at last turn the Avesta into a book.[120] And for a time Manicheism did succeed stupendously, propagating itself, with essential consistency[121] despite local divergences, from the Atlantic to the China Sea. If Mani had given his followers more to puzzle and argue about, it might have lasted until today.

Thanks to the Qur'ān's elliptic style, original lack of consonants, obscurities of vocabulary, and self-contradictions, Islam had no such problems, though its notions of scripturality and apostolicity may owe more to Manicheism than has been recognized. The Arabic scripture seeded the last of the great exegetical communities of the First Millennium (or since), in addition to itself being partly founded on exegesis of episodes from the Jewish and

115 *Kephalaia* [ed. and tr. (German) H. J. Polotsky and A. Böhlig (Berlin 1940–66); tr. I. Gardner, *The Kephalaia of the teacher* (Leiden 1995)] 7–8; cf. also M. Tardieu, "Le prologue des "Kephalaia" de Berlin," in Dubois and Roussel (eds), *Entrer en matière* [5:27] 65–77. On Mani's life see W. Sundermann, "Mani," *EIr*, www.iranicaonline.org.

116 *Kephalaia* [ed. W.-P. Funk (Stuttgart 1999–)—texts not in the Polotsky-Böhlig edition] 371 [tr. I. Gardner and S. N. C. Lieu, *Manichaean texts from the Roman Empire* (Cambridge 2004) 266].

117 *Kephalaia* [6:115] 6–7.

118 Gardner and Lieu, *Manichaean texts* [6:116] 9–11, 151–52.

119 I. Gardner, "Towards an understanding of Mani's religious development," in C. M. Cusack and C. Hartney (eds), *Religion and retributive logic* (Leiden 2010) 148–58, arguing mainly from the *Kephalaia* (quotation at 153); id., ""With a pure heart and a truthful tongue": The recovery of the text of the Manichaean daily prayers," *JLA* 4 (2011) 98–99.

120 Y. Elman, "Middle Persian culture and Babylonian sages," in Fonrobert and Jaffee (eds), *Talmud and rabbinic literature* [6:58] 167, 176–79.

121 Gardner, *JLA* 4 (2011) [6:119] 79–99.

Christian Bibles, notably the Psalms.[122] For its own reasons, European scholarship has traditionally dismissed the Qur'ān as an epigonal text, inferior to the Bible as both revelation and literature. This attitude is now being replaced by greater respect, in the same way later Aristotelianism and Platonism are no longer treated as so self-evidently inferior to the works of the founders.[123] Getting over such mental blockages is at the heart of the First Millennium periodization, and is indeed one of the major justifications for it.

Despite its apparent imperfections, Muslims perceive the Qur'ān as the actual uncreated speech of God, equivalent not so much to the Bible as to Christ himself, Muḥammad being but a mediator. In a sense, Islam's prophetic and scriptural phases are identical.[124] But just as the Qur'ān's being itself an exegetical text does not stop us recognizing that the post-Qur'ān commentary tradition is something different,[125] so too, at least for purposes of historical exposition, it is helpful to maintain the distinction between incipient Islam's prophetic phase from c. 610 to 632, when the revelations were delivered and then circulated orally and (probably) in writing too, and the period, perhaps equally brief, during which the complete text was gathered and edited into almost its present shape, with some fine tuning up to the 690s. According to abundant traditions, the Caliph ʿUthmān (644–56) circulated authorized codices of the Qur'ān, just as Constantine sent imperial codices of the Bible to the major Churches. A similar initiative is attributed, with still greater certainty, to the Caliph ʿAbd al-Malik (685–705), or more particularly to his governor of Iraq, Ḥajjāj.[126] John Wansbrough's attempt to posit a text still under construction as late as c. 800 has collapsed thanks in part to discovery and study of early Umayyad or even pre-Umayyad Qur'ān manuscripts.[127] The canonization process was strikingly faster and more straightforward than for the Jewish or Christian Bibles.[128] Yet Islam did not until recently[129] adopt the Christian habit of using the scripture codex itself to symbolize its inalienably textual faith. Instead, religious art focused on calligraphic passages taken from the Book—which was, after all, primarily an oral artifact.

122 E.g., Neuwirth, *Koran als Text* [1:6] 220–23, 414–17, 564–67, 606–7, 725–26, 744–52.

123 Neuwirth, *Koran als Text* [1:6] 42–43; cf. above, p. 136.

124 Neuwirth, *Koran als Text* [1:6] 158–81.

125 Sinai, *Fortschreibung und Auslegung* [1:8] X.

126 O. Hamadan, *Studien zur Kanonisierung des Korantextes* (Wiesbaden 2006) (a reference I owe to Aziz al-Azmeh) 170–74; Neuwirth, *Koran als Text* [1:6] 235–53; B. Sadeghi and U. Bergmann, "The codex of a companion of the Prophet and the Qur'ān of the Prophet," *Arabica* 57 (2010) 364–70, 413–14; A. Neuwirth, *Der Koran* 1: *Frühmekkanische Suren* (Berlin 2011) 24–26. On Constantine see Eusebius, *Life of Constantine* [3:54] 4.36–37.

127 Donner, *Narratives* [3:87] 35–63; F. Déroche, *La transmission écrite du Coran dans les débuts de l'Islam* (Leiden 2009); Sadeghi and Bergmann, *Arabica* 57 (2010) [6:126] 343–436, 516; Neuwirth, *Koran als Text* [1:6] 91–96, 249, 269–73; B. Sadeghi and M. Goudarzi, "Ṣanʿā' 1 and the origins of the Qur'ān," *Der Islam* 87 (2012) 1–129.

128 Neuwirth, *Koran als Text* [1:6] 235–36.

129 O. Grabar, "Art and architecture and the Qur'ān," *EQ* 1.172.

Besides being scripture, and exegesis of earlier scriptures, the Qur'ān was also itself the object of exegesis from a tender age. About the rationalizing and ultimately philosophical exegesis espoused by a learned minority, something was already said in chapter 5. More accessible and influential, as well as earlier, were the sayings or traditions (ḥadīth) attached to the Prophet or his Companions.[130] These brief, sometimes anecdotal texts, whether oral or written, set out to convey the Prophet's sunna or practice, to make vividly present (in the manner of a relic[131]) but also to routinize his charisma, and to remedy what were perceived as gaps or obscurities in scripture. The earliest specimens eventually received into standard collections seem to date from the late seventh century. They were especially in demand when it came to matters of religious practice, law, commerce, and personal conduct, also the political leadership of the community, about which the Qur'ān said nothing. Textual exegesis of the Qur'ān itself was also a major concern: exegetical ḥadīth were commonly attributed to the Prophet's companion Ibn 'Abbās (d. c. 686–88). Ḥadīth were also deployed to support divergent versions of history and doctrine proposed by the parties and sects which soon made their appearance. Many were inauthentic,[132] but obsession with this question in modern scholarship has not advanced appreciation of their sociohistorical context. The death in the 720s of Abū Ṭufayl, the last person who had enjoyed any personal contact with Muḥammad, did not restrain their proliferation.[133] It became customary by the end of the second Muslim century to validate each report by attaching a chain of authorities, or isnād.

Some early Muslim believers opposed (fruitlessly) the circulation and especially writing down of ḥadīth, fearing emergence in Islam, as in the other monotheist traditions, of a body of sacred literature competing with scripture, and consequent splits in the community—or wishing to maintain the oral monopoly of a rabbinic-style clique.[134] There were also, certainly by the late eighth century, many legal scholars who believed, like the Mu'tazilites, in rational reflection (ra'y), and cultivated antagonisms with the traditionists.[135] Thanks especially to the prestigious legal scholar Shāfi'ī (d. 820),

130 G. H. A. Juynboll, "Sunna," *EIs*[2] 9.878–81; C. Melchert, *Ahmad ibn Hanbal* (Oxford 2006) 19–57.

131 Cf. E. Dickinson, "Ibn al-Ṣalāḥ al-Shahrazūrī and the isnād," *Journal of the American Oriental Society* 122 (2002) 481–505 (mainly Ayyubid materials, but some earlier).

132 Donner, *Narratives* [3:87] 39–61, 89–93.

133 On Abū Ṭufayl, see al-Iṣfahānī, *Kitāb al-aghānī* [ed. 'A. 'A. Muhannā and S. Jābir (Beirut 1982)] 15.143–52.

134 Donner, *Narratives* [3:87] 93–94; Schoeler, *The oral and the written* [5:112] 111–41 (also comparing early Islamic with rabbinic orality); cf. T. Fishman, *Becoming the People of the Talmud* (Philadelphia 2011) 10, 20–64 (opposition to writing down of oral traditions in rabbinic milieu in Islamic Iraq).

135 Schacht, *Introduction to Islamic law* [6:47] 34–36; C. Melchert, *The formation of the Sunni schools of law, 9th–10th centuries C.E.* (Leiden 1997) 1–13.

ḥadīth were nonetheless accepted as an extension of revelation.[136] The most influential collections (written, but ideally first heard rather than read), were the *Ṣaḥīḥayn* composed by two pupils of Ibn Ḥanbal, Bukhārī (d. 870; active at Bukhārā and Nīshāpūr) and Muslim (d. 875, active at Nīshāpūr). These also contained biographical materials to facilitate authentification, and Qur'anic commentary. Since these are the best-known books in Islam after the Qur'ān, one sees that the religion's exegetical phase became one of its defining features. The attempt to make a closed, scholar-authorized canon out of what had hitherto been a more fluid, democratic oral tradition met with initial resistance—and the more informal approach continued as late as the twelfth century. But by the mid-eleventh century the authority of the two collections was established through consensus among scholars spreading from Khurāsān through the cities of Iran to eventually conquer Baghdad and then spread westward to Spain.[137] The canonization process's independence of central or conciliar authority we have already noted in the case of the New Testament canon; and one of the achievements of rabbinic scholarship has been to discredit the role once accorded the late-first-century "Council of Yavneh/Jamnia" in finalizing the Jewish Bible.[138] (The quick-off-the-mark and top-down 'Uthmanic edition of the Qur'an was another matter.)

Ḥadīth were the foundation of Islam's exegetical phase. Space allows us to touch here, briefly, on three major areas of Muslim thought and literary production which repose on their authority: Qur'ānic exegesis itself, law, and history.

I noted above that the Qur'ān already contains many passages that comment or elaborate on materials from the Jewish and Christian scriptures. Also that exegesis of scripture crops up in many branches of early Arabic literature, for example in ḥadīth and even in writers of philosophical tendency. But systematic commentary, as known to us from the philosophical and Christian traditions, took time to emerge.[139] By the late Umayyad period there was already beginning to be significant literary activity on this front, and it continued throughout the later eighth and ninth centuries. It probably mainly consisted of grammatical and lexical notes on the Qur'ān's many tex-

136 Schacht, *Introduction to Islamic law* [6:47] 58–60; Melchert, *Sunni schools of law* [6:135] 68–86.

137 Brown, *Canonization* [3:18], esp. 56–58 (elitism of canon); 60–64 (durability of living isnād); 103, 124–35, 374–77 (dissemination of *Ṣaḥīḥayn*); 209–61 (*Ṣaḥīḥayn* exemplars of authenticity and authority).

138 J. P. Lewis, "Jamnia revisited," in McDonald and Sanders (eds), *Canon debate* [6:90] 146–62. Fārābī insists, quite unhistorically, on the role of a council of bishops in fixing the canon of Christian Aristotelianism: above, p. 148.

139 On Qur'anic exegesis up to and including Ṭabarī, see C. Gilliot, "Exegesis of the Qur'ān: Classical and medieval," *EQ* 2.102–11. On the earliest period, see also Sinai, *Fortschreibung und Auslegung* [1:8] 161–288.

tual obscurities, narrative materials often of Jewish or Christian origin, and legal interpretation according to topics. Verse-by-verse commentary was not yet customary, but became so—with ḥadīth invoked to explain each verse's context—when Ṭabarī (d. 923), whom we have already encountered as an historian, wrote what quickly came to be regarded as the commentary par excellence on the Qur'ān. It was titled *The sum of clarity concerning the interpretation of the verses of the Qur'ān*. As in the *History*, Ṭabarī drew extensively on less systematic predecessors, and put them largely out of circulation. The Qur'ān commentary deploys not just theological and legal erudition—Ṭabarī trained as a jurist and was briefly the eponym of his own legal school—but also on grammar and lexicography, other fields essential to the understanding of scripture that were coming of age in the tenth century.[140] A carefully constructed monument of Sunni orthodoxy, *The sum of clarity* quickly became the focus of its own industry of epitomes, translations (into Persian), and supercommentaries. One might well wonder, whether Ṭabarī consciously borrowed the techniques of Aristotelian commentary in order to consolidate a very different style of thinking.[141]

But the most important field for the community as a whole was law. Shāfi'ī founded one of the four major legal communities (more traditionally called "schools") that dominate Islam to this day. Besides the Shafi'is and the Hanbalis, there are also the Hanafis derived from Abū Ḥanīfa (d. 767), and the Malikis named after Mālik ibn Anas (d. 795). One perceives ever more clearly the significance of the early Abbasid period in Islam's maturation—particularly through the formation of new scholarly elites keen to assert their autonomy from state authority.

As already remarked, Shāfi'ī introduced a stronger ḥadīth element into legal thought in order to secure an irrefragable basis for his rulings. This imparted a distinctive atmosphere to the legal communities, whose scholarly elites powerfully remind one of the rabbis of Pumbedita or Sepphoris. There is the same minute concern with elaborating law from scripture and constructing exhaustive *literary* corpora based on *oral* transmission of opinions from teacher to pupil. There is the same ambiguity about the status and authority of a nonordained scholarly elite lacking the Christian clergy's unique role in communal worship. And from at least the second century of Islam rabbis and ḥadīth scholars, at least those in the law schools' main center, Baghdad, dwelt in the same city and could have been alert to each other's activities.[142] It is likely that the rabbinical academies influenced Muslim

140 M. G. Carter, "Arabic lexicography" and "Arabic grammar," in M. J. L. Young and others (eds), *Religion, learning and science in the 'Abbasid period* (Cambridge 1990) 106–38.

141 The suggestion of Sinai, *Fortschreibung und Auslegung* [1:8] 278 n. 68.

142 On Hebrew grammar borrowed wholesale from Arabic, e.g., by Saadiah Gaon, see F. Pontani, ""Only God knows the correct reading!": The role of Homer, the Quran and the Bible in the rise of phi-

scholars' understanding of law both as organizing the whole of one's life, even its most intimate aspects, and as a field in which many authorities might have their say, no universal agreement being required on matters of detail, provided their general orientation was toward affirming the Islamic identity of their otherwise extremely disparate community, the umma.

The emergence of these four communities of interpretation was not without animosity and strife, and there were originally over a dozen of them; but the process of selection and consolidation was being completed in the later tenth and into the eleventh century, they were becoming mass movements, and different parts of the present-day Muslim world still acknowledge them.[143] Each community espouses a mature and self-sufficient exegetical system, appealing to the ultimate authority of God and his Prophet as evidenced in scripture and tradition (to the authenticity of which the works of Bukhārī and Muslim provided indispensable guidance), but imparting to that material the distinctive interpretative stamp of the school's founder and other authorities. Until this evolution is completed at the end of the First Millennium, it is not possible to talk about Sunni Islam. Contemporary Sunnism maintains a heterogeneity implicit in the diversity of tradition and the divergence of the legal communities, but is at the same time kept under control by the principle of the consensus (ijmāʿ) of the Sunni community as a whole, which is conservative because founded on tradition, but strong because it combines tradition with rational speculation. Christopher Melchert situates this "semirationalism" historically in the following words:

> The theology and law that al-Ma'mūn tried to establish evidently offered too little to the common people of Baghdad and other cities, but the pure traditionalism that Aḥmad ibn Ḥanbal and others opposed to it evidently offered too little to sophisticates at court. The jurisprudence taught by the classical schools of law did offer something to both sides.[144]

Apart from law, the other major area of Muslim thought dependent on collecting and assessing ḥadīth was history,[145] which likewise developed rapidly from the eighth century. Even the earliest ḥadīth might contain narra-

---

lology and grammar," in M. R. Niehoff (ed.), *Homer and the Bible in the eyes of ancient interpreters* (Leiden 2012) 72–74.

143 N. Hurvitz, "From scholarly circles to mass movements: The formation of legal communities in Islamic societies," *American historical review* 108 (2003) 985–1008. The maturation of the legal communities is variously dated: Bauer, *Ambiguität* [1:5] 21–22, 159–61, 205–6, has a formative period to 1000 and a classical period into the twelfth century; Brown, *Canonization* [3:18] 367–68, focuses on the eleventh century; Melchert, *Sunni schools of law* [6:135] 198, specifies "the beginning of the eleventh century."

144 Melchert, *Sunni schools of law* [6:135] 201.

145 Khalidi, *Arabic historical thought* [3:82] 17–82.

tive, and editorial comment, as well as the core saying. Prophetic biography was a natural development. Ibn Isḥāq, encountered in chapter 3, devoted immense energy not to collecting ḥadīth for their own sake, but to using them to contextualize each passage of the Qur'ān as part of a historical narrative. His book became a resource for exegetes. When in the ninth century historical writing took root, some works (like Ibn 'Abd al-Ḥakam's *Conquests of Egypt*) stayed dependent on the distinctively Arabic atomized style of composition imposed by ḥadīth,[146] while others (e.g., Wāqidī, d. 822; Ya'qūbī, d. c. 905) felt free to write in a more secular-political, less theological manner, and with less of that preoccupation with transmission implied by the isnād. Preference for the ḥadīth style did not stop the greatest Arabic historian, Ṭabarī, from constructing a narrative on a massive scale from creation to 915. Indeed, there are signs that he broke up more continuous earlier narratives in order to accommodate them to his traditionistic format.[147] But incorporating ḥadīth in a Qur'anic commentary meant to argue that the meaning of each verse was evident proved to be simpler than in the *History*, where there were multiple versions of each event and no criterion for sorting them. As he nears his own day, or strays beyond Arab history into Iranian, Ṭabarī's dedication to ḥadīth and isnād wanes, and he offers his own interpretative narrative in the more literary (adab) style already favored by some of his forerunners.

In Ṭabarī's oeuvre we see ḥadīth scholarship flowering into an impressive statement of the fullness of mature Arabic thought. But of still wider concern to the umma than these intellectual and scholarly maturations so typical of the tenth century[148] were on the one hand the emergence of an overwhelming Muslim majority in the population by the tenth/eleventh century, and on the other hand the schism between Sunnis and Shiites. This originated with the murder of the third caliph, 'Uthmān, in 656; opposition to his successor 'Alī, the Prophet's nephew and son-in-law; and particularly the slaying of 'Alī's son Husayn at Karbalā' in 681. The Shiites were those who backed the claims of the Prophet's family, and indeed on the authority of a distinctive exegesis of numerous passages in the Qur'ān. The Arabic historical tradition was not only alert to the significance of these events, it also viewed them in the broader context of First Millennium prophetic history. Already, Sayf ibn 'Umar (d. 796) linked them to a fantastical but to this day influential account of how the nascent early Christian community had been expelled from its homeland by the wicked Jewish King (!) Paul. Paul feigned repentance, gained the Christians' trust, and contrived to corrupt their pristine faith. But a minority rejected Paul and fled, to live as ascetics in the Syrian

146 Donner, *Narratives* [3:87] 255–58.

147 Donner, *Narratives* [3:87] 258–59.

148 Borrut, *Entre mémoire et pouvoir* [3:79] 107.

countryside until the appearance of Muḥammad, whose followers they became. Sayf's strange story was eventually taken up by Ṭabarī—minus Paul, and identifying the poisonous example given by the Jews with the role of the Shiites, to whom the historian was so opposed.[149]

The umma had remained politically unified until the mid-ninth century; and it was only toward the end of the tenth, from the 970s, that serious civil disturbances between Baghdadi Sunnis and Shiites led to irremediable rupture between them.[150] Paradoxically, just as the central strands of Arabic scholarship mentioned above were reaching a certain maturity, the end of the First Millennium marked the passing of any pretence at spiritual, let alone political, unity, except at the minimalist level represented by conventional lists such as the four legal communities, the four "rightly guided" caliphs (accommodating both Umayyads and Shiites), or the five pillars (faith, charity, prayer, pilgrimage, and fasting but not jihād).[151] Henceforth there was to be the Sunni majority with its exoteric appeal to Qur'ān, Prophetic tradition, the consensus of the community, and the authority of the powers that be, along with a growing taste for systematic dogma, catechisms, and creeds.[152] Ashʿarism emerged, from the tenth century, as the central, orthodox expression of this dominant current in Islam. Over against the Sunnis stood the Shiite minority (today it is about 10 to 15 percent of the Muslim world, but widely perceived to be again on the offensive, as it was in the tenth century too), with its belief in twelve (or, for some, seven) Imams after the Prophet, its hope for the return of the last, "occluded" Imam after his mysterious disappearance in 941, its esoteric conviction that the Qur'ān's inner meaning must be revealed through the Imam, and a consequent efflorescence of scriptural exegesis.[153] As for Shiite law, it differs in no essentials (except inheritance rules) from Sunni, the final split between the two branches of Islam having come after the formation of the four legal communities.[154]

There is irony in the coexistence in tenth-century Baghdad of the armed thuggery of Sunni and Shiite factions and the division of the city into sectarian neighborhoods on the one hand, with the open-minded circles around Kindī and Fārābī already evoked in the previous chapter and about which I

149 S. W. Anthony, "The composition of Sayf b. ʿUmar's account of King Paul and his corruption of ancient Christianity," *Der Islam* 85 (2009) 164–202; A. Barzegar, "The persistence of irony: Paul of Tarsus, Ibn Saba', and historical narrative in Sunni identity formation," *Numen* 58 (2011) 207–31. For further Sunni assertions of commonalities between Jews and Shiites, see S. M. Wasserstrom, ""The Šīʿīs are the Jews of our community": An interreligious comparison within Sunnī thought," *Israel oriental studies* 14 (1994) 297–324.

150 Kennedy, *The Prophet and the age of the Caliphates* [4:79] 228–29.

151 C. F. Robinson, "Conclusion: From formative Islam to classical Islam," in *New Cambridge history of Islam* [2:106] 692–93.

152 These last are examined by Wensinck, *Muslim creed* [3:24] 102–276.

153 Cf. M. A. Amir-Moezzi, "Le *Tafsīr* d'al-Ḥibarī," *Journal des savants* (2009) 3–23.

154 Schacht, *Introduction to Islamic law* [6:47] 16–17.

shall have more to say in the last. Both help define the First Millennium, the thugs announcing the maturation of an early schism in Islam whose durability recent events have illustrated; while the sages in their discussion circles point to the channels for dialogue opened up by the period from Christ to Ibn Sīnā, through contacts between traditions whose self-understanding—but also differences—had been deepened over the centuries by the exegetical communities surveyed in this chapter.

7

VIEWPOINTS AROUND 1000

ṬŪS, BAṢRA, BAGHDAD, PISA

I suggested in chapter 3 that the First Millennium periodization can be conceived of as an arch thrown from one support to another, but also as pivoted round a central event, here the rise of Islam. The First Millennium's usefulness does not depend on its start and finish being shown to have cosmogonic significance. Even freely chosen points in the flow of time may illustrate either what is common to all history, and the arbitrariness of periodization, or else—in microform—the characteristics of a particular phase of human affairs.[1] Nevertheless, in the minds of Christian theologians and historians the birth of Jesus and the reign of Augustus did acquire momentous significance, just as did the destruction of the Jerusalem temple for Jews, and for Muslims the career of Muḥammad set against the early seventh-century clash between Iran and Rome. Ignoring these intellectual constructions may look like a streetwise option for the historian keen to burnish materialist and skeptical credentials, but actually just undermines one's grasp of historical reality and causality.

But what of the First Millennium's cutoff point? Certainly the Millennium was eagerly anticipated, and freighted with apocalyptic hopes and fears. Unlike the coincidence of Augustus and Jesus, though, this construction turned out to be a deception and lacked historical posterity. It did not, in retrospect, change very much the way most people saw the world. Nor was the career of Ibn Sīnā, with whose name I have associated the end of the First Millennium, anything to compare with Augustus and Jesus, either in reality or imagination—despite his huge, centuries-long influence on thinking people from Central Asia to the Atlantic. The end of the First Millennium, or of the fourth Muslim century, did see, though, a maturation in the Muslim world, as it took on political and cultural contours much closer to what we are familiar with than the early Abbasid period. In this last chapter I treat the years around 1000 not exactly as another pivot—that would be a whole new project—but rather as a viewing point from which to look mainly back but

1 G. Traina, *428 dopo Cristo: Storia di un anno* (Rome 2007); H. U. Gumbrecht, *In 1926: Living at the edge of time* (Cambridge, Mass. 1997).

also a little bit forward, and to consolidate in this way our sense of the First Millennium's distinctiveness. I pick out certain themes broached earlier in the book, and elaborate them from the 1000 CE viewpoint. I have chosen four cities associated with momentous activity, not all of it conceptual, but in each case connected to far wider regions, whether spatial or mental. First comes another look at the Iranian perspective.

ṬŪS/IRAN

I have already touched on Iran's geographic, imperial, and strategic role, its cultural complexity, and the Iranian Commonwealth. Formal independence was lost with the Sasanids' collapse before Arab onslaught. Yet neither Iran's political subjection nor its people's gradual acceptance of Islam, which became the majority religion only during the tenth century, could extinguish its language or historical and cultural memory. These were the foundations of the "Iranian identity" that revived between the ninth and eleventh centuries and was resurgent by the thirteenth.[2] To Arabic scholarship and letters the Iranian contribution was so definitive that educated Iranians questioned whether there had been an Arab contribution at all—the so-called Shuʿūbīya movement in the eighth and especially ninth centuries.[3] The Shuʿūbīya had no problem with the Caliphate as a political structure. Rather they wanted to take advantage of it to assert the universal centrality of the Iranian tradition—not to mention the privileges of a particular scholarly elite.

To tenth/eleventh-century Islamic exegetical culture Ṭabarī made a classic contribution in the field of Qur'anic commentary, while Ibn Sīnā mastered and passed beyond it in that of philosophy. Ibn Sīnā's slightly older contemporary and correspondent Bīrūnī (d. 1048), also for a time a client of the Bukhārā Samanids, surpassed both in the breadth and catholicity of his skeptical erudition in the fields of history and chronology (his major contribution to this subject appeared about the year 1000), mathematics, astronomy, geography, pharmacology, mineralogy, history of religions, and Indology (showing here a sympathy and thoroughness unrivalled before modern times).[4] All three were Muslims and wrote in Arabic; but Ṭabarī's insistence that only Iran of all the nations had enjoyed a history "uninterrupted, constant and regular,"[5] Ibn Sīnā's "Eastern" philosophy and his trail-blazing composition of a popularizing philosophical treatise in Persian,[6] and Bīrūnī's

2 A. Ashraf, "Iranian identity i, iii," *EIr* 13.501–4, 507–22.

3 H. T. Norris, "*Shuʿūbiyyah* in Arabic literature," in J. Ashtiany and others (eds), *ʿAbbasid belles-lettres* (Cambridge 1990) 31–47; S. Enderwitz, "Shuʿūbīya," *EIs*[2] 9.513–16.

4 C. E. Bosworth and others, "Bīrūnī, Abū Rayḥān," *EIr* 4.274–87.

5 Al-Ṭabarī, *History* [3:85] 1.148, 353 (tr. Khalidi, *Arabic historical thought* [3:82] 78).

6 M. Achena, "Avicenna xi," *EIr* 3.99–104.

criticism of scholars who wrote in Persian, all in different ways acknowledged the distinctiveness of their heritage. There was also the old pre-Islamic Iranism to be encountered, and still evolving, among the Mazdeans, about whom Bīrūnī has plenty to say. By the end of the tenth century not only do we see the revival of Persian language and literature (including the Persian-language *Islamic* scholarship that turned Persian into the second language of Islam[7]), but Ferdowsi was re-creating the epic of pre-Islamic Iran both in response to the Arab conquests, and with one eye on his people's future.

Before glancing at that evolving Iranism, one may recall that the Iranian Commonwealth embraced much else besides, notably Manicheism. Mani's doctrine (once more, Bīrūnī is a major source) was strongly influenced by Judaism and Syriac Christianity. Such coloring as it took from its Mazdean environment was quite superficial, for instance the names of certain gods. The little Mani knew about Zarathushtra himself probably came from Syriac sources, especially Bardaisan.[8] Yet in the rescript he issued against Manicheism in 302, the Emperor Diocletian asserted categorically that it was a "Persian poison," so it was treated as a fifth column in the recurrent political and military conflict between Iran and Rome, just as Christians in the Sasanian Empire were at times treated as allies of Rome.[9] It is a striking example of how political prejudice might extend the range of a (perceived) cultural commonwealth. So too is the attack by the Christian polemicist Firmicus Maternus, writing in 346, on Roman worshippers of the Iranian god Mithras, whose religion had by then been totally acclimatized in the Roman Empire for a very long time:

> You then who claim that in these temples you celebrate your mysteries in the manner of the Magi, according to the Persian ritual, why is it only these customs of the Persians that you praise? If you think it worthy of the Roman name to follow Persian rituals and Persian laws . . . [10]

The supreme irony came when a Church of the East synod held on Sasanian territory in 612 claimed Manicheism had originated in the Roman Empire and thence been grafted into Iran, a land previously innocent of heresies![11]

Iranism is, then, a concept subject to interested manipulation. But at least

7 Fragner, *"Persophonie"* [4:58] 27–33.

8 W. Sundermann, "Manicheism ii," *EIr*, www.iranicaonline.org; A. L. Khosroyev, "Manichäismus: Eine Art persisches Christentum?," in Mustafa and Tubach (eds), *Inkulturation des Christentums* [4:65] 43–53; Gardner, in Cusack and Hartney (eds), *Religion and retributive logic* [6:119] 153–56.

9 Lieu, *Manichaeism* [4:24] 121–25; cf. *Eusebius, Ecclesiastical history* [3:35] 7.31.2: "a deadly poison that came from the land of the Persians."

10 Firmicus Maternus, *On the error of profane religions* [ed. and tr. (French) R. Turcan (Paris 1982)] 5.2.

11 J. B. Chabot, *Synodicon orientale* (Paris 1902) 584–85 (567 syr.).

the credentials of the Mazdean scriptures, the Avesta, can hardly be questioned.[12] Their oldest element, perhaps created c. 1000 BCE, is the Gāthās, poetic and cryptic texts attributed to the prophetic revelation of Zarathushtra himself. The Avestan scriptures were orally transmitted for a millennium and a half until Sasanian times, and then written down in a specially devised alphabet to guarantee their preservation and precise pronunciation, though the oral tradition probably remained predominant. This apparently came to pass progressively between the third and sixth centuries, and was presumably intended to reinforce Mazdaism against both its own heretics, and scriptural competitors such as Buddhism, Christianity, Judaism, and Manicheism.[13] Nevertheless, Sasanian Mazdaism avoided rigidification, and even accommodated a certain fluidity of doctrine.[14]

Besides writing down the original Avesta, Sasanid scholars produced a literal and glossed translation into Middle Persian, and commentaries. This zand, as they called it, was largely oral to begin with. It allowed the scripture to be taught publicly, and contribute to current theological debates. But it also reveals how far even the Mazdean elite now was from understanding its own heritage.[15] It also nurtured dangers—or might be perceived to. Their enemies linked both Mani and the notorious heretic Mazdak (d. 528) with the composition of zand texts. Perhaps this was why zand did not in Sasanian times become as deeply rooted a commentary culture as Torah or Qur'ān study.[16] Indeed, Khosrow I allowed the laity to study only the Avesta, not its zand,[17] which reminds one of his brother-ruler Justinian's distrust of both legal commentators and rabbinic exegetes (not to mention Origenists).

In the ninth- to tenth-century Avestan encyclopedic text known as the *Denkard* (*Acts of the religion*),[18] at the beginning of book 4, we find an account, dating back to the sixth century, of how the written Avesta (here assigned to the earliest phase of Sasanid rule) drew on a spectrum of scientific literature, including from other cultures, in line with the Iranian view that religion, dēn, embraces all human wisdom and knowledge.[19]

12 On the Avesta, see J. Kellens, "Avesta," *EIr* 3.35–44; H. Humbach, "Gathas i," *EIr* 10.321–27; S. Shaked, "Scripture and exegesis in Zoroastrianism," in Finkelberg and Stroumsa (eds), *Homer, the Bible, and beyond* [6:56] 63–74; A. Cantera, *Studien zur Pahlavi-Übersetzung des Avesta* (Wiesbaden 2004), esp. 162–63, 343–47.

13 On the third-century priest Kirdir's campaigns against alien religions, see his epigraphical record: P. Gignoux, *Les quatre inscriptions du mage Kirdīr* (Paris 1991) 60.

14 Shaked, *Dualism* [3:15] 14–15, 20, 57–58.

15 Humbach [7:12], *EIr* 10.321; cf. Shaked, *Dualism* [3:15] 6, 116–19.

16 Shaked, *Dualism* [3:15] 59, 79–80; C. G. Cereti, *La letteratura pahlavi* (Milan 2001) 23–24; de Blois [3:16], *EIs*² 11.510.

17 P. G. Kreyenbroek, "Exegesis i," *EIr* 9.115.

18 P. Gignoux, "Dēnkard," *EIr* 7.284–89; Cereti, *Letteratura pahlavi* [7:16] 41–78.

19 M. Shaki, "Dēn," *EIr* 7.279–81.

> The King of Kings Shapur [I: c. 241–72], son of Ardashir, collected again the writings deriving from the religion concerning medicine, astronomy, movement, time, space, substance, accident, becoming, decay, transformation, logic, and other crafts and skills, which were dispersed among the Indians and the Greeks and other lands, and he caused them to fit the Avesta. Every correct copy he ordered to be deposited in the treasury of the (royal) quarters, and considered establishing every province (?) upon (the principles of) the Mazdean religion.[20]

This grandiose project, aimed at gathering universal wisdom under the aegis of Zarathushtra, rests on the belief that Alexander the Macedonian had brutally disrupted the Iranian learned tradition and dispersed it to the four winds, and that all Greek wisdom was really Iranian. It also reflects the open, invigorating atmosphere of the sixth-century Sasanian court, known for its philosophical including Aristotelian culture. (There are indeed signs of both Indian and Greek influences in the surviving books of the Avesta, as well as in other Iranian literature of the period.[21]) Yet after the Arab conquest and with the beginning of Islamization, the core Avestan tradition will have seemed still more in need of exegesis than it had in Sasanid times. Even the compilers of the *Denkard* seem to have worked from the Middle Persian translation.[22] Examining the whole of the *Denkard* in all its haphazard variety, we see how much of it consists of summaries, glosses, and commentaries designed to illuminate the obscurity of the Mazdean scriptures. We also find the legend of Zarathushtra, an abundance of moral stories and precepts conveying the essence of the religion in digestible form, and a good deal of theology and law (but not ritual law[23]) alongside other sections on science and medicine. The *Denkard* often takes a rational or philosophical approach, and is polemical in its treatment of other religions, especially Judaism and Manicheism. At the same time, it seeks to save and make sense of the Avestan religion, at a time when it was under attack from Muslims for its alleged dualism.

We saw how the crystallization of Muslim theology and philosophy provoked in mature and dynamic Christian patristics a restatement of some of its themes in the new language of Arabic theologizing. In Judaism it triggered philosophical debate, and even made some impact in rabbinic circles (Saadia). In Mazdaism, though, the Muslim challenge stimulated a much more thoroughgoing reappraisal, an attempt to save what could be saved

20 *Denkard* [ed. D. M. Madan, *The complete text of the Pahlavi Dinkard* (Bombay 1911)] 4, 412–15 [tr. Shaked, *Dualism* [3:15] 100–101; limited divergences in Cantera, *Studien* [7:12] 109]; cf. Gutas, *Greek thought* [5:92] 34–45.

21 Shaked, *Dualism* [3:15] 104–6.

22 Cantera, *Studien* [7:12] 15–16.

23 Secunda [6:56], in Bakhos and Shayegan (eds), *Talmud in its Iranian context* [4:64] 152.

from permanent loss and to justify the religion's fundamental dualist assumptions. What we see in the *Denkard* is an exegetical culture polemical in tone, but more defensive than others we have looked at. Psychologically it is closer to the earlier (Mishnaic/Talmudic) rabbinical experience than to that of the Arabic Christian or Muslim "fathers," or the Muʿtazilite Jews. It was clear to many learned Iranians under the Abbasids that the future lay with Islam. Even so, they yearned to preserve something of their own identity within the new monotheist culture—as when Ṭabarī included not only the prophets of Israel but also the rulers of ancient Iran in his *History*.

Eventually, an Iranian efflorescence of Platonizing and Gnostic philosophy facilitated this compromise on the theological level too. A great deal of ancient Iranian mythology was given a Muslim orientation within the framework of Gnostic currents of thought. The influential "illuminationist" philosopher Suhrawardī (d. 1191) drew on episodes in Ferdowsi's epic poem the *Shahnameh* (*Book of kings*), especially the birth of Zāl and the combat between his son Rostam and Esfandyār, in order to tell the history of the soul, just as late Greek Platonists had read the *Odyssey* in a similar perspective.[24] The *Shahnameh* deserves a few words here, because just as the *Denkard* codifies Avestan culture at the close of the First Millennium, so the *Shahnameh* opens a new phase in Iranian historical and ethnic as well as spiritual consciousness—Islamic now, no longer Avestan—at the very beginning of the Second Millennium.

Of all the symptoms of Iranian cultural and especially literary revival we observe in the tenth century,[25] Ferdowsi's poem was the most spectacular and durable, its panorama of Iran's mythological and historical past in 50,000 lines making it seven times longer than the *Iliad*, and its use of New Persian causing it to stand out in a Middle East gradually letting go both its native languages and its pre-Islamic past. Ferdowsi was undoubtedly keen to revive Persian, but his restrained use of Arabic words may not be due to prejudice, given that some of those he does use are synonyms of common Persian words that occur elsewhere in his poem.[26] He himself, like Ṭabarī, Ibn Sīnā, and Bīrūnī, was a native of the Iranian East, which in his day experienced an upsurge of Iranian sentiment.[27] He was born and appears to have spent his whole life in the region of Ṭūs, near modern Mashhad, in Khurāsān.[28] (Ghazālī too was born there.)

24 H. Corbin, *En Islam iranien* (Paris 1971–72) 2.212–14; id., *L'archange empourpré* (Paris 1976) 197–200.

25 Daniel [4:81], in *New Cambridge history of Islam* [2:106] 1.502–3.

26 J. Perry, "Šah-nāma v. Arabic words," *EIr*, www.iranicaonline.org.

27 P. Pourshariati, "The Parthians and the production of the canonical Shāhnāmas," in Börm and Wiesehöfer (eds), *Commutatio et contentio* [3:84] 347–92, esp. 348–49.

28 D. Khaleghi-Motlagh, "Ferdowsi, Abu'l-Qāsem," *EIr* 5.514–23, www.iranicaonline.org (revised version).

Ferdowsi's epic closes with the great defeat suffered by the Sasanians at Arab hands at the Battle of Qādisīya c. 635–37. Before the fateful encounter, the Iranian general Rostam reads the stars and laments:

> I see what has to be, and choose the way
> Of silence, since there is no more to say:
> But for the Persians I will weep, and for
> The House of Sasan ruined by this war:
> Alas for their great crown and throne, for all
> The royal splendour destined now to fall,
> To be fragmented by the Arabs' might;
> The stars decree for us defeat and flight.
> Four hundred years will pass in which our name
> Will be forgotten and devoid of fame.[29]

When, soon after this, Ferdowsi closes the poem with words about his own fame, we sense he has taken upon himself sole responsibility for the historical consciousness of his people. Just as Yazdigird, the fateful last Sasanian ruler, ascended the throne "in the month of Sepandormoz, on the day of Ard,"[30] so Ferdowsi lays down his pen "in the month of Sepandormoz, on the day of Ard" exactly 400 years later, which corresponds to 25 February in the year 1010 of the Christian calendar:

> I've reached the end of this great history
> And all the land will talk of me:
> I shall not die, these seeds I've sown will save
> My name and reputation from the grave,
> And men of sense and wisdom will proclaim,
> When I have gone, my praises and my fame.[31]

BAṢRA/ENCYCLOPEDISM

I would like now to elaborate on the encyclopedic tendencies we have already encountered in the Aristotelian project, in Ulpian, the rabbis, and the *Denkard*, as also in several sixth- and seventh-century writers evoked in chapter 5: Boethius, Isidore of Seville, and Ananias of Shirak. This sixth- and seventh-century encyclopedism—of primarily pragmatic rather than hermeneutical knowledge—was a response in the spirit of Aristotle and Alexandria to a sense that civilization was under threat, and that the new Christian

29 Abolqasem Ferdowsi (tr. D. Davis), *Shahnameh: The Persian Book of Kings* (London 2007) 833.
30 *Shahnameh* [7:29] 832.
31 *Shahnameh* [7:29] 854.

worldview imposed a revision of the antique heritage.[32] The Alexandrian conspectus of human knowledge, filtered through the Qur'anic vision, remained influential in the Caliphate too.[33] Philosophers from Kindī onward pursued reconciliation of religious and rational studies, believing instruction in the sciences leads the soul to purification. Programmatic and classificatory statements were gradually fleshed out in treatises on individual sciences, including the vast translated library of Greek medicine, mathematics, astronomy and philosophy. Fārābī (d. 948) was a fundamental guide in all this activity, and his whole oeuvre can be seen as an encyclopedia founded on a macro-microcosmic vision of the divine and human spheres, revealed to the Prophet and designed to impart salvation. Ibn Sīnā's original, encyclopedic synthesis in *The cure*, based on the summation of the entire Alexandrian curriculum in his earlier work, was also evoked in chapter 5.

But to end the First Millennium with such as Ibn Sīnā and Bīrūnī begs accusations of intellectual elitism. Encyclopedism usually involves some attempt to make knowledge more available. That was a hard goal to achieve before printing, or indeed the circulation of cheap books in the twentieth century. But the largely anonymous milieu of the Brethren of Purity in Baṣra and Baghdad, around the 970s and 980s, gets us nearer the circles we are looking for.[34] The rich manuscript tradition of their *Letters* shows they were widely read, not in the orthodox Sunni world—for the Brethren were Shiites—but at least in the Isma'ili communities which took them up about two centuries after their composition, have continued to revere them to the present day, and to which they may themselves have belonged. (The enclosed and tightly defined Isma'ili community, with its well-guarded libraries only recently opened to—or at least exploited by—scholars, and bound to yield more surprises, can be placed alongside the Yemeni Zaydis and the Karaite Jews with their Mu'tazilite manuscripts, as another instance of a First Millennium literary and exegetical tradition's power to mold community identity and sustain it over long centuries.)

32 For a similar analysis of the imperially inspired compilation/encyclopedic literature of tenth-century East Rome, see Magdalino in van Deun and Macé (eds), *Encyclopedic trends* [5:86] 156.

33 G. Endress, "The cycle of knowledge: Intellectual traditions and encyclopaedias of the rational sciences in Arabic Islamic Hellenism," in id. (ed.), *Organizing knowledge* [5:87] 103–33, on what follows. More generally on Arabic encyclopedism, see G. J. van Gelder, "Compleat men, women and books," in P. Binkley (ed.), *Pre-modern encyclopaedic texts* (Leiden 1997) 241–59. On the literary trope of the encyclopedically learned slave girl (some compensation, however fictional, for the absence of women from the present book), see A. Talmon, "Tawaddud—The story of a majlis," in H. Lazarus-Yafeh and others (eds), *The majlis: Interreligious encounters in medieval Islam* (Wiesbaden 1999) 120–27.

34 C. Baffioni, "Gli Iḫwān al-Ṣafā' e la loro enciclopedia," *SFIM* 449–89; G. de Callataÿ, *Ikhwan al-Safa'* (Oxford 2005); F. Daftary, *The Isma'ilis* (Cambridge 2007²) 234–37; N. El-Bizri and others, *Epistles of the Brethren of Purity* (Oxford 2008–); D. de Smet, "Die Enzyklopädie der Iḫwān aṣ-Ṣafā'," *PIW* 531–39, 551–54. On the Brethren's activities in Baghdad, see Kraemer, *Humanism* [4:82] 165–78.

The Brethren of Purity's fifty-two (or fifty-one) *Letters* present themselves as the product of circles (majālis) that gathered to hold philosophical discussions. It is generally assumed, though nowhere explicitly stated, that several different authors were involved in their composition. The *Letters* have never been seen as belonging to the elite milieu of Arabic philosophy as represented by Kindī, Fārābī, and Ibn Sīnā (who is often said—on no good grounds—to have read the *Letters* in his youth[35]). The most telling analogies to them in the better-known realm of Greek philosophy would be the Pythagorean or Hermetic texts, which conveyed a general and relatively comprehensive philosophical worldview in an accessible language infused with religious values, without seeking to push back the frontiers of thought.

The *Letters* propose an ascending scale of knowledge divided between the "mathematical," "physical and natural," "psychological and intellectual," and "theological and religious" sciences. They minutely classify the various branches of human learning, largely according to the Aristotelian model, though their emanationist vision of knowledge and reality is redolent of late Platonism. Beyond these Greek philosophical debts, the *Letters* draw extensively on the whole intellectual heritage of the First Millennium, building a wide range of allusion to Babylonian, Iranian, Indian, Jewish, and Christian learning on a broad (albeit rather imaginatively deployed) bedrock of Qur'anic allusion. Their ideal man was

> learned, accomplished, worthy, keen, pious and insightful . . . Persian by breeding, Arabian by faith, a pure monotheist [ḥanīf] by confession, Iraqi in culture, Hebrew in lore, Christian in manner, Damascene in devotion, Greek in science, Indian in discernment, Sufi in allusiveness of expression [ishārāt], regal in character, masterful in thought, and divine in awareness.[36]

The *Letters* are by no means uncritical in their treatment of the various strands of thought on which they draw, even the Qur'anic. But the general impression conveyed is of a tolerantly eclectic approach to the whole spectrum of knowledge accessible to an educated tenth-century Iraqi. Since Iraq was still at this time close to being the center of the Eurasiatic world, or at least recalled having been that in the very recent past, the intellectual panorama offered by the *Letters* takes in the whole of the First Millennium. Note in particular the Brethren's tendency to treat the Jewish and Christian scriptures as more or less on a par with the Qur'ān.

The acquisition of this universal and comprehensive encyclopedia is to one single and undisputed end, namely the soul's salvation and its liberation

35 Gutas, *Avicenna* [5:150] 24 n. 7.

36 *Rasā'il Ikhwān al-Ṣafā'* 22.42 [ed. B. Bustānī, Beirut 1957, 2.376; ed. and tr. (here slightly adjusted) L. E. Goodman and R. McGregor, *Epistles of the Brethren of Purity: The case of the animals versus Man before the King of the Jinn* (Oxford 2009) ٢٧٨/313–14].

from the physical world. But this is conceived of in a Muslim context: Islam is the culmination of human experience. A roughly contemporary and again anonymous Syriac compilation, *The book of the cause of all causes*, likewise mobilizes encyclopedic knowledge in the service of a "universal religion" designed for all peoples, but this time necessarily Christocentric.[37] Sectarian allegiances remained undeniably strong, alongside an awareness of the congruence of notable traditions both human and divine.

BAGHDAD/RATIONALITY

As the "metropolis of Islam,"[38] Baghdad was home not only to philosophers and members of the Brethren, but to eminent Qur'ān scholars and experts on tradition and law. Among the Jewish population were to be found followers of rabbinical tradition, but also (as we saw in chapter 6) Karaites, philosophers, scriptural commentators, all—even the Talmudists—indebted to the fertilizing influence of the city's cultural life with its strong Muslim coloring. The Christian communities too were still vibrant, aware as ever of their own differences but also contributors, perhaps disproportionately, to philosophical debate.

Contacts might be abrasive, precisely because of these different groups' many shared concerns and traditions, and the doubts and temptations that arose from a situation of religious pluralism—too much choice. At least three types of discourse or debate resulted. Within the "minority" communities, educated elites were concerned to fend off doubt and apostasy by clearly articulating dogma and identity and proposing model arguments to be deployed against critics.[39] Then, between community leaders, formal debates might occur, or be staged for their own entertainment by caliphs or viziers. Such debates often involved the trading of Biblical or Qur'anic proof texts. If done with rhetorical and dialectical skill, this method might gain applause and even benefit one's community;[40] but it was philosophically sterile and redundant even by scripturalist standards if, as the Qur'ān stated, the Jews and Christians had indeed tampered with their holy books. Finally, some intellectuals were interested in getting at the "truth" behind the symbolic or

37 G. J. Reinink, "Communal identity and the systematization of knowledge in the Syriac "Cause of all causes,"" in Binkley (ed.), *Pre-modern encyclopaedic texts* [7:33] 275–88.

38 Al-Muqaddasī, *The best divisions for knowledge of the regions* (*Aḥsan al-taqāsīm fī maʿrifat al-aqālīm*) [ed. M. J. de Goeje (Leiden 1877, corrected reprint 1906); tr. B. Collins (Reading 1994)] 119.

39 See Saadia Gaon, *Book of beliefs and opinions* (*Kitāb al-mukhtār fī 'l-amānāt wa'l-iʿtiqādāt*) [ed. Y. Qāfiḥ (Jerusalem 1970); tr. S. Rosenblatt (New Haven 1948)], Prolegomena; D. Sklare, "Responses to Islamic polemics by Jewish mutakallimūn in the tenth century," in Lazarus-Yafeh and others (eds), *Majlis* [7:33] 141–42, 146.

40 Lazarus-Yafeh and others (eds), *Majlis* [7:33].

conventional language of scripture, and considered that the only way to do this was by rational argumentation—which offered advantages in the other two types of debate as well. One option was to use the mathematical or geometrical proofs Kindī pioneered, as in the theological correspondence between the Christian Qustā ibn Lūqā and the Muslim polymath Ibn al-Munajjim in the 860s.[41] Another possibility was to deploy Aristotelian logic, which was widely enough taught not to be the exclusive prerogative of philosophers.[42]

An Andalusian theologian, Abū ʿUmar Aḥmad ibn Muḥammad ibn Saʿdī, who visited Baghdad at the end of the tenth century, described this compromise between reason and revelation after attending an assembly of scholars which included

> every kind of group: Sunni Muslims and heretics, and all kinds of infidels: Mazdeans, materialists, atheists, Jews and Christians. Each group had a leader who would speak on its doctrine and debate about it. Whenever one of these leaders arrived, from whichever of the groups he came, the assembly rose up for him, standing on their feet until he would sit down, then they would take their seats after he was seated. When the assembly [majlis] was jammed with its participants, and they saw that no one else was expected, one of the infidels said: "You have all agreed to the debate, so the Muslims should not argue against us on the basis of their scripture, nor on the basis of the sayings of their prophet, since we put no credence in these things, and we do not acknowledge him. Let us dispute with one another only on the basis of *arguments from reason*, and *what observation and deduction will support*." Then they would all say: "Agreed." . . . When I heard that, I did not return to that majlis. Later someone told me there was to be another majlis for discussion, so I went to it and I found them engaging in the same practices as their colleagues. So I stopped going to the assemblies of the disputants, and I never went back.[43]

Ibn Saʿdī's observations are not isolated. He puts one in mind of Maʾmūn's dream: he asked Aristotle "What is the good?" and was told whatever is approved by intellect, or religious law, or the opinion of the masses, in that order.[44] The merits of reason/logic and grammar, in other words philosophy versus the Qurʾanic sciences, were publicly debated. Defenders of logic, who in Baghdad at this time were likely to be Christians such as Fārābī's teacher

41 Gutas, in Arnzen and Thielmann (eds), *Words, texts and concepts* [5:124] 208–9.

42 S. Stroumsa, *Freethinkers of medieval Islam* (Leiden 1999) 172–88.

43 Abū ʿAbd Allāh al-Ḥumaydī, *On Andalusian savants* (*Jadhwat al-muqtabis*) [ed. M. ibn T. al-Tanjī (Cairo 1953)] 101–2 (tr. Griffith, *Church in the shadow of the Mosque* [5:119] 64).

44 Gutas, *Greek thought* [5:92] 96–104, and cf. n. 35.

Abū Bishr Mattā (d. 940) or his pupil Yaḥyā ibn ʿAdī (d. 974),[45] appealed to the universality of reason compared to particular languages, while its opponents pointed out that it was formulated in Greek, and Arabs do not think like Greeks.[46] Fārābī held that religion addresses itself, through rhetoric and poetics (disciplines which were part of the full *Organon*) and varying images and similitudes, to differing peoples, whereas philosophy directly approaches the single intellectual truth that is universal.[47] One also finds in certain contemporary Jewish thinkers a conviction of the universality of reason. For moderates this meant that revelation, being known to us through reason, is also both universal and obligatory (and the Torah therefore not abrogated by Islam). To extremists it entailed religious relativism and skepticism, and excused neglect of traditional religion.[48]

One might also compare an arresting passage where Theodore Abū Qurra imagines himself a mountain dweller who descends to the cities of the plain, where he finds polytheists (there were notoriously some left in Theodore's see, Ḥarrān), Mazdeans, Samaritans, Jews, Christians, Manicheans, Marcionites, Bardaisan in person (!), and lastly some Muslims, all claiming they alone know the truth. Theodore was not the first to become a comparative religionist under the pressure of life in the Fertile Crescent. He concludes that the answer is rational reflection. He isolates three points all both agreed and disagreed on: God (but with what attributes?), plus commandments and rewards/punishments (but which, and for what?). Next he recommends that

> we must lay the books to one side and *inquire of the mind* how, from the likeness of human nature, we might know God's attributes [also his commandments and rewards].... When we have *discussed and come to understand* these subjects, we shall *compare those books* that are in our possession. If we find a book with these things in it, we shall *know* that it is from God. That book we shall confess and accept.

Theodore then describes how we may proceed from examining human nature to drawing conclusions about God, who transcends our condition in every respect.[49]

We must not be so impressed by the circles Ibn Saʿdī describes that we forget his own negative judgment, echoing the influential Ibn Ḥanbal or perhaps the emerging, more moderate Ashʿarite consensus, on their attachment

45 G. Endress, "Der arabische Aristoteles und seine Lehrüberlieferung in Bagdad," and "Yaḥyā ibn ʿAdī," *PIW* 290–324.

46 Kraemer, *Humanism* [4:82] 110–15.

47 J. W. Watt, *Rhetoric and philosophy from Greek into Syriac* (Farnham 2010) XVI.

48 The discussion by Sklare, *Samuel ben Ḥofni Gaon* [6:73] 99–165, repays detailed study.

49 Theodore Abū Qurra, *On the existence of God and the true religion* [ed. I. Dick (Rome 1982); tr. J. C. Lamoreaux, *Theodore Abū Qurrah* (Provo, Utah 2005) 165–74, 1–25, 41–47 (*sic*)] 200–40 (Dick)/1–18 (Lamoreaux).

to "reason, observation and deduction"; or Theodore's foreseeable conclusion, for all his rationalism, that "the Gospel alone contains what we learned from our own nature." Nevertheless, in tenth-century Baghdad there was still room at the majlis not only for theologians trained in logic, but also even for philosophers—we may imagine them among the "materialists and atheists."[50] And these philosophers were not just the earlier ecclesiastical Aristotelians whose concentration on logic we noted in chapter 5. The scholars of Baghdad deserve credit for taking on the whole corpus Aristotelicum as studied in the schools of Alexandria. Both Muslims and Christians might (or might not) still read Aristotle in the light of their scriptures; but in the ninth and tenth centuries philosophy regained, in Arabic, something of its old autonomy, thanks to the less clerical structure of authority in Islam and the interest of the Abbasid elite including several early caliphs. Arabic philosophers may not have been a very influential group in society; yet they are important to the historian because they were in a position to achieve an overview of the whole development of monotheism Jewish, Christian, and Muslim, but also of Greek science and the Aristotelian strand in Greek philosophy, not to mention the views of "Mazdeans, materialists and atheists." Much late Platonism was subsumed too, under the name of Aristotle the "First Master."[51] A prime motive for this openness to philosophy was the need felt by the influential Christian philosophers of Baghdad (and others, such as Elias of Nisibis discussed already in chapter 3), to create both a neutral space, transcending confessional identity, in which to go on talking to Muslim colleagues, and a reason-based, therefore truly humane social (as well as personal) ethic that might benefit their respective faith-communities more generally.[52] Something similar will have motivated Jewish philosophers too.[53]

The burning issues for philosophers were, after all, such as might, with good will, be discussed without straying beyond the common ground shared by Judaism, Christianity and Islam, or forcing participants to assume confessional labels. That is to say, there might be agreed proofs and results, consistent with all three scriptures, without need of quoting the divergent exegeses those scriptures had provoked. The unity of God; providence; the eternity or createdness of the universe—these were central, widely debated questions

50 Cf. Sklare, *Samuel ben Ḥofni Gaon* [6:73] 101: "Even though he [Ibn Saʿdī] was evidently reporting on a Kalām *majlis* rather than one which was philosophically oriented, his report reflects the atmosphere in the elite orbit of those connected to court society." Note also the specific examples Sklare adduces of scripturalist scholars open both to logic and to interfaith debate (114–18); and his parallel with the Brethren of Purity (136–37).

51 One might see the culmination and recapitulation of this ecumenical approach in ʿAbd al-Laṭīf al-Baghdādī's (d. 1231) heavily Platonized and Islamic Aristotelianism, reacting against Ibn Sīnā's synthesis and much indebted to Kindī: Martini Bonadeo [5:176], *SFIM* 648–59.

52 Griffith, *Journal of the Canadian Society for Syriac Studies* 7 (2007) [3:91] 55–73.

53 These may have been quite numerous: Kraemer, *Humanism* [4:82] 82–84.

about which it was possible to reach consensus (as much as philosophers ever had).[54] To glance briefly at the last of these, perhaps the worst sticking point between philosophers and scripturalists:[55] In the *Timaeus*, Plato had maintained that the world came to be in time. In the *Metaphysics,* Aristotle asserted the eternity of motion—and by implication of what moves. But in those days none thought the whole universe contingent. Among philosophers called on to face this Jewish and Christian notion, Proclus stood out for his insistence on the eternity of matter (which, following the principle of harmonization, he also read into the *Timaeus*). John Philoponus argued the Christian case—philosophically, though—against both him and Aristotle, and eventually, in Arabic translation, armed Muslim creationists too, notably Kindī—a student of Aristotle, but on this point perhaps concerned to underline the transcendent power of God and therefore the createdness of the Qur'ān, to which his caliphal patrons were committed. Such deference to scripture was not repeated, on this matter, by Fārābī or Ibn Sīnā, who saw the natural world as timeless and immutable (for nonbeing is an absurdity), while asserting its ultimate dependence on a causative divine act, emanation. Nor was it what Abū ʿUmar found. Probably he consoled himself among the mutakallimūn—though it has been shown that they too remained in some respects dependent on Philoponus, even in attempting to go beyond him and demonstrate the createdness not just of the universe as we see it, but of its substrate too, the atoms.[56] Philosophers like Philoponus or Kindī might choose to defend scriptural doctrines; scripturalists might exploit philosophical arguments. Real life was more often complex like that, than based on the self-conscious and no doubt temporary swap of faith for logic described by Abū ʿUmar. Whatever intellectual consensus was achieved had to emerge from a centuries-long accumulation of commentary and dialogue/polemic, to which the *Organon* was merely accessory (chapter 6). We see this nowhere more clearly than in the synthesis of kalām, philosophy, and Sufism eventually offered by Ghazālī (noted at the end of chapter 5).

The tenth century—in Baghdad, but elsewhere in the Islamic Commonwealth too, especially the East—saw a synthesis of ancient and modern

54 See, e.g., Adamson, *Al-Kindī* [5:148] 75–105; and the correspondence on problems in a range of Aristotle's writings between the Baghdadi Christian philosopher Yaḥyā ibn ʿAdī (d. 974) and the Jew Ibn Abī Saʿīd, without any reference to their confessional allegiances even when discussing Providence: S. Pines, "A tenth century philosophical correspondence," *Proceedings of the American Academy for Jewish Research* 24 (1955) 103–36.

55 M. Terrier, "De l'éternité ou de la nouveauté du monde: Parcours d'un problème philosophique d'Athènes à Ispahan," *Journal asiatique* 299 (2011) 369–421. On Philoponus's originality see R. Sorabji, "Waiting for Philoponus," in R. Hansberger and others (eds), *Medieval Arabic thought* (London 2012), esp. 195–96.

56 H. A. Davidson, "John Philoponus as a source of medieval Islamic and Jewish proofs of creation," *Journal of the American Oriental Society* 89 (1969) 357–91.

thought, and a cultural efflorescence, which found few if any rivals outside tenth- to twelfth-century Andalus—note especially the purist effort by Ibn Rushd (Averroes; d. 1198) to reinstate in commentary mode the Aristotelian/Farabian scientific outlook as the foundation of all understanding, after Ghazālī's and Ibn Sīnā's rereadings; and the influence achieved by the Jewish philosopher Maimonides (d. 1204) of Cordoba. From Toledo began the mainly Christian project of translating the Qur'ān and Arabic philosophical texts into Latin. But the former served mainly for launching ignorant polemics,[57] while the latter (along with James of Venice's renderings of the Greek Aristotle) fertilized thirteenth-century scholasticism, but were not seen by most Muslims as representative of their civilization, and anyway were vigorously resisted, as in the 1277 Parisian ban on doctrines derived from Aristotle (notably the eternity of the world) and his Arabic students such as Avicenna and Averroes (e.g., emanation). At the other end of Christendom the Syriac Renaissance—represented preeminently by the polymath Gregory Bar Hebraeus (d. 1286), whose *Candelabrum* has been compared to his contemporary Aquinas's *Summa theologica*—was of short duration and perhaps too tributary to Islamic scholarship, especially Ibn Sīnā.[58] Looking at other non-Muslim spiritual or intellectual syntheses achieved over the last millennium, whether in Renaissance Florence (in the shadow of the Ottomans!) or the salons of Enlightenment Paris frequented by Gibbon, or the secular universities of contemporary Europe and America, we can say that none has been in a position to encounter Islam as a known quantity, far less as a respected interlocutor. Those, especially in early modern Europe, who did achieve critical distance from all three monotheisms were more likely to spend their energies polemicizing "de tribus impostoribus" than actively pursuing truth through reason. This cliché too probably arose not far from tenth-century Baghdad, since where else could one ironize Moses, Jesus and Muḥammad impartially?[59] We still have a way to go before we replicate the wide-ranging discussions which occurred in that far-off place.

PISA/THE LATIN WEST

If, then, the First Millennium makes so much sense, does it make nonsense of other periodizations? The answer is a clear negative. I have already empha-

57 H. Bobzin, ""A treasury of heresies": Christian polemics against the Koran," in S. Wild (ed.), *The Qur'an as text* (Leiden 1996) 157–75; but on the stereotypes prevalent in this field of scholarship, see also D. Weltecke, "Emperor Frederick II, "Sultan of Lucera," "friend of the Muslims," promoter of cultural transfer," and K. Skottki, "Medieval Western perceptions of Islam and the scholars," in J. Feuchter and others (eds), *Cultural transfers in dispute* (Frankfurt 2011) 87–106, 107–34.

58 Teule and others (eds), *Syriac Renaissance* [3:89]; cf. H. Takahashi, "The reception of Ibn Sīnā in Syriac," in D. C. Reisman (ed.), *Before and after Avicenna* (Leiden 2003) 250–81.

59 S. Stroumsa, *Freethinkers* [7:42] 217; G. Stroumsa, *New science* [1:7] 138–39.

sized that it is no alternative to the already existing periodizations based on the Arsacid and Sasanian dynasties in Iran, the Roman Empire, late Antiquity, East Rome ("Byzantium"), and early Islam. It is a parallel periodization with its own logic and usefulness, which also helps contextualize the others just enumerated. But what of its effect on the periods either side of it, Antiquity more broadly conceived, and the Middle Ages?

Early Antiquity—the ancient Near East, "classical" Greece, and the Hellenistic period including the Roman Republic—will assuredly feel some gravitational pull from the arrival of this large and dynamic presence in place of or alongside "late Antiquity." It would make sense for students of the ancient world to pay more attention to those religious and intellectual systems which originated in the First or even Second Millennium BCE but developed or matured in the First Millennium CE: the Avestan from c. 1000 BCE, and the Mosaic from the first half of the First Millennium BCE. (The Vedas, from c. 1500 BCE, were already fixed before the Common Era.) Mazdaism and Judaism, but also Aristotelianism and Roman law, could do with being pulled closer to the focus of research, just as the broad category of ancient monotheism has been of late.[60] Among geographical regions, Iran and Arabia are obvious candidates for further integration. None of these subjects is so obscure or peripheral that interest in it can be dismissed as teleologically inspired; some even constitute independent disciplines; yet none can as yet be called central to the concerns of general ancient historians. One that can—imperial Rome—also demands reassessment in the light of the First Millennium, of which it is part. Ancient historians focus on its political history and the workings of empire; students of Judaism and Christianity also assign it high importance, but from their own sectarian perspective. Neither the compartmentalization nor the sectarianism is favored by the First Millennium viewing point.

It is historians of the medieval West, though, who will be most affected by attention to the First Millennium. The idea that important evolutions occur across Europe and West Asia in the period around the beginning of the Second Millennium has in fact been gaining ground of late, and it is widely agreed that if one is to identify what it means to be "medieval," it is to the period just after 1000 CE that one had best look, with the expansion of Christianity and the establishment of new polities in northern and eastern Europe, the extension and reform of ecclesiastical structures and religious orders, the formation of dynastic cults and the development of social categories, for example through the growth of bureaucracies, or the rise of a self-conscious aristocracy in the East Roman Empire.[61] The prominence attached

60 See, e.g., S. Mitchell and P. Van Nuffelen (eds), *One God: Pagan monotheism in the Roman Empire* (Oxford 2010).

61 G. Klaniczay, "The birth of a new Europe about 1000 CE," *Medieval encounters* 10 (2004) 99–129. J. R. Davis and M. McCormick, "The early Middle Ages: Europe's long morning," in J. R. Davis and

to Islam within the First Millennium framework, though, will be harder for medievalists to accommodate, given that they still see it as peripheral to their remit. First Millennium studies encourage us to chart a Eurasian dynamic, especially c. 1000 as the Eurasian Hinge, uneasily poised between the collapse of Abbasid power, the coming of the Seljuks and the intrusion of the Crusaders, opens up to interaction with the flanking but very different worlds of Central Asia and Latin Europe, and all are slowly integrated into a widening system of exchange culminating in the later thirteenth and early fourteenth centuries.[62]

I would emphasize the term "evolution" rather than the idea that there came a "turning point" into an entirely different era. There was a critical intensification of tendencies already under way, which had first become apparent through the Carolingian and Macedonian renaissances and the stimulation offered by Abbasid trade.[63] It is often said that the Muslim world has no need of renaissances; but here too we see, c. 1000 CE/400 AH, a maturation of Islamic civilization—and its obverse: Ibn Sīnā's impatience with writing commentaries on Greek texts, or the disappearance of churches from the urban tissue.[64] Then, the twelfth-century Renaissance in the Latin West reflects the rise of an intellectually, militarily, and commercially far more focused Europe, partly thanks to stimulus from the Muslim world. Between on the one hand the First Millennium and the dynamics arising from it, and on the other hand the Italian Renaissance anticipated in the twelfth-century Renaissance, the autonomy of the "Middle Ages" is undeniably squeezed.[65] Even more so when one takes into account the wish of some students of early modern Europe to annex the half-millennium from 1250 to 1750, or even a whole millennium, 800 to 1800.[66]

M. McCormick (eds), *The long morning of medieval Europe* (Aldershot 2008) 1–10, vigorously claim the whole period from 400 to 1000 as "the long morning of an expanding and changing world." Comparison with the civilizational level of the fourth-century Roman West, or the Caliphate's expansion, might have induced more sobriety. See below, n. 63.

62 J. L. Abu-Lughod, *Before European hegemony* (New York 1989).

63 The importance of Carolingian developments should not be underestimated. Comparison with the Abbasids (implied, notably, by Charlemagne's minting in the 780s and 790s of high-quality imitation Abbasid dinars: L. Ilisch, "Die imitativen *solidi mancusi*," in R. Cunz [ed.], *Fundamenta Historiae* [Hannover 2004] 91–106) is entirely legitimate, even if it throws up few resemblances, e.g., W. Drews, *Die Karolinger und die Abbasiden von Bagdad: Legitimationsstrategien frühmittelalterlicher Herrscherdynastien im transkulturellen Vergleich* (Berlin 2009). But until the eleventh century there is no justification for assigning the Latin West a role in the story of the middle and late First Millennium equal to that of the Greek, Arab, and Iranian worlds. On these, Central Asia from the Huns to the Seljuks exercised far directer influence: cf. Beckwith, *Empires of the Silk Road* [4:36], whose chap. 5 offers a conspectus of sixth- to eighth-century states from China to the Franks.

64 M. Guidetti, "The Byzantine heritage in the *dār al-islām*," *Muqarnas* 26 (2009) 1–36.

65 J. Banaji, "Islam, the Mediterranean and the rise of capitalism," *Historical materialism* 15 (2007) 47–74, dates the rise of European capitalism to the eleventh century already, and argues for its unmediated roots in the Muslim and late antique monetary economy and other commercial arrangements.

66 Osterhammel, *Verwandlung* [2:94] 100.

The boundary between the First Millennium and the Middle Ages is especially uncertain in Asia—as indeed is the applicability of medievalism at all, either here or elsewhere in the Islamic world. In arguing for a periodization ending around the year 1000, I have mentioned certain individuals whose work resumes the period and symbolizes that "end," but also stands for new developments pending or already under way. Ibn Sīnā fuses Aristotle and Muslim theology into a distinctive synthesis which, thanks also to Ghazālī's openness to the Sufi dimension, echoed for centuries to come. Bīrūnī draws his readers' attention to the utterly alien civilization of India, in acculturating to which Muslim invaders were to be challenged as nowhere else. Ferdowsi's historical epic sets the tone of Iranian national consciousness for a millennium to come, and still counting. All three of these men from Iran's eastern peripheries belonged to one of those fertile worlds where cultural zones overlap, in their case the Iranian and Islamic Commonwealths. Arabic remained the language of culture. Ibn Sīnā and Bīrūnī wrote Arabic, and Bīrūnī criticized scholars who used Persian. But the Arab lands between Tigris and Nile, although then as now more visible to the European eye, had lost both cultural and political impetus.[67] The East, by contrast, was confident, resilient and, above all, absorbent. Where the Arabs failed to assimilate the Crusaders (who took Christian brides, and paraded them in public instead of locking them up at home), the Iranian world made Sunni Muslims out of the Seljuks, and eventually the Mongols too. The Seljuks went on to create a vast empire in Iran and the Fertile Crescent but also Anatolia, where they drew cultural inspiration from East Rome and even the Crusaders as well as Iran and the Arab world, and were then absorbed by the Ottomans. The Mongols went down in Arabic and European history as a scourge, but they opened up Asian trade and brought a new efflorescence to the arts and scholarship of Iran. Their Ilkhanid and then Timurid states prepared the way for the Safavids; Iranized Mongols founded the Mughal dynasty in India. By the 1520s, all three of the great empires were in place which, as I observed at the outset of chapter 1, framed a self-confident Muslim world from the Danube to the Ganges into the eighteenth century and the age of European colonial conquest.[68]

In the 1780s Gibbon placed this Asiatic world at the culmination of what he must by then have realized was his thoroughly misnamed though (in part for its title) commercially successful *Decline and fall of the Roman Empire.*

67 For a recent, especially negative view of their eleventh-century state, see Ellenblum, *Collapse of the Eastern Mediterranean* [4:48] 168–70, 258–60.

68 The varied and creative postformative period of Islamic history, starting with the Seljuks, is a necessary counterbalance to the First Millennium perspective, given that attention to ninth/tenth-century Baghdad, or any other early "Golden Age" (e.g., Meccan-Medinan origins), tends to facilitate the Eurocentric agenda that dismisses the rest of Islamic history as "decline" ripe for colonialist rectification: cf. Bauer, *Ambiguität* [1:5] 53, 58–59, 161, 296–97.

Attention to the fall of Constantinople in 1453 served to excuse the title; but East Rome's cultural and symbolic status had long since ceased to be matched by any political clout. In his last chapters, Gibbon reverted to Old Rome on the Tiber and briefly gestured forward to the revival of classical culture which heralded the rise of Europe. Gibbon's emphasis on Oriental empires and bracketing of medieval Europe was evidently intended to provoke a Catholic historiographical tradition which saw the classical revival and European Modernity as having been prepared by the Church. One recalls, too, his emphasis on the rationality of Islam, in covert opposition to orthodox Christian Trinitarianism. No wonder Gibbon's posterity has generally declined to read beyond volume 3.

The First Millennium periodization should not be construed as sanctioning Gibbon's provocation, but rather as offering an alternative way out of Antiquity in the spirit of his innovative, neglected later volumes. The European/Christian and Asiatic/Islamic exits from Antiquity are not unrelated to each other. No amount of adulation of Charles the Great can persuade an impartial observer that "Europe" was born already in 800. Here, Catholic historiography truly overreached itself. But from the middle of the eleventh century onward it is indeed arguable that Europe comes into focus, and not in isolation from the world of Islam. I for a time considered acknowledging this by offering two Epilogues, one looking forward to the Eastern evolutions I have just sketched, the other returning to Pisa, at whose Scuola Normale Superiore these chapters were first tried out as three lectures in 2009. It seems preferable to emphasize instead the connectivity of these worlds; but Pisa is not at all a bad place to do that.

From about 1050, Pisa grew fabulously wealthy on its Saracen wars and the conquest of Corsica, Sardinia, and the Balearic Islands.[69] After the naval victory granted by the Virgin Mary off Palermo in 1063, the present duomo was begun the following year on a colossal scale with few parallels in Europe at that time. Inscriptions on the facade record that spoils of victory provided the funds, and compare the architect Buscheto to Odysseus and Daedalus (and Pisa therefore to ancient Greece).[70] The duomo's axial relationship to the new circular baptistery built in 1153, and their setting amid the Campo dei Miracoli, mirrored the Aqsā Mosque and the Dome of the Rock on the Haram al-Sharīf in Jerusalem. The Crusaders called the Dome of the Rock the "Temple of the Lord" and the Aqsā the "Temple of Solomon"; while the Pisans built an upgraded version in the heart of their city,[71] and imagined themselves latter-day Children of Israel struggling against the Midianites of

69 G. Scalia, "Pisa all'apice della gloria: L'epigrafe araba di S. Sisto e l'epitafio della regina di Maiorca," *Studi medievali* 48 (2007) 809–28; Abulafia, *Great Sea* [4:15] 271–86.

70 A. Peroni (ed.), *Il Duomo di Pisa* (Modena 1995) 1.336–37, 2.43–44.

71 J. E. A. Kroesen, *The Sepulchrum Domini through the ages* (Leuven 2000) 41–42.

Mahdīya, the Saracen emporium on the Tunisian coast.[72] Commercial competition and holy war were henceforth powerful mutually reinforcing motives, culminating in the First Crusade and ensuring a Latin presence throughout the Mediterranean for the first time since the fall of the Western Roman Empire. The foundations for the revival of Europe were being laid, and a first step had been taken toward the wider thirteenth-century Eurasian integration mentioned above.

Among other mementos of the East to be seen in Pisa was the famous mid-sixth-century codex of Justinian's *Digest*, plundered from Amalfi perhaps not long after the Pisan conquest in the mid-1130s, and now known after its present home as the *Littera Florentina*. This manuscript was to play a major part in the revival of Roman law in the West.[73] On the city's lesser churches—not the marble-clad cathedral—we can still admire numerous colorful glazed bacini (bowls) of Islamic origin, glinting in the sunlight and proclaiming rather more, perhaps, than just the Pisans' success in strong-arming themselves into the profitable North African and Levantine markets.[74]

As for the eleventh-century copper-alloy griffin that once adorned the apex of the cathedral's eastern pediment, and is now exhibited in the Museo dell'Opera del Duomo,[75] it not only is a very superior relation of the bacini, conveying the same message, but may also serve as an emblem for both the wider context and the distinctive character of our First Millennium. As a motif the griffin, half eagle half lion, goes back to the ancient Near East, whence it entered Greek art in the Orientalizing period. The Umayyads established an early vogue for metal animal sculptures in the Islamic world. The monumental Pisan specimen is probably a product of the eleventh century, and perhaps came from Mahdīya as booty when the Pisans captured it in 1087, or from Spain or the Balearic Islands. For all its ancient roots, the extreme stylization of the Pisa griffin makes its Islamic origin unmistakable, even without the Arabic benediction inscribed on it. The great mythical beast has fascinated art historians. They have assigned it every provenance from Khurāsān via North Africa to Spain (just as Ibn Sīnā's philosophical legacy was developed as much in Andalusia as in Iran). That in itself speaks volumes about the cultural coherence of the Islamic Commonwealth at the end of the First Millennium.

72 Abulafia, *Great Sea* [4:15] 280.

73 G. Cavallo and F. Magistrale, "Libri e scritture del diritto nell'età di Giustiniano," in G. G. Archi (ed.), *Il mondo del diritto nell'epoca giustinianea* (Ravenna 1985) 54–58 (arguing, though, that this particular manuscript may have been produced in sixth-century Italy).

74 D. Abulafia, *Italy, Sicily and the Mediterranean 1100–1400* (London 1987) XIII.

75 J. Sourdel-Thomine and B. Spuler, *Die Kunst des Islam* (Berlin 1973) 263 and plate 194; R. Ettinghausen and others, *Islamic art and architecture 650–1250* (New Haven 2001) 210; A. Contadini, "Translocation and transformation: Some Middle Eastern objects in Europe," in L. E. Saurma-Jeltsch and A. Eisenbeiss (eds), *The power of things and the flow of cultural transformations* (Berlin 2010) 50–57.

The merchants of Pisa well knew who the worthwhile enemy was, for plunder and trading concessions but also cultural prestige by association. It was Latin Europe, not the Islamic world, which felt the need to reconnect to the extraordinarily complex and rich civilizational dynamic that arose, mainly in the East, during the First Millennium. The rationale and history of this reconnection were gradually assigned to oblivion as the Second Millennium wore on, and the history of Europe came to be written according to other priorities and from different angles. The good news, at the beginning of the Third Millennium, is that this is no longer an option.

PROSPECTS FOR FURTHER RESEARCH

CHAPTER 1

Comparing the opening chapters of the *Cambridge history of Islam* (1970) with those of its successor, the *New Cambridge history of Islam* (2010), one observes how European and American Islamology now acknowledges the rise of late Antiquity, and studies the seventh-century Arab conquests and the birth of Islam against the background of Iranian and Roman rivalry in and around Arabia—also of the development, both separately and interactively, of the region's religious traditions, Mazdaism, Judaism, and Christianity. The Berlin-Brandenburg Academy of Sciences Corpus Coranicum project, and in particular Angelika Neuwirth's *Der Koran als Text der Spätantike: Ein europäischer Zugang* (Berlin 2010), applies this perception to study of the Qur'ān and its rabbinic and patristic antecedents. Late Antiquity and Islam are both emerging from the mutual isolation in which they once were studied. This makes research more demanding than when it was conducted independently, and with minimal mutual awareness, by students of Middle Persian, Greek, or Arabic, and mostly concentrating on either pre- or post-seventh-century events. But for a recent example of the payoff, see Parvaneh Pourshariati, *Decline and fall of the Sasanian Empire: The Sasanian-Parthian confederacy and the Arab conquest of Iran* (2008), revising our understanding of underdocumented Sasanid Iran by using both Arabic and Persian sources from the Islamic period to study continuities in social structures through the seventh century.

These wide horizons in both space and time had already been surveyed by Edward Gibbon back in the 1780s. After narrating the fifth-century decline and fall of Old Rome on the Tiber, Gibbon took two unpredictable decisions: first to follow the fortunes of New Rome on the Bosphorus rather than recounting the familiar tale of Papacy and Christian Germanic Empire; and second to allow himself to be distracted by the seventh-century Arab defeat of East Rome into investigating the rise of the Caliphate and Islam, and of subsequent Muslim empires down to the Ottomans. He penned a surprisingly positive assessment of both Muḥammad and the Qur'ān. This latter part of Gibbon's masterpiece is remarkably little read or appreciated, even by John Pocock in his monumental survey of Gibbon's thought world, *Barbarism and religion*. The sources, purpose, and repercussions of the treatment of Islam in *Decline and fall* are in need of examination.

CHAPTER 2

Along with the work of Pourshariati, another major attempt to draw the Sasanids into the wider picture is Matthew Canepa's *The two eyes of the earth: Art and ritual of kingship between Rome and Sasanian Iran* (Berkeley 2009), examining the impact of Sasanid art on East Rome from the third to the seventh centuries, and the mechanisms—commercial, diplomatic, and military—by which artistic motifs and styles were transmitted. Raised awareness of the artistic cross-pollination that existed between these two pre-Islamic empires ought to help Islamic art historians understand better the highly diverse origins of Umayyad art in particular. My own discussion of Umayyad style in chapter 10 of *Quṣayr ʿAmra* (2004) treated its Roman and Iranian antecedents too much as separate strands and took insufficiently into account the interactions Canepa has now described.

As I argue in chapter 2, art historians have played a leading role in fostering contacts between late antique and early Islamic studies. It is important, though, to understand the tensions between formalism and cultural, intellectual, and literary approaches to art and architecture. A major figure on the formalist side was Josef Strzygowski, and my engagement with him has made me aware how little we understand his controversial career and thought. Rejection of Strzygowski's racial theories has developed into a damnatio memoriae extremely damaging to the study of art historiography. There are signs this is lifting, which offers an opportunity to a courageous researcher.

Strzygowski's highlighting of the vigor of Oriental traditions called in question the "decline" that dominated Romanocentric perceptions of late Antiquity. There we see of course the influence of Gibbon—but, by contrast, one is struck how little Gibbon treats the Muslim world in terms of decline. The eclipse of the Abbasids is forgotten amid the magnificence of the Seljuks and the Ottomans' aspiration to deck themselves "with the trophies of the new and the ancient Rome" (68:3.976). Still, decline is the dominant theme in subsequent European histories of Islam, and is only now beginning to be questioned. The habit of "setting up" classical Islam by making it a Golden Age, and then writing off the next millennium of its history, conveys a rather obvious political subtext ripe for more systematic and incisive exposure than it has yet received (even by Edward Said).

CHAPTER 3

In developing my argument for the First Millennium, I show how this periodization, or at least certain mutually compatible elements of it, is implicit in several monotheist historians who lived during the centuries in question. Among these Christian and Muslim writers, by far the least known is Elias of Nisibis (d. 1046), who wrote in both Arabic and Syriac and covered the First Millennium—albeit as the culmination of a history that starts from Adam—with attention to Iran, Rome, *and* the Caliphate. As a bishop at the very heart of the Fertile Crescent who also engaged in theological debates with Muslims, this unusual bird's-eye view of our subject came naturally to Elias. With him, my argument begins to draw on the geo-strategic centrality and literary legacy of the Syriac world, an approach further elaborated in chapters 4 (geographical framework) and 5 (Aristotelianism). While a monograph on Elias is certainly a desideratum, a large-scale synthetic account of the Syro-Arabic Christian world, overlapping Iran, Rome, and Arabia, before and after Muḥammad, would revolutionize our historical perspective. A start has been made by Sidney Griffith, *The Church in the shadow of the Mosque: Christians and Muslims in the world of Islam* (2008), concentrating on theological and philosophical literature in Arabic.

CHAPTER 4

Closely linked to the role of the Syro-Arabic world is the question of cultural commonwealth, for the Iranian and East Roman spheres of influence overlapped both there and in the Caucasus. This overlapping of cultural zones raises in acute form the problem of how to define commonwealth, political as well as cultural. Once the vast Abbasid Caliphate succumbs to its centrifugal forces in the tenth century and generates a new commonwealth, the problem of definition acquires an Islamic dimension too. The concept of commonwealth, popularized by Dimitri Obolensky's *The Byzantine Commonwealth: Eastern Europe 500–1453* (1971) and developed with reference to the Christian East from the fourth century onward in my *Empire to commonwealth* (1993), has of late been critically reexamined, and somewhat undermined with regard to Orthodox Eastern Europe and Russia, with the impact of shared faith on political allegiance being called in question (see the works by J. Shepard and C. Raffensperger referred to above [4:74, 77]). There is also the question of whether the Latin West should be regarded as an extension of Constantinople's cultural zone, or an independent commonwealth. Given the current taste for comparative histories of empire, a more systematic comparison of cultural commonwealths seems to be called for.

The Iranian cultural zone reaches well into Central Asia, and the Sasanians were obliged to attend at least as much to threats from steppe empires as from East Rome. Central Asian population movements were also related to the fall of the Roman Empire in the West. Yet the tendency of European and North American historians to treat Latin Europe as the privileged exit from Antiquity, and the harbinger of modernity, works against serious attention to Central Asia in the overall historical narrative. By shifting the geographical frame of reference eastward, *Before and after Muḥammad* raises the question of whether these two peripheral regions, Central Asia and Western Europe, ought to be given more equal weighting.

CHAPTER 5

The final three chapters of *Before and after Muḥammad* illustrate how intellectual and spiritual traditions benefit from, and support, longer periodizations. In chapter 5 I highlight Aristotelianism because it was until recently upstaged by the Platonist strand in late Greek thought, but also for the role played especially by the *Organon* in polemic within and between Judaism, Christianity and Islam. Thanks to translation into English, the Alexandrian commentaries on Aristotle are now widely accessible; and even Syriac Aristotelianism has latterly been the object of intense research in Paris and Cardiff. It is still almost unheard of, though, for even a collaborative venture to cover the whole history of First Millennium Aristotelianism—and still that is not the whole story, since translations from both Arabic and Greek gave Aristotle a new lease of life in the Latin world too, from the twelfth century. There is also a major and influential group of pseudo-Aristotelian texts, which must be incorporated in this narrative, because for those who produced and read them they were genuine Aristotle, with remarkably few questions asked.

Although the translation of Aristotle from Greek via Syriac into Arabic is well-trodden territory, it remains unclear how exactly this project related to the rational reflection on the Qur'ān, which almost from the outset came naturally to some followers of Muḥammad and seems, at least initially, not to have been indebted to the Greek tradition. *Before and after Muḥammad* emerged, in part, from an earlier, unpublished book on *Rational Islam*. The project would be best continued by an expert on Arabic thought. Meanwhile, the Zaydi libraries of Yemen and the two Firkovich collections in Saint Petersburg continue to yield unexpected treasures of Muʿtazili theology; while the Intellectual History of the Islamicate World research unit, headed by Sabine Schmidtke at the Freie Universität Berlin, has been vigorously publishing and studying them since 2011.

CHAPTER 6

The Firkovich collections are also one of the main sources of new information about the revival of Jewish philosophy under the Abbasids, and the rationalist opponents of rabbinism known as Karaites. Both trends were influenced by Muʿtazilite theology, as were many Christian thinkers in the Caliphate. In tenth-century Baghdad there was considerable interaction between intellectual representatives of Judaism, Christianity and Islam. Putting together the new materials constantly coming to light, and the accounts in various sources, some well known, of the gatherings (majālis) at which scholars debated their differences, it ought to be possible to paint a more compelling picture than is yet available of this uniquely well-informed and tolerant moment in Eurasian intellectual history.

The parallel and to some extent comparative account, in chapters 5 and 6, of First Millennium exegetical cultures poses questions about the relationships between these traditions (especially the rabbinic and Muslim strands), and the role of reason as well as revelation. I have placed particular stress on philosophy and law, in order to underline that the First Millennium is more than just a periodization in the history of monotheism. In one very important respect, the legal strand is unique in that it produced a thorough codification in the time of Justinian, the *Corpus iuris civilis*. Nothing as all-embracing, systematic, and utterly authoritative (or deadening, depending on your viewpoint[1]) emerged from either the philosophy schools or the Talmudists, Christian fathers, and mutakallimūn. That raises an obvious and fundamental point about the political, organizational, and economic support presupposed by such wide-ranging intellectual syntheses. There needed to be imperial backing and interest—both Christianity and Islam disposed of that, at least at certain moments. But there had to be consensus too. That was infinitely more elusive in the sphere of religion than in that of law. In other words, a periodization may primarily be built on concepts, if they are of sufficient importance; but a narrative history must introduce the power factor, and ask how that molds as well as propagates the ideas. And when there is no central authority committed to fostering the tradition in question, as was the case for Judaism and later Greek philosophy, what role might be played by other, perhaps more local, social elites? These are questions I shall touch on, necessarily, in the narrative history of the First Millennium on which I am now at work.

To close these brief notes on future work: they and the book they con-

1 Cf. Y. Congar, "Du bon usage de Denzinger," in id., *Situation et tâches présentes de la théologie* (Paris 1967) 111–33.

clude are largely indebted to a tradition of European and North American research on Islam—and indeed everything else herein discussed. But the particularity of the tradition is conspicuous in the case of Islam, since on this subject there is a parallel tradition in the Muslim world. Western scholars' attention to this tradition is rarely very extensive, while contemporary Muslim scholarship in "Muslim" languages often ignores its Western counterpart or treats it with suspicion—see now Jacob Lassner's *Jews, Christians, and the abode of Islam: Modern scholarship, medieval realities* (2012). This is not to deny that the Muslim tradition has been considerably influenced, whether positively or reactively, by the West's more general secularism, rationalism and so forth. A thoughtful recent book by Thomas Bauer, *Die Kultur der Ambiguität: Eine andere Geschichte des Islams* (2011), draws attention to the way in which Muslim fundamentalist rejection of traditionally acceptable polysemy and ambiguity in the Qur'ān and elsewhere, in favor of only one meaning for each passage, is really a response to universalizing, hegemonial Western discourse. But the Muslim scholars who are more widely and profitably read in Europe and North America are those who work there and have absorbed that way of thinking, or at least express themselves in those terms, while often displaying a profounder acquaintance than their non-Muslim colleagues with research published in Arabic, Persian, Turkish, and so forth. Such scholars are ever more numerous, and probably offer our best hope for combining traditional and contemporary Muslim thought with the wide horizons imposed by the global turn in Western research.

Index